THE NUCLEAR REVOLUTION
IN SOVIET MILITARY AFFAIRS

THE NUCLEAR REVOLUTION
IN SOVIET MILITARY AFFAIRS

Translated and Edited, with Introduction and Commentary, by
WILLIAM R. KINTNER AND HARRIET FAST SCOTT

University of Oklahoma Press : Norman

LIBRARY OF CONGRESS CATALOG CARD NUMBER: 67-24620

Copyright 1968 by the University of Oklahoma Press, Publishing Division of the University. Composed and printed at Norman, Oklahoma, U.S.A., by the University of Oklahoma Press. First edition.

PREFACE

"THE REVOLUTION in Military Affairs" has been a common phrase in the Soviet military press in the last four years. Its implications are vital to United States military thinking, yet the meaning of that phrase is almost completely unknown in the United States. Its chief result, as explained to the Soviet people, is that "the basic fire and striking power of our [Soviet] armed forces now is the nuclear weapon and the chief means of delivery to the target is the rocket."[1] A primary premise, as stated again and again by Soviet military writers, is that the outcome of a future world war will be primarily decided by a nuclear rocket exchange.

The Soviets are writing of this revolution so often, so plainly, and, we might add, so forcefully, that any effort to transmit their views through our own analysis, or to restate them, would only detract from their impact. We have, instead, selected articles to show the continuity of the revolution from the Nikita Khrushchev period, during which it had its initial growth, through the first quarter of 1967. Our main emphasis, of course, is placed on the Leonid I. Brezhnev era. Selections have been made from the most authoritative sources available in the open Soviet press, and the most "approved" authors have been selected for inclusion.

What are these sources? Principally they are *Krasnaya Zvezda—Red Star*, the daily newspaper of the Ministry of Defense, and *Communist of the Armed Forces*, the fortnightly journal of the Main Political Administration of the Soviet Army and Navy. This is the only Soviet military journal devoted to military theory. Special note was made of those articles which were designated by the editors for study by Soviet officers, generals, and admirals. The

---

[1] Extracted from the definition of "The Revolution in Military Affairs," *Soviet Explanatory Dictionary of Military Terms* (Moscow, Military Publishing House, 1966), 393. Also see Glossary.

v

speeches of the late Minister of Defense, Marshal of the Soviet Union Rodion Ya. Malinovsky, and the Chief of the Main Political Administration, General of the Army Aleksei A. Yepishev, which were given at the March, 1966, XXIII Congress of the Communist Party of the Soviet Union, have been included as, presumably, the "word" for the next four or five years on the military and political orientation of the Soviet Armed Forces. Finally, selections were made from the Soviet *Officer's Library*, a series of seventeen volumes announced in 1965 to be published over a three-year period.[2] By March, 1967, nine volumes had been printed. Extracts also have been included from two other books published by the Soviet military press after October, 1964, and widely reviewed by Soviet authorities.

The authors selected were those who had been awarded the Frunze prize, given by the Ministry of Defense "for excellent writing on military theory," or who were listed as contributors to *Military Strategy* or to other recognized publications, or who are faculty members of the leading military institutions, such as Frunze Military Academy, the Academy of the General Staff, or the Lenin Military-Political Academy. Most of the authors are prolific writers whose works have been regarded as authoritative for many years. (The introduction to each selection frequently lists other writings by the same author.)

Every attempt has been made to present materials which the writers apparently intended for Soviet audiences. We have tried to avoid cutting any part of the original article even though this has resulted at times in including tedious propaganda. The military writings take on a somewhat different character when ideology and factual military doctrine are intermixed. To save space, we have omitted irrelevant introductions to one or two articles.

We have attempted to cover fully the time from October, 1964, to March, 1967, placing articles in chronological order so that the reader can discern readily when each statement was made, in case he wishes to relate the statement to an external event such as the various milestones in the Sino-Soviet split.

2 Books of the series are listed in the Appendix.

The translations are as literal as possible, to avoid risking distortion. Capitalizations are not uniform but are as found in the original Russian text so that the exact shade of meaning which Soviet military writers wished to convey would not be misunderstood.

The following Soviet reference materials and dictionaries were used to insure that each word reflects the current Soviet definition of the word rather than standard American usages. Readers are referred to:

Slovar' Russkovo Yazika (Dictionary of the Russian Language), S. I. Ozhegov, Moscow, "Soviet Encyclopedia" Publishing House, 1964.

Russko-Angliyskiy Slovar'—Russian-English Dictionary, 7th Edition, Professor A. I. Smirnitsky, Editor, Moscow, "Soviet Encyclopedia" Publishing House, 1965.

Kratkiy Anglo-Russkiy i Russko-Angliyskiy Voyenniy Slovar' (Short English-Russian and Russian-English Military Dictionary), Moscow, Voyenizdat, 1963.

Slovar' Osnovnikh Voyennikh Terminov (Dictionary of Basic Military Terms), Moscow, Voyenizdat, 1965.

Tolkoviy Slovar' Voyennikh Terminov (Explanatory Dictionary of Military Terms), Moscow, Voyenizdat, 1966.

Every translation has been made from the original Russian text. Although measures have been taken to assure accurate translations, we assume full responsibility for any error that may have been made.

Any jointly prepared book is a result of converging interests. Harriet Scott learned about Clausewitz, Douhet, Mahan, and Mitchell through her own reading and through listening to countless lecture rehearsals which her husband, Colonel William F. Scott, United States Air Force, prepared while on the faculty of the Royal Air Force College in England and the Air University in Alabama. From 1962 to 1964, Harriet Scott lived in the Soviet Union, where Colonel Scott had been assigned as the United States air attaché. By traveling and using the language daily, she gained an understanding of both the Russian language and the

Soviet people. Since her return to the United States, particularly after moving to Washington, she has been a regular contributor of translations and analyses to the Pentagon's *Friday Review of Defense Literature*; and an article, "Soviet Military Literature for 1966," appeared in *Military Review* in July, 1966.

The revolution in human affairs introduced by nuclear weapons evoked in William R. Kintner a sustained interest in the evolution of strategy in both the Soviet Union and the United States. This interest is reflected in a number of publications, beginning with *The Front is Everywhere* (Norman, Oklahoma, University of Oklahoma Press, 1950), an examination of Communist party organization, strategy, and tactics; *Atomic Weapons in Land Combat*, co-author, (Harrisburg, Pa., The Stackpole Co., 1953); *Protracted Conflict*, co-author, (New York, Harper & Brothers, 1959), an examination of over-all Communist strategy; *The Haphazard Years*, co-author, (New York, Doubleday & Co., 1960), a survey of the United States–Soviet technological confrontation; *The New Frontier of War*, co-author, (Chicago, Regnery, 1961), an analysis of Communist political warfare; *A Forward Strategy for America*, co-author, (New York, Harper & Row, 1960); *Peace and the Strategy Conflict* (New York, Praeger, 1967).

Professor Kintner's latest book, which was developed during the period 1963–67, required that he examine in depth Soviet doctrines and concepts for strategic warfare. While writing this book, he found a great paucity of published literature in the United States on this very important topic. He began to take advantage of the excellent translations that Harriet Scott was making of Soviet military literature, particularly for the period following the Cuban missile crisis. Since her work was valuable to him, he thought it would be equally valuable to American and Western students of Soviet affairs and, therefore, proposed that they produce a book of readings on significant and recent Soviet military writings. This volume on the revolution that is taking place in Soviet military affairs is the product of their joint endeavor.

The work was made possible by the assistance of many persons and organizations, particularly the Relm Foundation of Ann

Arbor, Michigan. We would particularly like to thank Mrs. Anne Jonas for her many valuable suggestions.

It is our hope that this work will help bring about a clearer understanding of contemporary Soviet strategic thinking.

WILLIAM R. KINTNER
HARRIET FAST SCOTT

September 13, 1967

CONTENTS

THE NUCLEAR REVOLUTION
IN SOVIET MILITARY AFFAIRS

INTRODUCTION
—THE REVOLUTION IN SOVIET MILITARY AFFAIRS
—A CHALLENGE TO AMERICAN SECURITY

If you [had] read our scientific journals, you would have known all about our plans to launch the first Sputnik at least a year before it was launched.[1]

AMBITIOUS PEOPLE tend to talk about and even to write about what they plan to do. Hitler outlined his hopes in *Mein Kampf*. The Communists have written what they expect to do in the economic and political fields. Soviet military leaders and theoreticians have presented with amazing frankness over the past several years the developmental direction and trends in their armed forces. They have told of the changes brought about by the nuclear weapon—of missiles and antimissiles—and have hinted at a military role in space. They have made clear their belief that: "The appearance of the nuclear rocket weapon and the arming of leading governments of the world with them evoked a modern revolution in military affairs. It signifies a profound qualitative jump not only in armaments and military equipment, but also in the methods and forms of armed combat."[2]

The purpose of this book is to make available English translations of some of the most significant Soviet writings that have been published on doctrine and strategy since the Cuban missile crisis of 1962.[3] Most selections were published after October, 1964,

[1] Professor A. I. Mikhailov, director of the Institute of Scientific and Technical Information of the U.S.S.R. Academy of Sciences, in a talk made to a group of American scientists in Washington, as reported in *The New York Times*, November 23, 1958, p. 3.

[2] General Major V. Voznenko, "The Dialectics of Development and Change in Forms and Methods of Armed Conflict," chap. 22, below.

[3] *Military Strategy*, Marshal V. D. Sokolovsky (ed.), was available throughout the Soviet Union in August, 1962, two months before the missile crisis. It was translated into English and was available in the United States in two editions in 1963. One publication was by Prentice-Hall, Inc., with an introduction by Herbert S. Dinerstein, Leon Gouré, and Thomas W. Wolfe, and another edition was by Frederick A. Praeger, with an introduction by Raymond Garthoff.

following the ouster of Khrushchev. We have tried to select, in the main, those military writings intended for Soviet officers and men. A glance at the table of contents or the reading of a few selections at random will indicate the Soviet preoccupation with nuclear weapons and their impact upon warfare.

The introduction of these weapons into the world political system has necessitated a profound change in the strategic thinking of both the United States and the Soviet Union. Because of this change the United States faces decisions about whether to deploy a heavy antiballistic missile system and to build complementary civil defense shelters—at a total cost of billions of dollars. In the most ultimate sense the consequences of these decisions will affect the future of civilization.

Meaning of the Revolution in Military Affairs

Many Soviet military theoreticians have divided the revolution in military affairs into three phases. The first was the creation of the nuclear weapon. The second was the development of the dominant weapon carrier, the missile. The third phase, sometimes referred to as the cybernetics revolution, still is under way and provides the guidance and control system. A primary result of the revolution is the emergence of the strategic nuclear forces, consisting of nuclear-armed ballistic missiles, atomic-propelled submarines armed with ballistic missiles, and long-range aircraft armed with air-to-ground nuclear missiles. Strategic defensive forces also have been developed to include antiaircraft, antirocket and antispace units.[4] Tactical nuclear weapons have been introduced into the Soviet Armed Forces.

The revolution in military affairs is a continuing process, undergoing constant change. According to the dialectic reasoning of the Soviet theorists, there is "the 'struggle' of tanks and antitank means, submarine and antisubmarine means, airplane and antiairplane defense, radio-means and means of jamming, rockets and anti-rockets."[5] In the process of developing weapons systems, they see

[4] For definitions of antiaircraft, antirocket, and antispace forces, see Glossary.
[5] Colonel S. I. Krupnov, "According to the Laws of Dialectics," chap. 16, below.

4

the phenomenon of opposite forces—of the contradictions to which they constantly refer—and of the dialectical operation of thesis and antithesis. There might be less surprise in the United States with frequently unexpected revelations of Soviet weapon system development if more attention was given to the dialectical intricacies of Marxism-Leninism.

Concern with China

What consideration is given to Communist China in Soviet military writings? Since the translations are presented in chronological order, a change can be detected in the tenor of the articles originally published in 1964, or early 1965, and those appearing in late 1966. Some concern is evident, although, until late in 1966, China seldom was referred to by name. The enemies presented to the Soviet military are the "imperialists," headed by the United States. The Soviet reader may have become a bit confused with the possible Chinese threat after being taught: "Wars have not always existed. They rose with the appearance of private ownership of the means of production and the division of society into hostile classes."[6]

In the latter part of 1966 Soviet writers appeared to be warning the Chinese with this statement: "The development of modern military affairs demonstrates the failure of the views of theorists who consider, it is said, even the most powerful weapons useless in the struggle against the masses of the people. That sort of opinion ignores the circumstances that the use of the nuclear rocket weapon . . . can have a decisive influence on the whole course and outcome of a war."[7]

The Soviet writers stress the concept that "a revolution in military affairs" can take place only in those nations with a high industrial and technological level. This observation appears deliberately designed to remind the Chinese that their masses of people do not

[6] Colonel S. V. Malyanchikov, "The Character and Features of Nuclear Rocket War," chap. 13, below.

[7] Lieutenant Colonel V. Bondarenko, "Military-Technical Superiority: The Most Important Factor of the Reliable Defense of the Country," chap. 25 below.

5

matter militarily and that they are not yet to be considered as a major nuclear power. Perhaps the speed by which Peking acquired a hydrogen bomb may change Soviet assessments.

Military Doctrine, Strategy, and Science[8]

As a frame of reference when studying Soviet military writings, the reader should know the Soviet meaning of such military terms as strategy, doctrine, and science. In the United States a pragmatic approach is taken toward doctrinal matters and insufficient attention is paid to precise terms. This is not the case in the Soviet Union.

Military doctrine, in Soviet terminology, is usually defined as embracing both political and military aspects of power. It has a state character and is considered by the Soviets as a system of "scientifically" based views on the nature of war. Military doctrine is essentially an expansion of the official policy of the state with respect to military matters. It is the same for all the armed forces.[9]

Military strategy occupies a subordinate position with respect to doctrine. The Soviets contend that their strategy is "guided by the advanced scientific theory of Marxism-Leninism."[10] In the opinion of some Soviet spokesmen, the most acute problem of strategy is the determination of the methods of waging nuclear rocket war.[11]

Military science develops the general principles of the organization of the armed forces in their various categories. Since "Soviet military science comes from Marxist-Leninist teachings and is governed by methods of dialectical-materialism," it may appear confusing and complex to the non-Communist strategist. Military science concerns itself with the combat capabilities of each type of force, concepts of troop organization, logistics, and operational training.[12]

8 A detailed definition of these terms, as defined by the Soviets, is contained in the Glossary.

9 Colonel A. A. Strokov (ed.), "Military Art in the Postwar Period," from *The History of Military Art*, chap. 15, below.

10 V. D. Sokolovsky and M. I. Cherednichenko, "On Contemporary Military Strategy," chap. 18, below.

11 *Ibid.*

12 See Glossary.

Political-Military Relations in the Soviet Union

Soviet military doctrine is promulgated by the Politburo and the Central Committee of the Communist party of the Soviet Union.[13] One of the many publications used to disseminate the views of the Communist party leadership to the Soviet military establishment is the journal *Communist of the Armed Forces*, the official organ of the "Main Political Administration of the Soviet Army and Navy" (in Soviet terminology, GlavPU [SA and VMF]). The authority of the journal derives in large part from the fact that the Main Political Administration is, in effect, a constituent part of the Communist party secretariat rather than simply an administration within the headquarters apparatus of the Ministry of Defense. Over the past several years this magazine has gone to considerable lengths to explain the nuclear revolution in military affairs to its readers.

It is not known to what extent Soviet military authors write according to specific instructions, just as it is impossible to know how much leeway they might have in presenting varying points of view. Conceivably, there could be certain issues that have not yet been resolved and about which different opinions might not only be permitted but even encouraged. As a general practice, debate over important issues is permitted up to the moment the party makes its decision. Consequently, we can assume that public divergencies on military matters are usually manifested only before the issue is resolved and the decision is incorporated into doctrine.

There does not appear to be one view on military matters held by the Communist party and another one held by the Ministry of Defense. All of the senior Soviet officers are party members, and a rather consistent 10 per cent of the membership of the Central Committee is made up of marshals and generals. Senior military officers also serve on the Central Committees of the various republics.[14] Moreover, a demotion from a political position may

13 I. Butsky, *Political Work in the Soviet Army* (Moscow, Progress Publishers, undated) 23.
14 *Ibid.*, 105.

7

herald a military demotion as well, and a political promotion may signify a promotion in military rank.[15]

When writing about military science (combat capabilities, operational training, etc.), Soviet officers seem to enjoy considerable professional freedom. There does not appear to be any basic conflict between the Soviet military and political leadership. The Soviet minister of defense, whose role roughly corresponds to that of the United States secretary of defense and to that of the chairman of the Joint Chiefs of Staff, is not a civilian but a career soldier, a marshal of the Soviet Union. Relatively speaking, the Soviet military seem to possess greater prestige than do their counterparts in the United States and have a greater voice in matters affecting the military profession.

Different views certainly must exist within the Soviet Union concerning military affairs and future war. There may be groups, both inside and outside the military, who feel that a nuclear war would mean disaster for the Soviet Union as well as for the other nations of the world. The official view, however, as reflected in the *Communist of the Armed Forces*, is that the Soviet Union would survive and be the victor in such a conflict. Disputes undoubtedly occur over other military matters, particularly concerning the allocation of scarce resources among and between military needs and the general economy. The chief protagonists of these divergent views probably have been members of the Politburo. This does not imply that the party leaders arbitrarily tell the military what they should do, without taking into account the responsibilities with which the military have been entrusted and the problems they face in discharging their responsibilities. It is necessary to bear in mind that there are no neat distinctions between the military and civilian elements of Soviet society such as those which exist in the United States.

15 Marshal of Aviation Vladimir A. Sudets, former commander in chief of PVO (air defense), was dropped as a candidate member of the Central Committee during the XXIII Party Congress in April, 1966. In July, 1966, he was relieved of command. His replacement, General of the Army P. F. Batitsky, was promoted from a candidate to a full member of the Central Committee at the same party meeting in April, suggesting that the decision to remove and to replace a commander in chief might have been a party decision.

Sources

In the main, we have selected for translation Soviet military writings which were published for reading and study by members of their armed forces. The "letopis," or the master index, published in the Soviet Union and containing listings of all authors and their works, to include newspapers, magazines, and books, was utilized as a bibliographical aid. Extracts have been taken from books which can reasonably be identified as being prepared for military study, such as the series called the *Officer's Library*.[16] Magazine selections, except in certain cases which will be noted, are from those printed for military personnel. Insofar as newspapers are concerned, *Red Star*, the official daily publication of the Ministry of Defense, has been the most fruitful. Other newspapers, such as *Pravda* and *Izvestia*, have been checked for articles of significance.

It is recognized that some important articles on various matters may appear in obscure publications. These may be trial balloons for new ideas, or be written to attack an individual or group. Any discussion of the subtle maneuvers used in the Soviet Union to carry on internal power struggles would be beyond the scope and purpose of this book.

Sources which have been deliberately avoided are magazines and newspapers which the Soviets print in English. For example, there is a magazine called *Soviet Military Review* which is printed in English and in French. There is no Russian-language version of this magazine, and it is not read by members of the Soviet Armed Forces. Hence it must be regarded as published for propaganda and disinformation. There are some journals of note, such as *International Affairs*, which are printed in Russian, as well as in English and French, but they are not directed at the Soviet military reader.

Ideological Aspects of Soviet Military Doctrine

The Soviet Armed Forces were first forged as the combat tool of

16 A series of seventeen books, being published by the Ministry of Defense, to cover doctrine, strategy, tactics, and military art. For listing of titles and publishing status, see Appendix.

a revolutionary party. They profess to retain this role today. Until the advent of the nuclear age, Communist theoreticians believed that all wars were not only inevitable but a progressive political phenomena. Consequently, war for them had been what [Karl von] Clausewitz claimed it was, the continuation of politics by other means. Because of the destructive potential of nuclear weapons, Khrushchev introduced the doctrinal modification that war was no longer "necessarily" inevitable and that the triumph of communism could possibly be achieved without war. The condition for this bloodless triumph is that the capitalists recognize the intrinsic superiority of the Communist system and peacefully acquiesce to their own demise.

Within three years after the ouster of Khrushchev, it became apparent that the Soviet Union was not settling for a position of strategic inferiority but appeared to be striving to change the strategic balance in its favor. The authoritative *Communist of the Armed Forces* began to chide those earlier writers who had argued that Clausewitz might be outmoded.[17] Articles in this magazine claim that special advantages accrue to the military leaders of the Soviet Union because of their adherence to Marxist-Leninist ideology, particularly by their employment of the dialectical approach in analyzing the problems of strategy.[18] These concepts are consistently reflected in Soviet writings on the subjects of military research, development, and weapons procurement and deployment.

Manipulative Aspects of Soviet Doctrine

We must consider carefully the possibility that these Soviet writings are written primarily to communicate with the West, or per-

[17] In 1965, Lieutenant Colonel Ye. I. Ribkin published an article in the *Communist of the Armed Forces* entitled "On the Nature of the World Nuclear Rocket War," which attacked by name N. Talensky and his article "Thoughts on Past Wars," *International Affairs*, April, 1965. In 1966, Colonel I. Grudinin, writing "On the Question of the Essence of War," *Red Star*, July 21, made a rather obscure attack on Ribkin and singled out Talensky for particular wrath and scorn. N. Talensky was a Soviet general major in 1944, and in 1965 was one of the editors of *International Affairs after the Second World War*, published by the Academy of Sciences. Note Ribkin's article, chap. 9, and Grudinin's attack, chap. 24, below.

[18] This belief is stated in a number of translations in this book, such as "On Contemporary Military Strategy," chap. 18, and "Military Art in the Postwar Period," chap. 15, below.

haps to deceive or to influence it by propaganda. Obviously, any book written by a Soviet officer, conceived in the framework of Marxist-Leninist ideology, will contain intrinsic propaganda similar to any other Communist work. Thus, the motives of the principal Communist adversary, "imperialistic" United States, will be described in terms of propaganda, as will also the issues of "just" and "unjust" wars. Any war fought to advance the cause of communism is by definition "just," whereas those who oppose the expansion of communism by force, as the United States has done in Vietnam, wage an "unjust" or "reactionary" war. Soviet writers also tend to stress the destructiveness of nuclear weapons when applied against non-Communist targets, and to minimize the effect of such weapons when targets are located in the "progressive, socialist" Soviet Union.

Some students of Soviet affairs contend that the Soviet military writings available to the West actually are a form of psychological warfare. At the other extreme are those who believe that Soviet military writings are entirely for internal consumption. They would argue that the changes brought about by "the revolution in military affairs" are so far reaching that they could not be communicated covertly even within the Soviet Union. The indoctrination of several million troops could not be accomplished entirely through classified documents any more than such a vast change could secretly be brought about in the United States.

We believe the basic purpose of the selected military writings which we present in this book is to inform the existing and emerging Soviet military leadership and to serve as the basis of troop indoctrination. The newspapers, magazines, and books from which these articles are taken are readily available throughout the Soviet Union. A secondary purpose of a number of the writings, one that is impossible to assess accurately, may be to communicate to some degree with the United States and Communist China.

Evaluation of Soviet Military Doctrine and Science.

Westerners who have studied Soviet military writings have frequently reached the conclusion that they are unsophisticated or

11

naïve, without really knowing the restrictions under which the writers must operate. Nothing could be more dangerous than to categorize Soviet military writings as backward. The Marxist-Leninist phraseology may make many of the selections boring and difficult to follow. But the reader who thinks that the articles can be ignored need but remind himself of the reality of the Soviet nuclear weaponry.

There are Soviet military concepts that differ in certain functional respects from our own. For example, their theoreticians seem to place greater stress on strategic defense than the United States does. The rationale justifying a "defense" orientation will be seen in a number of translations throughout this book.

The level of Soviet military discussion does not seem to be below Western standards. Soviet writings often are quite generalized and written, at least in part, in Aesopian language. One may marvel at the single-minded obsession with security and even become amused at the fact that the Soviet press feels compelled to describe new military development only in terms of achievement by non-Soviet forces.[19] Soviet military writers do not illustrate their ideas with specific examples pertaining to their own forces, apparently in the belief that these might give Western leaders an indication of their operational thinking.

Has Soviet military thinking adapted to the problems imposed by a constantly changing technology as rapidly as non-Communist military thought? In attempting to answer this question, we must measure Soviet military literature against military doctrinal writings by non-Communist theorists, available in the open press of the United States and elsewhere. It should be noted that every word in any Soviet publication is carefully censored, and much of what would be regarded as unclassified in the non-Communist world is a carefully guarded secret in the Soviet Union.

It will be seen that many important issues are treated more am-

---

19 The Soviets have two huge military parades each year. A primary purpose of the parades in Moscow is to show certain of their missiles, tanks, and other military equipment to foreign attachés and the foreign press. In order that the Soviet public have some conception of how an antiballistic missile system functions, detailed photographs and explanations are given of proposed United States systems.

biguously in Soviet writings than in those of the West. Sometimes there are blatant contradictions contained in the views presented in a single article. Certain of the contradictions may have been introduced deliberately, while others may be a result of the complexity of the problem. Other "contradictions" may reflect the Soviet dialectical approach to strategic thinking. Soviet military writers undoubtedly are aware of the significance of possible new weapons systems which they do not and cannot discuss publicly. For example, their writings reiterate that they are considering the use of space solely for peaceful purposes, while asserting that the aim of the United States space efforts is to gain military control.[20] To communicate to their readers an understanding of the importance of space, they translate many articles from the open and uncontrolled press of the United States.

Despite these shortcomings and omissions, Soviet military writings do provide a perspective through which we can at least see the surface of their military preparations and planning. At the same time, views obtained from Soviet writings must be reconciled with information from other sources before we can reach any firm conclusions regarding what the Soviet military forces are really designed to accomplish. This caveat notwithstanding, much can be gained by carefully analyzing Soviet doctrine, even if one must draw conclusions by inference or deduction in lieu of precise revelations concerning Soviet military thinking.

Doctrine and Capabilities

We have become reasonably certain of many things concerning Soviet military capabilities. Yet, the unexpected rapidity with which they developed nuclear and thermonuclear weapons was a shock to the scientists of the United States. In 1950 their number of advanced fighters, the famed MIG-15, propably exceeded those of our own comparable fighter, the F-86. By the mid-1950's they were ahead in missile technology. They launched the world's first

---

[20] See Colonel P. Plyachenko, "The Cosmic Big Stick of the Pentagon," *Soviet Warrior*, No. 15, 1965, and Colonel M. Golishev, "The Pentagon Strains for the Cosmos," *Izvestia*, September 28, 1965.

Sputnik and the first cosmonaut. Future surprises can be expected.

Leonid I. Brezhnev and Aleksei N. Kosygin have been far more restrained in their public utterances concerning Soviet military strength than their predecessor, the flamboyant Khrushchev. It would seem prudent, therefore, to take their claims that the U.S.S.R. enjoys superiority in one or more strategic areas more seriously than we have in the past. Although Soviet Armed Forces operate within the context of budget restraints and limitations of resources, Soviet strategic capabilities appear to have been growing more rapidly than those of the United States, and the gap between these two nations' forces is diminishing, perhaps at an accelerated pace. The Soviet Union seems to be catching up with respect to strategic offensive and is forging ahead in the defensive sector. A Soviet defensive advantage, based on a deployed antiballistic missile system, could become a crucial factor in the over-all strategic balance between the two superpowers.

Despite Soviet successes with missiles and in space during the 1950's, there were few Soviet writings of any note on doctrine or strategy in that decade. The initial reason for this was Stalin's belief in the "permanently operating factors" crucial to the outcome of war.[21] "The dogmatization of a series of military theoretical theses stated at different times by Stalin hindered the creative development of Soviet military thought and promoted certain stagnation of it, especially in the sphere of strategy."[22] For example:

> The factor "quantity and quality of divisions" in war was considered in isolation from concrete historical conditions. . . . In the period when war chiefly bore the character of a struggle in land

[21] General Major Svyatoslav N. Kozlov, General Major Mikhail V. Smirnov, Colonel Ivan S. Baz', and Colonel Petr A. Sidorov, *On Soviet Military Science*, 209. Also see Raymond Garthoff, "*The Soviet Image of Future War*, 24–25, which lists "the 'permanently operating factors which decide the course and fate of wars.' " They are:

1. The stability of the rear;
2. The morale of the army;
3. The quantity and quality of divisions;
4. The armament of the army;
5. The organizing ability of the command personnel.

[22] General Major N. Ya. Sushko and Colonel S. A. Tyushkevich, *Marxism–Leninism On War and the Army*, 343.

theaters of military actions, the basic military might of governments was composed of ground forces and their combat capability was determined by the quantity and quality of tactical commands or divisions. Now the decisive factor of military force is the new technical means of armed struggle and chiefly the nuclear rocket weapon. . . . All this shows that "quantity and quality of divisions" cannot be considered abstractly outside of concrete historical conditions.[23]

Not only did Stalin have to die before a sophisticated discussion of warfare could take place; he also had to be discredited. Khrushchev denounced Stalin, *in camera*, at the XX Congress of the Communist party on February 25, 1956. This was the "revitalizing influence" that was needed.[24] For Stalin's military views to be openly renounced, he had to be publicly discredited as well. This was not done until the XXII Party Congress in October, 1961. Within a few months, in March, 1962, Sokolovsky's *Military Strategy* was typeset and sent to the printers two months later.

There has been sufficient time since 1962 to appraise Soviet military capability and force posture over the intervening years. How well have their military writings during this time anticipated or paralleled the development of the evolving Soviet force posture?

We leave the answer to this question to the reader. Translations which follow are presented in chronological order, starting with a post-Khrushchev book published in late October, 1964, by the Soviet Ministry of Defense. In the presentation of succeeding articles every attempt was made to select varying opinions dealing with different areas of strategy, doctrine, and tactics.

Each translated article is preceded by a brief description of the author, a list of other articles which he has written, and an indication of why the particular work is included in this book. Many equally informative articles had to be omitted for lack of space. These translations will afford the reader an opportunity to examine for himself Soviet views on their "revolution in military affairs" and to relate this to the future security of the non-Communist world and to the United States in particular.

23 Kozlov, *et al.*, *op. cit.*, 292.   24 *Ibid.*, 209.

I · The Doctrinal Legacy from Khrushchev

THE GOVERNMENT'S evening newspaper, *Izvestia*, was late the night of October 15, 1964. This was the first hint Muscovites had that something was amiss. By morning, the world knew that Nikita Khrushchev had "resigned" his post as Communist party first secretary and premier of the Soviet government. The loss of a world leader always produces a shock, whether he is liked or not. The world watched Moscow with a certain nervousness. How could this have happened? Exactly four days later the Chief of Staff of the Soviet Armed Forces, Marshal of the Soviet Union Sergei S. Biryuzov, along with other high-ranking officers, was killed in an air crash in Yugoslavia. Nerves already taut were stretched even more. Was this part of a plot?

But nothing more followed, and Brezhnev and Kosygin took over the reins of government without a hitch. The army noted that the new chief of staff, sixty-six-year-old Marshal Matvei V. Zakharov, replacing the chief of staff who had been killed in the aircraft accident, was simply being returned to the job he had vacated in February, 1963.

In less than a month, however, charges of "harebrained scheming, subjectivism, and arbitrariness" were leveled against Khrushchev. In 1957, when the presidium had tried to remove him, Khrushchev had called the Central Committee and had rallied them to his support. This was not to be the case in 1964. A plenum of the Central Committee in mid-November dropped several of Khrushchev's coterie; but Alexander Shelepin, former head of the Komsomols (the Young Communist League) and the secret police (1959–61), now party secretary, won a seat on the presidium, as did Petr Shelest. Eight men achieved full member status on the 330-man Central Committee. One of these was Vladimir Semi-

16

chastny, former Komsomol leader and present chief of the KGB,[1] the secret police, and another was General of the Army Alexsei Yepishev, once a deputy of the KGB under the notorious Lavrenti P. Beria and presently the chief of the Main Political Administration of the Soviet Army and Navy, the party's watchdog in the armed forces.

A new book, *Problems of the Revolution in Military Affairs*, which went on sale in early 1965, had been prepared prior to Khrushchev's downfall. Three of its chapters make up Section I of this book.

---

1. THE REVOLUTION IN MILITARY AFFAIRS AND THE TASK OF THE MILITARY PRESS
By Marshal of the Soviet Union
Rodion Ya. Malinovsky (1898–1967)
Minister of Defense, U.S.S.R. (1957–67)

Editors' Notes

Chronologically and topically, Marshal Malinovsky's article is an ideal point of departure for the Soviet military writings which follow. In it the late Soviet Minister of Defense shows the continuation of the military policy from the Khrushchev regime into the new one; it is short, to the point, and states why articles on doctrine and strategy are needed by the Soviet military forces.

This selection is taken from *Problems of the Revolution in Military Affairs*, a collection of articles published by the Military Publishing House, Moscow, in 1965.[1] The book was typeset before Khrushchev's ouster, and a check of the original articles discloses

---

[1] KGB means Komitet Gosudarstvennoi Bezopasnosti or Committee of State Security (secret police). Yuri V. Andropov succeded Semichastny as head of the KGB on May 18, 1967.

[1] Colonel P. M. Derevyanko (ed.), *Problems of the Revolution in Military Affairs*, 3. First printing 16,000 copies.

that only few changes were made after his removal from power. The timing of the appearance of the book suggests it was meant as a reassurance that there were to be no basic changes in military policy under the new regime. The Soviet revolution in military affairs, already well under way, was regarded as irreversible.

All of the articles in *Problems of the Revolution in Military Affairs* previously had appeared either in *Red Star* or in *Communist of the Armed Forces* during 1963 and 1964, while Khrushchev was in full command. We have selected three for inclusion in this book, the first by Marshal Malinovsky and the two immediately following, entitled "The Revolution in Military Affairs and Its Results" and "New Means of Fighting and Strategy."

Clearly and concisely, Marshal Malinovsky points out the impact of the nuclear weapon on warfare and tells of the creation of the strategic rocket forces. He does not consider that a plateau in weapons development has been reached, but he emphasizes that new weapons constantly are being substituted by those even newer and that there is always the possibility of a technological breakthrough.

As minister of defense, he indicates the role of military newspapers and magazines, as well as the publications of Voyenizdat, the Military Publishing House, in explaining to the Soviet Armed Forces the nature of the revolution in military affairs. He states that "some units of military personnel still live with old, outmoded notions about the nature of modern warfare." Soviet leaders "must by all means prepare the personnel for fighting with a strong, technically highly equipped enemy who possesses the nuclear rocket weapon and other means of destruction . . . ." To achieve this, "the feeling of the new must appear in everything issued by our press."

Since the selections in this book are in chronological order, Malinovsky's views will again appear under a later date. His address to the XXIII Party Congress in April, 1966, will show his continuity of thought.

At the time the following article was written, Marshal Malinovsky already had served over fifty years in uniform. Born in 1898, he entered the Tsarist Army in 1914 and saw action with the Russian Brigade in France. After his return to Russia, he joined the Red Army and fought in the Civil War. He went to Spain during its civil war and commanded various Soviet forces during World War II. He was in the Soviet Far East from 1945 to 1955 and there played a key role in Soviet planning and support for the Korean conflict. In 1957 he replaced Marshal Georgi K. Zhukov as minister of defense. Marshal Malinovsky died March 31, 1967.

THE SOVIET ARMED FORCES are supplied with first-class military equipment and powerful modern weapons. In the last few years we have had a revolution in military affairs, thanks to outstanding successes in the development of the Soviet economy and science and technology. Fundamental qualitative changes have taken place in all the basic areas of military activity: armaments, organization, combat methods, and methods of training and educating personnel. This has been caused, first of all, by the wide introduction of the nuclear rocket weapon and new equipment assuring its use. *Atomic and thermonuclear weapons now compose the basic firepower and striking power of our Armed Forces. Rockets, which in minutes can cover great distances and carry devastating blows to the enemy at any point in the world, are the main means of delivering these weapons on target.* An absolutely new service of the Armed Forces has been created: the Strategic Rocket Forces. National PVO [air defense] has been basically changed, as well as the Ground Forces, Air Forces, and Naval Forces.

The following innovations, and many others, have radically changed the face of the army and navy: intercontinental and global rockets; atomic and thermonuclear charges equivalent in power to several thousands up to fifty or one hundred million tons of TNT and more; supersonic aviation, including rocket carriers; atomic submarines armed with ballistic and homing rockets; the most exact devices and instruments for observation, computation, guidance, and communications.

19

But new weapons are both being perfected and being substituted by even newer. One cannot exclude the possibility of the appearance of a weapon that is new in principle.

The history of war and military art teaches that changes in military equipment and weapons have a decisive influence on the changes in combat methods and that they unavoidably lead to new forms of troop organization. The level of development of military equipment determines the battle picture and the character of combat operations. Is it necessary to say that the absolutely new, hitherto unheard-of nuclear rocket weapon and other technical means have radically changed the nature of contemporary combat actions and have added fantastic scope and violence to them as well as enormous destructive force and transitoriness?

New means of armed combat radically change the nature of modern war. A new world war, if it should break out, will envelop all the continents and water areas of the world. There will be no protection from nuclear strikes anywhere. Any military base, any city, any industrial area might be not only destroyed but so covered with radioactive fallout that people could not live in that locality for a long time. The time required for the solution of the basic mission of war with contemporary means might be very short, perhaps hours or even minutes. All this makes a definite imprint on the activities of all services of the Armed Forces.

New, greater demands are being made for training the Armed Forces; for the repulse of aggression; for the training of troops, commanders and staffs; and for educating personnel. The guaranteeing of high vigilance and constant combat readiness—the readiness to frustrate a surprise attack by the enemy and swiftly carry out a retaliatory blow—is moving into the forefront.

The significance of military technical training of all categories of military servicemen has grown immeasurably, which in turn demands from them a basic knowledge of nuclear physics, mathematics, electronics, and other sciences.

Extremely great is the significance of the morale and the hardening of the will of the soldier whose moral and physical strength will undergo severe trials. Our socialist structure and Communist ide-

20

ology are creating the most favorable conditions for fostering a strong spirit in the soldier. But these possibilities must be converted into action and put into effect. The revolution in military affairs produced new demands for the disciplining and the organization of troops. Battle will now be distinguished by the most unusual transitoriness and swiftness, demanding from each soldier special accuracy, co-operativeness, and fulfillment of duty.

As never before, the preliminary development of all basic questions of future military actions in peacetime takes on great significance. Indeed, putting into practice the principle "study that and only that which is necessary for present-day war" has now become a matter of life and death.

Military newspapers and magazines, and Voyenizdat, our military publishing house, can and must do a great deal for the thorough explanation of the nature of the revolution in military affairs and the resulting demands produced in the training and education of personnel of different branches and services of the Armed Forces.

The correct understanding of the nature of modern war, battle, operations, the potentials of the new means of warfare, the methods of their use in delivering crushing blows to the enemy and also measures for protection from weapons of mass destruction—these are very important for training our soldiers to fulfill missions given them by the party and government for the sure protection of the state interests of the builders of communism of the Land of the Soviets.

The task of propagandizing the progressive views and conclusions of Soviet military doctrine is highly important because some units of military personnel still live with old, outmoded notions about the nature of modern warfare. This fact is reflected in various published articles, brochures, and books. It is necessary to chop down and discard more boldly everything that hinders the creative development of progressive military thought, the formation of correct, innovating views in military affairs. In connection with this, creative, lively discussions in the press of the actual questions of military theory and practice, ending with detailed, qualified conclusions and generalizations, would be useful. It is important that the widest possible circle of servicemen take part in these discussions: theorists and practical workers, from both scientific establishments and military schools, and from the troops.

Thus the first problem is military, theoretical, propagandistic, and explanatory in nature. But it is not enough to declare, to proclaim the demands and conclusions of contemporary military science thought; it is necessary to struggle actively, insistently, persistently, and constantly to put them into practice, to help soldiers follow them in daily studies and service, to unite theory and practice for the sake of the most important thing: the raising of the combat training and the combat readiness of units, ships, formations, and the Armed Forces as a whole. Here is the immense field of activity for all of our military press.

The combat training of the personnel, organized to take into account the new demands, must always be in the center of attention of newspapers and magazines. Special attention in this training must be given to military-technical preparation and field training of the troops. To these ends, it is very important to improve and perfect the activities of the press in the generalization and diffusion of innovations, propaganda of progressive methods of teaching and educating soldiers—this should be considered as the most important continual task of all of the military press. The movement for producing outstanding soldiers, for raising class ratings, and for advanced subunits and units must be expanded; war must be declared on indulgences and oversimplifications; the shameful facts of eyewashing must be burned out with red-hot irons.

The correct moral and psychological training of personnel is exceptionally important. Our soldier is an ardent patriot of the Motherland, an individual with high political consciousness, and he must believe in the force of Soviet weapons and have pride in the might and glory of our Armed Forces, but at the same time avoid conceit, complacency, and a scornful attitude towards the enemy. We must by all means prepare the personnel for fighting with a strong, technically highly equipped enemy who possesses the nuclear rocket weapon. The highest combat readiness and the highest vigilance—this is the iron law of our army and navy.

The feeling of the new must appear in everything issued by our press. More attention must be given to the Rocket troops and rocketeers, submarines, and submariners. Highly important, too, is the role of the operators of military and transport machinery on whom so much depends, but our press so far has given them little attention. In a word, cultivate more feeling for the new; study life more deeply; aim to be closer to the rich, instructive examples of military practice.

2. THE REVOLUTION IN MILITARY AFFAIRS AND ITS RESULTS
By General Lieutenant of Aviation N. A. Sbitov
Candidate of Military Sciences[1]

Editors' Notes

THIS ARTICLE, as well as the one preceding by Marshal Malinovsky, is taken from *Problems of the Revolution in Military Affairs*. Originally, it had appeared in *Red Star* on February 15, 1963, less than six months after the Cuban missile crisis.

Sbitov begins his paper by pointing out the necessary conditions in which a revolution in military affairs takes place. Among these are "a high level of economic development and outstanding achievements in science" as well as "the opportune foresight by the political leadership of the tendency in the development of new military equipment and weapons systems."

The author places in italics that "*the Communist party and its Leninist Central Committee were the organizers and leaders of this revolution.*" He then goes on to state:

> The party reached the conclusion that the Armed Forces and the country, as a whole, must prepare for a war in which nuclear rocket

1 See Glossary.

23

weapons will be widely used; which will represent a decisive, classic collision of two opposed world social systems; and which will be distinguished by unseen violence, dynamic force and high maneuverability of combat operations.

According to Sbitov the mass production of nuclear weapons has been achieved, the rearming of both the army and navy with these weapons has been completed, and all troops, especially officers, generals, and admirals are trained in the use of the new weapons. The "revolution in military affairs is an accomplished fact" and "marks a turning point in the theory of military art."

With what appears as rather grim pleasure, Sbitov calls attention to the fact that "nuclear rocket strikes will deprive the U.S.A. of that geographical inaccessibility which it had earlier." He goes on to state the Soviet targeting philosophy for nuclear weapons: "The enemy's strategic means of nuclear attack, economy, system of government and military administration, and also main groupings of troops and naval forces in the theaters of military action, will undergo massive nuclear rocket strikes." Sbitov concludes his article, as most Soviet writers on military affairs do, by giving credit for Soviet military successes to the party and to the guiding principles of Marxism-Leninism.

General Sbitov was the author of "The Nature of World Nuclear Rocket War and the Laws Governing It," which appeared in *Naval Collections*, March, 1964. *Red Star* announced late in 1966 that his new work, *The Contemporary Revolution in Military Affairs*, soon would be published.

I

THE SOVIET ARMED FORCES possess invincible fighting strength, great discipline, and high combat readiness. In every way, they are at the level demanded by contemporary conditions. And this is one of the most important results of the revolution in military affairs which has taken place in recent years.

A revolution in military affairs can take place only when the necessary conditions are there. The most important of these are:

1. A high level of economic development and outstanding achievements in science and technology which permit the creation of an absolutely new military-technical base and new weapons for the armed forces;

2. The opportune anticipation by the political leadership of the trends in the development of new military equipment and weapons, the disclosure of the nature of a future war, and the carrying out of basic reforms in military affairs;

3. The availability in the armed forces of such personnel, especially of leaders, who will have the ability to master quickly the new means of armed fighting and use them in any combat conditions with the greatest effectiveness.

All of these conditions existed in our country. It is well known with what a furious tempo the economy of the U.S.S.R. developed and continues to develop. In the Soviet Union, important branches of industry, such as atomic energy, rocketry, and radioelectronics, were created. We have precise instrument-making, special metallurgy, highly developed jet airplane production, atomic ship construction, production of the means of automation and telemechanics, and electronic computers.

The Soviet Union has amazed the whole world with the new heights of its technical science progress. The launching of an artificial Earth satellite, the flights around the world of Soviet cosmonauts in Soviet space ships—these are the best evidence of the flourishing of our science and technology, of our industrial power. The Soviet Union has not only caught up with but has surpassed the leading capitalist countries in the training of scientific and technical engineering cadres.

The Communist party and its Leninist Central Committee were the organizers and leaders of this revolution. Guided by the wealth of military theoretical heritage from V. I. Lenin, the creative development of the teachings of Marxism-Leninism on war and the army, taking into account the arrangement of the class forces in the world arena, the basic changes in military affairs, the military potential of our probable enemies, and the potentials of the U.S.S.R. and of all the socialist camp, our party and its Central

Committee gave clear scientifically based answers to the questions of what the nature of a new world war will be if the imperialists succeed in unleashing it; what direction the structure of the Armed Forces of the U.S.S.R. must take; what the trends of the development of the means of armed conflict and the ways of waging it will be.

The party reached the conclusion that the Armed Forces and the country, as a whole, must prepare for a war in which nuclear rocket weapons will be used widely; which will represent a decisive, classic collision of two opposed world social systems; and which will be distinguished by unprecedented violence, dynamic force, and high maneuverability of combat operations.

Thanks to the constant concern of the Central Committee of the Communist party, the Soviet government, by firmly putting the military policy into practice, created everything necessary to place the Armed Forces of the U.S.S.R. and the defense capabilities of the country at the level of contemporary demand.

Of great significance for the creative solution of the problems of the defense power of the Soviet government and the further strentghening of the might of its Armed Forces was the fact that the Central Committee of the CPSU[2] bravely and decisively did away with the harmful consequences of the personality cult of Stalin, including those in the military-theoretical area.

The revolution in military affairs, brought about under the leadership of the party, solved the following problems:

1. The mass production of the nuclear weapon, as the main means of mass destruction, was organized; and the mass production of rockets of various designations, as the basic means for delivering the nuclear ammunition to the objectives of destruction, was accomplished.

2. The equipping of the Soviet Army and Navy with the nuclear rocket weapon was fully completed, and the basic reorganization of the Armed Forces, connected with the introduction of the weapon, was carried out.

3. Modern Soviet military doctrine, which determines the new

2 Communist party of the Soviet Union.

principles of Soviet military strategy, operational art, and tactics, was developed; and on the basis of the guiding instructions of the Communist party, the Soviet government, and the achievements of leading military-scientific thought, regulations and manuals were reprocessed, taking into account the peculiarities and requirements of nuclear rocket war.

4. The retraining of all troop personnel, especially of officers, generals, and admirals, was carried out; a systematic and purposeful character was given to the mastering of the new sorts of complicated and powerful military equipment and weapons by the servicemen; this same thing was done in mastering new methods of combat operations; in the process of all this work, the high political consciousness, the military-theoretical and military-technological preparation of our military cadres, and their ability to be always at the level demanded by contemporary theory and practice was once again demonstrated.

Thus, *the revolution in military affairs is an accomplished fact. It led to basic quantitative and qualitative changes in the military-technological base of the Armed Forces and in its structure. It marked a revolution in the methods of waging war, a revolution in the theory of military art and actual combat training of the troops.*

II

At a time when the Soviet Union and all the other socialist countries are firmly following a policy of peace and persistently and consistently struggling for the prevention of nuclear war, the imperialist governments are opposing the idea of peaceful coexistence, forcing the arms race, and are preparing to unleash nuclear rocket war. This is what is forcing us to be ready for nuclear rocket war as we have already stated above. Therefore, this readiness must not be lower but higher than the readiness of the aggressors. Otherwise it will be impossible to frustrate their criminal plans in the very embryo stage and, if war becomes a fact, to smash the aggressors.

Nuclear rocket war signifies that the main means of armed combat, the main means of defeating the enemy, will be the nuclear weapon, and the basic means of delivering it to the target will be the rocket. The nuclear rocket weapon possesses gigantic destructive force, unlimited range, and enormous speed of movement in space. For example, a modern strategic bomber, according to the figures of American specialists, needs eight to ten hours to cover a distance of eight thousand kilometers; and a naval ship carrying nuclear means of attack needs eight to ten days; but an intercontinental ballistic rocket needs only thirty to thirty-five minutes.

The characteristics of the nuclear rocket weapon also cause the appearance of a new law in nuclear war which lies in the fact that war will be accompanied by massive extermination of people and massive destruction of resources. The action of this law calls for a change in the means of waging combat actions. The basic, determining method of waging war is not the attack of the Ground Forces, as it was earlier, but the *delivery of mass nuclear rocket strikes*. For instance, nuclear rocket strikes will deprive the U.S.A. of that geographical inaccessibility which it had earlier. In the event of war, the vital centers and stategic nuclear offensive weapons of the belligerents, which are located throughout enemy territory, might turn out to be the main objectives of military actions. This means that the line of separation between the front and the rear will disappear. The very meaning of "interior of the country" will become untenable because *the focus of armed combat will move to the interior of the territory of the belligerents.*

The long range of strategic means makes it possible to achieve strategic military and military-political goals at the very beginning of the war. The enemy's strategic means of nuclear attack, economy, system of government and military administration, and also main groupings of troops and naval forces in the theaters of military action, will undergo massive nuclear rocket strikes. Operational and tactical successes will depend on strategic nuclear rocket successes. (In the past, war was the other way around: the stategic successes were achieved or built up gradually, according to the tactical and operational successes.)

The results of strategic nuclear rocket strikes must be used by the Ground Forces in full measure. The task of accomplishing the defeat of remaining groupings of enemy forces, occupying the enemy's territory, and protecting one's own country from invasion by the enemy's troops, is given to them. Combat operations in naval theaters might have as a goal the defeat of the enemy's naval groups of forces, destroying his communications, and protecting one's own communiciations and coasts from nuclear strikes from the sea.

The scale and nature of combat operations of Troop PVO [air defense of troops] grow according to the development of nuclear rocket weapons.

The sum total of these and other laws and demands of nuclear rocket war has enormous significance for determining and solving the *practical problems* of the structure of the Armed Forces and for strengthening their fighting power and the defense potential of the Soviet government. Proceeding from the fact that intercontinental and global rockets will serve as the most powerful means for repulsing the aggressor and for bringing about his decisive defeat, the Central Committee of the Communist party and the Soviet government created a new service in the Armed Forces, the Strategic Rocket Troops. This is the leading service of the Armed Forces, the troops of constant combat readiness.

From time to time bourgeois propaganda sets up a clamor about the military weaknesses of the U.S.S.R., claiming that the U.S.A. supposedly is ahead of the Soviet Union in the realm of development of nuclear rocket means.

People can now scarcely be found in the world who would seriously believe such twaddle. The excessively zealous representatives of imperialist militarists should remember several facts which amazed the whole world in their time.

It is well known that the Soviet Union was the first to begin the storming of the cosmos with the use of rockets. On the fourth of October, 1957, it launched the world's first sputnik of Earth. Since that time, each year has given a sufficient demonstration of the enormous progress of Soviet rocket construction. The launching of rocket systems for solving more and more complicated tasks follows according to schedule. The U.S.S.R. was the first to put a cosmic ship satellite with a man on board into a near Earth orbit. Several dozen Earth sputniks of the "Cosmos" type have placed a mass of valuable scientific facts in the hands of scientists. Our cosmic rockets have penetrated lunar space more than once and have started to planets of the solar system. Sputniks of the "Electron" type, and also the maneuverable sputniks, "Polyot" and interplanetary station "Mars," and so forth, have been made by the hands of Soviet scientists, engineers, and technicians.

It is obvious that such launchings of heavy sputniks and cosmic stations would be impossible to carry out with a weak rocket technology. So far, many of the problems solved by us are beyond the power of American specialists.

The Soviet Union has carried out a test of nuclear ammunition the equivalent of fifty million tons of TNT. At the XXII Congress of the CPSU it was said that we have a bomb equivalent to one hundred million tons of TNT, but we will not test it. These facts testify to the fact that we possess powerful nuclear ammunition and that our rockets can deliver them to any point in the world. For this reason the significant growth and invincible power of the Armed Forces of the U.S.S.R. is not propaganda but real, indisputable fact.

Our highly developed economy, our industrial power, and our advanced science and technology permitted the construction for the Strategic Rocket Troops of such a quantity of launchers, the creation of such a quantity of rockets and charges for them of enormous power, that we, if it is demanded, are in a position to sweep any aggressor from the face of the earth no matter at what point of the earth he is located or what military power or territory or economy he controls. *The infliction on the aggressor of retaliatory mass nuclear rocket strikes by strategic means, or to speak more frankly, by the Strategic Rocket Troops, is considered by us to be the main aspect of strategic operations.* To them is given the decisive role in achieving victory in war if the imperialist aggressors risk unleashing it.

Also taken into account is the fact that the diversity of objectives and the conditions of military operations require the presence of the other services of the Armed Forces. No matter how significant the role of the Strategic Rocket Troops, full victory over the aggressor can be achieved only as a result of the combined actions of all the services of the Armed Forces, of all sorts of weapons, and with the active support and participation of all of the people in the struggle for victory over the enemy. That is why we are perfecting, strengthening, and developing in every way possible all of the services of the Armed Forces and service arms.

Take, for example, the Ground Forces. The basis of their force now is the operational-tactical rocket formation and unit. The Ground Forces possess excellent conventional weapons, the power and capabilities of which have grown. The facts testify to this: Soviet motorized infantry divisions are considerably less in number of personnel than the division at the end of the last war. But to make up for it, the weight of one of its salvos, without adding rocket weapons, has increased by more than four times. In modern Soviet motorized infantry and tank divisions, there are more tanks than in the mechanized and tank corps of the period of the last war or in corresponding divisions of any NATO country.

One of the most important results of the revolution in military affairs has been the birth of a *qualitatively new* service of the Armed Forces, the National PVO [air defense] and PRO troops [antirocket defense]. Characteristic for these troops at the contemporary stage of their development is their being equipped with surface-to-air missiles of different ranges, new types of fighter aircraft, long-range radar equipment, and automatic means of guidance. The rearming of Troop PVO [troop air defense] with antiaircraft artillery and surface-to-air missiles produced a very great effect. During the last war an average of four hundred to six hundred shells were expended by antiaircraft artillery on destroying one enemy plane. A modern airplane, possessing great speed and more than twice the altitude which can be reached by the shells of antiaircraft guns, can be shot down by one or, at the most, two rockets.

Those enormous quantitative and qualitative changes which have taken place in the Air Forces are widely known. We have at our disposal excellent jet aircraft, supersonic long-range bombers and formidable aerial rocket guns. Rocket-carrying aviation capable of delivering nuclear strikes to the aggressor from far dis-

31

tances, without entering the PVO zone of the enemy, is being more and more widely introduced.

The revolution in military affairs has brought changes to our Navy. Its basic strength is the submarine of various designations, which is incomparably more effective in nuclear rocket war than a surface ship. The basis of the submarine fleet is the atomic submarine armed with nuclear rocket weapons. The modern submarine has the ability to bombard and demolish important strategic targets and destroy the warships of the aggressor with ballistic and homing rockets. Naval rocket-carrying aviation can successfully wage combat actions in co-operation with submarines.

From all this, it is possible to reach the following conclusion. As a result of the revolution in military affairs, *the Armed Forces of the U.S.S.R. have been turned into a powerful factor in preserving the peace, into a reliable stronghold of security of the people. In the competition for arms' quality forced on us by the aggressive forces, we are not only not inferior to those who threaten us with war, but in many ways we excel them. The Soviet Armed Forces surpass imperialist armies in their military might.*

III

As long as the danger of aggressive war from the side of the imperialists is not liquidated, while agreement on general and complete disarmament is not achieved, we must keep our powder dry, we must display the greatest vigilance and maintain high combat readiness. Our party views the protection of the socialist Fatherland, the strengthening of the defenses of the U.S.S.R., and of the power of the Soviet Armed Forces as our sacred duty, as the task of tasks of all the Soviet people, as the most important function of the socialist government.

The party and the government display tireless concern so that the Armed Forces of the U.S.S.R. in the future will be powerful and will have at their disposal the most modern means of protecting the Motherland.

The trends in the further development of the Armed Forces, in military affairs as a whole, are determined by the progress in all areas of natural and technical sciences. This progress will stipulate the *continuous* perfection of the existing sorts of arms. At the same time *new* means of fighting and *new* sorts of military equipment might be created. Science does not exclude the possibility of creating kinds of weapons, which are new in principle, for destroying various targets. In the interests of assuring the military supremacy of our country over the imperialist aggressors, newer and newer problems in developing and equipping the Armed Forces with more effective sorts of armaments will be raised and solved in the future.

The gigantic revolution in military affairs, the further growth of the technical equipping of the troops, and the appearance of new means of armed struggle make very high demands of the personnel of our army and navy, and of our guiding military cadres. And this is understandable. No matter how powerful the military equipment, people will decide the fate of the high combat readiness of troops and the result of the armed conflict. Our party gives great attention to the preparation of military cadres, to the combat training and political education of all Soviet soldiers.

Educated by the party, boundlessly devoted to the people, the Motherland, and the cause of communism, our officers, generals, and admirals are successfully solving the problems which have been given to them. But successes must not give rise to complacency, carelessness, and conceit in our ranks. Rapid development of military affairs and the interests of strengthening the combat readiness of the troops demand that we systematically, persistently, and with a feeling of high responsibility, continue to master Marxist-Leninist theory, raise our military-theoretical and military knowledge, and perfect the political and businesslike qualities of skillful organizers and educators of personnel.

The task of tasks of all troop personnel was and is the maintenance of constant high combat readiness. High combat readiness in contemporary circumstances has taken on decisive significance. And this is directly connected with the significance of the beginning period of war which is growing in an enormous degree. The accumulated reserves of nuclear weapons and their carriers,

33

rockets, can be used by the belligerents in the very first minutes of the war. Therefore, the possibility cannot be excluded that the initial period will be the decisive period, which in many ways will predetermine the development and outcome of the war. And if this is the case, then it is necessary to display exceptionally high vigilance and maintain exceptionally high combat readiness in order to give a crushing repulse to the aggressor at any moment, to frustrate his intentions, and to defeat him completely.

It is necessary that each Soviet soldier thoroughly understand that our combat readiness is embodied in our soldiers' skill and high moral-political qualities, and in exact calculations in hours and minutes which cannot be violated. This is a law, born of the revolution in military affairs.

Soviet soldiers are deeply aware of their responsibility for the reliable protection of the Motherland and the great accomplishments of the people. They now and henceforth will devote all their knowledge, energy, and labor to selflessly serving the people, the cause of the Communist party, and the cause of communism.

---

3. NEW MEANS OF FIGHTING AND STRATEGY
By Colonel V. V. Larionov
Candidate of Military Sciences

Editors' Notes

ANOTHER SELECTION from *Problems of the Revolution in Military Affairs* is this one by Colonel Larionov which originally appeared in *Red Star*, April, 1964. Its subject is the impact of the nuclear rocket weapon upon strategy.

Larionov calls attention to the uniting of all the strategic offensive forces in the United States, to include ballistic missiles, strategic bombers, and atomic submarines. In the Soviet Union the strategic rocket forces were formed, and they were from the very start considered the main service of the armed forces.

The revolution in military affairs, resulting from the atomic weapon, has changed leadership roles. This Soviet view has far-reaching implications. In the past, strategic leaders attempted to influence the course of a war by moving reserve units. It was believed that successes achieved in battle in various theaters might result finally in general strategic successes. With supreme command now having the use of nuclear weapons, Larionov states that "decisive results can frequently be achieved without even the use of forces and means of tactical and operational elements, that is, it [the supreme command] is independent of the outcome of battles and operations."

Larionov notes that radical changes have taken place in *strategic deployment* and in *strategic maneuver* as a result of the nuclear weapon. Deployment of forces can no longer be accomplished after a war has started; strategic groupings of armed forces must be formed in times of peace for the beginning of the war. Strategic maneuver is accomplished mainly by retargeting nuclear rocket strikes.

The author of the article indicates that previously "war had a relatively stately beginning, the strained culminating point, and the closing period, bringing one of the sides to victory." Hence, a loss in the beginning period did not necessarily mean defeat in the war. In World War II the Soviet Armed Forces had managed to take the strategic initiative from the Germans and conclude the war successfully. In contemporary times, however, "the outcome of the armed struggle in the beginning period can have a decisive influence on the outcome of the war as a whole."

Colonel Larionov is one of the most prolific writers on military subjects in the Soviet Union. In 1962, he was one of the contributors to the famed *Military Strategy*, edited by Marshal V. D. Sokolovsky.

In March, 1963, Soviet leaders called a conference on Soviet military doctrine. There was some speculation at the time whether this conference was to review the events of the Cuban missile affair, which had taken place a few months earlier, or to approve a second version of *Military Strategy*. Colonel Larionov was listed as one of those attending the conference.

35

Larionov also was one of the four authors who wrote "Against Slanders and Falsifications," *Red Star*, November, 1963, which criticized the United States comments on *Military Strategy*. He remained in favor under the Brezhnev regime and, in 1966, was awarded a Frunze prize for his writings on military theory.

"New Weapons and the Duration of War," by Colonel Larionov, also is included in this book. Among his many other articles are the following:

"Missiles and Strategy," *Red Star*, March, 1962;
"Outer Space and Strategy," *Red Star*, March, 1962;
"In Search of a New Strategy in Vietnam," *Red Star*, September 24, 1965;
"Through the Prism of War," *Red Star*, September 11, 1966.

I

THE DISTINGUISHING FEATURE of the revolution in military affairs is that in the first instance it enveloped the decisive areas of the practice and theory of military organization. To such areas, first and foremost, must be attributed strategy, which occupies a leading place in the theory of military art. As a result of the appearance of a new means of armed combat, it has perhaps undergone the most radical changes.

What explains this? As is known, each new change in the ways of waging war and, therefore, also in strategy, is caused first of all by the development of the economy and by progress of military equipment. These improvements and discoveries in the sphere of military equipment and the creation and introduction into the armed forces of its new forms serve as the determining factor of those basic changes in military affairs, the evidence of which we will report.

Thus, for the original cause of the revolution in military affairs, it is necessary mainly to search in the material sphere, in the development of production caused by contemporary technical science progress.

This progress, the beginning of which was laid down in the

forties of our century, has its own special features which find a reflection in the development of military art and its component parts.

The mastering of atomic energy represents a revolutionary jump in the means of armed combat in contrast to the evolutionary process of change in the means of war in the nineteenth and the beginning of the twentieth centuries.

The appearance of new, highly effective means of destruction gave a push to the rapid development of all other branches of military equipment. Corresponding means of reaching the target and new equipment for directing the weapon were needed. The tempo of technical progress rose sharply, and reviews of criteria for evaluating one or another set of technical tactical information on the new forms of the weapon began to be made more often.

And finally, yet another characteristic feature of contemporary technical science progress must be pointed out. This consists of the fact that this progress literally envelops every area of man's activity. Almost simultaneously the most radical changes in equipment took place and are taking place, outstanding results in research were achieved, and new discoveries were made in physics, chemistry, radioelectronics, and in other branches of science and industry.

All these discoveries have enormous significance for military affairs. Nevertheless, the achievements connected with the creation of the nuclear weapon, rocket equipment, and automatic guidance systems produce special interest, however, from the point of view of military art.

The nuclear weapon by force of its high combat effectiveness was recognized at once as a *means of strategic significance.* In combining long-range and high accuracy in the agents of delivery, such as in intercontinental ballistic and global rockets, the nuclear weapon turned into one of the decisive factors of waging war and basically changed the nature of strategy. It was not by accident that among nuclear rocket means the most development was received by weapons having strategic significance, located under the direct authority of the supreme commands. The appearance, development, and mass introduction into the armed forces of means of

37

military radioelectronics, which opened up the possibility of directing the nuclear rocket weapon and processes of armed conflict, also had a great influence on the nature of strategy.

Since the role of strategic means began to grow more and more noticeably, the striving arose to isolate these means with regard for their specific character. Thus, in our country the Strategic Rocket Forces were created, which became the main service of the Armed Forces. In the U.S.A., it was considered useful to unite all formations and units of strategic bombers, atomic submarines with the "Polaris" missile, and ballistic missiles using the strategic nuclear weapon, together in strategic offensive forces with special commands.

This means that strategy somehow finds its own material strength. In the event of war, this will permit the strategic leadership to have a direct influence on the course of the armed conflict with their own autonomous means. Such autonomy in no way means that strategy in this case is isolated from the other component parts of military art: operational art and tactics. But to a certain degree it changes the very essence and content of strategy and also the methods of achieving the final result in world war.

Before the appearance of the nuclear rocket weapon, strategic leadership usually had available directly under its command such means, the range and combat effectiveness of which allowed them to be used only in conditions of operations and battle. Therefore, in order to influence the course of armed combat in one or another strategic direction or theater of military operations, the supreme command had to give these reserves to strengthen fronts or separate armies. Particular successes achieved in battle and operations in various directions and in diverse spheres of military operations (on land, sea, and in the air) subsequently took shape in general strategic successes. Now, when in the highest instance the command has nuclear means at its disposal, decisive results can frequently be achieved without even the use of forces and means of tactical and operational elements, that is, it is independent of the outcome of battles and operations.

In contemporary conditions, war from the very first minutes can start by means of the use of decisive strategic means of armed combat. It follows that victory in war will now be formed not so much from the sum of separate successes as in the totality of the effective application of the maximum power of the government at the very beginning of the war. This new relationship between strategy, operational art, and tactics must not fail to be taken into account in the theory and practice of military organization.

II

The essence and content of strategy cannot remain unchanged. According to the possibilities of material and moral form, that is, of the forces and means which have been put under the command and also of the military-political aims being pursued by the government in war, the basic categories of strategy, its principles and rules, are undergoing a review.

According to the development of the technical means of armed combat and the introduction of the latest forms of military equipment into the armed forces, even decisions taken at the beginning of the technical revolution can become obsolete. Thus, several strategic concepts and decisions which were formed in the first years after the appearance of the atomic weapon are now viewed differently than at the beginning of the fifties. It is sufficient to disclose the definitions of such basic strategic categories and concepts as the strategic aim, the strategic deployment, strategic maneuver, strategic co-operation, theater of military operations, and means of achieving strategic goals, in order to understand the level of influence of the new means of combat on strategy.

Before the appearance of the nuclear rocket weapon, *the strategic aim*, just as now, included defeating the enemy and depriving him of his ability to wage organized armed resistance. Consequently, in this relationship, there has been no sort of change. But what was meant by depriving the enemy of the ability for armed resistance, what was the criterion for achieving this goal? Earlier it was sufficient to defeat the armed forces, since an enemy who was morally and materially undermined usually capitulated. Now this may prove to be insufficient. Until the enemy government or enemy coalition which unleashed the aggressive war is deprived of his ability to produce the nuclear weapon and the means of its delivery, until the economic and moral political potential is brought to naught, and his administrative and military control destroyed, the enemy will be able to resist and do damage to the opposing side. One of the military ideologists of imperialism, H. Kissinger, writes: "The idea that victory in war is secured by destroying the industry of a potential enemy and undermining the moral spirit of the civilian population is the basic principle of English and American strategic thought."

Thus, the strategic goal is not a separate aspect in world nuclear rocket war but a decisive link in achieving a general military-political goal.

In order that the armed forces can enter war in an organized way, usually measures are taken for their strategic deployment. In the definition of the understanding of *strategic deployment* radical changes have also taken place.

The idea existing right up to the Second World War of strategic deployment and the systematically carried out procedures for covering, mobilizing, concentrating, and combat deployment of forces is now undergoing a review. The majority of these measures are brought about in good time in many governments of opposing coalitions. In any case, the basic means of waging war are always kept in constant combat readiness. In the modern definition, strategic deployment, as a matter of fact, turns into the process of creating strategic groupings of armed forces for the beginning of the war in agreement with the plan of war and the probable conditions of its unleashing.

The perfection of the means of delivering the nuclear weapon to the target, its great range, and the possibility of retargeting nuclear strikes from one object to another also changes the earlier definition of *strategic maneuver*.

Strategic maneuver in the last war occurred when troops and equipment from one strategic direction or theater of combat operations transferred to another by train or automotive transport. In contemporary conditions, with the great vulnerability of communications and lack of time for similar regroupings, such manner of maneuver would be difficult to make and in many cases would be of little expediency. Of course, it cannot be written off the books, insofar as it can be widely used in regrouping within theaters of military operations by the forces of ground troops, aviation, and navy. But as a decisive means of war, strategic maneuver with these means can be defined as moving forces from one strategic direction or objective to another, mainly by means of retargeting nuclear rocket strikes.

The definition of another concept is directly tied to the definition of strategic maneuver: *strategic co-operation.*

In modern strategy the transition from the classic forms of strategic operation is revealed not in the sphere of armed combat, as was observed earlier (military operations on land fronts, on sea, and in the air), but in the breaking down according to objectives: the strategic objectives, the objectives of a general character, the objectives of security, and so forth. This tendency leads to the fact that in the scale of all of the armed forces participating in the war co-ordination of forces will be constructed more on objectives and time than on place. Consequently, the earlier formula here also undergoes changes, although one must not forget that if nuclear war starts, then in it, as in wars of coalitions, a great role will be played by strategic co-operation of allied armies where new correlations and principles will have already come into effect.

The contemporary meaning of *theater of military operations* should also be dwelt on. This category of strategy arose almost before the definition of strategy itself. In the sixteenth century, Machiavelli, in his work *On Military Art,* among the general demands of the military leaders, pointed out the necessity of their knowledge of the theater of war.

In the classic definition, which was not disputed until the appearance of the nuclear weapon, the territory or aquatory on which military operations were directly unfolding was understood under *the theater of military operations.* The borders of the theater were determined in dependence on the aims and plans of the war, on the limits of the range of means of firing action, and on the possibil-

41

ities of destroying objectives in one or another theater of military operations. These limits and possibilities, right up to the development of long-range bomber aviation, then rarely reached beyond the depth of the operational rear. Thus the strategic rear and all of the remaining territory of the belligerent countries was beyond the limit of these borders.

The new means of armed combat has led to a new concept of the definition of the theory of military operations. In the modern understanding it might include all of the territory of the belligerent countries or coalitions, whole continents, and even the expanses of the sea and air spaces.

III

Special significance in contemporary strategy is given the question of *the ways of achieving strategic aims in war*. If earlier the correct determination of the most effective ways of waging war played a decisive role in achieving victory, then it is not hard to understand how it has grown with the appearance of the nuclear rocket weapon.

The history of the development of military art confirms the position that each belligerent government always tries to achieve the aim of war in the shortest possible time and with the minimum expenditure of forces. Prolonged war never has been advantageous to any belligerent country. At the same time, not a single government could ever admit its defeat until all its possibilities had disappeared and until all its economic, military, and moral powers had been put to the test. V. I. Lenin stressed that war is the comprehensive testing of all the material and spiritual forces of each nation.

The problem of the most effective use of all of the government power in the name of achieving strategic aims in conditions of nuclear war has become especially acute. Before the appearance of the nuclear weapon this was not so because the outcome of the concluding battle usually crowned the war. War had a relatively stately beginning, the strained culminating point, and the closing period, bringing one of the sides to victory. Then, a loss in the be-

42

ginning period of the war still did not indicate a defeat in the war. It is well known that the Soviet Armed Forces—in spite of the beginning period of the Great Patriotic War [World War II] which turned out unsuccessfully for them—managed to wrest the strategic initiative from the hands of the Fascist German Army and win.

Another condition is formed now when the outcome of the armed struggle in the beginning period can have a decisive influence on the outcome of the war as a whole. The very first surprise nuclear rocket strike can lead to unprecedented destruction, destroy an enormous quantity of troops in the places of their usual quartering, and annihilate a significant part of the population of the leading cities. It is understood that one must take into account that, depending on the circumstances of the origins of the war, the armed life-and-death struggle is not limited just to strikes of the nuclear weapon. War can be drawn out, and it can demand prolonged and maximum effort of all the forces of the army and the country.

In accordance with the changing role of results achieved in the very beginning of nuclear war, the ways of waging it are now taking shape. *The simultaneous strike on the armed forces, including strategic nuclear means, and on the objectives of the enemy's economic potential for achieving the aims of war in a short period of time—this is what moves to the forefront.* This method finds expression in different forms of military operations: in strategic nuclear strikes, in strategic operations in theaters of military operations, in operations of the navy, and in combat operations of national PVO [air defense] troops. Each of these forms will adapt itself according to conditions taking shape with the participation of formations and units of the different services of the armed forces.

In the above article only the military technical side of the question has been briefly examined. For the all-round study of the problem, it is necessary to understand the dialectical laws of the process of change in the sphere of armed conflict, the dependence of strategy on politics, the character of the mutual relationships between strategy and economics, strategy and morale-political factors, and so forth. The knowledge of these and other questions enables our military cadres to study more deeply the nature of the revolution in military affairs and to decide better the problems of raising the military potential and combat readiness of the Soviet Armed Forces.

PREMIER KOSYGIN increased Soviet military support commitments to North Vietnam during a visit to Hanoi in February, 1965. Chief Marshal of Aviation Konstantin A. Vershinin, commander in chief of the Soviet Air Forces, accompanied him on this visit. Sixteen months later, the time required to select and train jet pilots, the results of this visit were demonstrated as Soviet-trained Vietnamese took to the air in the famed MIGs, vastly improved over those that had fought American aircraft over Korea some fifteen years previously.

Soviet presses were getting ready for the celebration of the twentieth anniversary of the end of the Great Patriotic War; they stressed the "liberating" role of the Red Army in Eastern Europe. Especially active were the marshals of World War II, who showed remarkable energy for men nearing seventy. Among them were Marshals Ivan S. Konev, Konstantin K. Rokossovsky, Vasili D. Sokolovsky, Semyon K. Timoshenko, and Andrei I. Yeremenko, all now general inspectors for the Ministry of Defense. Far from being retired, these senior consultants still retained seats on the Central Committee—Konev as a full member, the others as candidates. The most famous marshal of all, Georgi K. Zhukov, idolized hero of World War II, banished as minister of defense in 1957 by Khrushchev, came out of the deepfreeze to take a place on the reviewing stand in Red Square for the anniversary parade.

May 9, 1965, was a great day in the U.S.S.R. It not only represented a smooth half-year for Brezhnev and Kosygin, but marked a milestone for the Soviets. Twenty years after the German unconditional surrender the Soviet leaders by imposing terrible sacrifices on their subjects had catapulted the broken shambles of their country to a position from which to challenge the U.S.A. as the dominant world power. A rash of articles appearing in the military press in 1965 soon proved that they meant to keep, and to improve, that position. Nuclear-tipped missiles of intercontinental range were described in Soviet military writings as a logical and inevitable dialectical phenomenon. Quotes from Engels gave the impression that as gunpowder had spelled the end of the feudal system, thermonuclear weapons marked the end of capitalism and imperialism.

General Colonel Sergei Matveyevich Shtemenko reflected the line of the new regime by mentioning Stalin in a casual way. Shtemenko also launched the year with an article on the primacy of the strategic rocket forces. Two other authors, Colonel V. V. Larionov and Colonel V. V. Glazov, were to win Frunze prizes for writing "excellent military theory" articles in 1965. The book, *Marxism-Leninism on War and the Army*, part of the *Officer's Library* scheduled for completion in 1967, also won commendation from the Ministry of Defense. Selections by these officers and a chapter from that book follow in this section.

---

4. THE QUEEN OF THE BATTLEFIELD YIELDS HER CROWN
By General Colonel Sergei Matveyevich Shtemenko

Editors' Notes

> I certainly do not pretend to make a discovery by saying that our grandfathers successfully defeated their enemies without even a suspicion of the existence of a scientific category called military doctrine.—Shtemenko

THERE ARE VERY FEW writers in the Soviet Union who would have the courage and wit to start an article with such a sentence. Even fewer could get such an article published.

There are a number of other unusual things about this work by General Shtemenko. The title itself is different, and even many United States military leaders and writers of World War II vintage may bristle at the thought expressed. Additionally, it was published, not in a respectable military newspaper or journal, but in *Nedelya* (The Week), the magazine section of *Izvestia*, one of the two leading Soviet newspapers.

Shtemenko opens his article with a discussion of doctrine: "The political side of the doctrine is the main thing and *de facto* determines the military-technical side which embraces purely military tasks, armament and military technology, and the training and education of the troops." He further points out that "Soviet military doctrine has been worked out by the Communist party and Soviet government on the basis of Marxism-Leninism, by utilizing the best military experience and by introducing what is new and modern in warfare."

According to Shtemenko the military-technical side of Soviet doctrine at the eve of World War II, on the whole, was correct. However, because of Stalin's arbitrary method of command, "the best military cadres were exterminated or separated from the army." (One cannot but wonder about the inner conflict of an individual who speaks of his comrades being "exterminated" under Stalin, and yet he himself served as Stalin's chief of operations of the general staff, as well as chief of the general staff after World War II.)

Throughout the article Shtemenko discusses "doctrine" and takes but little note of "strategy" and "tactics." Among his views: "According to our doctrine war is not inevitable, but if war is unleashed by the imperialists it will be the last war—one in which imperialism will be reduced to ashes." He goes on to state that "our military doctrine considers a constantly high combat readiness as the primary task of the Soviet army and navy because the aggressive imperialist forces, particularly the United States, are primarily banking on a sudden 'first strike.' "

In 1964, General Shtemenko was chief of staff of the Soviet Ground Forces. Sometime in the spring of that year the ground forces were reorganized and Shtemenko was given another assignment. Less than a year later, he wrote, "It is obvious that today the ground troops can no longer be of decisive importance as in the past and that the queen of the battlefield has now yielded her crown to the strategic rocket troops."

An interesting comment concerning this statement, taken from an interview with representatives of the armed forces, appeared in *Pravda* on April 15, 1965. The interview, one of a series held with the services, was connected with the celebration of the twentieth anniversary of the end in Europe of World War II. In "The Armored Shield of the Motherland," Chief Marshal of the Armored Troops P. A. Rotmistrov was introduced by:

> He is a professor, a doctor of military sciences, and the author of a series of works on the theory of military art. He has trained and educated many tankers who now successfully command tank units and formations. Speaking of the role of tanks in contemporary conditions, P. A. Rotmistrov conclusively and severely criticized views which are creeping into the press that supposedly "the queen of the battlefield—the ground forces—is yielding her crown to the rocket weapon."
>
> "One must not belittle and set off one arm of service against another," he said. "The ground forces, armed with powerful tanks and artillery, always, in any condition, will play a major role in achieving victory over the enemy."

How does Soviet military doctrine apply to other Communist nations? Shtemenko claims that their doctrine is "of a truly international nature and in keeping with the basic interests of all socialist countries." However, there is "the necessity to preserve in each socialist country the respective country's national peculiarities in military development, a fact which strengthens the military alliance of the socialist states."

Shtemenko is not an ordinary writer; he is a remarkable Russian character with an unbelievable career. During World War II, he became, in his own words, "the fifth successive chief of operations of the general staff." In a series of articles published in the *Military Historical Journal* in 1965–66, Shtemenko describes the planning and the battles during the last days of World War II. As a member of the "Genshtab" or the general staff, he relates how he worked for Stalin, whom he considers to have been neither an ogre nor an idol. Rather, he portrays Stalin as being arbitrary and dogmatic but not without shrewdness.

About the time of the beginning of the Korean War, Shtemenko became chief of the Soviet General Staff. Frustrated by events in Korea, among other things, Stalin's last months appear to have been filled with madness, typified by his obsession with the "Doctors' Plot" to kill high military and political officials. Shtemenko reportedly was to have been a victim of this plot. Ten days before Stalin's death, Shtemenko disappeared, and Marshal Sokolovsky took over as chief of staff. Shtemenko turned up in Berlin later in the week. He then dropped from sight until 1957, when he appeared in Moscow. In 1966 he was serving as deputy chief of the general staff of the Ministry of Defense.

Shtemenko is a refreshingly original writer and, by being at the nerve center of important events at crucial times, his historical articles are most interesting. Equally, he appears to have gained a keen grasp of technical developments associated with the revolution in military affairs. His article entitled "Technical-Science Progress and Its Influence on the Development of Military Affairs" was one of the selections reprinted in *Problems of the Revolution in Military Affairs*, described earlier in this book. Among his other articles are:

"Ground Forces in Modern War and Their Combat Preparation," *Red Star*, January 3, 1963, and
"New Requirements Posed for the Combined Arms Commander," *Red Star*, January 16, 1964.

Shtemenko's memoirs were to be published in 1967.

I CERTAINLY do not pretend to make a discovery by saying that our grandfathers successfully defeated their enemies without even a suspicion of the existence of a scientific category called military doctrine. This term was born about half a century ago when wars became world wars and when multimillion-man-armies with rapid-fire artillery, tanks, aircraft, and other machines, with electric wire and wireless communications, went to the battlefields. Victory in such a war was impossible without mobilizing all forces of the state and primarily its economy and science.

Now it becomes necessary not only to draft operational plans of armies and their maintenance but to work out a system of uniform governmental views on the nature and purpose of a war in given historic conditions and on the bases of military organization and military art, and to prepare the country and the armed forces for war. Such a system of views has received the conventional name military doctrine. Of course, it primarily reflects the interests of the ruling class in a country and has a class character. This class orientation also determines its political side, that is, all that concerns the political aims of war and the general class evaluation of the military tasks. The political side of the doctrine is the main one and, in fact, determines its second side, the military-technical side which includes purely military questions such as, let us say, the choice of means and methods of fulfilling military tasks, armaments, and military equipment, and the training and education of the troops. If a government is reactionary and adheres to an adventuristic policy, all this is reflected in its military doctrine. Such was, for example, the doctrine of the German Fascist Army.

Soviet military doctrine has been worked out by the Communist party and the Soviet government on the basis of Marxism-Leninism by utilizing the best military experience and by introducing what is new and modern in warfare. V. I. Lenin formulated the basic principles of its political side. He made a great contribution to the elaboration of its military-technical side too. His ideas that the people are drawn into modern war, which inevitably assumes world-wide proportions and extreme violence, are still valid. He stressed the decisive influence of economic and moral factors and of a strong rear on the outcome of the war. But in drawing attention to the special importance of military equipment, Lenin pointed to the decisive role of the soldier, full of initiative and consciousness, for achieving victory. He assigned an important place to military science, without which it is impossible to create a modern army, as well as to the art of mastering all methods and forms of combat, resolute attack, retreat, and defense.

50

The prominent party and military leaders, M. V. Frunze, S. I. Gusev, A. S. Bubnov, and M. N. Tukhachevsky, also contributed much to the development of Soviet military doctrine.

Speaking of the military-technical side of our doctrine, one can say that on the eve of the Great Patriotic War it solved the complex problems correctly on the whole. The role of tanks, aviation, artillery, and other means of combat was correctly evaluated. The untenable Western theories, such as the theory of [General Giulio] Douhet, who overestimated the role of aviation, or that of [General] Eimannsberger and [Major General J. F. C.] Fuller, apologists of the "tank" war, were resolutely rejected.

In accordance with this, a military science developed which resolved the questions of training and carrying out of deep operations and battle. Artillery was regarded as the main firepower and infantry, cavalry, and tanks as the main striking force.

Unfortunately, during the personality cult period, the Leninist military legacy was ignored and distorted. The laws of armed struggle were not disclosed deeply and correctly enough, and military theory was basically formulated to the dictates of J. V. Stalin. Some of the best military cadres were exterminated or separated from the army.

The possibility of enemy invasion of our territory was completely excluded. Therefore, the problems of strategic defense, retreat, and mobilization of the country's forces were not given due attention, and this negatively influenced the course of the initial period of the war. Only the collective will of the party and unprecedented heroism of the Soviet people and soldiers were able to overcome the errors.

Our military doctrine is worked out on the basis of a scientific analysis of the correlation of forces in the international arena and of the military economic possibilities of the U.S.S.R. and of a potential enemy. The Communist party leadership of the Armed Forces, the Program of the CPSU shows, is the precise basis of military organization. At the same time, of course, conclusions of Soviet military science and recommendations of the supreme military command are given due consideration.

The concrete substance and orientation of the work in preparing the country and the army for effective defense of the state are determined in accordance with military doctrine. Thus, our military doctrine is a sort of basic military law of the U.S.S.R. in the country's defense against outside attack.

Naturally, at present its problems must be solved in a completely different way than before, if for no other reason than that now a completely different correlation of forces exists in the international arena and rapid technical progress has caused a revolution in military affairs. Nuclear and thermonuclear weapons, rockets of various classes, atomic rocket-carrying submarines, supersonic jet aviation, radioelectronics, and other new weapons and equipment have caused radical changes in the training and methods of conducting armed struggle.

But, in its political substance, our military doctrine, as before World War II, reflects basic Leninist principles, proceeding from an appraisal of the contemporary epoch. It excludes the possibility of any predatory war by us and corresponds with the interests of the Soviet people, the socialist camp, and all peace-loving peoples.

According to our doctrine, war is not inevitable. But, if it is unleashed by the imperialists, it will be the last war, one in which imperialism will be reduced to ashes. It will be the decisive clash between two different social systems and will become a world war and a coalition war.

It is not impossible that the protagonists of aggression will try at the beginning to unleash in some area a "small," "limited" war. Such wars are fraught with the enormous danger of growing into thermonuclear world war. Therefore it is dangerous to underestimate them, and constant vigilance is necessary.

The new material technical base of the army and navy brings about substantial changes in the military-technical content of Soviet doctrine. Concerning means of warfare, the war will be a nuclear rocket one. Nuclear weapons will play a decisive role in achieving the goals of war, and their main carriers will not be aircraft, as in World War II, but rockets.

The territorial range of the war will increase beyond measure.

It will not involve thirty-six or sixty-one countries as in the two past world wars. Into its orbit inevitably will be drawn far more countries. War will be all embracing and intercontinental, waged on the land, on the sea, and in the air. And what is particularly important, the former border line between front and rear will disappear.

Our military doctrine considers a constantly high combat readiness as the primary task of the Soviet Army and Navy. This is because the aggressive imperialist forces, particularly the United States, are primarily banking on a surprise first blow. Our doctrine takes into account the danger of such a blow but does not confine the entire war to such a blow. It teaches how to repel the first blow and to repulse the enemy's attack as a whole and also devotes great attention to the necessary defensive measures to insure the U.S.S.R.'s security. Hence the fundamental demand posed to the armed forces: to be always ready and capable every minute to fulfill any task of defending the Motherland.

The question of the length of the war is posed in a new way. For today the huge stockpiles of nuclear weapons make it possible to reach targets quickly. Yet our army cannot merely assume an easy and speedy victory, although it possesses a recognized military-political superiority. Under certain conditions the war can become prolonged and demand extremely tense efforts from the people and the army.

The views on the role played by the various services of the Armed Forces have also changed. It is obvious that today the ground troops can no longer be of decisive importance as in the past and that the queen of the battlefield has now yielded her crown to the strategic rocket troops, which possess the most powerful nuclear weapons and carriers of unlimited range. Long-range rocket-carrying aviation and rocket means of the ground forces and the navy will assist the strategic rocket troops.

Yet, to achieve full victory over the aggressor, all services of the armed forces will be needed. If the aggressor unleashes a war it will be necessary to crush his armies, including the ground armies, preventing them from reaching our own territory, and to seize the nuclear rocket base and other bases and capture the most important objectives and key areas of the enemy's territory. This is why our doctrine gives an important role to the ground forces, the navy, and the air forces. As before, their close co-operation is considered an important guarantee for victory.

The new technical means have changed the methods of waging war. The mass use of nuclear rocket weapons has brought about a different interrelation between strategy, operational art, and tactics. In previous world wars, strategy attained the aims of the war only through numerous and prolonged battles, combat, and operations, in others words, through the tactical and operational means of the services of the armed forces. Today the strategic leadership has at its disposal powerful long-range means of fighting—the strategic rocket troops. By means of massed nuclear blows inflicted by these troops, it is now possible—without waging combat operations, and, I would say, without interference of tactical or operational art—to directly achieve extremely important results. All this changes the conditions and nature of the operations of other services of the armed forces and also the scope of their combat tasks.

Above all, the army and navy must know how to advance determinedly and actively. But the fact is taken into consideration that in a number of cases, in certain sectors, transition to defense is possible.

Great attention is being devoted to antimissile defense, to the struggle with the enemy's submarine rocket-carrying atomic fleet and his other latest inventions.

As a whole, Soviet military doctrine corresponds to the modern material-technical base of the army's and navy's armament. It exists side by side with our military science, guiding its development, and, in a sense, "crowning" Soviet military strategy.

Our doctrine poses high demands upon the country's and the population's preparation in the military sense. The national economy will not have as much time as before to reorganize itself in the course of military operations. Everything necessary for work under war conditions must be prepared in advance. The possibilities of industry, agriculture, transportation, science, and culture will be utilized even more fully in the interests of victory.

The development of the military might of the U.S.S.R. and the socialist camp has influenced the evolution of the military doctrines of the imperialist countries, particularly the United States, where plans for world domination were being forged during the time of its nuclear monopoly. Now both this monopoly and the United States' superiority in the sphere of nuclear armament have been lost.

This is why not only principles of military doctrine more flexible in form and contents have emerged in Washington—principles such as the "strategy of flexible reaction" and the "counterforce strategy"—but there are more and more frequent references to a war without nuclear weapons or in which only tactical nuclear means will be used within the framework of "local" and "limited" wars. Soviet military doctrine does not exclude such wars, but we are against the use of any nuclear weapons in general and in the talk of the imperialist militarists about tactical nuclear weapons we see only a trick intended somehow to help motivate and legalize the use of the atom against mankind.

The generals of all imperialist countries without exception believe that nuclear forces will play the main role in a large-scale war if it should break out. Therefore the United States undeviatingly increases its nuclear potential; the imperialists of France are creating such a potential; and the *revanchists* of the Federal Republic of Germany are struggling to obtain access to nuclear weapons. All of these nations strive to keep abreast of the latest achievements in the development of nuclear weapons and search for methods of using them which are more and more aggressive and dangerous for peace. This is evidenced by the increased intrigues around plans for establishment of "multilateral nuclear forces," the creation of which increases the threat of emergence of a nuclear war, particularly in Europe since this plan would not only insure first place for the United States among nuclear imperialist countries but would also increase their number, at the same time essentially hindering control over the use of the nuclear weapon by placing it in the hands of *revanchist* West German circles.

Along with the nuclear rocket forces, all principal imperialist countries devote much attention to developing their ground armies, air forces, navies, and all other branches of service which will not only use nuclear weapons widely but will also carry out combat tasks with the aid of conventional armaments.

In conclusion, it must be noted that Soviet military doctrine is of a genuinely international nature and answers to the basic interests of all socialist countries including those united by the Warsaw Pact. The doctrine bears in mind the necessity to preserve in each socialist country its own national peculiarities in military organization which strengthens the military alliance of the socialist states.

Soviet military doctrine is linked to history. It will become unnecessary and wither away as soon as war is excluded from human society. Under contemporary conditions, however, its improvement and development—in keeping with the international situation and with scientific-technical progress—must continue henceforth on the basis of the wise policy of the CPSU.

---

5. NEW WEAPONS AND THE DURATION OF WAR
By Colonel V. V. Larionov
Candidate of Military Sciences

Editors' Notes

Colonel Larionov has been discussed already in connection with his article "New Means of Fighting and Strategy," listed as the third writing in this collection.

"New Weapons and the Duration of War" appeared in *Red Star* in March, 1965. The author uses a rather transparent device, that of answering a letter purportedly written to the editor, to introduce and to discuss the matter of a short, swift-moving war, keeping the discussion at a theoretical level.

Larionov starts with a historical summary of World Wars I and II, showing how, in both, the opposing sides had counted on a short war. Also, in both, the Germans won initial victories but lacked the resources to wage a prolonged conflict. The moral is that a nation must be prepared for both short and protracted struggles.

As in his earlier article, Larionov emphasizes the three phases of the traditional war—"the beginning, the following period, and the final one." The second period was the "culmination point of the war, the result of which made clear to which side the scales were tilted." In nuclear rocket war, however, "the white-hot culminating point will move to the beginning period of the war." During this decisive phase, "the surprise mass use of nuclear rocket weapons can bring utter defeat to an enemy in the shortest time." Some countries of the enemy coalition might capitulate as the result of even a single strike of nuclear weapons. "The short, swift-moving war is becoming now the usual category of military art."

The increased significance of the initial period of war on the outcome of war as a whole gives the military theorists new problems. For the initial period of the war to be decisive, maximum force must be used from the outset. If maximum force is used, what kind of reserves are required in the event of failure to achieve victory in this beginning period?

Larionov quotes General Maxwell Taylor and "the American military ideologist H. Kissinger" to support his allegation that the United States is counting on a short war. He erroneously observes that "the strategic attacking forces take up the lion's share of the military budget," which shows, according to Larionov, that the United States is planning "the completion of war in the shortest time." Simultaneously with this, however, he says the leaders of the United States also "are perfecting and increasing the forces of general designation for waging protracted operations."

What about the Soviet Union? "Such a non-aggressive government as the U.S.S.R., never dreaming of a treacherous attack, has good reason in its military art to allot a place to the study of means of waging not only protracted but also short, swift-moving war." One gathers, therefore, that Soviet troops must be prepared for wars of any duration.

"IN OUR MILITARY theory literature," writes Captain F. Pritokin in his letter to the editor, "one often meets the attitude that a new world war, if it is successfully unleashed by the imperialists, might be either protracted or short and swift-moving. We conceive the general characteristics of a protracted war. But what might be those of a short, swift-moving war?"

In our time the problem of the duration of war has become especially acute. This is explained primarily by the appearance of nuclear rocket weapons possessing colossal destructive force. The Soviet Union and other socialist countries, and all progressive mankind, are constantly and persistently struggling to avert world nuclear rocket war. But if, in spite of this, the imperialists succeed in unloosing this war, then its length will depend on a series of circumstances and conditions. The main one consists of the fact that our Armed Forces were and will be ready to repulse the aggressors decisively and to wage victoriously and win both short, swift-moving wars and long wars.

In answering the question of Comrade Officer Pritokin, I will dwell only on the problem of short, swift-moving war. On this I will state at once that such a problem will be examined on a purely theoretical level.

I

I think that in the interest of a correct analysis, it would not hurt to begin with a historical glance into the past.

Earlier, while picking this or that method of action in a prospective war, a government proceeded from its economic, moral, political, and military power, appraising the level which would be reached immediately before the war. They also took into account the potential possibilities of a probable enemy. In this, the general staffs took as a basis of calculation chiefly a time indicator, that is, they calculated, for example, how long a war might last, what the probable losses might be, and consequently, the average demand for their supplies during a definite period or year of war.

This method of planning was used in particular by the general staffs of the countries of the Entente before the First World War. As is known, they came to the firm conclusion that war could not be prolonged.

The Kaiser's Germany, which also planned on a short, swift-moving war, proceeded from other calculations. The inspirers of the German plan, based on finishing the war "before the leaves fell," attached decisive significance to a massive surprise attack with concentrated forces. They hoped thus to smash the enemy, not giving him time to collect himself and gather his forces.

But the calculations of that side and the other were unsound. This became clear at the end of 1914, that is, in a few months after the war began. There was no doubt that the war had turned into a protracted and exhausting struggle on land fronts where positional form of waging war prevailed.

Thus, the errors of the German plan, not materially provided for, became evident. It also became evident that there had been an untrue evaluation of the nature of the prospective war by the general staffs of the Entente.

It is important to stress in this that the countries of the Entente, taken as a whole, had at their disposal incomparably greater potential possibilities for waging prolonged war, because of which they turned out as the victors. It is very characteristic that the final results of the war favored the Entente in spite of the mistakes in the initial calculations and plans. These mistakes at that time were not fatal.

To a certain extent nothing analogous was observed in the Second World War. True, the countries of the "Axis" achieved more serious results in adopting the strategy of "blitzkrieg." However, as was shown by the further march of events, the misfortunes of the Anglo–Franco–American bloc in the beginning stages of the war by no means decided its result.

While urging Hitler's Germany onto the Soviet Union, having carried out the Munich policy of encouragement of aggression, the ruling circles of the West underestimated the growing attacking force of the Fascist German armies with which they were forced in the end to fight. They were guided in their conclusions by the experience of positions of the First World War and did not create therefore large maneuverable forces for waging swift operations at the beginning period of the war. It is sufficient to say that not long before the beginning of the Second World War, France had only twenty-five fully equipped divisions, and England and the U.S.A. only six divisions each. France counted on the strength and insurmountability of her "Maginot" defense line. England, as always, made a stake on accumulating forces during the course of the war and on winning final victory. The idea of "gathering" forces after the "first shot" was seen, by the way, in the prewar doctrine of the United States of America.

"From the time of the First World War," wrote the American military ideologist H. Kissinger, "our strategic doctrine has always been built on the proposition that the forces which we have at the beginning of the war must guarantee us only the possibility of avoiding a catastrophe. The defeat of the enemy is proposed only after the full mobilization of our industrial potential, that is, a long time after the beginning of military actions."

In the Second World War, the plans of German Fascists for "lightning-like defeat" of the Soviet Union suffered complete failure. In spite of the fact of the loss in the very beginning of the war of strategic initiative and that the outcome of the beginning period was not in our favor, the Land of the Soviets and her Armed Forces managed to seize the initiative from the hands of the German Fascist command, to gather forces, to make a basic break in the course of the war, and to win victory. Here, in full force, is shown the superiority of socialism, the better organization of society, the high morale of the Soviet people, and the ability to overcome the most difficult experiences of war. A definite role was also played here by the vast spaces of our country and time, which worked for us after the failure of Hitler's plan of blitzkrieg.

These examples show that mistakes in evaluating the nature of prospective war from the point of view of its duration, and defects in prewar planning were not decisively dangerous in the past or, in any event, [they were] correctable. If plans for a short, swift-moving war suffered a failure, the government could, drawing on its potential possibilities, reorganize to wage a long war. In the conditions of nuclear rocket war, it would be very difficult, even impossible, to do this. And so, because of this, the question has been raised of the acute necessity to be fully prepared to wage both short, swift-moving, and prolonged wars.

II

In the theory of strategy and in the planning of war, three basic periods are usually distinguished: the beginning, the following period, and the final one. The beginning period was signified by the development of military actions; the second period was considered the culminating point of the war, the result of which made clear to which side the scales were tilted. The final period was the crowning victory of the war.

Can such a maintenance of periods in nuclear rocket war be preserved if it is short and swift moving? Scarcely. First of all, it can be supposed that the white-hot culminating point will move to the beginning period of the war.

The effectiveness of modern means of armed combat has no comparison with any prenuclear-period means of defeat. The massive and surprise use of nuclear rocket weapons can bring utter defeat to an enemy in the shortest time. Separate countries of the enemy coalition might be brought to the verge of capitulation as the result of even a single strike of strategic nuclear rocket means.

This forces an absolutely different evaluation of the time factor in today's war. And this is being studied now in all the highly developed countries of the world. Much attention is being given to this by the leaders of the aggressive imperialistic bloc of NATO. The opinion that nuclear rocket war would be completely devastating, and at the same time short and swift moving, is voiced not only by separate authors but also by official representatives of the ruling circles of Western countries. True, the official doctrine of the U.S.A. also foresees the necessity of preparing the armed forces for waging prolonged war. But it stresses in every way possible the significance of the advantages achieved in the first stages. And, in our military theory researches, this must not fail to be considered.

The short, swift-moving war is now becoming the usual category of military art, stipulated by the objective process of the development of the means of armed combat. By the way, there are a few

61

differences between the meaning of "korotkaya"—short—and "skorotechnaya"—short, swift-moving—and "bistrotechnaya"—transient. The term "short" war, or the expression "the achieving of the goals of war in a short time period," mainly indicates the time in the course of which war is actually waged. But this index in our view is not exactly characteristic of nuclear rocket war and does not reflect its nature. You see, there were short wars in history without the use of nuclear weapons. If we speak of a possible nuclear rocket world war as [likely to be a] relatively short [one], then we proceed from comparing it with past *world* wars.

The meaning of "short, swift-moving war" points out the *dynamics* of the development of military events, on the absence of any kind of pause between active operations of the armed forces. This term also signifies that in each definite unit of time the government which is waging war applies the maximum force. It is rather an index indicative of tension, the intensiveness of military actions. Those military efforts which in past wars could be waged, for example, during four or five years can now be realized in armed battle in a few days or weeks. Consequently, time comes forth now as a gauge of expended combat efforts.

Thus the duration and tension of war is defined now as if in two dimensions: according to the actual time of its waging and according to the coefficient of the effectiveness of the utilization of forces and means in a definite unit of time.

The more efficiently a government uses the accumulation of forces and means before war, the greater the results it can achieve in its very beginning, and the sooner it will gain victory.

III

The growth of the significance of the beginning period of war on the outcome of war as a whole also placed before the military theorists this problem. It has become highly complicated to reconcile two points: the questions of the degree of economy of forces and the advisability of their economy. Truly, in order to win the armed struggle in the shortest time, the government must apply maximum effort in the course of this period.

But what does maximum effort contemplate in the modern era? It is a fact that the fighting countries always aim to gain victory in war at the price of minimum expenditure of material means and morale efforts. In war it is difficult to get a guarantee that these efforts are not excessive and, in the event of failure, not to deprive those reserve forces of the resources which are necessary for the successful continuation of a protracted war.

Several bourgeois military theorists consider that the simultaneous preparation for waging both a protracted and a short, swift-moving war is difficult to accomplish. Therefore, they say, one must give preference to one method of preparing for and waging war.

Highly characteristic of this theory is the point of view of several persons in the U.S.A.—a view expressed by the former Chairman of the Joint Chiefs of Staff, General M. Taylor, in his book *The Uncertain Trumpet*. He writes: "Since it is necessary to prepare only for a general war and since a general war will be short, it is not necessary to create in the United States a large mobilized reserve."

In the view of several American military ideologists, the staking on a short, swift-moving war conjectures the creation of all the necessities for effective use of forces and means at the beginning of war. This supposedly makes it possible to achieve decisive goals in a very short time and without large additional development of armed forces. It goes without saying that industry must work intensively to satisfy the needs of war before it begins, and that the armed forces, necessary for achieving decisive goals in the very beginning of the war, must also be developed and brought to combat readiness in good time.

The American military ideologist H. Kissinger writes: "General war waged with the use of modern weapons will be decided by actions of the armed forces available for the disposal of the adversaries at the beginning of the war."

True, the aiming by a number of imperialist leaders and theorists *only* at a short, swift-moving war does not find full and uncompromising realization in practice. As already said above, in the U.S.A., during the time of the accumulation of forces and means for a short, swift-moving war, preparation is also going on for a protracted war. This is not hard to prove in examples of the military budget of the U.S.A. The maintenance and development of strategic attacking forces takes up the lion's share of the military budget. This says that the U.S.A. is leaning to the side of making and amassing means, permitting, in the opinion of the military ideologists of imperialism, the completion of war in the shortest time. But simultaneously with this, they are perfecting and increasing the forces of general designation for waging protracted operations.

Sometimes one reads an affirmation that the idea of a short, swift-moving war exists only in aggressive governments. Nonaggressive governments, supposedly, cannot develop ways of reaching the goals of war in a short time. This, in our opinion, is an untrue supposition—which comes from a confused understanding of the unleashing of a surprise war and of the methods of its waging.

Such a nonaggressive government as the U.S.S.R., never dreaming of a treacherous attack, has good reason in its military art to allot a place to the study of waging not only a protracted but also a short, swift-moving war. In the first place, it is conditioned by aspirations to give an appropriate repulse to aggression and to be always ready to defeat a surprise attack of the enemy in a short time. In the second place, nonaggressive countries also must always reckon with the fact that a protracted war demands more sacrifices and material reserves than a short, swift-moving war.

War with the use of modern nuclear rocket weapons, both short, swift-moving and drawn out, will be notable for its exceptional violence and the resoluteness of combat actions. Because of this, it demands from the people and the army unprecedented effort of moral and physical strength, steadfastness, and heroism. From this comes the great importance of high military mastery by all personnel and of their military and moral-political qualities. Unquestionably, troops possessing all-round abilities to wage swift battles and operations can more successfully carry out missions in the event war takes on a protracted character.

In the midst of troops one can sometimes hear the opinion thus: in short, swift-moving war, victory will be won, they say, by one strike of strategic rockets. This is a mistaken opinion. In protracted as well as in short, swift-moving wars, victory over the enemy can be achieved by the united efforts of all the services and branches of the armed forces. At the same time, the peculiarity of a short, swift-moving war will be that its colossal significance will be acquired by exceptional accuracy, co-ordination, and interaction of the services and branches of the armed forces and the clear, firm, highly qualified leadership of troops and the implementation of plans of military operations. From this comes the task: in the course of operational-tactical training of troops, in practice in the field, in the air, and on sea voyages, to laboriously perfect the co-operation of all the fighting organizations.

Thus, the idea of unprecedented effort, maneuverability, and swift armed conflict must penetrate every process of the training and education of the troops. This is one of the most important demands of the combat training of the troops.

---

6. ON THE CHARACTER AND TYPES OF WARS IN THE MODERN ERA
By General Major K. S. Bochkarev
Candidate of Philosophical Sciences

Editors' Notes

For those who hope for a lasting *détente* with the Soviet Union, the 1967 Middle East crisis notwithstanding, the reading of this translation may be a sobering experience. This article appeared in *Communist of the Armed Forces* in June, 1965. Bochkarev's words become even more disquieting when the reader realizes that he is an official spokesman for the Communist party and the Ministry of Defense.

Bochkarev opens with a discussion of how communism is becoming stronger, while the "class war in capitalist countries is intensifying." In the contemporary international situation a "scientifically valid evaluation" of the character and types of wars is needed. A passive, contemplative attitude toward war as well as the condemnation of any sort of armed conflict is incorrect and harmful. In particular, the position of the pacifist is weak and passive because he "condemns war in general, irrespective of with whom and for what it is being waged." Instead of a negative attitude toward all war, the pacifist should be struggling against the main source of war, which Bochkarev asserts is the capitalist system. The correct way, he says, to solve the problem of war is to provide for the triumph of socialism and communism. This is the only way to achieve a durable peace. According to this author, the greatest antiwar force of today is the Communist movement.

To understand the nature of war, one must first analyze its social-political character. This analysis of the "class-content" of war may be a bit difficult for the non-Communist reader. "All this complicated interlacing of classes, nations, and states, and their contradictory aspirations find reflection in war and determine its nature and political content."

Bochkarev's discussion of just and unjust wars is simple and straightforward. The Soviet Union and her allies fight only "just" wars. Their opponents fight "unjust" wars. World War II, Bochkarev says, "began as an imperialistic, aggressive, unjust war from both sides." There was a fundamental change, however, "from the moment of the forced entry into it of the Soviet Union which placed itself at the head of the just, liberating struggle of the nations against fascism." In Vietnam the "unjust" American "interventionists are using poison gases, that is, putting into action such barbaric weapons as even Hitler did not dare use."

In the Communist view, if a future war does start, it will be a class war, universal in scope, and the main means of fighting will be with nuclear weapons. A future war will be a "monstrously criminal" act on the part of the imperialist powers but "most just" on the part of the countries of socialism.

The author's portrayal of "national-liberation war" follows the approved Communist party position. Such wars, as a rule, "develop from the inside of a country and are wars of insurrection." They are similar to partisan warfare "and often are carried out with poor technical equipment." This was not the case for some nations,

66

such as Algeria and Indonesia, where "the aid of the highly developed socialist governments permitted the equipping of such armies with completely modern equipment."

The "imperialists" make a mistake in trying to deny the connection between their own wars against "people's liberating movements" and a new world war. Local wars, whatever their nature, always have the possibility of changing into nuclear world war. For that reason the Soviet Union must carefully watch all local conflicts and "suppress the attempts of the enemies of peace to fan the spark of such conflicts into universal nuclear fire."

General Major Bochkarev is a well-known writer on Soviet military matters. Among his other works are:

"Several Questions on Lecture Propaganda," *Communist of the Armed Forces*, February, 1963.

"The Struggle for Peace and the Development of the World Revolutionary Process," *Communist of the Armed Forces*, November, 1964.

One of the most significant publications by the Ministry of Defense in 1966 was *The Program of the CPSU on Defending the Socialist Fatherland*. General Bochkarev was listed as one of its three editors. Extracts from this book are included later in our selection.

WORLD EVENTS are now developing in a direction which is, as a whole, favorable for the cause of peace, democracy and socialism. The might of socialism is steadily growing stronger, the Communist and national-liberation movement is growing, and the class war in capitalist countries is intensifying. However, imperialism, torn apart by deep inner contradictions, suffering one defeat after another in the historical contest with the forces of progress, will not voluntarily yield its position. World reaction and its chief stronghold, American imperialism, continues to exert every effort to save the capitalist system from final bankruptcy, to prevent changes in the world which are not advantageous for them.

In their attempts to turn back history to bygone days of omnipotent capital, the imperialists are pinning special hopes on the military method of solving social problems and on their creation of a gigantic war machine. While persistently preparing for nuclear world war and while aiming their spearheads primarily against the U.S.S.R. and the other countries of socialism, the aggressors do not give up any sort of local aggressive actions but consider them as "probes" and "training" of their forces for more important military campaigns and simultaneously use them as a means of strengthening their position in this or that region of the world.

In the international situation which has taken shape, especially important significance is acquired by the scientifically valid evaluation of the character and types of wars which are possible in the modern era and of an explanation of their probabilities and conditions of beginning. A proper understanding of these questions has a direct relationship to the solution of crucial tasks which have been given to the Armed Forces of our country.

Marxism-Leninism, the most influential and humane teaching of the present, is against the military method of deciding international problems which are now fraught with exceptionally serious danger for all peoples and countries. But, at the same time, it recognizes as incorrect and harmful the passive, contemplative attitude toward war, the abstract condemning of any sort of armed conflict. Marxism-Leninism considers that, as long as war is coming to a head or has already become a fact, it is necessary to reveal clearly its character, the aims of the struggling sides, the possible influence of a given war on the fate of the revolutionary movement and social progress—in order to determine exactly on this basis the ways and means of active influence on the course of events.

The Marxist-Leninist approach to war is different in principle from pacifism. Pacifism (we have in mind the sincere supporters of peace between nations and not the hypocritical "peacelovers" among the ideologists and political figures of imperialism) is also against war, but it condemns war in general, irrespective of with whom and for what it is being waged. The pacifist does not connect his negative attitude toward war with the struggle against its main source, the capitalist system. This makes his position inwardly weak and passive. Pacifism is not able to indicate a real and effective course of struggle with military danger.

While considering the defense of peace as the most important general democratic task of nations, Marxist-Leninists render to the forces of all sincere opponents of war between governments their due and try to achieve unity with them regardless of what slogans they go under: pacifist, religious, or other. However, Marxist-Leninists themselves go further in solving the problems of war and peace. They connect the struggle for durable peace, universal security, and the curbing of aggressors with the struggle for the revolutionary reformation of society, for social progress and for the triumph of socialism and communism on earth. The leading role of the Communist movement is foreordained by them as the greatest antiwar force of the day.

Marxist-Leninists approach each war in a specific historical way, on the basis of an analysis of its content. All occurrences of public life are considered from the point of view of the principal leading forces of modern times, the international working class, and its offspring, the world system of socialism. From these positions, Marxist-Leninists consistently evaluate the character and types of wars.

Wars are a complicated and contradictory phenomenon. They can be characterized from various sides. Wars are distinguished by their political content and by the aims which the fighting sides pursue. At the same time, they are distinguished by the scale of the armed struggle, the modes of military operations, and the technical means which are used. In concretely evaluating one war or another, a person should not lose sight of any of its essential features or signs. But it is always necessary in the evaluation to distinguish particularly between *the social and the political character of wars* and under no circumstances to substitute for either the military-technical content of war or the spatial scope of the armed conflict. This distinction is desirable because only an analysis of the social and political character of war permits the correct ex-

69

posure of its essence, the definition of the relationship of the various classes and masses of people to it, and its possible influence on the development of society.

Such an approach to evaluating the character of war takes into account that although the social causes of all modern wars are the same (rooted in the very nature of the exploiting systems), their real political and class content might be far from being the same in the majority of instances.

Politics, of which all wars are a part and a continuation, include the sphere of relationships of classes, nations, and governments. But classes are different according to their special nature, as nations and governments are different—different and sometimes opposed in their aims and interests and role in the development of society. There are classes of the exploiters and classes of the exploited, the reactionary and the progressive, just as there are nations of the oppressors and nations of the oppressed falling behind or marching forward in their development. In its turn, the state, depending on the nature of the ruling classes in it, in certain instances acts as the instrument of forward, progressive politics, in one way or another answering the interests of the people, and in other instances, it proves to be the instrument of a reactionary and antinational policy. All this complicated interlacing of classes, nations, and states, and their contradictory aspirations finds its reflection in war and determines its nature and political content.

The aim of war in certain instances is alien and hostile to the progressive forces of society, the masses of the people, and takes shape in contradiction to the development of society; in other cases it fully or partly corresponds to the interests of the workers, to the objective tendencies of historical progress.

Thus, having chosen especially the question of the social and political content of wars and having analyzed their nature from this viewpoint, classic Marxism-Leninism points out that it is necessary to divide war into two kinds; just and unjust. "There are wars that are just and unjust," pointed out V. I. Lenin, "progressive or reactionary, wars of the progressive classes and wars of the backward classes, wars which serve to strengthen class op-

70

pression and wars which serve for its overthrow. (*Works*, Vol. 29, p. 315.)

This conclusion has fundamental significance for the understanding of the class nature of this or that war and, it follows, for determining policies in relation to it.

Furthermore, insofar as each war is a two-sided process in which opposing hostile forces clash with each other, then often duality is found in its social and political nature. War may be reactionary and unjust from both sides, as is the nature of all imperialistic wars because of division and pillage of property of other nations and countries for world supremacy. War may be just from one side and unjust from the other. Such a position is characteristic, for example, of liberation wars which are waged by the masses of the people against invaders and internal forces of reaction.

In the course of the development of war, highly essential and deep changes in its social and political nature are possible, such as there were in the period of the Second World War. This war began as an imperialistic, aggressive, unjust war from both sides. However, subsequently, as the monstrous intentions of the German militarists, who had set their goal on the enslaving of the whole world, were displayed more and more distinctly, the struggle against the introduction of Hitler's "New Order" into Europe grew stronger and it became deeply just and progressive. In the conditions which took shape, the war of the Anglo-American bloc against Hitlerism began to acquire an objectively progressive character although the ruling classes of this bloc by no means renounced their mercenary, reactionary goals. The process of basic change of the nature of war was completed from the moment of the forced entry into it of the U.S.S.R., which placed itself at the head of the just, liberating struggle of the nations against fascism.

As we have already said, it would be wrong to confuse the evaluation of war as just or unjust, with its aspects, such as ways, means, and scale of military operations, which are different questions. But, at the same time, these questions must not be separated from each other and be all the more contrasted. If the aim of war is unjust, reactionary, and antinational, then thereby the

71

foundation for taking into consideration the vital interests of the people and demands of social progress, for selecting ways and means of realizing this goal, is also removed. It is not by chance that the aggressors of all times were ruled by, and are ruled by, the formula "the end justifies the means," and wars unleashed by them are distinguished by monstrous cruelties and barbarities. The graphic confirmation of this is the present "dirty war" of the American imperialists in Indochina. This war is unjust in its very essence, and its criminal nature is still more aggravated by bandit attacks of the American interventionists on the peaceful civilian population. While flouting the elementary norms of international law and civilized morals, they are using poison gases, that is, putting into action such barbaric weapons as even Hitler did not dare to use.

From the other side, if the aim of the war is just and progressive, then this exerts a definite influence on the ways and means with the help of which it will be achieved. Of course, even in a just war, achieving victory is impossible without severe, ruthless actions, directed at the decisive defeat of the enemy's troops, because this is the nature and law of any armed conflict. However, the nature of the goals of given wars prompts the avoidance of extremes in armed combat only of that which is not directly dictated by military necessity.

Marxism-Leninism demands a concrete approach to the evaluation of the goals of the struggle and ways of achieving them, of the obligatory calculation of their interconnections, and the results of one action or another on the fate of the peoples. In light of what has been said, it is clear why Communists consider that politics and its goals cannot be legal, just, and progressive if they are deliberately calculated on kindling world war, or in this case, the way itself of achieving the goals would turn out to be in contradiction to its just character. One cannot justify nuclear world war, which would put in question the fate of whole nations and states and would create a threat to the very existence of human civilization, by concern about the happiness of peoples and about social progress.

From this, however, it does not follow that peace-loving peoples do not have the right to use all the power of modern weapons for the purposes of self-defense and the suppression of aggression. The imperialist madmen must be aware that if they, despite the will of the people, unleash nuclear world war, then they cannot go unpunished. An aggressor will swiftly receive a shattering, annihilating retaliatory nuclear blow. And this will be a fully justified, lawful retribution to the enemies of peace, democracy, and socialism.

The tactics of Marxist-Leninists in the questions of struggle with military danger are in definite relation to the correlation between the forces of war and reaction and the forces of peace and progress which are taking shape in the world arena.

Earlier, under the undivided rule of capitalism, when peace-loving nations did not have the necessary means for deterring aggressors and war was in essence the sole means of the radical solution of acute international problems, Marxists raised the question thus: The victory of which side in a given war would be more preferable from the point of view of the interests of the workers' movement and social progress? This also explains why some wars of that period organized by the *bourgeoisie* and directing their spearheads against absolutism and feudalism were recognized by Marxists as progressive, although at that time they protested the solution of intergovernment contradictions by the force of arms.

The epoch of imperialism stirred up wars for the redivision of an already divided world. At the same time, the revolutionary workers' movement became significantly stronger. In conformity with imperialistic wars for world rule, it was already forbidden to pose the question of the preferableness of victory of some one side insofar as from both sides the war was reactionary and predatory. In the given conditions, Marxists advanced the slogan for the transformation of imperialistic war into civil war.

In our time, another situation was radically formed, insofar as the forces of war no longer undividedly rule on earth. In connection with the creation of a world system of socialism, with the growth of the Communist, workers', and national-liberation movements, the possibility of averting intergovernmental wars was created. This means that now the progressive tendencies in the development of society can force their way ahead, not through the victory of one side or another in intergovernmental war, and not through one type of war or another, but without war, in conditions of peaceful coexistence and competition of the two systems. New forms of social progress, born in the modern era, in full measure answer to the interests of socialism, the international working class, and all mankind. World war has become especially intolerable because armed conflict has taken on an unusually destructive character due to the military-technical revolution which has taken place.

However, the possibility of peaceful forms of socio-historical development in the actual conditions of our time by itself does not exclude the danger of wars and armed conflicts. While the capitalist system exists, while imperialism is preserved, the fertile soil for war also remains, and it follows the necessity does not pass for correctly evaluating its nature.

In contemporary conditions, the wars of the imperialist *bourgeoisie* against the countries of socialism, against the revolutionary movement of the working class, and against the national-liberation movement of oppressed peoples, and also the wars of the imperialists for redividing the spheres of influence and world rule, are primarily regarded as reactionary, unjust wars. Wars to protect the socialist Fatherland, civil wars of the working classes against the *bourgeoisie*, national-liberation wars of colonial peoples and dependent countries, and also peoples of bourgeois states who have become victims of aggression from the side of the imperialist powers, are considered just.

Our party and other Marxist-Leninist parties attach primary importance to the analysis of the nature of war and the unveiling of its political and class nature, because from this depends our relationship to one war or another, the correct determination of the concrete problems and actions connected with it.

"The CPSU and all the Soviet people," states the Program of the CPSU, "will henceforth protest all and any predatory wars, including wars between capitalist governments and local wars directed at stamping out national-liberation movements, and consider it their obligation to support the sacred struggle of oppressed peoples in their just, liberating wars against imperialism." (*Material of the XXII Congress of the CPSU*, p. 365.)

A concrete analysis of wars includes not only an evaluation of their socio-political nature but also the definition of the *kinds and types of war* dependent upon the historical conditions of their origins and on the nature and roles of the societies and class forces taking part in them. And this is understandable, since wars having one and the same socio-political nature very often differ considerably in their actual composition and influence on the social process.

For example, wars to defend the socialist Fatherland and national-liberation [wars], being just and progressive, are not alike in their class and political content. In the first of these we are talking about defending socialism. The chief force in such wars is the working class which is acting in conjunction with all the laboring masses; but in conditions of full and final victory of socialism, the task of defending the Fatherland is solved by the people as a single whole, led by the Communist party. In wars of national liberation, the basic aim is the liberation of the country from foreign enslavement. This goal answers to the interests of not only the working class and working peasants but, in many cases, to those of the *bourgeoisie* and of all the progressive forces of the nation. Depending on the conditions which are actually taking shape, the leading role in such a war might be played by either the proletarian masses or the national *bourgeoisie*.

Unjust wars also have their distinctions which are evoked by different class forces and have different degrees of negative influence on the development of the society.

V. I. Lenin pointed out many times that war is a varicolored, diverse thing which cannot be measured by a common yardstick, that it is theoretically a mistake and practically harmful not to distinguish types of wars, and that a given war cannot be understood without understanding the epoch. (See: *Works*, Vol. 35, pp. 155, 180, 219.)

75

An analysis of the historical types and sorts of wars shows that their specific character and variety of form was stipulated by the content and features of those antagonistic contradictions which have a place in one period of social development or another and which carry in them the possibility of the origin of armed conflicts and wars.

This conclusion is fully applicable to wars in the contemporary era whose basic content is the change from capitalism to socialism. The report given by the conference of the representatives of Communists' and workers' parties in 1960 evaluated the modern era as an era of the struggle of two opposed systems, an era of social and national-liberation revolutions, an era of the downfall of imperialism and the liquidation of the colonial system; the change-over to the path of socialism of all new nations, the triumph of socialism and communism on a universal scale—this evaluation gives the key to the understanding of the probable varieties and types of modern wars.

Most typical for the contemporary era are *the wars of imperialist powers against peoples and countries struggling for their social and national liberation or defending the freedom and independence which has been won and their right to build a new society.* At the same time the aggressiveness of imperialism, the anti-Communist direction of its military preparations, foreordains the possibility of war to protect the socialist Fatherland, to protect all the socialist camp; these wars will be forced and retaliatory from the side of the countries of socialism.

War between two social systems, in the event that the imperialists unleash it, would be a decisive armed clash of two systems. According to its socio-political nature it would be a class war, monstrously criminal, extremely reactionary from the side of the imperialist powers, and most just from the side of the countries of socialism. In scale, it would unavoidably take on universal scope, and the main decisive technical means of waging it would be the nuclear rocket weapon.

Marxist-Leninists are sure that, thanks to the creation of nuclear rocket power, the U.S.S.R. in the relationship of forces now taking shape in the international arena has a real possibility of carrying a crushing defeat to imperialism and of achieving the victory of socialism. But, at the same time, they take into account the unprecedented destructive nature of such a war and consider that unleashing it is the greatest crime against mankind. That is why the CPSU and other Marxist-Leninist parties are taking decisive steps for curbing the aggressors and preventing world war. This noble aim serves the Lenin principle of peaceful coexistence which guides the U.S.S.R. and other socialist governments in their relationships with capitalist countries. This principle proposes as two of its important measures *the strengthening of the defense potential of the socialist camp and the high combat readiness of its armed forces.*

The antagonisms of the two opposed social systems, socialism and capitalism, are basic, and they are the main ones in the modern world, but it does not lessen the contradictions between capitalist governments. Such contradictions exist and operate and above all they have a tendency to intensification insofar as at the present time the territorial sphere of the rule of capital has been sharply reduced and the action of the law of the uneven development of capitalism is becoming stronger, which is changing the relationship of forces between governments. In the imperialist camp, a bitter competition for sales markets, for spheres of investing capital, and for raw materials and cheap manpower is deepening the contradictions between the main imperialist powers.

The peculiarity of the present situation of the world capitalist system is that in spite of the intensification of contradictions in this system, there are no opposed groups of leading powers in it ready to begin armed conflict among themselves. Almost all of the capitalist countries are united in reactionary unions and military political blocs aimed against the countries of socialism, international communism, and national-liberation movements. However, the imperialists are not in a position to eliminate completely the inner contradictions of the world capitalist system, and it follows that there is no guarantee against the intensification and deepening of the antagonisms existing in it or against the transformation of the latter into armed conflict.

The relationship of Marxist-Leninists to war between bourgeois governments would depend on its actual causes and aims. Insofar as it most likely will be imperialistic from both sides, then Marxist-Leninists will unmask the unjust character of such a war and decisively struggle for the revolutionary outcome of the people from it and against turning it into a world nuclear conflict.

With the fundamental internal class antagonisms of the capitalist system—the contradictions between the proletariat and the *bourgeoisie*—is associated the possibility of *civil war* in the countries of capitalism. This contradiction does not have to take the form of armed struggle, because in certain circumstances it might be resolved without the use of military means. In the modern era, which is characterized by basic changes in the relationship of forces between the two systems in favor of socialism, the perspective has opened in a number of capitalist countries for the achievement of power by the working class without civil war. However, while admitting the real possibility of peaceful accomplishment of the socialist revolution, Marxist-Leninists take into account that in countries where the exploiting class has created a powerful military-political machine, the proletariat, in their struggle for revolutionary reform of society, can run across violent resistance of the reactionary classes in their attempts to hold power in their hands by force of arms. And then the proletariat and the working masses have no other choice left but to answer force with force. In these conditions civil war becomes unavoidable. From the side of the working class it is fully warranted, legal, and just.

The lesson of history shows that the reactionary *bourgeoisie* in resorting to force against the people rely not only on their own internal possibilities and resources. Being unable to oppose the steadily strengthening forces of democracy and socialism, they more and more often resort to the help of imperialists of other governments. Most of all, even in peacetime, in desperation over inevitable loss of their supremacy, the *bourgeoisie* often grant territory of the country for basing alien troops on it and creating foreign military bases. The *bourgeoisie*, disregarding national sovereignty, try to oppose the inner forces of the revolution with the united power of all of the imperialist camp. This is one of the main functions of the present military-political blocs of the capitalist countries. This means that in the event of civil war, the conflict cannot be limited to armed struggle between classes of a given country but will combine with a war against foreign invaders, acting in combination with the inner counterrevolutionaries.

The growing threat of the union of forces of internal and external reaction for the purposes of a forced stamping out of a revolution in one country or another poses with all acuteness the question of rallying the forces of the international working class, strengthening the international unity of workers. Against the aggressive blocs and unions of imperialists, the working class and the peoples' masses must set the brotherly solidarity and unity of all their national vanguards in order not to allow the imperialistic export of counterrevolution.

One of the most acute antagonistic contradictions of the modern era is the contradiction between the world systems of imperialism and the peoples of colonial and dependent countries and young national governments. *In its soil grow the local colonial wars of imperialism and the national-liberation wars of oppressed peoples.*

A given contradiction does not have to take the form of armed struggle. In conditions taking place now, of the basic change in corresponding forces in the world arena, it can also be solved in favor of the people without use of military means. However, the sources for armed conflict and war, in the sphere of the relationship which has been pointed out, have not disappeared, because imperialism has by no means reconciled itself with the weakening of its position in regions of former colonies and semicolonies and it continues to hold on tenaciously to the remains of its ownership.

Present day reality gives many proofs that the imperialists, dashing against the fact of the wreck of the colonial system and the formation of dozens of young sovereign states, are going to any base action, barbarity, and crime in order to put off the demise of colonial enslavement. The imperialists of the U.S.A. have even

79

created special troops which are especially designated and prepared for punitive raids and terroristic diversionist operations against peoples who are rising up in liberating struggles.

Characteristically, the present colonizers are trying to create their pillaging military campaigns insofar as possible with the hands of the most dependent nations and peoples. While supporting separatist tendencies in certain feudal-bourgeois strata of the population of young governments and igniting tribal and racial differences, the colonizers thereby are creating conditions and grounds for conflicts and frictions inside countries and, in addition, for interfering in their affairs from outside. While leaning on local reactionary forces, they usually organize puppet governments subservient to them, supply their troops with military equipment and arms, and include in the ranks of these troops many groups of their own military instructors, advisers, and specialists; they recruit mercenaries from any kind of riffraff and so forth.

How this is done can be easily seen in the example of South Vietnam. The imperialists of the U.S.A. have, for more than ten years, waged there a most real, although officially undeclared, colonial war, hypocritically portraying the business as fulfilling "a partner's obligation" and helping the "legal" rulers in their struggle against internal "seditionists" and "Communist aggression from the North." This is a false device and a pirate tactic. In reality, the ruling circles of the South Vietnamese represent a corrupt clique of puppets which the Americans themselves formed and placed in power. The army of the Saigon puppets is wholly supported by the U.S.A. and fights with American weapons under the leadership of American military men.

Recently in connection with the combat successes of the South Vietnamese patriots, the mask of "advisers" of the Saigon regime was no longer organized by the American imperialists, and they openly put into action their own armed forces. Moreover, the ruling circles of the U.S.A. started on the path to widening the aggression by straight military provocations against the Democratic Republic of Vietnam, Laos, and Cambodia. The bandit actions of the colonizers in Indochina evoked irate indignation and decisive protests in the whole world. The workers of the Soviet Union and other countries of socialism, all honest people of the world, branded American imperialism with shame and expressed their solidarity with the patriots of Vietnam. They are rendering real help to the Vietnamese people in their just struggle for freedom and independence.

The aggressors adhere to the plundering tactics also in the Congo (Leopoldville), [a country] which the American imperialists, together with Belgium and other partners of NATO, are trying to turn into a second Vietnam—and also in the Dominican Republic and in a number of other countries.

The bloody actions of the neocolonizers and local reactionary circles naturally are forcing the patriotic forces of these countries to resort to arms in order to achieve victory over the enslavers. *Thus arise the national liberation wars of oppressed peoples which are the lawful, just, and progressive wars of our time.* These wars have clearly expressed anti-imperialistic natures and often combine with revolutionary struggles of the mass of the people for radical social reforms against feudal orders and reactionary regimes.

One of the essential features of national-liberation wars is that they develop as a rule from inside a country and are wars of insurrection. The aim of these wars is not the seizure of the territory of others but the clearing of their own land of colonizers. In the methods of combat action, national-liberation wars bear the usual partisan character and often are carried out with poor technical equipment. But this is not always so. In a number of countries struggling for independence there have been created strong, centralized national-liberation armies as there were for example, in Algeria and Indonesia. The aid of the highly developed socialist governments permitted the equipping of such armies with completely modern equipment.

Speaking of national-liberation wars, it is necessary to have in mind that they are possible not only in areas of former colonies and semicolonies but also in developed capitalist countries. In societies where the voracious laws of imperialism operate, the people of these countries can also prove to be victims of the predatory policies of a stronger aggressive power, and this forces them to carry on a desperate battle with alien enslavers. Thus in the years of the Second World War, the attempts of the Hitlerites to enslave the whole world evoked a powerful liberating movement in the countries occupied by them, including such bourgeois governments as France, Italy, Greece, and others.

In what way are the wars of the imperialists against peoples' liberating movements connected with their political preparation for a new world war? The ideology of imperialism strongly denies such a connection. They are trying to prove that the given wars do not have any sort of relationship to the danger of world war insofar as the armed struggle is limited in aim and in scope, that is, a local war. Such affirmations are basically false. In actual fact, local wars of imperialists, irrespective of what sort are in question, carry in themselves the real possibility of growing into nuclear world war.

In our country, when the tightest economic and political ties have been made between all governments and peoples, everything that takes place in one area of the world, in one or in several countries, is unavoidably reflected in the situation of other countries sometimes many thousands of miles away. A flare-up at one point on the planet, a local conflict, can affect important political and economic and strategic military interests of opposed groupings of powers and evoke armed clashes between them.

The possibility is not excluded that the imperialists, having unleashed a local war, will use nuclear weapons in it. The more shameless of them have already fought for such actions. But if nuclear bombs begin to burst in some region of the earth, this will evoke its own sort of chain reaction. As a result of a "local" nuclear adventure of the imperialists, it might gain global scope. This is why the CPSU and other Marxist-Leninist parties call the peoples of all countries to regard the flare-up here and there of military clashes with the greatest vigilance and suppress the attempts of the enemies of peace to fan the spark of such conflicts into a universal nuclear fire.

Marxist-Leninst analysis of the character and types of wars has enormous significance for working out and determining strategic and tactical aims of the Communist movement in the question of war, peace, and revolution. The conclusions flowing from the analysis compose one of the most important theoretical bases of military policy of the CPSU and Soviet military doctrine. They help to determine correctly the direction of the structure of our Armed Forces, the nature of training and educating the personnel of the army and navy. The main conclusion which Soviet military cadres can make for themselves and all of our soldiers from the analysis of the character and types of wars in modern times is to be constantly alert, to raise their readiness in order to frustrate the evil plans of the enemies of peace in any condition, at any moment, and to carry a decisive defeat to the aggressors if they decide to attack the U.S.S.R. and the great socialist brotherhood.

7. THE REGULARITY OF DEVELOPMENT AND CHANGES OF METHODS OF ARMED CONFLICT
By Colonel V. V. Glazov

Editors' Notes

Colonel glazov, like Colonel Larionov, was one of the nineteen Soviet officers who attended a conference on Soviet military doctrine in March, 1963. Also, he was awarded a Frunze prize in March, 1966, for his writings on military theory. The publication of this article in *Communist of the Armed Forces*, June, 1965, attests to a high acceptance of his work by both the Communist party and the Ministry of Defense.

The first two-thirds of "The Regularity of Development and Changes of Methods of Armed Conflict" is a historical treatise, starting with a discussion of war in a "slave-holding society." Brief reference is made to the "revolutionary-liberation war of the American colonies for independence (1775–83)." Finally, the author begins a discussion of World War II.

In our translation we are omitting the first part of this article.

We are striving to present the views of the Soviet military writers as accurately as possible and do not want to edit their work unnecessarily. We do not believe, however, that failing to print the first part of this article will result in a distortion of the author's views as presented in the latter part of his work.

Glazov, in contrast to the majority of Soviet writers, does not condemn the allied strategic bombing attacks in World War II. In that war he states that "aviation and rocket strikes on objectives in the deep rear of a country marked the beginning of a new sort of strategic action and, together with it, also a method of waging war that was new in principle, which included defeating both the opposing groups of forces and the military-economic base of the enemy." With conventional warheads, however, this bombing did not lead to major changes in the methods of waging armed conflict.

The atomic weapons were another matter. "The use by the United States of America of two atomic bombs against Japan 'under the cover' of the Second World War" confirmed the concept of strategic action and basically changed the methods of war. "A new stage in the development of military affairs began."

According to the author, in any future world war there will be the imperialist countries on one side and the coalition of socialist countries on the other. There is never any speculation about the possibility that a nation like China, would not be fully on the socialist side. "The acute class character" will result in decisiveness of both political and military aims.

Glazov, as do many other Soviet writers, speculates on how such a war might start. First, he considers that the "imperialist aggressors" will open with a mass nuclear attack on the Soviet Union. Or again, world war might begin as a result of a local war, in which nuclear weapons initially might not be used. But once war starts, "everywhere, the nuclear weapon can be used."

The article closes with the message that "The Communist party calls on all generals and officers to study in the most serious manner the problems of military theory in the light of the demands of

84

modern war." We can be reasonably certain this admonition is being followed.

Some of Colonel Glazov's other works are:

"What is Local War?" *Red Star*, May 16, 1961;
"Illusion and Reality," *Red Star*, April 3, 1963;
"Some Features of Conducting Military Actions in Nuclear War,"
Communist of the Armed Forces, February, 1964;
"The Concentrated Shock Force of the U.S.A. in Europe," *Red Star*, March 22, 1966.

IN THE SECOND WORLD WAR, the defeat and annihilation of the enemy was achieved chiefly as a result of strategic attack. Attack operations had various forms. In particular attack operations aimed at cutting, encircling, and annihilating large enemy groupings were widely used.

The Second World War, in contrast to the First, was distinguished by the maneuverability and dynamics of combat operations, and strategic attack received a clear preponderance over strategic defense.

The belligerent sides also, in addition to defeating the armed forces, made serious attempts to undermine the enemy's economy. In the past war, aviation strikes on military-industrial objectives, cities, and communications were practiced on a large scale for lowering military-economic potential, wrecking strategic transportation, and disorganizing administration. In addition, in bombing London, after breaking off its air strikes on England, Germany first used the FAU–2 ballistic rocket, which had a range of flight of about three hundred kilometers.

Aviation and rocket strikes on objectives in the deep rear of a country marked the beginning of a new sort of strategic action and, together with it, a method of waging war that was new in principle, which included attacks on both the opposing groups of forces and the military-economic base of the enemy. But because rockets and aviation bombs were equipped with, at that time, conventional warheads, their strikes on objectives in the rear, as the experience of war testifies, did not give tangible results, did not assure the fulfillment of strategic missions, and thus did not lead to sharp changes in the methods of waging armed conflict.

At the same time, in the period of the Second World War, it became evident that strikes directed at achieving the strategic aims of war on economic objectives and especially on large political and administrative centers and road centers, in conditions of significantly increased means of destruction, might basically change the methods of armed conflict. This conclusion received actual confirmation on the basis of the use by the United States of America of two atomic bombs against Japan "under the cover" of the Second World War.

Reviewing the methods of armed conflict in different historical epochs makes it possible to explain the regularity of their development and change depending on the weapons of waging war and also on the moral spirit and level of preparation of the mass of soldiers. In the same way that old weapons were not at once but gradually replaced by new ones so also methods of armed conflict were not changed in a flash. They are perfected and basically modified only with the massive equipping of the troops with new military equipment and weapons. This process, as a rule, takes place not during one and the same war but extends into the beginning of the next war. This is explained by the fact that war takes place faster than the time needed for creating new weapons in massive quantities, for the full understanding of their properties, and for organizing transformations of the armed forces.

The achievement in the perfection of the nuclear weapon, the building up of an enormous reserve of nuclear bombs of various powers and of different designations, the creation of ballistic and global rockets as the carriers of the nuclear warheads having colossal destructive force, the rapid development of other military equipment, and the creation of automatic guidance systems marked such a revolution in military affairs as had not been known in all history. A new stage in the development of military affairs began. That is why our military thought, coming from the experience of wars and an analysis from the position of Marxism-Leninism, considers that the methods of waging armed conflict in a future war, if the imperialist aggressors unleash it, will be basically different from all wars of the past. A new world war will bear a clearly defined class character and will be a decisive armed clash of two opposed social systems. On one side will be the coalition of imperialist countries and, on the other, the coalition of socialist countries. The acute class character of such a war will predetermine the extreme decisiveness of political and military aims.

How such a war will begin is hard to guess. It is fully possible that the imperialist aggressors will unleash it with a direct attack on the Soviet Union by using weapons of mass destruction in the very first minutes of the war. It is not excluded that the prelude to world war will be a local war in which in the beginning nuclear weapons will not be used. There might be other methods of beginning world war. But it is now already obvious that no matter how a world war begins, the basic changes which have taken place in the material-technical base of war, without fail, will stipulate the appearance of new methods of armed conflict. Indeed, the presence of modern means makes it possible to involve in the sphere of war all continents, seas, and oceans. Combat actions can unroll on land, on sea, under the sea, in the air, and in space. And everywhere, the nuclear weapon can be used.

But the most essential principle in the change of methods of armed conflict in the strategic range is that nuclear strikes can now be simultaneously directed at the undermining of the economic potential of the enemy, the destruction of his administrative and industrial centers, energy centers, sources of raw materials, transport systems, and at the destruction of the armed forces no matter where they are located. The distinguishing feature of the new method of armed conflict might be the maximum participation of nuclear weapons of all the services of the armed forces for the destruction of stated objectives in the shortest time.

The use of the nuclear weapon also affects changes in the methods of armed conflict on an operational and a tactical scale. But the correlation of the role and the significance of the armed conflict which is being waged in the zone of direct contact with the enemy to that of the zone beyond in the interior of the belligerent states is sharply increasing to the side of the latter. In connection with this, large strategic results in favorable circumstances can now be achieved at once by means of delivering powerful strategic nuclear strikes, the preparation and realization of which is the most important mission of the armed forces.

Nuclear rocket strikes will have a decisive significance for achieving the greatest successes in battle and operations. The powerful nuclear strikes will create conditions for the rapid and full completion of the defeat of the enemy by firepower and strikes of tanks, artillery, aviation, and motorized infantry troops. The armed struggle and methods of its waging by all the services of the armed forces and service arms with the use of the nuclear weapon will be characterized by exceptionally large movement, maneuverability, and purposefulness. The task of overcoming areas contaminated with radioactive substances will be placed before the troops.

Nevertheless, it cannot be denied that along with new methods of action of troops, methods which were established in the last war will also be used widely, based on weapons which, even though improved, are in principle the same weapons with which the armies were equipped earlier. This is especially true in the event that the transfer to world war takes place gradually, by means of expansion of local aggression. Therefore, it is now extremely important in the course of combat and operational training to have combined the study of the new and the perfected existing methods of armed conflict.

The Central Committee of the Communist party teaches military cadres to follow attentively the further development of military art, to imagine distinctly the perspectives of the use of the new weapon and military equipment, and to seek boldly and creatively, in accordance with real conditions, new methods of armed conflict.

The Communist party calls on all generals and officers to study in the most serious manner the problems of military theory in the light of the demands of modern war. The Soviet Armed Forces must be always ready to give a decisive repulse to any aggressor.

8. NATIONAL-LIBERATION WARS—
MARXISM-LENINISM ON WAR AND THE ARMY[1]
EDITED BY GENERAL MAJOR N. YA. SUSHKO AND
COLONEL S. A. TYUSHKEVICH

Editors' Notes

THIS BOOK, published in 1965, was the fourth to be issued of the new series of the seventeen-volume *Officer's Library*. It contains 367 pages and fifty thousand copies were printed in the first edition. For the excellence of this work, the two editors, General Major Sushko and Colonel Tyushkevich, were awarded gold watches and commendations by the commission for the awarding of Frunze prizes.

No short selection can fully cover the range of subjects discussed in *Marxism-Leninism on War and the Army*. We have chosen the selection dealing with "national-liberation wars," and this book contains one of the best discussions on the subject we have found. The reader will note, however, that the Soviets never go into specifics as to how wars of national liberation should be fought.

Their writers claim that national-liberation wars did not become significant until after World War II. Then, *"the downfall of the system of colonial slavery under the onslaught of the national-liberation movement is second in historical meaning after the formation of the world system of socialism."* Initially, in the struggle for independence, "all the patriotic forces of the nation are united, the proletariat, the peasants, the national *bourgeoisie*, and the democratic intelligentsia."

The authors state that in underdeveloped countries conditions are not ready for the "leadership of the proletariat." The peasants are the most numerous class and form the basis of the "revolutionary democratic forces." Since there are few of the proletariat in such countries, who supplies the leadership? The authors suggest that the "national *bourgeoisie*" be used for this but that they "can

[1] Compiled by the Lenin Military Political Academy, Department of Marxist–Leninist Philosophy, 1965.

stand at the head of the national-liberation movement only in the first stage." Then, however, the *bourgeoisie* may "lean toward conciliation with imperialism." It is "only with the help of the international working class [that the struggle] in the final count takes on a socialist character."

The book discusses several types of national-liberation wars and quotes the conclusion reached by Engels that "people who want to win their independence do not have to be limited to *conventional* methods of waging war. Mass uprisings, revolutionary war, partisan detachments everywhere, this is the one method whereby a small people can overcome a large."

Both General Sushko and Colonel Tyushkevich, the two editors of this book, have other writings to their credit. Among General Major Sushko's other works are:

"The Laws Determining the Course and Outcome of Wars," *Red Star*, January 31, February 4, and February 7, 1964;

"Marxist-Leninist Philosophy, the Soul of Soviet Military Science and Practice," *Communist of the Armed Forces*, August, 1965;

"The Development of Marxist-Leninist Teaching on War Under Modern Conditions," *Communist of the Armed Forces*, September, 1961;

"Soviet Military Ideology and Its Contrast to Bourgeois Military Ideology," *Sovetskii Flot*, March 22, 1957; and

(With Major T. Kondratkov), "War and Politics in the Nuclear Age," *Communist of the Armed Forces*, January, 1964.

Colonel Tyushkevich has written:

"The Contemporary Revolution in Military Affairs—Sources and Nature," *Communist of the Armed Forces*, October, 1966.

[Chapter Two.

The Social Character and Types of Wars of the Modern Era]
Section Four. National-Liberation Wars

THE REVOLUTIONARY STRUGGLE of the working classes for socialism is closely bound with the national-liberation movement of

90

people of colonies and dependent countries. V. I. Lenin theoretically based the law of the emerging of social revolution in capitalist countries with the national democratic struggle of peoples of colonies into a single world stream of the revolutionary downfall of imperialism. "Socialist revolution," he said, "will not be simply and primarily a struggle of the revolutionary proletariet in each country against its own *bourgeoisie*, no, it will be a struggle of all colonies and countries oppressed by imperialism, of all dependent countries against international imperialism." (V. I. Lenin, *Works* (5th ed.), Vol. 39, p. 327.) Such a union of anti-imperialist forces is inherent in the modern era.

The October Revolution in our country produced a deep crisis in all the colonial systems of imperialism. It pointed out to oppressed people the path to national liberation and socialism. The working masses of colonies and dependent countries became an active force of international politics and of the revolutionary destruction of imperialism. V. I. Lenin foresaw that: "In the coming decisive battles of the world revolution the movement of the majority of the inhabitants of the earth, originally directed toward national liberation, will turn against capitalism and imperialism and perhaps play a much larger revolutionary role than we expect." (V. I. Lenin, *Works* (5th ed.), Vol. 44, p. 38.)

A new powerful blow to colonial slavery was carried out by the socialist revolutions in a series of countries of Europe and Asia after the Second World War. Resting on the world system of socialism, the liberation struggle of oppressed peoples for the full annihilation of the colonial system became an enormous moving force of historical progress. *"The downfall of the system of colonial slavery under the onslaught of the national-liberation movement is second in historical meaning after the formation of the world system of socialism."* (*Program Documents of the Struggle for Peace, Democracy and Socialism*, p. 64.)

The Social Forces of the National-Liberation Struggle

The revolutionary national-liberation movement is a highly complicated social process in which the formation of varied anti-

91

colonial forces takes place and their co-operation is established. In this, contradictions unavoidably arise about the interlacing and clashing of the interests of various social and ethnical groups, classes, and parties. In the course of the struggle for government independence and for the solution of common democratic problems, all the patriotic forces of the nation are united: the proletariat, the peasants, the national *bourgeoisie*, as well as the democratic intelligentsia.

The working class of a colony in an economically underdeveloped country usually is small and not always sufficiently organized. In many African countries, as a result of colonial economics and of a low level of productive forces, a working class has not been formed as an independent political force. Conditions there do not yet exist for the realization of the leadership of the proletariat. Only as these countries move on the path of economic independence and social progress are national cadres of the working class formed and their political roles raised. Around the working class will rally the semiproletariat masses and peasants. In some liberated countries the union of the working class with the peasants composes the nucleus of the national front; the conduct of the national *bourgeoisie*, who often play a leading role in the national front, depends on the strength of this union.

In a mass movement for national independence and social progress, an important place is occupied by the peasantry. Being the most numerous class, they determine the antifeudal general democratic nature of the revolutionary liberation movement. Without the revolutionary movement of the peasantry one cannot eliminate remains and holdovers of feudalism. The peasant working masses make up a powerful social base for forming the revolutionary democratic forces under the leadership of which, in present-day conditions, the transition of an underdeveloped country to the path of noncapitalist development is also possible.

The national *bourgeoisie* play a great role in the liberation movement. They have a significant possibility of struggling against imperialism, and their interests do not correspond with the interests and politics of foreign monopoly. But in their make-up there

92

is a reactionary element which tries to halt the development of the liberation struggle. Therefore, in politics the national *bourgeoisie* are inconsistent and two-faced. The *bourgeoisie,* fearing the revolutionary upsurge of the peoples' masses, can come to an agreement with the imperialists. The national *bourgeoise* can stand at the head of the national-liberation movement only in the first stage when the question of the government independence of the country is being decided. From then on, according to the development of the anticolonial struggle and the aggravation of the class contradictions inside the country being liberated and, according to the strengthening of the economy and political positions of the *bourgeoisie,* several of their sections more and more lean toward conciliation with imperialism and internal reaction. This is clearly demonstrated by events in the Congo (Leopoldville), a former colony of Belgium.

The contradictory arrangement of social forces of the national-liberation movement complicates the process of the development of the country which has been liberated. After the gain of government independence, the revolutionary struggle is not finished. Life poses new social problems and questions of strengthening the sovereignty of the young national government. Political freedom will be unstable and turn into a fiction if the revolution does not lead to deep changes in social and economic life and does not solve the vital problems of national revival.

The forces of the world system of socialism are decisively promoting the struggle of the peoples of colonies and dependent countries for liberation from imperialist oppression. The whole world knows of the unselfish help which our country is giving to the national-liberation movements of oppressed peoples and to the development of young national governments. The President of the Republic of Ghana, Kwame Nkrumah, said in one of his speeches, "If it wasn't for the Soviet Union, the movement for liberation from colonial yoke in Africa would have wasted all its strength on cruel and rough suppression." The social system has become the reliable shield of independent national development of countries which have been liberated.

The international working class renders great support to the national-liberation movement.

Meanwhile "left" revisionists declare that supposedly the leading role in the world revolutionary process is played not by the international workers' movements but by the national-liberation struggle.

No doubt the national-liberation movement is an enormous force in the world revolutionary process. But it decides, first of all, the general democratic task of national liberation. Only with the help of the international working class does this struggle, in the final count, take on a socialist character. Therefore, it is necessary to not oppose one revolutionary force of the present with another but to strengthen their unity as the leading role of the world socialist system and the international working class.

The War of Oppressed Peoples for Government Independence

The forms of national-liberation struggle of oppressed peoples are sufficiently diverse, from a national armed uprising, for example, in Algeria and Angola, to a comparatively peaceful achievement of independence of the former French colony of Guinea. The choice of methods and the forms of anticolonial struggle depend not on the desires of the people but on the degree of force with which the colonizers try to strengthen their rule.

Thus, for example, after the defeat of imperialist Japan, the Vietnamese people were freed from occupation and took the government power in their own hands. But the French colonizers began open aggression against Vietnam; the American imperialists gave them active support. The Vietnamese people were forced to carry on a long armed struggle for their independence (1946–54). With the help of the [Vietnamese] Revolutionary Liberation Army, they achieved victory in the northern part of the country and started on the path of building a socialist life.

The same conditions had been formed in Indonesia after it was proclaimed a republic in August, 1945. The imperialists of the U.S.A., England, and Holland decided to suppress the national-liberation struggle of the Indonesian people by force of arms. At the end of 1945, English troops occupied several regions of the islands of Java and brutally dealt with the local population. The Dutch troops, with the support of English-American imperialists, twice (in 1947 and 1948) made treacherous attacks on the Indonesian Republic. In answer to this, the people of Indonesia unleashed revolutionary partisan warfare against the occupationists and achieved victory.

Reactionary imperialist forces also unleashed war in Malaya. The armed struggle began (1948) with the repression against the people by the English troops and with the declaration of a siege situation in the country. Partisan war against the English colonizers was unleashed in all Malaya. In 1949 partisan detachments united with the [Malayan] Liberation Army under a single command. The people achieved success; in 1957, Malaya became an independent government. However, England forced an agreement on Malaya by which an English military base was kept in the country. With the formation of the Federation of Malaysia (1963), the base became a support of English imperialism in southeast Asia.

National-liberation war always bears the nature of a retaliatory action for the oppression and violence of the colonizers. The colonial policies of the imperialists were and remain the source of popular uprisings and national-liberation wars.

A series of resolutions of the United Nations stress the unconditional recognition of the right of nations to self-determination and formation of their own independent government. Present-day international law recognizes the legality of armed uprising of the people against oppression and tyranny. In the general declaration of the rights of man it is stressed that tyranny and oppression force people to turn "to uprising as a last resort." (*International Law in Selected Documents*, Vol. 1, Moscow, IMO Publishing House, 1957, p. 207.)

Communists always recognize the progressive significance of wars of liberation. They are the most active fighters for national freedom and social progress. It is written in the Program of the Communist party of the Soviet Union that "The CPSU considers it its international obligation to help people who are on the path of achievement and strengthening of national independence, to all people struggling for the full destruction of the colonial system." (*Material of the XXII Congress CPSU*, p. 357.)

Anticolonial national-liberation war includes (a) armed struggle of oppressed people for their own independence; (b) war of newly independent governments against imperialist aggressors trying to restore colonial regimes.

Anticolonial war of the first variety directly continues the policy of the revolutionary national-liberation movement and smashes the last bastion of colonial slavery. An example of such a war is the war of the Algerian people against the French colonizers (1954–62). Another example is the struggle of the people of Kenya against the forces of English imperialists (1952–56).

The popular nature of anticolonialist wars determines the methods of their being waged and their tactical forms of mass uprisings and patriotic struggles. F. Engels on the experience of national wars of his own time reached the conclusion that "people who want to win their independence do not have to be limited to *conventional* methods of waging war. Mass uprisings, revolutionary war, partisan detachments everywhere—this is the one method by which a small people can overcome a large [people]" (*K. Marx and F. Engels, Works*, Vol. 6, p. 416), and resist its stronger army.

The national-liberation struggle in Algeria took on an especially acute form. The Algerian people started on the path of armed struggle for their independence (on the night of November 1, 1954) after ten years of trying to achieve the realization of their national aspirations by peaceful means. They began a liberation war in order to make an end to the unbearable colonial regime established 130 years earlier. From the side of France, the war with Algeria was an aggressive, plundering war. From this flows the decisiveness of the goals and the acuteness of the form of the liberation war of the Algerian people against their oppressors.

In the course of the armed struggle a liberation army was formed, a struggle ensued which enjoyed the wide support of the people. Along with regular units, temporary partisan formations were created which acted in certain regions.

96

A special upsurge of partisan warfare in Algeria marked the uprising of the peasants in August, 1955. It marked the spread of the liberation war to the whole territory of the country and the attraction to armed struggle of a significant mass of the people, with the poorest peasants in the first ranks. The war took on the nature of an anti-imperialist, agrarian revolution.

The selfless struggle of the people of Algeria for their independence and the angry protests of the workers of France against the dirty war in Algeria forced the French government to start talks with the Algerian patriots, which led to a cessation of combat actions in all of the territory of the country on March 19, 1962.

The Algerian people, heroically struggling with arms in their hands for seven and on-half years, victoriously concluded the just war and defended their government's independence. As a result of this victory, the Algerian Peoples' Democratic Republic came into existence.

The Struggle of Newly Independent Governments Against Imperialist Aggressors

The colonial system of imperialism established for centuries came to an end. In place of former colonies and semicolonies, new sovereign states arose and will continue to arise.

Almost all of them decisively stated a reluctance to join with the aggressive military blocs and proclaimed neutralism as the basis of their foreign policy. Many of them followed a consistent anticolonial policy. However, some newly developing governments are dependent on foreign monopoly and still have not torn themselves away from the world capitalist economy, although they occupy a special place there. Now more and more significance is being acquired by the struggle of the people of these countries for economic independence and for the abolition of military bases and imperialist strong points in their territory.

On the contrary, the basic efforts of the colonizers are directed at holding the people of the countries who have broken the bonds of the colonial yoke in the framework of the world system of capitalism. Capitalistic monopolies try not to let the key positions in

97

the economy of the liberated country slip from their hands. They try to seize new positions by means of loans, credit, and other forms of "aid." At the base of the policy of neocolonialism lies the aim of the imperialists to achieve economic enslavement of countries which have won political independence. "Thus," says the Program of the *CPSU*, "imperialism remains the chief enemy and main obstacle on the path of solving national problems which stand before young sovereign states and all dependent countries." (*Material of the XXII Congress CPSU*, p. 354.)

Along with the policy of flirting with the national *bourgeoisie* of the newly independent states, the imperialists often resort to methods of intimidation by military means. Such military conflicts as the aggression against Egypt, armed intervention in Lebanon and Jordan, conspiracies against Syria and Laos, and aggression in South Vietnam and the Congo arose in connection with the attempts of imperialists by force of arms to prevent the national development of young governments. The aggressive policies of the colonizers put the peace and security of the people, not only of these countries or in certain regions but also in all of our planet, under a threat.

Especially characteristic in this relation was the Anglo–Franco–Israeli aggression against Egypt in 1956. The aggressors wanted not only to seize the Suez Canal but also to liquidate the revolutionary gains of the Egyptian people and frighten the peoples of all Arab countries who were striving for national renaissance.

The aggression against Egypt brought a serious threat to the general peace and security of the peoples. Therefore all the progressive forces supported the struggle of the people of Egypt. The protest by the overwhelming majority of the countries and the especially firm position of the Soviet Union forced the imperialists to cease firing and to remove their troops from Egyptian territory. The Suez battle occupied an important place in the history of the revolutionary liberation struggle of peoples of colonies and dependent countries. It suffices to say that after that time about thirty African countries achieved government independence, and they are struggling now to destroy the shameful colonial yoke in all of the African continent.

The national-liberation struggle of the peoples of Africa is being complicated further by the fact that now not just one sort of colonial power is against them but coalitions of imperialist states are against them. It is absolutely obvious that without this union and its support such a country as Portugal, being a weak, under-developed country of Europe, could not hold in submission African colonies twenty-three times larger than her territory and one and one-half times [larger] in population.

The aggressive actions of a series of imperialist powers are abso-lutely obvious in the repeated armed interference in the internal affairs of the Congolese people. For example, in November, 1964, for reprisal upon insurrectionist patriots, Belgian paratroopers were transported to the Congo, on American planes, from the English island of Ascension. Convinced of the inability of their henchman, Tshombe, to cope with the situation in the country, the imperialists rendered armed support to him in suppression of the national-liberation movement and to protect the interests of foreign monopolists.

The aggressive intrigues of the imperialists are directed against other African states also—states which not long ago achieved na-tional independence—and against all the peoples of South America struggling for democratic freedom. This is clearly shown by the armed interference of the U.S.A. in the internal life of the Domini-can Republic.

Each act of imperialist aggression is a call to liberated states and independent countries which are holding to a policy of non-alliance —a call to all peace-loving forces. Aggression will not strengthen the position of imperialism but will weaken it even further and still will more tightly unite all true strugglers against colonial slavery. The imperialists are powerless to prevent the full disintegration of the shameful colonial system.

III · The Adaptation of Clausewitz to Nuclear War

THE COMMUNIST Chinese Minister of Defense, Lin Piao, proclaimed to the world on September 2, 1965, the Chinese revolutionary strategic concept which declared that the "rural" areas of the world (Asia, Africa, and South America) would overwhelm the "cities" of the world (the U.S.A. and Western Europe) and win final victory. The U.S.S.R. came in for severe criticism in Lin Piao's statement for "revising" Lenin's ideas on war. Lenin had adopted Clausewitz' idea that war is "a continuation of politics by other (that is, more violent) means." The Red Chinese claimed that the Khrushchev "revisionists," because of their fear of nuclear war, were trying to do away with this idea. The leaders in Peking profess to believe that nuclear war should be welcomed rather than feared.

In the fall of 1965, the military press in the Soviet Union stressed its devotion to Lenin. A central theme of the Soviet revolution in military affairs is that mere ability to set off an atomic bomb (as the Chinese had done in October, 1964) does not signify that a country is capable of nuclear war. The economy must be strong; rocket and electronic technology needs to be highly developed. Aircraft and submarine technology must be advanced. In a warning to East and West alike, possible nuclear rocket war was discussed as a foregone conclusion; nuclear rocket war had fundamentally changed every aspect of military art.

It was announced on October 1, 1965, that the Indonesian Army had defeated a Communist coup. India and Pakistan were observing a shaky truce. Vietnam was experiencing bitter fighting and rail-delivered Soviet aid to Hanoi was causing trouble with Communist China about transshipment rights. Brezhnev announced the long-awaited XXIII Party Congress would take place on March 29, 1966. As 1965 came to a close, articles began to reflect the importance of the party's role in establishing Soviet military doctrine. The stronger the armed forces, the greater the deterrent potential. Clausewitz seemed to have been modernized to read, "War is the continuation of politics by other (that is, thermonuclear) means." As if to show that they meant business, civil defense was stressed by its chief, Marshal V. I. Chuikov, of Stalingrad fame.

---

9. ON THE NATURE OF WORLD NUCLEAR ROCKET WAR
By LIEUTENANT COLONEL YE. I. RIBKIN
Candidate of Philosophical Sciences

Editors' Notes

THE EDITORS of the authoritative *Communist of the Armed Forces*, September, 1965, placed this article of Ribkin's in the section of their magazine "Lectures and Consultations," and recommended it for study of the theme "nuclear rocket war and politics." With the known Soviet concentration on nuclear missiles and antimissile systems, such an official view "On the Nature of World Nuclear Rocket War" is of particular interest.

The article deserves attention for several reasons. First, as stated, it is recommended for study. Second, it presupposes that a nuclear war can be fought and won by the Soviet Union.[1] Third, it seems to make a plea for a first strike, advocating a "one-act war"; the side which puts the greatest force into the first strike will have the greatest chance of success. Fourth, this writing was subject to renewed attention after these views of Ribkin's were attacked in a somewhat ambiguous manner in an article, published in *Red Star* in July,

[1] In this regard Ribkin takes issue with retired General Major N. Talensky, Soviet Army, and his contention that thermonuclear war cannot serve as an instrument of politics. Talensky's article appeared in April, 1965, in *International Affairs*, a Soviet monthly journal which is published in Russian, French, and English. Since this magazine is found in many United States libraries, a translation is unnecessary. Talensky does not appear as a spokesman for the Ministry of Defense, and his article is not directed at a Soviet military audience. He has not written for military journals for several years.

1966, by Colonel I. A. Grudinin, another well-known Soviet military writer. A translation of this article by Grudinin will be found at chapter 24.

Ribkin attempts to identify the different groups in the United States and in Europe who disagree among themselves about war and its relation to politics. Among those persons who believe that war can be successfully waged with nuclear weapons are Herman Kahn, Robert Strausz-Hupé, William Kintner, Stefan Possony, and General Thomas Power. There is another group who believe that "war has stopped being a continuation and tool of politics." The late President John F. Kennedy was in the second group, as well as B. H. Liddell Hart, Henry Kissinger, Maxwell Taylor, British Air Marshal E. J. Kingston-McCloughry, and Robert Osgood. The "pacifist reactionary-utopian group" who declare that "war has paralyzed itself" and that peaceful coexistence is guaranteed by the "balance of nuclear power" are Paul-Henri Spaak, Sternberg, F. Schuman, and others. Kind words are given to "those active supporters of the radical struggle for peace," such as "members of the Pugwash movement," and to Bertrand Russell, Jean Paul Sartre, and Linus Pauling.

Should the "imperialists" unleash a nuclear war, the Communist response to it will cause mankind to suffer enormous losses, but it will be a "just" war. The more rapidly the aggressive acts are suppressed by the forces of Communist weapons, "the fewer negative results of war will be found." The need for the single blow, the "one all-destroying blow of a 'battle-ax'" has become paramount in waging world nuclear war. (One might wonder how this idea compares with the opposite concept of "escalation," so much discussed in the United States.) "The a priori rejection of the possibility of victory is bad because it leads to moral disarmament, to disbelief in victory, to fatalism and passivity. The Soviet people are sure of their victory over the forces of reaction."

Ribkin stands high on the list of Soviet military writers. In 1959, when he was a major, his book *War and Politics* was published. In 1964 he contributed a chapter entitled "V. I. Lenin 'On the Causes and the Nature of Wars Under Imperialism,'" which was a part of

On the Military Theory Legacy of V. I. Lenin, edited by V. G. Tsvetkov. "The Laws of Armed Conflict" was in *Communist of the Armed Forces*, April, 1965.

SINCE THAT TIME when the danger of nuclear catastrophe hung over mankind, articles on the question of the nature of contemporary war have not ceased to come from the pages of the foreign press. The authors of many statements try to explain how much those qualitative changes which have taken place in the character of contemporary weapons and methods of their application have influenced the political and social nature of a possible world war; if one can, as before, consider war as a continuation of politics; whether there has been any sort of change in the inner correlations of war and politics, or have these relations remained unchanged.

Contradictory views of this connection are found now and then in the Soviet press also. And although, in our opinion, on the whole, correct answers are given on the questions raised, the problem cannot be considered settled. That is why there is reason to return to it.

We say "return," because in *Communist of the Armed Forces*, No. 2, 1964, an article was published entitled "War and Politics in the Nuclear Age." Its authors [General Major N. Ya. Sushko and Major T. R. Kondratkov] indicate their point of view that the availability of nuclear weapons did not lead to a basic change in the relationship of war and politics, although it introduced several corrections or "improvements." The authors urge us not to mix the question of the nature of war with the question of the advisability of its use as a weapon of politics, correctly reasoning that nuclear war ought not to be such a weapon.

While basically sharing the ideas of the authors, we would like to continue the examination of the problem in question.

Indeed, the appearance of the nuclear weapon as a means of armed struggle, new in principle, could not fail to have brought some sort of improvement in the understanding of the nature of war and its relationship to politics. But what are those improvements? Has the revolution in military affairs had an influence on the profound connections of war and politics?

This problem today is acquiring more ideological and political significance. Within bourgeois society the discussion of it affects the interests of different social strata and political forces. In one or another interpretation of the nature of war, the relationship to war of the various classes is expressed and, consequently, out of it comes various political conclusions. This adds a special pungency to the problem.

The leading trend in the attitude to war among the imperialist *bourgeoisie* appears to be aggressive and militaristic. Its spokesmen use, as a basis of understanding the nature of war, Clausewitz' famous formula: "War is a continuation of politics by other (that is, violent) means." Until recently the basic tendency in the interpretation of this formula by the ideologists of the militaristic trend came to numerous corrections toward *rapprochement*, of identifying the concept of war and politics, and of even turning around Clausewitz' formula to read, "politics is war."[2] Thus spoke the British military theoretician, [J. F. C.] Fuller, in particular, in advancing the idea of blending war and politics. His followers maintain that in the "cold war" the differences between war and peace disappeared.

In the theories of the ultramilitarists, the formula "war is the weapon of politics" remains on a firm base since it answers the plans of imperialism. A few years ago when the idea of a crisis in war and political force began to spread among the bourgeois military ideologists, the government of the United States even created special research centers and political committees which, in their conclusions, sharply condemned every assumption that war had stopped being a weapon of politics. The official point of view was fixed in a document approved by the government of the United States under the name "The Development of Military Technology and its Effect on the Strategy and External Politics of the United

---

[2] Mao Tse-tung in his book, *On Protracted War*, states, "Politics is war without bloodshed while war is politics with bloodshed." (Quotation at page 59, *Quotations from Chairman Mao Tse-tung*, Peking, 1966).

States" (December, 1959). In conformity with the military doctrine, the works *On Thermonuclear War*, and *Thinking About the Unthinkable* by H. Kahn; *A Forward Strategy for America* by Strausz-Hupé, Kintner, and Possony; *Design for Survival* by [T. S.] Power, and other books, the possibility of successfully waging war with the use of nuclear means was proved, and any sort of change of principle in the nature of contemporary war was denied.

For this reason, the aggressive wing of the imperialist *bourgeoisie* not only firmly defends the point of view of the nature of war as a continuation of politics, even in the "nuclear age," but also is prone to identify war with politics, i.e., considers war a basic, universal means of politics.

However, in the social conscience of the capitalist world, ever greater dissemination is being given the view of radical changes in the nature of war; and that "war has stopped being a continuation and weapon of politics." Such an opinion is held by people of the most varied political leanings. Among them are also the staunch supporters of imperialism who recognize, nevertheless, the fatal nature of nuclear war and accept the policy of peaceful coexistence in one degree or another. The late President of the United States, J. Kennedy, for example, inclined to their opinion. This opinion is held by the military theorists and ideologists Liddell Hart, H. Kissinger, M. Taylor, E. Kingston-McCloughry, R. Osgood. They, of course, do not deny the policy of militarism and are fighting for the preservation of nuclear weapons, although they fear the results of their use.

A large group of spokesmen sharing the point of view that war has stopped being a continuation of politics make up the pacifist, reactionary-utopian element. They (P. Spaak, F. Sternberg, F. Schuman, and others) declare that "war has paralyzed itself" and that at the present time peaceful coexistence of nations is guaranteed by the "balance of nuclear power." To this same group belong many bourgeois and *petit bourgeois* "peacelovers," writers, and philosophers of decadent doctrine. The imperialist aggressors would have no objections to using their passive contemplative position for lulling to sleep the vigilance of the peace-loving forces.

105

The sincere pacifists, those active supporters of the radical struggle for peace and for the banning of nuclear arms, deserve different estimates. For example, there are the many scientists, writers, and political figures of nonaligned governments, members of the "Pugwash" movement, and progressive representatives of the movement for preserving the peace, as B. Russell, J. P. Sartre, L. Pauling, and others.

Therefore, it would be improper to place all the supporters of a review of the Clausewitz formula on one list. From a political point of view, the formula "nuclear war has stopped being a continuation of politics" expresses the admission of the fatalness and undesirability of nuclear war. Most of all, it serves in a few cases as a peculiar form of protest against the threat of a new war. The acceptance of this formula for a person of bourgeois society can mean at least a realization of the crisis of militarism, adoption of the principles of peaceful coexistence, and might even lead to active fighting for peace against imperialist aggressors. Therefore, we cannot help but admit the well-known progressive importance of this formula for drawing into the antiwar movement the most healthy-minded people from the proletariat levels of bourgeois society. The Program of the Communist Party of the Soviet Union states, "All organizations and parties aiming at the prevention of war, neutralist and pacifist movements, bourgeois circles supporting peace and the normalization of relations between countries—will find in the Soviet Union understanding and support." (*Material of the XXII Congress CPSU*, p. 365.)

However, it must be remembered that the humanistic, social-democratic movement in the bourgeois world rests, as a rule, on unscientific, idealistic, and metaphysical methodology. It would be wrong in practice to carry into the theoretical content of this problem as a whole the positive meaning of the formula "war has stopped being a continuation of politics."

The Content of the Idea—"War is a Continuation of Politics"

Theoretically, the proposition of the possibility of a change in the nature of war should not bring any objection. V. I. Lenin stated

106

that "not only is appearance transient, moving, flowing, and separate only by agreed borders, but even the *nature* of things as well." (*Works*, Vol. 38, p. 249.) Since everything in the world moves and changes, then the nature of things generally is also mobile. The whole question lies in the degree and character of this change. In order to explain this, it is necessary to specify the subject of our research. Many doubts and vaguenesses in the understanding of the nature of nuclear war are rooted in the oversimplified interpretations of the very idea itself.

The formula "war is a continuation of politics by violent means" (methods of armed struggle) grows out of a very intricate complex of existing connections and relationships. This formula is composed of three elements: "politics," "continuation (of politics)," and "violent means" ("armed struggle"). Each of these elements is full of profound meaning.

Politics in the interpretation of V. I. Lenin is (a) "participation in the business of government, the direction of the government, the determination of the form, the problems, and the content of the activities of the government" (*Lenin Collection*, XXI, p. 14); (b) "relationship between classes" (*Works*, Vol. 32, p. 205); (c) "the concentrated expression of economics" (*Works*, Vol. 32, p. 62). The fundamental question of politics is the question of governmental power and its use.

Marxism-Leninism sees in politics two sides: objective and subjective. The objective side consists of the presence of classes, nations, and social layers, which find themselves in various interrelationships formed independently of the will of the people. The basis of demarcation of political forces lies in the social structure of society, in the gradual development of its material production, and in the economic interests of classes. The subjective side is the activity of the government, the power struggle, and the use of power to protect the interests of one or another class inside and outside the country. This side of politics is supported by the objective side and appears as its expression.

The nature of political activity consists of the struggle for changes in the objective arrangement of the social-political force in the interest of a given class, government, or nation. This struggle takes different forms, the most acute of which is war. In the understanding of the Clausewitz formula by bourgeois ideologists, politics is only the activity of government, mainly of the leaders—personalities in whose make-up lie psychological, geographical, biological, mystical, and what-have-you motives. The role of economic factors and class struggle, if recognized, has a distorted, misunderstood viewpoint.

Under *methods (means) of armed violence* we divide the struggle into forces especially designed for this (army, navy), secured by measures of economic, moral, and diplomatic character. In understanding this element there is also an untrue interpretation. In bourgeois-military theoretical literature more and more often one meets attempts to widen excessively the understanding of means of violence (and even war) right up to the inclusion in it of "the cold war," subversive activities, methods of military threat, blackmail, and so forth. (See, for example, E. Kingston-McCloughry, *Global Strategy*, Military Publishing House, 1959.) Such a point of view is directed essentially at the theoretical basis of politics balanced on the brink of war and might serve as justification for "creeping into" nuclear war.

The analysis of the idea *"continuation of politics"* is of great interest. Namely, in it is reflected the deep connection of politics and armed conflict, which exactly constitutes the nature of war.

Between politics (as the governing impulse, the basic substances of war) and armed struggle at least five relationships are revealed.

First: *War is the result of politics.* It begins, in part, when aggressive politics, led by the interests of the exploiting classes, in one form or another, demands military conflict, and external and internal political agreements do not hinder it forcefully enough.

The second relationship: Politics by means of its aim *adds a definite direction to armed struggle* and consequently even to war as a whole—progressive or reactionary. Namely, this relationship has in mind the Marxism-Leninism demand, "In each separate instance, for every war especially, determine its [each war's] political make-up." (V. I. Lenin, *Works*, Vol. 23, p. 187.)

The third relationship: *Politics rules military strategy.* It "controls" the waging of war and (considering, of course, the objective logic of armed struggle) does not let its results go counter to the interests of politics. The nature of political goals has a decisive effect on the waging of war.

The fourth relationship: The armed struggle in turn becomes in practice *a means of changing political conditions,* "pushing slightly" its development in a direction convenient for the victors. In this way, they speak of war as a "weapon of politics." But war can only play the role of a political weapon when victory is achieved. If there is no hope of victory, then war objectively stops being a political weapon, although it may keep up its role in the first three relationships.

Finally: The fifth relationship indicates *the spontaneous reverse influence of armed struggle on politics,* as a result of which war may leave the framework undertaken by its politics. The reverse influence of armed struggle is expressed primarily in the fact that it leads all society to special, even "frantic" conditions, it brings in, as a result, aggravated class contradictions in an antagonistic society, and in corresponding conditions it might evoke a revolutionary situation, a social crisis. The reverse influence on the political development of society takes place also as a result of the enormous sacrifices and the destruction, which always negatively affects the historical process.

All this converts war from a consciously used "weapon of politics" (as a "rapier or sword" as Clausewitz imagined it) into an "enormous historical process," and a peculiar "summation of politics." (See V. I. Lenin, *Works,* Vol. 26, p. 350, and Vol. 30, p. 202). In this process many opposing forces are at work. From this it is clear that it is absolutely wrong to identify the concepts "continuation of politics" and "weapon (or means) of politics." *War is always the continuation of politics, but it cannot always serve as its weapon.* Besides, war leaves a mass of "side effects" while putting politics under its own sort of examination and test and while exerting on it a reverse, often unseen, influence.

For this reason, the formula "war is a continuation of politics by violent means" can acquire different meanings in connection with one or another interpretation of "politics," "continuation of politics," and "armed violence." While explaining the genuine nature of war, we must confine ourselves strictly to its dialectical-materialistic sense and completely analyze its connections and relationships.

The Nature of the Changes in the Connections of Politics and War

Now let us look at each of the given relationships of politics and war in light of the change caused by the revolution in military affairs, by the rise of nuclear danger, and also by the development of socio-political factors.

First relationship. Thanks to the rise of the socialist system, the sphere of action of the sources of war now are seriously restricted. The presence of nuclear weapons in the U.S.S.R. serves as an enormous factor deterring the aim of the imperialists to start a world war. However, the contradictions capable of leading to such a war continue to exist and the possibility of its arising remains. And what is more, as a result of the appearance of systems automatically resulting in operation of rocket equipment and in view of the constant adventuristic acts of the imperialists, the danger has grown of an "automatic" beginning of war even as the result of an unimportant international conflict. Therefore, the real possibility of nuclear war, now as before, fashions itself only out of the economics and politics of imperialism. And so, to speak of changes in the nature of war in this relationship cannot be done; if war starts, it will be a result and a continuation of politics.

With the *second relationship* matters are somewhat more complicated. Nuclear weapons lead to reactionary and unjust war from the side of the imperialists up to the culminating point. War, having as an aim the stopping of social progress and the physical annihilation of people who are struggling for revolutionary transformation of society cannot be compared with anything in the past in its reactionary and inhuman nature. This is clear. But how to consider the acts of those forces which must bring down on the aggressors the retaliatory, crushing nuclear strike and, by this, cause great sacrifices and destruction? Is the fact not being excluded that the use of nuclear weapons is possible and necessary in waging a just war?

Bourgeois pacifists come to the conclusion that the use of nuclear weapons changes war from any side and under all conditions into an unjust and reactionary war. On this basis they speak of a "self-negating war." With such a conclusion, of course, it is impossible to agree. So long as nuclear war, if the imperialists despite the will of the people unleash it, will have the goal, from our side, of the annihilation of the aggressors, and the liquidation of the perpetrators of war—imperialism—then, from this side, it will bear a just character.

Of course, also in this forced, just war from the side of progressive forces, mankind will suffer enormous losses. But it must be kept in mind that the degree of damage which inevitably will be brought to civilization by such a war, in many ways, depends on the speed of the armed struggle. The more decisively and quickly the aggressive acts of imperialism are suppressed by the force of our weapons, the fewer the negative results of war. This conclusion must prompt the Soviet military cadres to every sort of raising of vigilance and combat readiness, to decisive and relentless acts against imperialist aggressors.

From the discussion, it is obvious that nuclear weapons do not abolish the second relationship of war and politics either, although the application of these weapons, obviously, restricts the possibility of achieving immediate progressive results in a just war.

The third relationship—politics controls the military actions—also is not abolished by the presence of nuclear weapons, although it suffers sizable changes. They consist of this, that the possibility of politics to maneuver in space and especially in time with nuclear forces is more limited than under conditions using conventional arms. Military theory agrees with the idea that the most effective variant of nuclear strategy must be, as theorists say, "one-act war," that the government which more quickly paves the way to victory, which puts the bigger force in the first blow, will use its results more effectively.

Clausewitz in his time wrote, "With the all-destroying element of war (a million times weaker than now!—Ribkin) politics turns into only its own simple instrument: the terrible fighting battle-ax, which demands that it be raised with both hands and strains every force for carrying out of one unique blow which, thanks to politics, is converted into an easily maneuverable sword which becomes now and then even a rapier, and they fence with it according to all the rules of the art." (*On War*, Vol. II, Military Publishing House, 1932, p. 99.)

At the time, the inner logic of armed conflict did not demand the *compulsory* concentration of forces of the belligerents in one all-destroying blow of a "battle-ax." Now, in the conditions of the application of nuclear weapons, the demand for such a blow really has become the most important law of the methods of waging world war. Of course, politics under all circumstances will aim at keeping military actions under its control and, in this sense, its role and responsibility has grown colossally, but the possibility of maneuvering, "fencing" with weapons, in the course of a nuclear war has been sharply reduced. Therefore, *the center of gravity of the efforts of politics for the guidance of strategy is carried over into peacetime*, especially in threatened periods. So, the third relationship in conditions of nuclear war undergoes serious modification and limitations.

And what happens with the nature of war in the *fourth and fifth relationships*? Do the armed forces remain the means of clearing the path for politics—to secure for it the possibility of achieving its goal?

In the West many authors of various persuasions have arrived at the idea of the impossibility of victory in nuclear war. "To try to win the war, to set as one's goal victory," writes the British military theoretician Liddell Hart, "is sheer madness because total war with the use of nuclear weapons will be disastrous for both sides." (*Intimidation or Defense?* Military Publishing House, 1962, p. 55.) Encountered also are similar ideas of several Soviet authors. N. Nikolsky, in the book *Today's Basic Question*, writes, "The disappearance of the possibility of victory in world thermonuclear war as a means of achieving political aims of governments, the denial of all military categories of the institution of war in thermonuclear war, testifies to the fact that world thermonuclear war is already in nature, not war, but self-negating war. This is that dialectical limit of the development of phenomena when they stop being phenomena" (*Today's Basic Question*, IMO Publishing House, 1964, p. 381.)

"In our days," writes N. Talensky, "there is no more dangerous illusion than the idea that thermonuclear war can still serve as an instrument of politics, that it is possible to achieve political aims by using nuclear weapons and at the same time survive, that it is possible to find acceptable forms of nuclear war." ("Thoughts on Past Wars," *International Affairs*, No. 5, 1965, p. 23.)

The supporters of such views usually refer to the political results of nuclear war which form spontaneously and get out of control. Such facts actually are inevitable, and they hamper the control over events in significant measure. The destruction of people, the razing of factories and energy systems, the poisoning of topsoil and water, the spontaneous movement of radioactive clouds, the changes in the biosphere of the earth, enormous fires, and so forth—all these threatening forces, of course, can give birth to doubts concerning the real possibility of achieving victory and about the survival of the victors themselves. No one has a right to close his eyes to all the serious results of nuclear war. Exactly therefore, the Communist party and the government of the U.S.S.R., all of our people, the peace-loving people of all the planet, propose a maximum effort in order to not permit the unleashing of war, and to curb aggressors. However, to maintain that victory in nuclear war is in general impossible would be not only untrue theoretically but dangerous from a political point of view.

It must be remembered that victory in war depends not only on the character of the weapons but on the *correlation of forces* of the belligerent sides. The achievement of a quick victory over the aggressors that will avert further destruction and calamity might depend on this correlation. There is a possibility of developing and producing new means of waging war which would be able to safely counter the nuclear blows of the enemy.

In addition, other factors and forces which inevitably enter into operation in the event of the unleashing of world war cannot be left out of one's reckoning. These primarily are the decisive anti-imperialist actions of the masses of the people, diplomatic and other acts aimed at deterring the aggressors.

The a priori rejection of the possibility of victory is bad because it leads to moral disarmament, to disbelief in victory, to fatalism and passivity. It is necessary to carry on a struggle with such views and attitudes of mind. The Soviet people are sure of their victory over the forces of reaction. This sureness is based on the real power of our government and of all of the socialist system, with prepossessing economic, moral, and military–technical opportunities for the rapid, utter defeat of aggressors.

At the same time, it would be a mistake to assert that the presence of potentialities in themselves already predetermines our victory. Such an assertion lowers the role of subjective factors, the role of the activities of the masses and the leaders. The objective advantages of the socialist structure and the strength of its material and moral forces act not by fate but are realized only by the activity of the people.

Recently the party and its Central Committee put to severe criticism worthless methods of management which issued from the idea that the objective advantages of our advanced structure almost automatically assured our rapid successes. Nothing is more dangerous, especially in military affairs, than such ignorant ideas. Any advantages are only potentialities which are turned into reality solely by tenacious labor supported by deep scientific understanding of phenomena and processes. This means that in order for victory to be safely assured, it is necessary to have high daily vigilance of all the personnel of our Armed Forces, further raising of military preparedness, constant development of military science and equipment, and perfection of miltary art.

Such an understanding of the question of victory in nuclear war promotes the correct training of soldiers and mobilizes their

strength on all-round military preparedness, on the further strengthening of discipline and organization in forces, on decisive action
in fighting situations, and, at the same time, warns against the
danger of "swell-headedness."

So, nuclear war, because of its consequences, leaves the framework of previous ideas about the relationships of politics and war.
Remaining as the continuation of politics, such a war now, because
of the effect of the consequences of the nuclear means of struggle,
is *limited as a weapon of politics.* This fact does not negate either
the possibility of the unleashing of war by aggressors or the possibility of our victory in it. The main conclusion from the analysis of
this problem consists of the necessity of doing everything for the
preclusion of world nuclear war. Along this line, the Program of
the Communist Party explains to us in this way, *"War should not
and must not serve as a means of solving international argu-
ments."* (*Materials of the XXII Congress CPSU,* p. 364.) Together with the Program of the Communist party of the Soviet
Union, the decision of the party and government obliges our
Armed Forces to be constantly in a condition of full readiness to
frustrate with their decisive actions the plans of the agressors and
to carry a shattering retaliatory blow to them.

These are a few of the practical conclusions from a dialectical-
material understanding of the nature of nuclear rocket war.

---

10. THE MODERN REVOLUTION IN MILITARY AFFAIRS AND ITS MEANING—*THE PROGRAM OF THE CPSU ON THE DEFENSE OF THE SOCIALIST FATHERLAND*[1]

By General Major K. S. Bochkarev, Colonel I. P. Prusanov, and Colonel A. A. Babakov

---

Editors' Notes

Marxism-Leninism teaches that for the success of the revolutionary movement it is necessary to be master of all forms and

1 Published by the Military Publishing House, Moscow, 1965.

115

means of struggle; peaceful and not peaceful, parliamentary and non-parliamentary; legal and not legal, and to use those which the concrete situation dictates.

THIS EXTRACT TYPIFIES the tone of The *Program of the CPSU on the Defense of the Socialist Fatherland.* The book appeared in Soviet bookstores in February, 1966, just before the opening of the XXIII Party Congress in March. Regretfully, we can include only a small portion of this interesting work in our collection here. We have chosen a section, taken from the second chapter, entitled "The Modern Revolution in Military Affairs and Its Meaning."

The authors emphasize the relationship between the over-all technological development of a nation and its military capability. A high level of science and industry is a necessary prerequisite of the military-technical revolution. The development of scientific knowledge is directly tied with production.

Through Communist eyes, the course of the technological revolution in the countries of capitalism differs from that of socialism. Under capitalism, scientific progress "takes on a misshapen form" and is used "primarily for military purposes." Scientific progress in the Soviet Union "has a peaceful direction and is used for the good of the workers."

The authors discuss the "revolution in military affairs" in considerable detail. Its "most important results have been achieved in two countries only, the Soviet Union and the United States of America." Although there are other nations that have nuclear weapons, they have not changed the relationship of nuclear forces.

The nuclear rocket weapon has altered all aspects of war to include organization, strategy, and tactics. Even if conventional weapons are used, the troops "must constantly be ready to repulse the nuclear strikes of the enemy." Both attack and defense are radically changed. In fact, "defense as a method of action on a strategic scale will lose its meaning, for going over to strategic defense when the enemy has nuclear weapons at his disposal and is counting on attack means voluntarily placing the country and the army under nuclear execution."

The Soviets generally profess not to have the slightest interest

116

in the military use of space. They accuse the "American imperialists" of trying to "boost a race for space weapons," and claim that "it would be a great mistake not to take into account the possibility that cosmic means of attack might turn out to be in the hands of the imperialists. The interests of the security of our Motherland and the other socialist countries demand the detailed study of the whole sum of questions connected with organizing PKO [anti-cosmic defense], with working out effective methods of battle with the 'cosmic strategy' of the aggressor."

The authors' discussion of military doctrine is of particular interest. "Military doctrine, as a definite system of views on the questions of military structure, exists in each state." American readers might be reassured to find, "At the present time, the imperialists, especially the Americans, in their military doctrine, are trying to escape the mistakes of the past and extract the lessons from the past war. They are making great efforts in order to analyze as fully and deeply as possible the revolution taking place in military affairs and to approach the problem of military structure in a new way." However, their writers tell us, defects in the American approach will still remain and, in contrast, Soviet military doctrine is being developed "on a genuinely scientific basis."

The authors present the view that a future war "will be a decisive armed clash of two opposed social systems, capitalism and socialism, in which both sides will pursue the most decisive goals, excluding any sort of compromise." Attention is given to the importance of the beginning period of the war, "which can have a decisive effect on its whole course and outcome." In this regard, the reader should note that "the role of the surprise factor in combat operations will increase sharply."

General Major Bochkarev, one of the three authors of this book, already has been discussed in chapter 6.

Colonel Prusanov is the author of several articles published in *Communist of the Armed Forces*:

"The Work of the Party in the Strengthening of the Armed Forces in Terms of the Revolution in Military Affairs," February, 1966;

"The Development of Leninist Principles of Building the Armed Forces in the Program of the CPSU," April, 1962; and

"The Party in the Period of the Great Patriotic War," February, 1964.

Colonel Babakov has written for the same publication:

"An Important Condition of the Effectiveness of Studies," February, 1962;

"V. I. Lenin on the Military Organization of the Proletariat Government," October, 1964; and

"Anti-communism in the Service of Imperialist Reaction," August, 1966.

[*Chapter Two. The Defense of the Socialist Fatherland—*
The Most Important Function of the Soviet Government]
Section Three. The Modern Revolution in Military Affairs and its Meaning

WHILE STRENGTHENING the defense of the country, our party strictly took into account the latest achievements of military theory and practice and the changes going on in the material-technical basis of military affairs.

In the postwar period, as is well known, military equipment underwent very great changes. According to their consequences, these changes were more significant by far than those which were evoked, in their time, by the invention of gunpowder and shooting irons, and, later, the appearance of automatic weapons, tanks, and airplanes.

The present military-technical revolution was prepared for by all the previous development of the material-technical base of military affairs and the increased possibilities of productive forces, science and technology. "Nothing so depends on economic conditions," wrote F. Engels, "as the army and navy. Armaments, structure, organization, tactics, and strategy primarily depend on the achievement at any given moment of the level of production and on the means of communication." (F. Engels, *Selected Mili-*

118

tary Writings, The Military Publishing House, 1957, p. 11.) The development of military affairs in present day circumstances serves as a convincing affirmation of this conclusion by F. Engels.

Prerequisites and Basic Features of the Military-technical Revolution

Our time is characterized by the unusually rapid development of science and industry. In the system of scientific-technical knowledge, revolutionary transformations have taken place in the genuine sense. Exceptionally great successes have been achieved in such branches of natural science as physics, mathematics, chemistry, and biology.

As a result of the study of the inner structure of the atom and its nucleus, the chain reaction and the thermonuclear process were discovered. This formed the foundation for making powerful nuclear energy. The study of the physics of solid bodies led to basic changes in the realm of electrotechnology, electronics, and radio-technology. The successes of cybernetics permitted the making of swift-acting computing machines and electronic guidance systems and opened the widest possibilities for the introduction of automation in various branches of industry.

Achievements in working out theories of the chemical structure of material, in the field of kinetics, catalysis, and research of high molecular combinations, helped create new, unknown before, substances and materials with characteristics set beforehand.

Successes of mathematics, physics, and a series of other branches of knowledge permitted the development on a large scale of the research of cosmic space and created manned space ships, quantum generators, and artificial sputniks of Earth.

In contemporary circumstances, the relationship of science and technology has acquired new features. The development of scientific knowledge is more tightly bound with production. From one side science has been industrialized, insofar as its successes to a decisive degree now depend on the use of new means of research produced by industry (powerful instruments for splitting the nucleus of the atom, computer equipment, and various forms of

119

instruments); from the other side, the development of technology and industry to an ever greater degree depends on the results of scientific research. Science now does not simply follow the demands of production, serving it. It is invading the very process of production and directly taking part in it.

Science is more and more turning into the direct productive force of society. This new role of science clearly appears especially in the solution of such technical production problems as the automation of technological processes, the use of atomic energy, the establishment of intercontinental radiotelephone communications, the research of cosmic space, and so forth.

The *rapprochement* of science and production is opening grandiose perspectives for the subjugation of nature's forces by man and for the ever greater satisfaction of the material and spiritual needs of people. "Mankind," it is pointed out in the Program of the CPSU, "is entering a period of scientific-technological revolution connected with the mastering of atomic energy, the opening up of space, the development of chemistry, the automation of production, and other major achievements of science and industry." (*Material of the XXII Congress CPSU*, p. 339.)

The scientific-technological revolution is taking place in both countries of capitalism and of socialism. But, under the conditions of capitalism scientific-technical progress takes on a misshapen form and creates extreme contradictions. It increases the army of the unemployed and destroys ever newer sections of small manufacturers.

The capitalist system, as a whole, is more and more fettering the development of productive forces and giving a one-sided character to the development of science and technology. "Imperialism," it says in the Program of the CPSU, "is using technological progress primarily for military purposes. It is turning the achievements of mankind's intelligence against mankind itself." (*Material of the XXII Congress CPSU*, p. 339.)

In contrast to capitalism, socialism is creating all the conditions for the unlimited development of science and technology. This is proved by the experiments of our country. The first artificial sput-

120

nik of Earth and a cosmic ship with a man on board were launched by the Soviet Union; the first ice-breaker in the world with an atomic engine, an atomic electric-power station, the largest accelerator of elementary particles, the world's most powerful hydro-electric station, jet engine, and so forth were built in the Soviet Union.

Scientific-technical progress in our country, as in the other countries of socialism, has a peaceful direction, and it is used for the good of the workers. However, socialist governments must not forget that international imperialism is placing at the service of its reactionary policy all the achievements of science and technology. In the face of the danger of imperialist aggression the peoples of the countries of socialism must use scientific-technical progress for strengthening the defense potential of the socialist camp. *Imperialism is the sole culprit in causing the greatest scientific-technical achievements of our time to be used in great measure and often, in the first place, for military purposes.*

What is the nature and peculiarity of the revolution which is taking place in military affairs?

The main thing in the present military-technical revolution is the creation of the nuclear rocket weapon and the organization of its mass production.

The nuclear rocket weapon in its combat qualities and potentials sharply differs from all kinds of weapons previously existing. It has colossal destructive force, surpassing by many thousands and even millions of times the striking force of conventional combat means. It is a weapon of combined actions. Its striking factors are: powerful shock waves, light radiation, penetrating radiation, and radioactive contamination of the area.

According to foreign figures, a nuclear bomb the power of ten to twenty megatons exploding in the air creates a zone of complete destruction for a radius of fifteen to twenty kilometers. A bomb with the power of fifty megatons creates such a zone in an area of fifteen hundred to three thousand square kilometers, and with the power of one hundred megatons, an area of four to five thousand square kilometers.

121

Powerful light emanations, produced as a result of the nuclear explosion, can cause fires and serious burns at a distance of dozens of kilometers from its epicenter. Thus, with the explosion of a one hundred megaton bomb, this radiation creates a zone of destruction in an area of seventy thousand square kilometers. Also, exceptionally great danger is presented by the penetrating radiation and radioactive particles left after the nuclear explosion which can be spread by wind and other factors for hundreds of kilometers and keep their fatal properties for a long time.

With the nuclear rocket weapon, a strike can be carried out in a short time on practically any point in the world. As is known, the average speed of flight of a strategic rocket is twenty times higher than the speed of an airplane and ten times the starting speed of an artillery shell. Such a rocket can cover a distance of ten thousand kilometers in thirty minutes. Rockets have a high degree of invulnerability in flight, and protection from them is extremely difficult and complicated. Finally, the action of the nuclear rocket weapon, as distinguished from conventional weapons, depends very little on geographic, climatic, and other natural conditions, and it can be used at any time of the year and day, in any weather.

The nuclear rocket weapon, as is evident from the very name, consists of two parts: The nuclear charge and the rocket mechanism. At first both parts were created independently of each other, which mutually limited their combat possibilities.

It is well known that rockets at first were used for getting warheads carrying conventional explosives to the target. This lowered the significance of rockets as a combat means insofar as the zone of destruction of such warheads did not cover the area of dispersion in the place of their landing. In turn, the atomic bomb was perfected as one of the kinds of aviation bombs, insofar as it was proposed that the airplane was the most convenient carrier of the nuclear device. But, in fact, this weakened the combat effectiveness of the nuclear charge, because carrying it to the target was done relatively slowly and at a limited range, not to mention that the nuclear ammunition could be destroyed comparatively easily before it reached the target.

The turning point in the development of the new weapon was the union of the nuclear charge with a rocket, as a result of which the nuclear bomb acquired a nature corresponding to the combat possibilities of the means of delivery to the target and at the same time the enormous significance of the rocket device in armed combat was uncovered. As is known, this was first done in our country.

With the creation of the nuclear rocket weapon, the changes now taking place in the technical basis of military affairs were not exhausted. Serious changes have taken place in so-called conventional weapons: tanks, aviation, submarines, surface ships, artillery and shooting weapons, and so forth.

Modern tanks, compared with tanks of the last war, have much greater speed, power and accuracy of fire, armored protection, and mobility. They can independently overcome various obstacles—including water barriers—and successfully operate in complicated radioactive conditions.

Aviation has undergone major changes in converting from piston engines to jets. The altitude of airplanes has been greatly increased—and the duration and range of their flight and the power of their strike weapons. Airplanes have appeared with sonic and supersonic speeds, with ceilings of flight up to thirty kilometers and more. Helicopters have been widely developed.

Atomic submarines, armed with nuclear weapons, that increased considerably the duration of their voyages, invulnerability, and firepower, have appeared in the navy.

The range of fire, rate of fire, and striking force of cannon artillery have grown. Recoilless, and jet artillery especially, and various types of guided missiles, such as antitank, antiaircraft, and so forth, have received further development.

The motorization and mechanization of troops has been sharply reinforced. Infantrymen are carried in machines which increase by far their combat potential.

Automation for guidance of military equipment and troops is becoming widely diffused. Automatic arrangements of the so-called self-programming system are a structural part of the guidance of rocket systems, cosmic apparatuses, and airplanes.

123

The most important changes in conventional forms of armed combat are caused primarily by the fact that these weapons are adapted to an ever greater degree for the use of nuclear charges.

The change taking place before our very eyes in military equipment is unrolling on an exceptionally wide front, and it is affecting literally every sort of weapon and piece of military equipment, every element and side of military affairs. This is one of the most important features of the modern military-technical revolution.

Its other special feature is that the tempo of the perfection of military equipment and weapons has increased. While in the past, more or less important changes in military equipment were made in the course of tens or even hundreds of years, now more significant changes have taken place in about one and one-half or two decades.

Not long ago, for example, the atomic bomb represented a rather bulky and clumsy arrangement. Now bombs of even megaton power are very compact. The caliber of atomic charges has become diverse, as has the assortment of nuclear explosives; and what is particularly important, thermonuclear charges have appeared which exceed by many times the power of the first atomic bomb.

The rate of perfection of rocket devices is just as high. In recent years a great quantity of types and classes of rockets were created, distinguished from each other by the construction and power of engines, type of fuel used, range of flight, combat designations, methods of guidance, and many other features. Rockets now exist which have engines using both liquid and solid fuel and with ranges of flight from several dozen to many thousands of kilometers. Some of these can be launched from land, others from the air, and still others from under water.

The rockets are guided by various systems. For example, in rockets with automatic guidance, the given program of flight is assured by the aid of special devices placed on board. In rockets having systems of long-range guidance, radioelectronic apparatuses constantly determine the location of the target and the projectile, and between the rocket and the ground-control point distant ties are maintained. There are self-navigating rockets, rockets with combined systems of guidance, and others.

Ballistic rockets, the guidance of which is done only in the beginning period of flight, have particularly important significance; their further movement follows the laws of free-falling bodies. The multi-stage ballistic rocket can reach an altitude higher than a thousand kilometers. These rockets (they are called intercontinental) represent a complicated complex in which have been placed the latest achievements of automation, telemechanics, electronics, computer technology, instruments, metallurgy, chemistry, and other branches of science and technology.

The world's most powerful rocket is the Soviet rocket-carrier, with the help of which the cosmic ships with men on board were launched. It is well known that the first Soviet "Vostok" rocket had six engines with a total power of twenty million horsepower. The basic power plant of the rocket carrier—with the help of which the scientific space station "Proton–1" was launched—developed power of more than sixty million horsepower.

Repeated tests have shown that Soviet rockets have exceptional accuracy of landing on the given point. Even at a distance of thirteen thousand kilometers, dummy rocket nose cones have not gone out of the limits of a two kilometer square.

The present changes in the technical base of the armed forces are not limited to the further development of recently created forms of weapons. The persistent search for newer and newer forms of weapons continues. In particular, work is going on for using quantum generators (lasers) for military purposes, creating so-called ionic and plasma rockets, atomic engines of a lighter type, and other technical means, based on the latest achievements of scientific thought.

Finally, one of the characteristic features of the present-day military-technical revolution is its uneven development in different countries. The most important results have been achieved in only two countries, the Soviet Union and the United States of America. As concerns other governments, some success in making nuclear weapons has been achieved by France, England, and, recently, the

CPR (Chinese Peoples' Republic). However these successes, so far, have not made any essential change in the relationship of nuclear forces which have taken shape in the world.

The Military-technical Revolution and the Problem of Methods and Forms of Armed Struggle

The changes which have taken place in military affairs have had the very deepest influence on the methods and forms of armed struggle and, at the same time, also on the nature of war as a whole.

It is generally known that the forms and methods of armed struggle were different in different historical eras and, at times, even in wars in one and the same era. As a matter of fact, in each war one or another feature in the methods of its waging is always discovered. This is natural, for many factors have an influence on armed struggle.

The forms and methods of armed struggle are determined in large degree by the content and nature of the political goals which are pursued in a war. The more radical this goal, then usually the more decisive the actions of the troops and the more fierce the battle. Indecisiveness of the political goal inevitably weakens the combat activity of the troops and results mainly in the urge for defensive operations.

The moral-political state of the troops depends on the character of the goal of the war. Just goals of war raise and unjust goals lower the moral spirit of the soldiers, and this is directly reflected in their fighting activities. The higher the moral state of the troops, the higher their offensive impulses and persistence in battle. Troops with high moral spirit more easily endure the difficulties of marching-fighting life and surprise attacks, are less susceptible to enemy flank attacks, and fight more steadfastly in encirclement and other complicated conditions of combat circumstances. Troops with low moral spirit cannot display genuine selflessness and bravery in battle. Several sorts of combat activity, for example, partisan methods of armed struggle, generally will not receive any serious development with a low moral-political state of the troops and if the population of the country has a negative attitude toward the goals of the war.

126

The forms and methods of armed struggle depend on their range, the special features of the theater of military operations, and the natural conditions. Wide spatial range of armed conflict, when large masses of troops are involved from both sides, makes necessary definite forms of their organization, for example, the creation of frontal, army, and other operational commands, the necessity for which might not exist under a smaller range of combat actions. As concern natural conditions, their influence is obvious: armed conflict in sea theaters of military operations is one thing, in land theaters, another. And combat actions on land, for example, in wooded mountain regions, will be waged differently than those on a plain or in the desert.

Finally, military equipment and weapons have an exceptionally great influence on the forms and methods of armed conflict. The perfection of material means of armed conflict is raising the firing and striking force of the troops and their mobility and is creating an objective base for widening the scope of combat actions and for unleashing them in the most diverse conditions of the earth's surface and air space.

"The successes of technology," wrote F. Engels, "only just become applicable and actually used in military affairs, and immediately, almost by force, often against the will of the military commander, they evoke changes and even revolutions in the methods of waging war. (K. Marx and F. Engels, *Works*, Vol. 20, p. 176.)

All factors which influence the methods and forms of armed conflict are inwardly tied together and act jointly. But the role of each of them proves to be first more, then less, in different historical eras and in different wars, and at times, also, in different stages of one and the same war. At the present time, especially important meaning has been acquired by those changes in the forms and methods of armed struggle which have been evoked by the appearance of the nuclear rocket weapon. Let us look at these in a little more detail.

The nuclear rocket weapon fundamentally changes the whole course of a war and the general picture of armed struggle. It smashes the ordinary, seemingly firm notions of waging war, its beginning period and length, spatial range of armed struggle, theaters of military actions, methods of carrying out fire strikes and their objectives, the character of the actions of troops, the role of the different services and branches of the armed forces.

Indeed, in the past there was not a sufficiently reliable technical means of carrying out strikes in the interior of the belligerent states and of unleashing armed struggle on an intercontinental scale. The state of equipment also did not permit the carrying out of combat operations in the air at great altitudes or at great depths of the seas and oceans.

It is not accidental that in the past even world war was waged on only a comparatively limited part of the earth's surface. Both in the First and in the Second World War, neither America nor Australia were in the sphere of combat actions; the armed struggle in Asia and Africa was territorially limited. In both world wars, the main events took place in the land theaters of military operations in Europe. The use of bomber aviation, and then the German guided missiles, the FAU–1 and the FAU–2, and the American atomic bombs did not bring about radical changes in the scale of armed struggle.

The situation that has arisen at the present time is absolutely different. *Modern military equipment and weapons literally permit the waging of combat actions on every territory on earth, on every continent, sea, and ocean.* If world nuclear war is unleashed, then the American continent also would be in the sphere of powerful fire strikes; it would be the arena of bitter battles. The possibilities become very real of waging combat operations at great depths of the seas and oceans.

Of course, the range of armed struggle is in direct dependence on the economic power and the number of states which enter into the war and on the aims of the war. But this does not lessen the primary role of military equipment and its combat potential.

The changes which have taken place in military equipment and weapons again raise the question of the direct object of armed struggle. In wars of the past, the main forces were directed at the defeat of the armed forces of the enemy. The results of these efforts to a decisive degree determined the whole course and outcome of the war. The destruction of the armies of this or that state or coalition of states usually meant their defeat in the war. The winner was that side which achieved the given goal while preserving the combat capability of its own troops.

Now, wide possibilities have been opened for carrying out destructive blows not only on the armed forces of the enemy but also on those sources which feed them, on the industrial economic objectives, the centers of government administration, and so forth. This sort of strike acquires great significance insofar as, in the event of their success, the weakening or even the complete undermining of the military power of the state will be inevitable. In nuclear war the center of gravity of the armed struggle will shift from the region of direct contact of the armies of the belligerent sides to their rear areas. All of the territory of the belligerent countries will prove to be in the sphere of the theater of military operations.

In modern war, the interconnections and interdependencies of strategic and operational-tactical actions of the armed forces have become different. In the past, when battle in the frontal zones was actually the sole means of defeating the enemy and achieving the decisive goals of war, strategic successes took shape gradually from the favorable conduct of battles and operations. At the present time, the nuclear rocket weapon allows the carrying out of crushing blows on the enemy without waiting for the results of separate battles on the front.

Of course, even in nuclear war, finally smashing the resistance of the enemy and carrying the struggle to victory is impossible other than through the actions of the troops on the front, through separate battles and operations carried out on land, at sea, and in the air. However, it is absolutely obvious that the place and role of armed conflict in the form of the direct clash of troops has changed. This form of battle now acts as part of the general military effort of the government and, moreover, depends on the strategic nuclear strikes. Thus the nuclear rocket weapon gives strategic operations a relatively independent character and immeasurably increases their influence on the whole course of the armed struggle.

The use of the nuclear rocket weapon essentially changes the beginning period of the war. The Second World War has shown already that the time has passed when the beginning period amounted to weeks and even months, in the course of which mobilization and concentration of the troops of the states entering into battle took place. Foreign specialists calculate that now the armed forces must be kept in that structure and that condition in peacetime which will allow the achievement of strategic goals to be expected in the very first days of the war.

Although in the past war started with battles in the border regions and the main objectives of combat actions were the groupings of the armed forces along the front lines, war, as has already been pointed out, most probably will begin with surprise attacks in the interiors of the belligerent sides, on their most important vital centers. Now such specific sorts of combat actions, unknown in wars of the past, as the carrying out of nuclear rocket blows of colossal destructive force and the exchange of such strikes, will acquire decisive significance.

The nuclear rocket weapon again poses the question of how to use the chief quality of the armed forces, firepower. The effect of firepower on the enemy once served as the basic means of securing the actions of the ground forces and other services of the armed forces. Now it has grown out of this framework and has acquired the importance of the determining factor of armed battle as a whole. And this is understandable, because the aim of combat actions after nuclear strikes might be only to complete the defeat of the dispirited enemy by means of occupying his territory and establishing appropriate control over it. From this comes the necessity for the ground forces and other services of the armed forces to time their actions to the periods of execution of strategic nuclear strikes and to use these results to the maximum. This is an objective demand dictated by the very nature of the new weapon, which neither one of the belligerent sides can overlook.

130

In nuclear war, the combat activities of the troops will inevitably be distinguished by great activity, swiftness, and exceptionally high maneuverability, for only in such conditions will the results of their own nuclear strikes be used in full measure on one hand; on the other, the carrying out of similar strikes by the enemy will be made difficult. Armies will widely use all mobile means of fighting: tanks, armored transport, airplanes, helicopters, and others. The skill of the troops in overcoming areas of the localities contaminated by radioactive fallout will acquire special significance.

In nuclear war, attack and defense will be drawn up in a new way. Attack, as before, will remain the chief method of solving problems of armed struggle, but it will even more than in the last war regain control over defense. The form and order of attack will change. Attacking troops, most likely, will meet on their path not continuous zones of defense fortifications but only centers of resistance and more or less extensive zones of radioactive contamination. However, they must constantly be ready to repulse the nuclear strikes of the enemy. Therefore, attacking troops must: first, be dispersed as much as possible but so that the ability for co-operation and joining forces at the necessary moment is preserved; second, attack at high tempos and advantageously in tanks, armored transport, and helicopters; third, widely use maneuver and evasion of the centers of enemy resistance; fourth, create one's own strike groups on withdrawal from the enemy.

Thus, attack will obviously not be connected with the traditional breakthrough of the enemy's defense, with forces "gnawing through" the defense zone, as it was in the Second World War. It will take the shape of rapid movement of columns of soldiers simultaneously in several directions. In the course of attack, pockets of resistance will develop and engagements will take place, often without the troops dismounting.

Defense also will have another character in conditions of nuclear war. Defense as a method of action on a strategic scale will lose its meaning; because going over to strategic defense when the enemy has nuclear weapons at his disposal and is counting on attack means voluntarily placing the country and the army under nuclear execution. Such a strategy does not answer to the nature of contemporary war.

But defense keeps its significance on a tactical scale and, to a certain degree, operational scale. It will be used in separate areas and on those occasions when the force for attack is not sufficient. It goes without saying that defense, when the necessity for it arises, will shape up in a new way. While defense in the Second World War was built on a continuous front, including a series of positions and zones with solid forces and facilities for defense built up within them, now it must be built beforehand with a calculation of the use of the nuclear weapon and the maneuvering actions of the troops.

Defense will be first and foremost against the nuclear rocket weapon, that is, intended for the preservation of the personnel and equipment from the nuclear strikes of the enemy—and also against aircraft and against tanks. On the main lines of advance, the troops will occupy very important isolated regions and positions dispersed along a front and in the interior, and the protection of the spaces between them might be secured by the fire of various weapons. Defensive action, in the ways (firepower strikes, counterattacks and counterstrikes) that it is conducted, will be close to offensive action.

In nuclear war, the forms and methods of combat actions of PVO [antiair defense], the air forces, and the navy will radically change.

The basic efforts of the troops of PVO and PRO [antiair and antirocket defense] will be directed toward frustrating enemy aerospace attacks, that is, toward the timely detection of his planes and rockets and toward their destruction before reaching important centers of the country.

Aviation will destroy and demolish important objectives in the enemy's rear, carry out air reconnaissance, and co-operate with ground forces and naval forces in their operations. The role of aviation in the landing of airborne troops and in transporting them great distances is growing.

The navy, to a greater extent than formerly, will independently perform tasks not only close to shore but on the vast areas of the

132

seas and oceans. Its main force will be directed at destroying the enemy's fleet, disrupting his sea and ocean communications, carrying nuclear rocket strikes on shore and interior objectives, and, also, co-operating with its own ground troops, and assuring the protection of its own sea communications. The leading role will be played by the actions of submarines and rocket-carrying aviation.

Rapid scientific-technical progress is opening wide the possibilities for developing military equipment and weapons. Nuclear charges, rocket equipment, and other sorts of weapons continue to be perfected. In the armed forces, atomic energy plants, means of automation, telemechanics, and radioelectronics are used more and more widely. The work directed at finding ever newer and newer military means is continuing with great persistence. Therefore, the forms and methods of armed struggle will inevitably undergo essential changes in the future.

It is well known that in recent years the American imperialists have persistently tried to boost a race for space weapons. They have spent enormous amounts on the creation of various cosmic systems—spy-satellites, navigational satellites, communications satellites, anticosmic means, especially satellites carrying nuclear charges in them.

It would be a great mistake not to take into account the possibility that cosmic means of attack might turn out to be in the hands of the imperialists. The interests of the security of our Motherland and the other socialist countries demand the detailed study of the whole sum of questions connected with organizing PKO [anticosmic defense] and with working out effective methods of battle with the "cosmic strategy" of the aggressor.

Such, in brief, are several of the most important features characterizing the problem of developing forms and methods of armed conflict in contemporary circumstances.

The Growing Role of the Scientific Management of Troops

The deep changes which have taken place in the development of military affairs have acutely raised the significance of the scientific approach to the solution of the problem of the structure of the

Armed Forces and the management of all their lives and activities.

Management, in general, consists of the co-ordinated actions of people, in joining their efforts for achieving one goal or another. It is the same also in the military field, but here it takes place in the specific conditions of armed conflict, of constant opposition of the enemy, when the lives of the people are subject to mortal danger, and when maximum effort of all physical and moral strength is demanded from them.

The most important thing in management is making a decision and organizing its execution. Obviously management will be equal to and will fully meet its purpose only when the goals advanced by it are real and the indicated path of its achievement is the most effective. In other words, management will be successful when it is built not on chance observations and fruitless phantasies but on the sober stocktaking of objective factors and correlation of forces on the battlefield, and when it is accomplished creatively and skill- fully, really scientifically.

Even in the past, especially at the time when the motorization of troops began, creating multimillion man armies and increasing the range of armed conflict, the solution of military problems de- manded great scientific competence from the commander per- sonnel. Even V. I. Lenin pointed this out, stressing that "without science one cannot build a modern army." (V. I. Lenin, *Works*, [5th ed.] Vol. 40, p. 183.) In present conditions, the given de- mands have taken on, one might say, an absolute character. *Mili- tary theory and practice can now move ahead only on a strictly scientific basis.* Scientific management has become one of the most important prerequisites of fighting efficiency of the troops and of achieving victory in armed conflict. In nuclear war, one cannot manage troops on the off-chance, setting one's hopes on "a lucky star" or only on empirical knowledge.

The growth of the role of scientific management is stipulated primarily by the very nature of present-day weapons. Being the concentrated embodiment of the latest achievements of science and technology, they demand genuinely scientific treatment. And this is possible only when not just the army engineer service

134

but the commander and his staff as well understand the bases of nuclear physics, electronics, cybernetics, and other sciences. The military leader who does not have deep scientific-technical knowledge cannot correctly evaluate the possibilities of the new weapons, determine the most efficient method of their use, cannot confidently orient himself in conditions which are created on the battlefield as a result of the use of nuclear weapons.

And more. The probability of a gigantic increase of spatial range of armed conflict, the necessary training of troops to operate in the most diverse conditions, at a great distance from the places of their constant deployment, obliges military cadres to know well the political and economic map of the world, the social structure, national characteristics, and geographical situation of many countries, land, sea, and air communications, and so forth. Modern military commanders must have a wide general science and cultural outlook and have all-round education. This is an indispensable prerequisite for the successful management of troops.

The necessity of scientifically-based management is dictated also by the growing significance of foresight in military affairs. Never before has the question of the correct evaluation of the nature of a future war and the possible forms and methods of armed conflict acquired such acuteness and, in addition, been so complicated and difficult as at the present time. This is explained primarily by the radical and unusual revolution which has taken place in military affairs and the briefness of the period of time of its existence.

In the past, one or another type of new weapon or of military equipment usually was tested in practice in the course of a war. This made it possible, by leaning on the experience of the combat use of the new equipment which was introduced at the front, to bring to light its merits and defects, and to introduce the necessary changes in the organization and methods of the combat actions of the troops. That is just the way it was with the machine gun, tanks, and aviation, which were revealed in a series of wars, and, as is well known, were more or less correctly evaluated very slowly.

At the present time the situation is different. Although the

American imperialists used two atomic bombs at the end of the last war and the results obtained permitted judging the colossal combat potential of the new weapon, still this experience had limited meaning. This was a test of an isolated and not a mass use of the new weapon, and, besides, it was in the first stage of its technical development when atomic bombs could be delivered to the target only by airplanes.

Insofar as the nuclear rocket weapon is concerned, then, as a combat arm in a real war, it has not been tested. Nevertheless, tests on testing ranges and various studies are giving extremely valuable material for evaluating the nature of nuclear war, but it is far from being sufficient for revealing the full picture of such a war. Here science and theoretical thought must come to the rescue. They are called upon to penetrate deeply into the nature of nuclear war, evaluate its probable course and—in the event it is unleashed by the imperialists—determine the trend of the military structure which would in the greatest degree answer the interests of a reliable guarantee of the security of the Soviet government.

Scientific management of troops proposes:

First, the mastery by the military cadres of Marxism-Leninism and the latest achievements of military theory and practice, for only on this basis can there be confident orientation in the events which are taking place and correct determination of the tendencies and perspectives of the development of military affairs;

Second, all-round validity of the decisions which are made, whether they concern the organization of troops, the training and education of personnel, or the technical equipping of units and ships. In other words, scientific management is incompatible with the smallest appearance of subjectivism, arbitrariness, rashness, and superficiality both in the raising of problems and in the determining of the way of their solution. Subjectivism is always dangerous in any area of man's activity, but it is especially dangerous in military affairs and especially at the present stage of its development in conditions of unprecedented growth of the power of the new weapon;

Third, firm direction of subordinate subunits, units, and ships based on a deep knowledge of the field and of the concrete conditions of the situation, and on the creative fulfillment of the demands of the regulations and manuals;

Fourth, constant support of the collective thought and the collective experience of the soldiers. This in no way is contrary to the principle of unity of command. The commander is given the right to make individual decisions, but these decisions can be fruitful only when they take into account the opinion and the experience of the collective;

Fifth, an attentive attitude to the new and progressive; a decisive struggle against conservatism and routine, blind adherence to the old. Bold and persistent search for more nearly perfect forms of troop organization and the most effective methods of their combat activity, and critical appraisal of the results achieved must be the inalienable feature of commanders and chiefs of all degrees.

The scientific approach to the solution of military problems is indeed the demand of the times. Our party and its Central Committee demonstrate constant concern so that the leadership of all branches of the governmental structure, including developments of military affairs, takes place on a strictly scientific basis. This concern is clearly shown in the documents of the XX and XXII Congresses, in the Program of the CPSU, in the decisions of the October (1964) [plenum] and subsequent plenums of the Central Committee CPSU.

The scientific approach of the party to the solution of the more important questions of military theory and practice finds its own actual conversion into fact in its conclusions on the special features of contemporary war, on the organization of the defense of the country, and on the ways of combat actions of the Armed Forces in the event aggression from the side of international imperialism becomes a fact. These conclusions make up the starting point and the basis of Soviet military doctrine.

Military Doctrine of the Soviet Government

Our military doctrine represents an aggregate system of views on the nature of a possible war, which guides the Soviet government in taking measures for the reliable guarantee of the security of the U.S.S.R. and of all the socialist camp.

Military doctrine includes in itself two sides: Political and military-technical. The political side determines the chief purpose of all of the military structure in the U.S.S.R., the role of our Armed Forces as a weapon of the socialist government. It discloses the political goals for the sake of which the Soviet Armed Forces might be used—in other words, the political goals of a future war if it is thrust on us by the imperialists.

The military-technical side of the doctrine is composed of the views and postures which have a specific military character, that is, which determine the organization of the defense of the country, with a stocktaking of the demands of a probable war as well as of the number and inner structure of the army and navy, the methods of training the troops, and the forms and methods of armed conflict.

Military doctrine, as a definite system of views on questions of military organization, exists in each state. It is worked out under the influence of general conditions of development of the country, its economic, political, and military possibilities, and it reflects the character, goals, and missions of the policies of the ruling classes. The different sorts of conditions in which countries find themselves, including those of the same type of social structure, give rise to different sorts of military doctrines also.

Once formed, military doctrine does not remain unchangeable. Changes in the economy, in the arrangement of political forces inside the country, as well as outside it, and in the development of military equipment and weapons, sooner or later evoke changes in the military doctrine of the government as well.

It must be noted that conclusions and recommendations contained in military doctrines of capitalist countries do not always correspond to the real possibilities, the objective demands flowing from the nature of war, and the level of development of military affairs which has been achieved. History knows of many examples when countries entering into armed conflict have had to reject one or another of the lines of their own military doctrine or even completely revise them. The imperialist powers which took part in the First World War proved to be in such a position.

As is known, the military doctrines of these countries did not give a correct evaluation of the peculiarities of the war which was starting, of its duration, of the roles of the services and service branches, and of defense and attack. The passive wait-and-see strategy of the French General Staff did not justify itself; it manifestly underestimated the German forces and their potential for carrying out major attacking operations in the ground theaters of the war. The hopes of the military and the political leadership of England to decide the fate of the war by means of sea operations and to escape having their troops being drawn into an armed conflict on the Continent were not justified; the English had to deploy a massive land army while still in the beginning of the war. The calculation of the Kaiser's Germany that it would succeed in defeating its enemies one by one by means of successive lightning blows and in finishing the war in a short period of time failed.

In spite of expectations, the First World War took on a prolonged and a positional character. It continued for more than four years. The military doctrines of the imperialist powers went bankrupt by reason of not studying in sufficient measure the changes which took place at the beginning of the present century in the means and conditions of armed conflict.

The lessons of the Second World War are also highly indicative in this regard. In its course, the French military doctrine which had exaggerated the role of long-lasting defenses and had oriented the army to positional war turned out to be untenable. The adventuristic military doctrines of Hitler's Germany, Fascist Italy, and militarist Japan—all betting on lightning war and surprise attack—suffered a failure.

In essence, the military doctrines of all of the imperialist powers on the eve of Second World War were little different from their military and strategic purposes in the period of the First World War, although political conditions in the world and the material-technical base of waging armed battle at that time had undergone deep changes.

139

The experience of the Second World War again confirmed that the military doctrine of bourgeois states, while sometimes correctly noting changes which had taken place in the development of military affairs, still could not escape the limitations inherent in the ideology and the policies of the *bourgeoisie*. This limitation is reflected in subjectivism and one-sidedness in evaluating the factors and perspectives of armed struggle, especially the role of the masses of the people, of man and equipment in war, and of adventurism and conservatism of military thought.

At the present time, the imperialists, especially the Americans, in their military doctrines, are trying to escape the mistakes of the past and to extract the lessons from the last war. They are making great efforts in order to analyze fully and deeply as possible the revolution taking place in military affairs and to approach the problem of military structure in a new way. However, even in the present military doctrines of the imperialists, the defects—in a more concentrated form but all the same defects—make themselves known in subjectivism, one-sidedness, adventurism, by exaggerating their own potentials, and by underestimating the potentials of the other side.

In contrast to the military doctrines of imperialism, Soviet military doctrine from the very beginning, in all stages of its development, is being worked out on a genuinely scientific basis.

Guided by Marxist-Leninist methodology, our military doctrine aims with maximum fullness and objectiveness to evaluate conditions and factors in order to determine a way of strengthening the defense might of the Soviet government. Such conditions and factors are: The situation of the U.S.S.R. in the general system of governments; the arrangement and relationship of political and military forces in the world arena; the nature of the probable clash with world imperialism; the goals which will be pursued in a war by the belligerent sides; the potentials (military, economic, moral, and political) of the probable enemy; the potentials of the Soviet state and of all of the socialist camp; the achieved level of development of military affairs, primarily military equipment and weapons. Soviet military doctrine takes into account the experience of

140

the last wars but does not overestimate it. It is giving special attention to everything new that contributes to the development of military theory and practice.

The merits of our doctrine were clearly revealed in the years of the Second World War. Long before the beginning of this war, Soviet doctrine with great exactness determined its character and features and the possible arrangement of military and political forces in the world. In it was soundly stressed the growing significance of motorization and the mechanization of the army, the necessity of harmonious development of the services and service arms, the exceptional importance of the maneuverable form of armed conflict and of deep attacking operations; and defense was considered as a necessary, although subordinate, kind of combat action. Our doctrine proceeded from the fact that war cannot be accomplished in one lightning-like strike and inevitably will assume a prolonged character, and victory in it demands enormous effort of all the forces of the army and the people.

These and other ideas of Soviet military doctrine found their reflection in various documents of that time, in the regulations, manuals, orders, and directives of the People's Commissariat of Defense and the General Staff, in plans and programs of combat training. They were clearly formulated in the projected *Field Manual of 1939* in which was especially stressed the necessity of high combat activity in the actions of troops and of conducting war until the enemy was completely defeated.

The Great Patriotic War revealed a series of weaknesses (underestimating the possibility of enemy invasion of Soviet territory, insufficiently taking into consideration the growing role of the beginning period of a war, the possibility of great losses, and so forth) in our doctrine, but at the same time it convincingly showed the correctness of its basic premises, its superiority over the military dictrine of Hitler's Germany and of other imperialist governments. This conclusion in no way contradicts the fact that the Soviet Armed Forces in the first stage of the war suffered failures in battle with Hitler's armies and were forced to withdraw. The failures of our troops were stipulated in large measure by the inter-

141

national military-political situation which was unfavorable for the U.S.S.R., having built up on the eve of the war and by crude errors in its evaluation having taken shape under the influence of the personality cult.

Soviet doctrine, basically, passed the severe test of the great war. Its ideas, enriched by the conclusions and lessons of the Second World War, also had a deep influence on the development of the Armed Forces of the U.S.S.R. after the war. However, in the post-war period, a serious re-examination of many positions of our doctrine was demanded. The necessity of such a re-examination was dictated primarily by the fact that new factors, which earlier either were absent or had only just appeared, came into action.

As a result of the formation of the world system of socialism, the foreign policy position of the Soviet government radically changed. The creation of the thermonuclear weapon signified the deepest revolution in all areas of military affairs. The threat arose of the unleashing by the imperialists of thermonuclear war against the U.S.S.R. and the other countries of socialism. All this necessitated the working out of new directions on the questions of the organization of the armed protection of the socialist Fatherland.

Of what does the peculiarity of the present stage in the development of Soviet military doctrine and the essence of its new ideas consist?

To begin with, it should be stressed that in the fundamental concepts of our doctrine, as formerly, the question is exclusively about the measures against the aggressive aims of imperialism, about measures which are retaliatory and forced, aimed at the protection of the most lofty and just goals, answering to the vital interests both of the Soviet people and of all progressive mankind. *Soviet military doctrine is undergoing changes, is being perfected; but it was and remains the doctrine of a peace-loving socialist government, of socialist armed forces imbued with the spirit of the ideology and the policy of the Communist party.*

Basing itself on a scientific analysis of the peculiarities of the contemporary international situation and the development of military affairs, Soviet military doctrine gives *an evaluation of the na-*

142

ture and range of the war which the imperialist powers, headed by the U.S.A., are preparing and are trying to unleash against the U.S.S.R. and the other countries of socialism.

Our doctrine is guided by the fact that no matter how war begins, with an attack of the imperialists on the socialist camp as a whole or on separate countries belonging to it, or as a result of the unleashing by the imperialists of a local conflict, affecting the vital interests of the U.S.S.R. and of all of the socialist camp, it will inevitably draw into its orbit the peoples of all countries and continents, that is, it will become world-wide.

From the social point of view, this war will be a decisive armed clash of two opposed social systems, capitalism and socialism, in which both sides will pursue the most decisive goals, excluding any sort of compromise. From the military technological point of view, the war inevitably will be thermonuclear, the chief means of destruction will be atomic and hydrogen bombs, and the basic means of delivering them to the target will be rockets. All this stipulates the unprecedentedly destructive and annihilating character of the war and the exceptional intensity and fierceness of combat actions.

Soviet military doctrine takes into account that the appearance of the nuclear rocket weapon signifies not a conventional change in the technical equipment of the troops but a basic revolution, a genuine revolution, in military affairs. In war with the use of nuclear rocket weapons the whole course of the armed struggle and the role and significance of most, if not all, of its sides, elements, and factors are radically changed.

The power of the nuclear weapon and the possibilities of almost instantaneous delivery of it in massive quantities on the target predetermines the aim of both sides to carry out strikes of maximum force in the very first minutes of the war. In view of this, the beginning period of the war acquires a qualitatively new significance which can have a decisive effect on its whole course and outcome.

The role of the surprise factor in combat operations will increase sharply. New features will be acquired by the interrelationship of man and equipment in battle. The significance of combat activity of troops—their stability, resolution, initiative—and the scientific,

143

technical, and military competence of the commander and the rank and file will be raised. The nuclear rocket weapon in its very nature does not permit sluggishness, flabbiness, uncertainty, pauses, or clichés in the actions of troops. Daring and decisive attack and swift and skillful maneuver will not only assure the defeat of the enemy but will be the best means of protection from his nuclear strikes.

An important feature of Soviet military doctrine is that it *considers the factors of armed struggle in their organic interrelationship and comprehensively takes into account possible variants of this struggle, its forms, methods, and stages.*

While stressing the decisive role of the nuclear rocket weapon and the Strategic Rocket Troops as the main service of the Armed Forces, our military doctrine by no means minimizes the significance of conventional weapons. It considers that victory in modern war can be achieved only by the combined forces of all of the services of the Armed Forces and branches of service.

Indicating the growing importance of the beginning period of the war and the possibility of its short duration, Soviet military doctrine does not exclude the fact that under certain conditions war might become long and drawn out; consequently, the country and the army must be ready for such a variation of armed struggle.

In Soviet military doctrine the circumstance that a future war will have a coalition character from both sides, that is, in it the united forces of the imperialist powers will oppose the powerful coalition of socialist states, is fully taken into account.

Such a nature of war obliges all countries in the socialist camp to give serious attention to the co-ordination of their efforts in the areas of military structure and to questions of the co-operation of the armies of socialist states. In the struggle with aggression, the countries of socialism and their armies must act with united force as a single whole.

It is especially important to stress that, while recognizing the colossal power of the new weapon, Soviet military science by no means falls into technicism and one-sidedness, inherent in the bourgeois theories of "push-button war." It considers that nuclear

144

war will be waged by massive multimillion man armies, that in this war, in spite of the sharp growth of the destructive forces of the new weapon, the main role, as before, will be played by man.

Taking into account that the enemy will try to carry out strikes of enormous force, primarily on the vital centers of government, bases, and regions of the positions of nuclear rocket weapons, our doctrine demands high combat readiness of the Armed Forces and the timely preparation of the country to repel aggression. This preparation includes the solution of a whole complex of important problems.

A characteristic feature of Soviet military doctrine is that *it soberly and objectively evaluates the potentials of the probable enemy,* resolutely warns against thoughtlessness, subjectivism, counting on an easy victory, and tossing one's hat in the air. In war, if the imperialists unleash it, we will be confronted with a strong and crafty enemy armed with all the modern means of fighting, one having large reserves, enormous territory for maneuver, and able to resort to the most decisive and merciless actions.

Our military doctrine is the reliable orientation point for the military cadres, helping them to correctly organize combat training and education of the troops and to resolve successfully all questions of military structure. It arms the personnel of the army and navy and all of the Soviet people with a single view on the nature of the military tasks and methods of their solution by means of common purposes and demands.

The party by no means considers military doctrine as something settled, given once and for all, and incapable of further development and perfection. It teaches that under the condition of the revolution in military affairs which has taken place it is necessary to analyze critically combat experience of the past, to reject boldly worn-out concepts and views, to consider attentively the new, to explore deeply the influence of the nuclear weapon on the nature, ways, and methods of armed struggle. The demands for criticism and for an inventive, creative approach to military affairs are contained in the very nature of our doctrine, and in this is one of the sources of the correctness of its views and recommendations.

11. LAND FORCES, THEIR ROLE AND FUTURE
BY COLONEL V. V. MOCHALOV
Candidate of Military Sciences

Editors' Notes

SOVIET MILITARY DOCTRINE or strategy is not the main subject of this article; rather, it is about the United States Army. It might be intended as a presentation of views from United States sources which some Soviet military leaders wish their own country would adopt. At any rate, it is typical of the meticulous attention given to every nuance and change of United States military policy by the Soviet military leaders. The need to know the strong and the weak sides of the "probable enemy," the United States, is an admonition taken very seriously by the Soviets, judging from the number of books, articles, and brochures devoted to this subject.

Colonel Mochalov himself is an interesting choice for bringing to light such a view. In July, 1954, his article "Peculiarities of Offensive Operations of a Field Army in Contemporary Circumstances" was published in *Voyenniya Mysl'* (Military Thought), a classified Soviet publication on military matters. Other noteworthy articles are: "Mobile Defense," *Red Star*, March 30, 1956, and "The Smokescreen of American Imperialism" (with Major V. Dashichev), *Red Star*, December 27, 1957. In March 1963, Mochalov was one of the seventeen officers attending a conference on military doctrine. His participation was reported as follows:

> He (Mochalov) stressed that in the West the tendency toward an integrated military doctrine has recently gained strength. There is much in common in the military doctrines of the U.S.A., England, France, and FRG. It is admitted that a future war will be a nuclear rocket one. At the same time, the possibility of waging local or limited war is not denied. Comrade Mochalov remarked that the views held by probable enemies on the nature of future wars should be taken into account by us [the U.S.S.R.] in working out questions of armed conflict.

146

Mochalov followed up with a book, *The Big Lie About Little Wars*, in September, 1965. The advertisement for the book read,

> *The Big Lie About Little Wars.* On the bourgeois theory of limited war. The theory of limited wars—born of American imperialistic reaction—is the officially acknowledged and accepted conceptual armament of the Pentagon and the military departments of other NATO countries. In the brochure, the aggressive nature of this theory, the means and forms of planning by the imperialists of little wars, is bared, unmasking their reactionary character and anti-Communist direction.

"Land Forces, Their Role and Future" is a typical example of Colonel Mochalov's keen interest in the United States Armed Forces and an equally good example of what the Soviet military is told about our military policies. This Soviet view of the United States Army should be measured against official Soviet doctrine presented again and again in these translations.

On January 19, 1967, *Red Star* launched a series of articles which told of the combat actions of the United States Armed Forces in Vietnam. The first article, dealing with the ground forces, was entitled "When There are No Front Lines," and it was written by Colonel Mochalov.

AMERICAN MILITARY leaders long ago rejected the idea that war is won by aviation alone or by nuclear rocket weapons. "Waging war cannot be completely done by any one service of the armed force. . . . We must never tie our military policy to any one weapons system or one theory of waging war," writes General [Harold K.] Johnson in the *Army Information Digest* magazine, the official organ of the American Army. However, it was further emphasized in the magazine, "This basic concept in no way reduces the primary role of the land forces as the decisive and basic element of national power."

Land forces do not take part in carrying strategic nuclear blows, and this led several bourgeois military theorists to the idea that they could not play a large role in contemporary war. The regulations of the Pentagon and the majority of the military specialists in the U.S.A. confirm that a strategic nuclear strike, although it is the most important stage of the war, does not finish it. Forces are needed which will be able to use the results of a nuclear strike in order to finish off the enemy and to seize his territory. For such forces, only land troops are considered.

Official military circles of imperialist countries came to the firm conclusion that without infantry, artillery, and tanks, nuclear rocket war cannot be waged, not to mention local wars. In the American press, it is noted that war is waged on the ground— for the main aims of military operations are ground objects. These objects must be taken by infantry with the support of other services and branches of the armed forces. Before a soldier's foot steps on the enemy's territory, victory cannot be considered complete. In the magazine *Military Review*, it is said that "irrespective of the fact that damage will be carried to one or the other government, the result of the war will be decided when his land forces are defeated."

The highest operative-strategic united land forces in the theatre of military operations in the majority of imperialist countries are the army groups which may consist of two to four field armies and one tactical aviation command. In the army are usually included from two to four army corps each of two to five divisions. The army groups, field armies, and corps have no constant organization. Their fighting structure depends on the problem facing them. Only infantry, armored, mechanized, and airborne divisions have constant organization, since they are the basic tactical formations of the land forces.

The development and reinforcement of land forces in the imperialist countries occupies one of the leading places in the arms race and in the planned preparations for aggressive adventures against freedom-loving peoples. This is also confirmed by the nature of the structure of their armed force. According to the *New York Journal American* for July 31, 1965, the armies of the U.S.A. have 970,000 soldiers and officers (not counting marines). On orders of President Johnson, in connection with widening the aggression against Vietnam, the number in the American Armed Forces will be enlarged by 340,000 men from which 235,000 will be assigned to the army, which will then have 1,205,000 men.

The West German *Bundeswehr* has up to 438,000 men. Their land forces have about 278,000 men. Numerous land armies are held by other NATO countries. Out of a general armed force of 5,000,000 men, they compose more than half—3,200,000 soldiers and officers. Land forces in the armed forces of France are 67 per cent, Greece—72 per cent, Turkey—83 per cent, Portugal—74 per cent.

According to the words of the Chairman of the Joint Chiefs of Staff of the U.S.A., General [Earle G.] Wheeler, the military doctrine of the Pentagon demands powerful regular land forces which, in case of necessity, could be used in any theater of military operations. To prepare these forces the Defense Department of the U.S.A. points out the necessity of solving three basic problems:

1. The concentrate in peacetime in overseas theaters of military operations sufficient forces which could be quickly used in world or local wars.

2. To have mobile strategic land forces in the U.S.A. ready for rapid transfer to reinforce units which have started military operations in one region or another.

3. The training of reserve troops of the army and national guard to be done so that at any time they might be swiftly transferred to the regular forces.

The land forces of the U.S.A., as reported in the magazine *NATO's Fifteen Nations*, are scattered in ninety countries of the world. The number of personnel in these units and subunits composes 40 per cent of the general army numbers. Eight of sixteen American divisions are located near the borders of socialist countries. The land troops situated in the territory of the U.S.A. compose the strategic reserves, held in full readiness to reinforce American Armed Forces being deployed beyond the borders of their own country. These forces are made up of two corps with four divisions in each one.

The imperialists are aware that their land troops, intended for

149

dirty aggressive adventures, cannot have such high moral qualities as the armies of freedom-loving people. Therefore, the military departments of the states, which are partners in the aggressive blocs, constantly search for newer and newer means of deceiving the soldiers, persistently work on contriving more powerful weapons with which it would be easier to move on their predatory march. In order to somehow compensate for the weak links of their own armies, these strategists work on the principle of maximum saturation of the troops with the latest equipment and arms. This is especially so for the American Armed Forces.

Habits are established in the soldiers and officers of active offensive operations. Basic attention in this preparation is focused on using the results of nuclear rocket strikes, which could be carried to great depth. Therefore, the demand for mobile troops is being raised. Formations and units must quickly concentrate for the blow and just as quickly spread out in order not to place themselves under the nuclear blows of the enemy. The infantry is equipped with armored transportation and machines of high practicability. They are armed with automatic arms. Artillery with mechanized traction is being transformed to self-propelled. Tanks are made with such calculations that they have great firepower, comparatively little weight, and could move quickly to the battlefield for infantry support or for fulfilling other aims.

But the main firepower of the land forces is nuclear rocket weapons. Small caliber nuclear ammunition is being developed for them with a power of from two to one hundred thousand tons. Infantry, mechanized, and armored divisions of the army of the U.S.A. have for armaments the nonguided rocket "Honest John," and howitzers of 155 millimeter and also 203.2 millimeter caliber which can take nuclear charges. In divisions, they number twenty-six units. For use in arming the land forces, "Sergeant" and "Pershing" rockets are being introduced. The first is designated for giving fire support to the level of army corps; the second, for field armies. The rocket "Sergeant" has 150 kilometers range; the "Pershing," up to 800 kilometers. The West German Army, the most reactionary and aggressive force of the imperialists in Europe, is being equipped with these rockets.

As a result of the saturation of contemporary land forces with nuclear rocket weapons, their fighting power, as write the military magazines of the U.S.A., has grown significantly. While earlier, the general troop units with their firing means could carry a blow to a depth of twenty to twenty-five kilometers, now their rocket weapons can neutralize enemy defenses at a depth of four to five hundred kilometers or more—not to mention the power of the nuclear blast. According to information of the American press, four divisions with the "Sergeant" rocket, which might be given to field armies, would have more firepower than all the American artillery in World War II.

The Pentagon is not satisfied with existing nuclear rocket weapons. To replace "Honest John" and "Little John" for division use, a new, guided rocket "Lance" (with a range of up to seventy-five kilometers) is being made. It will be introduced, beginning in 1968, into the arsenal of the army of the U.S.A.

At the same time, as the firing power of the army is being reinforced, the imperialists of the U.S.A. are constantly trying to enlarge the infantry's mobility so that they can suddenly appear fully armed wherever the command sends them. For answering such problems, special airborne divisions have been formed. General troop units can also be transferred by air. Military transport aviation is being developed in answer to the demands of the Pentagon—to be able to transfer troops with heavy arms from the American continent to any area on earth. Recently, the Secretary of Defense of the U.S.A., McNamara, gave the order to start developing a new transport plane, the C–5A, with a flying weight of 350 tons. At the time, in 1963, of the training exercise "Big Lift," carried out by the Pentagon, 204 transport planes transferred from the U.S.A. to West Europe fifteen thousand soldiers in sixty-three hours; forty-two C–5A's could have fulfilled this requirement in thirteen hours.

In the American press it is said that land forces could not achieve maximum mobility if they were transferred only on dry land. It is well known that local terrain in many areas of the world precludes the possibility of using tanks, armored transport, and sometimes even cross-country vehicles. Therefore, primary importance, in the opinion of American military specialists, is acquired by air mobility. If troops have air mobility, writes the military press of the U.S.A., then this would shorten the time spent on scouting the enemy, quickly spread forces and again collect them for a strike, bring reserves to threatened regions, strengthen successes, and block enemy units in their retreat.

All these problems are designated to be solved by army aviation, the development of which is being given much attention by the Pentagon. Going into its make-up are light planes and helicopters. In 1961 the army aviation system of the U.S.A. had more than fifty-five hundred planes and helicopters. At the end of 1966 it is proposed that they will have about eight thousand. Each division now has one hundred and one planes and helicopters. In military operations in South Vietnam, says the magazine *Air and Cosmos*, army aviation has three hundred 'copters and two hundred planes.

The foreign press raises the question of what land forces will be in the future. It is noted that, in these, the role of the engineer will be raised each year, the number of electronic computer machines and other complicated equipment will be enlarged. There is a discussion about whether it is better to have a small but well-trained professional army or numerous troops formed on the basis of a draft. The argument on the solution of these problems is raised in connection with the introduction into the armaments of the land forces of such equipment, the running of which demands much time and special knowledge. The short length of active service (of two years) gives little chance to have a well-prepared army of draftees. But an increase in length of service has its own minuses.

The military theorists of the West aim to find such an organization of land forces that would answer all contemporary demands and—most of all—plans for unleashing world and local wars. But any war demands mass armies. This is admitted by the majority of bourgeois military specialists. And the search continues. In imperialist countries they are settling on massive armies, intended for the suppression of the workers protesting against the exploiting classes and for realizing the aggressive foreign policy of monopoly.

12. THE INFLUENCE OF SOVIET MILITARY DOCTRINE ON THE DEVELOPMENT OF MILITARY ART
By General Colonel Nikolai A. Lomov
Professor, Doctor of Military Sciences

Editors' Notes

General Lomov is a professor at the Soviet General Staff Academy and a doctor of military sciences. He is the author of *Soviet Military Doctrine*, which appeared in brochure form in May, 1963. In December, 1965, the Military Publishing House of the Soviet Ministry of Defense announced that Lomov would edit *Military Doctrine*, a new book which would discuss the military doctrine of various governments as well as that of the Soviet Union. This was planned as one of the *Officer's Library* series of seventeen books. As of January 1, 1967, the book had not been published. The article which follows appeared in *Communist of the Armed Forces*, November, 1965.

Lomov presents the usual Soviet contention that "imperialism" is the sole source of war and that the "imperialists" are preparing for, and may start a war against the "socialist camp." Such a war would be a world nuclear war in which "the most decisive impact on its course and outcome will be rendered by the results of the armed combat in the beginning period." Local wars, also, are being waged by the imperialists and, as a rule, they are fought with conventional weapons. There is always the possibility that a limited war will develop into a world nuclear war. This is of particular concern "in the event of the involvement of nuclear powers in local conflicts," in which the possibility of world nuclear war "is always great, and under certain conditions, it may become inevitable."

The article takes issue with statements in "bourgeois military literature" that nuclear missiles have led to the "liquidation of military art." Lomov writes that, on the contrary, the nuclear weapon does not abolish conventional weapons but is a self-sufficient type of weapon used in conjunction with the conventional means of fighting. However, "The decisive role belongs to nuclear rocket weapons."

In the contemporary period, "The rapid development of science and technology, the revolution in military affairs, which served as a material base of the position of modern military doctrine, lifted strategy to a higher, qualitatively new level of development." An important feature of this strategy is that nuclear war is "characterized by the sweep of intercontinental space." The mass use of nuclear weapons gives a real possibility of forcing "the quick removal from the war" of several countries without seizing their territory with land forces or airborne troops.

Lomov continues with further explanations of the role of military doctrine, strategy, science, tactics, and art in the nuclear age. He points out that the revolution in military affairs has increased the need for operational and technical preparation, for discipline, and for individual training.

Among Lomov's other writings are, "New Weapons and the Nature of Actions of the Armed Forces" and "Basic Tenets of Soviet Military Doctrine," which appeared in *Red Star* on the 7th and 10th, respectively, of January, 1964. These two articles, slightly edited, appeared in *Problems of the Revolution in Military Affairs*, which was discussed earlier in this book. Another paper, "The Fundamentals and Principles of the Organization of the Soviet Armed Forces," appeared in *Communist of the Armed Forces*, November, 1966.

THE ORGANIZATION OF THE MILITARY of each government is determined by its politics. It is linked inseparably with the economy and depends on the trend and the level of development of the economic, social, and political life of the country. The practice of this organization in the last few years is confirmation of the integral ties of our military organization with the political course of the Soviet government.

Indeed, the materials of the XXII Party Congress and the new Program of the CPSU have inestimable significance in this. The party Program states that the CPSU considers the defense of the socialist Fatherland, the strengthening of the defense of the U.S.S.R. and the might of the Soviet Armed Forces as the sacred duty of the party and of all the Soviet people and as the most important function of the socialist government.

In fulfilling this most important government function, the direct preparation of the Armed Forces for waging contemporary war and their ability and readiness to give a shattering repulse to imperialist aggressors at any moment has great significance. As is known, the basic trend of this preparation is determined by Soviet military doctrine, in which views accepted in our country on the nature of war in the modern era, on the aims and methods of conducting armed conflict in these wars, and, consequently, on the principal demands for preparing the country and the army and the navy for war are interpreted.

From what sort of evaluations on war and armed conflict does modern Soviet military doctrine come?

Generally these evaluations come from the following: Imperialism, being the sole source of war, is preparing and may unleash war against the countries of the socialist camp. In the event of a clash of the military coalitions of the two antagonistic world social systems, which include nuclear powers, such a war would be a world nuclear war, in which both fighting sides would pursue the most decisive political aims with all the resultant consequences.

Armed struggle in a world nuclear war acquires intercontinental scope and may be waged simultaneously in several land and sea theaters of operation. The modern arrangement and relationship of political forces in the international arena and the special characteristics of nuclear weapons permits conjecture that a world nuclear war will be short and swift-moving, one in which the most decisive impact on its course and outcome will be rendered by the results of the armed combat in the beginning period. However, in certain conditions, war might take on a protracted character, the waging of which also will demand corresponding preparations.

But in the contemporary era the imperialists are waging, and may unleash in the future, local wars. As is openly testified by the American strategy of "flexible response," such a war might be in Europe also. Local wars, judging from those which are already taking place, are waged as a rule with the use of conventional means of armed combat. However, this does not exclude the possibility of the use in them of tactical and operational nuclear weapons. For everyone, including imperialist theoreticians of local wars, obviously the probability of the development of limited war into world nuclear war, in the event of the involvement in local conflicts of nuclear powers, is always great and, under certain conditions, it may become inevitable.

Taking into account the nature of imperialism and its present course in foreign policy, Soviet military doctrine defines as the main trend of the perfection of the Soviet Armed Forces their ability and readiness to successfully wage armed combat in conformity with the demands of world nuclear war.

Therefore, the most important feature of Soviet military doctrine is that it is oriented not to past but to future war, taking into account its features, which pose specific demands on the art of the use of armed forces.

It must be noted that in foreign bourgeois military literature there are statements which in essence come to this, that supposedly nuclear rocket weapons lead to the liquidation of military art, that waging armed combat in nuclear war does not require any military theory preparation of an officer cadre.

Soviet military science categorically rejects such groundless and over-simplified assertions about the nature and methods of conducting armed conflict with the use of nuclear rocket weapons. While appearing as the decisive means of waging armed combat, the new weapon does not abolish conventional weapons, does not become an adjunct, a supplement; it comes forth as a self-sufficient type of weapon used in combination with conventional means of armed combat.

This point of view finds its expression in one of the basic positions of modern Soviet military doctrine, in accordance with which final victory over the enemy may be achieved on the basis of the combined, united efforts of all services of the armed forces, using all contemporary means of combat with the decisive role belonging to nuclear rocket weapons. The acknowledgment of this position serves as a basis for working out the theories, practical forms, and methods of waging war with the services of the armed forces; that is, military art, in response to the concrete conditions of modern war, rests on the firm scientific bases and principles of military doctrine.

What sort of influence does modern Soviet military doctrine have on the development of our military art?

The realms of military art—strategy, operational art, and tactics—in principle include in themselves common scientific positions regarding the theory and practice of using the armed forces in different levels of waging war. The most important positions defining the nature and the methods of preparing the armed forces and of waging war as a whole make up the content of our military strategy. These enter as main positions into the principles of Soviet military doctrine, thus determining the trend of the theory and practice of operations and tactics of the services of the armed forces.

The offensive nature of Soviet military doctrine logically evokes offensive strategy which corresponds to the views on operational and tactical use of the services of the armed forces. The rapid development of science and technology, the revolution in military affairs, which served as a material base of the position of modern military doctrine, lifted strategy to a higher, qualitatively new level of development.

The first distinguishing characteristic of modern Soviet military strategy is that it represents a system of views on the strategic use of not one service but of all services of the armed forces. Not only sea strategy but also the strategy of land forces which dominated the last world war has gone into the historical category. Onto the

157

scene came the common strategy of the armed forces based on the decisive role in it of nuclear rocket weapons. Each service of the armed forces is examined together with the other services in the general system of armed combat; at the same time each preserves relative independence in deciding military problems within its sphere of combat activity by virtue of the inherent superiority of its service within the armed forces.

The Strategic Rocket Troops are the main service of the Armed Forces of the Soviet Union. But it absolutely does not follow from this that other services of the Armed Forces will fulfill combat functions to the advantage of the Rocket Troops. In turn the Strategic Rocket Troops are intended for resolving the main, independent problems of armed combat in the interest of achieving the general goals of war. That is, the results of the nuclear strikes of the Strategic Rocket Troops serve as a basis on which is built the utilization of the other services of the armed forces in carrying out operations. As has already been stressed, the achievement of final victory over the enemy is possible only on the basis of the joint effort of all services of the armed forces in using nuclear rocket weapons as the decisive means of combat.

Another distinguishing characteristic of our modern military strategy is its coalition character, which also results from Soviet military doctrine. The doctrine characterizes a possible future war as a world war resulting from the existing circumstances of political forces in the international arena. Two worlds—capitalistic and socialistic—already oppose each other, not only as two social systems but also as two military-political coalitions: on one side the imperialistic bloc, headed by the U.S.A. (and NATO, CENTO, and SEATO), and on the other, the coalition of socialistic countries in Europe, united on the basis of the Warsaw pact, and also the coalition of socialistic countries in the East, which have pacts of friendship and mutual assistance.

From the Marxist-Leninist definition of war as a continuation of politics by violent means, it follows that the strategy of a state is formed by its politics. The experience of past wars shows that in all coalition wars, the strategy of the fighting sides inevitably car-

158

ries in itself coalition traits. It reflects both political and military interests common to all partners of the coalition and their private, narrow state aims.

These traits fully preserve their importance for the modern, aggressive, military-political coalitions. The anti-Communist direction of the struggle against the socialist camp serves as the general political basis of the existing imperialistic blocs. This, however, does not eliminate the contradictions either inside each state of the aggressive blocs or between the governments of one and the same bloc.

The principal features of the strategy of the countries of the socialist coalition consist, first of all, of the unity of their foreign policy course, which is determined by the unity of the political aims which will stand before the coalition if the imperialists unleash a new world war. More than once V. I. Lenin stressed that the nature of the political goal which composes the "real essence" of war has a decisive influence on the waging of war which in turn determines the decisive role of military strategy in the preparation of the armed forces and in using them in war.

The absence of inner political contradictions in the socialist coalition thus causes the *unity* of its military strategy. This allows the most effective use of the combined armed forces for the achievement of the goal which will be placed before them by the coalition's political leadership.

The cause of such unity of national and general interests lies in the fact that the socialist coalition was formed *to protect* the revolutionary gains from imperialist aggression and not to seize territory, spheres of capital investment, sales markets, or to enslave the people of other countries—for which the capitalist government coalitions were created. The noble aims of the socialist countries, in a war which imperialism might force on them, permit the evasion of clashes and frictions between members of the brotherly collaboration in the use of armed forces and direct members' efforts in solving common problems. The moral-political and ideological unity of the society arising in the countries of the socialist collaboration, the unbreakable bond between the Communist and work-

159

ers' parties, the government and the people, endlessly raises the moral potential of brother armies. This allows the military leadership of the socialistic coalition in the event of imperialistic aggression to set decisive aims in armed combat and confidently to go into bold and important operations.

A specific feature of modern military strategy is the direct dependence of strategic concepts on nuclear weapons and, first of all, on the equipping of the armed forces with strategic nuclear means. Although the waging of armed combat with conventional means, even in the event of the participation in it of a nuclear power as one of the fighting sides, is typical in respect to local wars, for world war the possibility of nonnuclear armed combat becomes abstract.

Of course, in conditions of nuclear war, such circumstances might occur when military problems would be decided by conventional means. However, until the time that international agreement on full and complete disarmament is achieved, or even agreement on excluding nuclear weapons from the arsenal of modern means of armed combat for governments in existing military-political coalitions, including also countries not having nuclear weapons, the coalitional strategy of nuclear war is real.

The ignoring of this new feature of military strategy, or attempts to lessen the catastrophic results of its use, cannot be justified or explained. On the contrary, the most objective representation of the possible nature of armed combat with unlimited use of nuclear weapons, the knowledge of the effective methods both in using this weapon and in fighting against it, must serve as an important condition in achieving a level of preparedness by our Armed Forces corresponding to the demands of nuclear war.

The important new feature of military strategy is that armed combat in nuclear war is characterized by intercontinental scope. Intercontinental ballistic missiles, whose combat properties are sufficiently well known, in half an hour can cover the distance between two continents most distant from each other and they have the practical ability of carrying nuclear charges to any region on earth. As a result of the mass use of strategic nuclear means, the possibility becomes reality for the quick removal from the war of a series of countries of one or another coalition even without the simultaneous seizing of the territory of the countries by land forces and airborne troops.

This new feature of modern military strategy decisively influences the nature of waging war. The use of intercontinental means of combat can at once, from the very beginning of the war, achieve results of great strategic meaning. These results are achieved by the immediate use of strategic nuclear weapons, avoiding the methodical successive development of tactical successes into operational, and finally strategic, and in its turn, political results.

In nuclear war, more sharply than in past wars, the natural dependence of the course and outcome of war on the economic and moral-political factors becomes apparent. The ability of governments to resist is found in direct relation to the ability of the people and economics to stand the growing strains of armed combat which absorb the basic mass of products of the productive labor, not only of current labor activity but of all the past.

Besides problems unknown in the past, which have already been discussed, the strategy of short, swift-moving war runs into the most complex problems of protecting the country from the blows of nuclear weapons and other means of mass destruction. Air defense of the country in modern conditions is an exceptionally crucial area of military strategy. In a nuclear war each of the fighting sides will try to act so that the effect of nuclear weapons will curtail to the maximum the political, economic, and military base of the resistance of the enemy. Therefore, to repel the nuclear blows of the enemy, especially in the beginning of the war, when he evidently will try to use the maximum of his nuclear power, is a problem of great national significance.

Theoretically it is possible to conjecture that the length of nuclear war will be directly proportional to the ability of the country or the coalition of fighting nations to resist the nuclear blows of the enemy. And this ability will depend basically on two conditions: First, on how much the nuclear power of the enemy will be strengthened or weakened; and, second, on the effectiveness of protecting the country from nuclear blows in the widest sense of the word, that is, on active PVO [air defense] and civil defense.

Soviet military doctrine, orienting its strategic leadership to such complicated conditions of waging war, takes into account that the powerful progressive forces, which are able at the present time to avert the start of a new world war, in the event of its unleashing, can actively assist the countries of the socialist camp in gaining decisive victory over imperialism in a short time. Of course, in the first place Soviet military doctrine takes into account the real fighting power of the armed forces of the countries of the socialist camp and, first of all, of the Armed Forces of the Soviet Union, equipped with the most modern weapons and the newest military equipment. The Communist party of the Soviet Union, turning its attention to the aggressive intrigues of imperialism, revealed in its Program adopted by the XXII Congress of the CPSU that "the Soviet government will see that its Armed Forces will be powerful, equipped with the most modern means of protecting the Motherland— atomic and thermonuclear weapons, rockets of all ranges of action, supported to the necessary level by all sorts of military arms and equipment." And this pronouncement is being realized with all decisiveness and consistency. Our army and navy is equipped with everything necessary for the defeat of any aggressor.

Soviet military science takes into consideration also that world nuclear rocket war, if not successful in being averted, will produce exceptionally high demands on mankind, on his moral, political, and fighting qualities. Soviet soldiers must command high conscientiousness and vigilance, discipline and organization, bravery and decisiveness, steadfastness and physical fortitude. The forming of such qualities demands the constant improvement of ideological education of the troops ensuring the moral-political superiority of our troops over any enemy. Therefore, the commanders, political organs, party and Komsomol organizations are called to henceforth persistently raise the level of party-political work, directing it so that the soldiers of the Soviet Army and Navy will be infinitely loyal to their own people and the cause of communism, ready to give all their strength, and, if necessary, even life, to protect the socialist Motherland.

Such, in short, are the consequences of the influence of our modern military doctrine on Soviet military strategy.

From the understanding of military art as a theory and practice of armed combat at different levels, based on common principles, it follows that military doctrine also plays a decisive role in determining the direction of the development of operational art and tactics. Owing to the integral ties of the content of military doctrine and strategy, which were spoken of before, the position of military strategy will determine the bases of operational art and tactics. In addition, each of these fields of military art has its own inner logic of development flowing from the nature of the problems of operational and tactical use of services of the armed forces and the means and methods of their resolution. Not having the possibility of examining the multiplicity of innovations of Soviet operational art and tactics, we will pause only on a few important sides of their contemporary content.

The operations of each service of the armed forces and also their combat actions for the achievement of operational goals are characterized by features common for all of the services and features appearing specifically for each service of the armed forces.

To the number of common features of contemporary operations which characterize the influence of military doctrine on the development of operational art of all the services of the armed forces might be attributed: The decisive significance of nuclear rocket blows which compose the basis of operational formation; the simultaneous defeat by nuclear weapons and conventional methods of the whole depth of the operational formations of groupings of armed forces in land and in sea theaters of military operations irrespective of the character of this formation, offensive or defensive; the sharp and quickly changing operational correlation of forces of the sides, breaking up the stability of the groupings of armed forces in operations; the high dynamics of military operations; the maneuverability of forces taking part in the operations; the short duration of fighting, of battles, and of operations; the large range of operations; the high percentage of loss from nuclear blows.

In the make-up of operations with the use of nuclear rocket weapons appeared a new, major element of waging war—the nuclear strike. It serves as the basis on which is built contemporary operations. Fighting and battles, as component elements of operations, are planned and developed depending on the results of nuclear strikes, which were intended for the fulfillment of important and independent fighting problems.

For this reason, the position of military doctrine that a new world war according to its means of waging armed combat would be nuclear war, finds a suitable expression in operational art. For example, the construction of a front or army operation with the use of nuclear rocket weapons represents the modern development of the theory of deep operations developed in its own time in the Soviet Army. The simultaneous defeat by means of nuclear blows, and blows of conventional means, of the whole interior of operational constructions of groups of armed forces of the enemy, converts modern operations into the simultaneous waging of war on several circles of operational interiors. Apparently such a form of carrying out operations, when it disintegrates into a series of relatively isolated centers of battle and fighting, is characteristic not only of operations of land forces but also of sea operations and of the fighting of National PVO Troops.

The decisive influence of nuclear rocket blows on the scale of operations consists of this, that the results of these blows, first, might very acutely and quickly change the relative forces of both sides, and second, will cause a no less acute and quick breach of stability of the operational formation of groupings of armed forces. Also favoring this is the revival, in operational large units of ground forces, of a proportion of tank forces which could invade the operational interior of the enemy using the gaps formed as a result of nuclear blows. A substantial influence on the loss of the enemy's stability could be rendered by the airborne troops, whose actions, coming after nuclear blows, could be highly effective.

In past wars, battles and actions very often were of a highly

164

drawn-out character, were bloody, and led to great and heavy losses of personnel, weapons, and equipment. But then these losses consistently grew in the course of a relatively protracted time. This continually permitted, at the expense of reserve formations, the re-establishment of the fighting ability of troops and correlation in forces and weapons in the course of operations and, for this reason, preserved the stability of the operational formation of the fighting groups on a satisfactory level and on a sufficiently long term.

The blows of nuclear rocket weapons are able to bring such a defeat that whole formations (units) might completely lose their fighting ability in the course of a few minutes. As a result, it might undergo a radical breaking up of all systems of operational formation of groups of forces which would demand a radical revision of the problems of the fighting forces and of the order of their fulfillment. The plotting of such a blow to the enemy opens wide possibilities for energetically and quickly accomplishing the defeat of the forces of the enemy. From the other side, similar losses of one's own forces demand decisive measures of counteracting the enemy in order to hinder him in using the results of his nuclear blows and at the same time to secure the possibility of reviving one's own forces. In passing, it must be said that the system of reviving the fighting ability of formations and units, which existed in the past, can hardly answer the conditions of nuclear war.

The nuclear strike is the basic method of combat action of the rocket troops and the basic constituent element of operations for formation of ground forces, air forces, and naval forces. Besides the immediate annihilation and destruction, nuclear strikes, in definite circumstances, might simultaneously be used also for the creation of an operational zone of radioactive contamination with a high level of radioactivity. Overcoming such zones in the course of operations is a new aspect in the operations of land forces. Aviation must also contend with these factors, although in a lesser degree.

While examining the operational art of nuclear war, it is necessary to take into account that the classic form of operation might also significantly vary depending on the peculiarities of the theater

165

of military operations, on the time of conduct of operations (at the beginning of a war or in its course), and on the composition of forces and means used by the fighting sides. In particular, the armed forces must master the methods of waging operations in existing organizations with limited use of nuclear weapons and without them, that is, with the use of conventional means.

Highly significant is the influence of military doctrine on the structure of the Navy and the character of naval operations. The basis of its fighting power now is the missile submarine and naval rocket-carrying aviation. This allows it to decide successfully the most complicated problems of fighting with enemy attack aircraft carriers and rocket-carrying fleets, to carry blows to his important objectives located on land, to attack actively the ocean communications of the enemy in remote regions of ocean theaters, and to wage, together with other services of the armed forces, landing and counterlanding operations. The connection of naval actions with aviation, especially long-range actions, will be more closely connected than in the last war; and also a new factor, strikes of rocket forces on naval objectives, brings new features into the content and form of waging war in sea and ocean theaters of military operations which determine the active character of combat of a modern navy and its greater self-sufficiency than in the past in deciding combat problems.

Also, there must be mentioned, even though briefly, those specialties which characterize the fighting actions of the National PVO Troops in operational relationships. For National PVO Troops, having become one of the most important services of the Soviet Armed Forces, the character of their operational use is determined by a series of new factors, among which the combat potentials of modern means of attack are decisive. Ballistic and winged rockets and high-speed airplanes, which compose an arsenal of active means of attack from the air, land, and sea, have basically changed the system of PVO. Moreover, they are supplemented by highly effective activity of technical means directed at making obstacles in systems of radio communications—locating, aiming, and guiding. "Radio War," as it is called overseas, has become one of the ways of the systematic organization of air defense.

No less important an influence on the organization and conduct of air defense is shown by the combination of such means of PVO as surface-to-air rocket troops and modern fighter-interceptors. From an operational point of view, the organization of air defense, as with large units of other services of armed forces, is subordinated to the general demands of planning combat operations. However, the difference is that the plan of the operational use of National PVO Troops is notable for its great stability, caused by the features of forces and means of attack, whose speed of flight extremely limits the possibility for maneuver by forces and means of defense.

Finally, the features of the conditions of waging war of those units of National PVO Troops, which by the force of their distribution will have the task of operationally protecting the groups of armed forces in the theaters of military operations, must be pointed out. The dynamics of the situation, integral ties with the fighting actions of other services of the armed forces and the raised demand in respect to maneuver by forces significantly reinforces the operational element of combat activity in National PVO Troops.

Summarizing the examination of a few features of modern operational art above, one may reach the following conclusions:

First, the laws of armed combat connected with the military-technical revolution received the same general scientific conclusion in the principles of operational art as in the realm of strategy.

Second, the theory and practice of operational art, based on the use of nuclear rocket weapons, in essence differentiates itself from the theory and practice of past wars, preserving, however, the continuation in the range of forms and methods of waging war.

Third, the influence of the posture of military doctrine on the further development of operational art of the services of the armed forces continues, promoting a fuller disclosure of the military possibilities of large operational units and more effective co-operation in operations. More and more clearly the typical features are appearing which characterize contemporary operations as combined operations of several services of the armed forces.

The basic changes in military affairs which gave the initial momentum in determining the most important positions of Soviet military doctrine have a common character; along with strategy and operational art they have spread to tactics.

The exposition of the questions of the development of tactics in the contemporary stage is a most difficult problem, since it would demand discussion of tactics not only of the services of the armed forces but also of the branches of the service and the forces. But this can be done only in a separate article. Therefore, we are limiting the review only to those common characteristics which are typical for contemporary tactics as the theory and the practice of combat in conditions using nuclear weapons.

The appearance of operational-tactical nuclear weapons has not changed the nature of battle as a combination of firepower and movement. Qualitatively its content has changed: The basis of battle has become the nuclear strike. The waging of modern combat is built for using the results of nuclear blows, the chief problem of which seems now to be the completion of the defeat of army groups of the enemy subjected to nuclear strikes. The use in battle of nuclear strikes in combination with firepower of conventional means has raised the effectiveness of combat and its activity far beyond comparison with the past and has given it a new sweep of tempo and depth.

Simultaneously, there have been changes in the form of waging war especially assisted by the significant growth in the proportion of tanks and the complete motorization of the land forces. Of primary importance has been the high maneuverability of the active forms of battle—encounter and attack. The methodic, measured actions of troops have changed to fighting in different directions, as a result of which the place held in the past by a continuous front line is now absent; combat is waged simultaneously in a series of centers at various depths on the modern battlefield.

The fighting of ground forces—this is a combination of nuclear strikes with the movement of troops in tanks and armored transport, carrying out fire from conventional weapons—and the high dynamics and maneuverability of modern battle lead to its brief-ness, to the change from one form and method to another—to encounter battle, followed by attack, and to defense. Defense is characterized, also, by high activity and briefness, enabling troops to quickly change from defense to attack.

The high speed and long range of fire of modern weapons has decisively influenced the content and form of waging war with aviation and sea power and in the character of the mutual support between them and with land forces. Thus the realm of tactics and the art of waging modern war has been subject in theory and practice to the powerful influence of the revolution in military affairs.

The revolution in military affairs has raised high the meaning of operational-technical and military-technical preparation and the resolute qualities of the commanding cadres. It has immeasurably raised the role of the organizational abilities of the commander, his ability to work with people. It is possible to guarantee the unity of will and action of all the personnel only on the basis of conscientious discipline of each and every one, by unremitting demands of the commander, by his party principles, by his care of subordinates.

From Soviet military doctrine flow the serious demands for the style of work of any military commander, his way of thinking and nature of acting. During the last war decisions which were not exactly correct could be corrected during the course of battle by the commanders themselves or the senior leaders. In modern, brief, dynamic battle, the help of the commander, or from time to time his deputy, can hardly be counted on. This means one must be equipped with full knowledge, be deeply understanding of the nature of combat, and aim always to have the maximum facts that are necessary for the self-contained direction of units and subunits.

Soviet military art, developing in accordance with the conditions of modern military doctrine, in the last few years has accomplished the advance to a new, higher level. The results achieved in this development serve as a real basis for the further raising of military preparedness of the Soviet Armed Forces in the interest of strengthening the defense of our Motherland.

169

13. THE CHARACTER AND FEATURES
OF NUCLEAR ROCKET WAR
By Colonel S. V. Malyanchikov
Candidate of Military Sciences

Editors' Notes

Each soldier in the Soviet Armed Forces must devote four hours a week to political indoctrination. This writing, "The Character and Features of Nuclear Rocket War," provides the basis for six hours of study directed by the political instructor. For this particular topic two hours are to be allowed for lectures and another four on seminars. Publication of the article was in *Communist of the Armed Forces*, November, 1965, in the magazine's regular section for political studies.

This selection is a typical example of a political indoctrination theme. The student referred to throughout is the serviceman who will attend the lecture. Full directions, setting forth even such details as ". . . reading . . . should be organized in the evening hours," are given to the instructor. The article outlines the basic questions to be discussed, such as, "Why are nuclear rocket weapons the chief means of waging war?"

In the instruction, war is considered as a social-historical phenomenon according to the Marxist-Leninist view, and the statement is made that wars did not arise until the appearance of private ownership. "Capitalist monopolies" make profits "from the exploitation and robbery of the people of their own countries." In order to make these profits, "Imperialists are ready to do everything right up to starting wars."

Malyanchikov repeats the Soviet dictum that "future world war will assume the character of nuclear rocket war. It will be the most destructive in its consequences, the most devastating that has ever been known in history." In particular, the beginning of the war is of special significance. "The first mass nuclear attack in great measure predetermines all the following course of the war. . . . The

Soviet Armed Forces are able to frustrate the aggressor's attack and carry to him shattering blows."

The threat of the use of nuclear weapons requires dispersal of the troops, strict observance of the rules of camouflage, and increased attention to night operations. The individual soldier must be able "without fuss to take the necessary measures at the signal notification of radioactive, chemical, and bacteriological contamination of the locality, to liquidate the traces of the use by the enemy of weapons of mass destruction."

Colonel Malyanchikov is a frequent contributor to *Red Star*. In March, 1966, he was awarded a Frunze prize "for writing excellent military theory papers."

Political Studies Department

As A RESULT of the study of this theme, the student must understand the nature of war as a social phenomenon and the characteristic features of nuclear rocket war, better understand the necessity of increasing to the maximum the combat readiness of the Armed Forces and be more deeply imbued with consciousness of his own obligation in fulfilling the mission of strengthening the military power of our government.

Six hours are given to study of this theme. Of these, it is recommended that two hours be used on lectures and four hours on seminars. Independent reading of the literature should be organized in the evening hours.

In the lectures it is necessary to deal with the following basic questions:

1. Marxist-Leninist understanding of the nature of war. Soviet military science on the character and features of nuclear rocket war.

2. Nuclear rocket weapons—the main means of carrying out combat actions in contemporary war.

3. The role and place of different services and branches in nuclear rocket war.

4. The features of combat actions of units under conditions

171

using nuclear rocket weapons. The raised role of each soldier in modern battle.

5. The constant combat readiness, high moral spirit of troops, the organization and disciplining, the ability to use military equipment perfectly—these are necessary conditions for victory over the enemy.

At the seminar these questions must be discussed:

(a) What is war as a social-historical phenomenon?

(b) What are the characteristic features of modern war stipulating the use of nuclear rocket weapons?

(c) Why are nuclear rocket weapons the chief means of waging war?

(d) How do you explain the fact that the beginning period of war might decide the course of all the armed struggle?

(e) What missions are given to the Strategic Rocket Forces, the Ground Forces, National PVO [air defense], the Air Forces, the Navy?

(f) What are the features of actions of squads, teams, crews, and fighting units in conditions of the use of nuclear weapons?

(g) Why does modern warfare produce increased demands of each soldier and what are they?

(h) Of what does the role of sergeants and starshinas [petty officers] consist in modern war?

(i) What more can be done (in conformity to the conditions of service of the students) to raise the combat readiness of one's own elements and units?

During the *independent study* period, the students should study the first part of the resolution of the XXII Congress of the CPSU, in the account to the Central Committee CPSU, the eighth section of the first part of the Program of the Party [CPSU]. . . . In addition, soldiers and sailors should read the twelfth chapter of the textbook, *On Guard of the Motherland Building Communism*, and sergeants and starshinas, the second chapter of *Sergeants and Starshinas of the Armed Forces of the U.S.S.R.* [Further recommendations omitted in this translation.]

1. In dealing with the *first* question, one must stress that Marxism-Leninism views war as a social-historical phenomenon. Wars have not always existed. They arose with the appearance of private ownership of the means of production and the division of society into hostile classes, into the exploiters and the exploited. Relations between these classes are built on private ownership of the means and tools of production, on the exploitation of man by man. These features are especially displayed in capitalistic societies. Capitalist monopolies try to get the most profits from the exploitation and robbery of the people of their own countries as well as from the people of other countries. For this, imperialists are ready to do everything right up to starting wars. Wars, just as an arms race in peacetime, bring capitalists huge profits.

The receiving of maximum profits is the aim which monopoly pursues. Capitalist governments try to achieve their aims by political, ideological, economic, and other means. When this is not sufficient, then they use means of armed struggle. Political goals remain the same, but the means of achieving them are different.

V. I. Lenin teaches that war is the continuation of politics of interested governments and classes inside them by other, that is, violent means. War is armed violence, armed struggle between classes, governments, or groups of governments, waged for the achievement of definite political aims. Depending on what aims are pursued in war, what classes prepared and will wage it, Marxism-Leninism divides war into just and liberating wars and unjust, reactionary, and expansionist wars. In the Program of the CPSU it is stressed that our party and the Soviet people decisively speak out against all expansionist unjust wars and support just, liberating wars against imperialism.

In examining the character and features of contemporary war, one must first of all proceed from the presence in the world of two systems—socialist and capitalist. Here it is appropriate to recall the instructions of V. I. Lenin that while imperialism remains the danger of wars starting also remains. The rapacious nature of imperialism has not changed. Therefore the imperialist bloc, headed by the U.S.A., might make attempts to reach their mercenary aims by means of war, directed against the socialist camp, but primarily against the Soviet Union.

In its political nature, world war, if it is started by the imperialists, would be a strongly pronounced class war, a war of two world systems. This is stipulated by the decisiveness of political and military aims which both sides would place before themselves. In such a war, compromises are impossible; the question might relate to the existence of one or the other world system.

The correlation of forces which has taken shape at the present time in the political, economic, and military areas in favor of the socialist camp gives us the basis on which to confirm that victory in a future world war would go to our side. The political content of world war is caused by its coalition character. The bloc of imperialist governments will oppose the powerful coalition of socialist countries.

Future world war will assume the character of nuclear rocket war. It will be the most destructive in its consequences, the most devastating that has ever been known in history. Therefore the Soviet soldier must be thoroughly trained to wage strenuous military operations, to overcome enormous difficulties, to display self-control, heroism, and resourcefulness.

The massive use of nuclear weapons and the long-range means of their delivery makes for an enormous spatial area of war. Military operations will include the territory of all fighting governments no matter on what continent they are located and will be waged on land, at sea, and in the air. War will assume an intercontinental character. The Soviet Union, by possessing a large quantity of powerful rockets, is in a condition to rain down shattering nuclear blows on the aggressor no matter where he is located.

The qualitatively new means of armed combat have evoked basic changes in the strategic goals and methods of waging war. In past wars, strategic goals consisted of crushing the armed forces of the enemy, for the main part, in land theaters of military actions, which finally led to his capitulation. In nuclear rocket war the main goal of armed battle will be the simultaneous annihilation of the armed

174

forces of the enemy, the destruction of his economy, and the disorganization of his governmental direction. The achievement of these goals will be realized by the carrying out of massive nuclear rocket attacks, which will be the basic means of waging war.

The correct understanding of the possible nature of contemporary war produces great interest for the solving of theoretical and practical questions in the area of military affairs. It also acquires great political significance. People must know from where the military danger comes and for what reason the imperialists are amassing monstrous means of the mass destruction of people. The deep understanding of these questions will promote the intensification of the struggle to avert war.

2. The main feature of the development of our Armed Forces is the wide introduction of nuclear rocket weapons. The arming of the army and navy with these weapons produced a revolution in all areas of military affairs. The revolutionizing significance of these weapons is determined, in truth, primarily by its unlimited destructive power. Nuclear weapons make possible the achievement of immeasurably larger results than any other means of destruction and the solution of problems in a very short time.

So that the students can picture this for themselves, a few examples must be introduced. Here are a few.

As a result of the explosion of the twenty kiloton atomic bomb at Hiroshima, more than 78,000 people were killed and more than 37,000 wounded; out of 75,000 homes in the city, 62,000 were completely destroyed and burned. In all, the explosion of two atomic bombs at Hiroshima and Nagasaki killed more than 100,-000 people and more than 60,000 were wounded.

The destructive power of nuclear weapons can be shown also by comparing it with actions of conventional aviation bombs. Thus, as a result of the bombardment by American aviation of Tokyo on March 9, 1945, when 279 bombers dropped seventeen hundred tons of demolition and fire bombs, 83,000 people were killed, that is 17,000 less than from the two atomic bombs at Hiroshima and Nagasaki.

At the present time, the destructive force of nuclear weapons has immeasurably grown. Nuclear charges have been created with a power of fifty and even one hundred megatons. It is noteworthy that nuclear charges of a ten megaton power exceed by five times the force of all the bombs dropped on Fascist Germany in the four years of the last war. As reported in the American press, nuclear attacks on fifty large U.S.A. cities, in which about half of the population of the country live, could bring a loss of fifteen to twenty million people killed and still more wounded. In addition, about 60 per cent of all industrial establishments would be completely destroyed. And according to the calculations of English scientists, eight nuclear charges of a power of three to five megatons are enough to knock out a country like Western Germany. All the main industrial centers of England can be annihilated with five to ten hydrogen bombs.

It is also necessary to take into account such destructive features as thermal radiation, the explosion of a ten megaton nuclear charge can start fires and deeply burn people within a radius of forty kilometers. No less dangerous is the radioactive fallout.

In using nuclear weapons the most decisive influence is given to the development of means of getting to the target—rockets of various designations. They are completely different from other delivery methods. Rockets possess enormous speed and practically unlimited flight range. It is enough to say that objects located at a distance of ten thousand kilometers can be destroyed in thirty minutes after the start of the rocket, which would take strategic bombers more than ten hours to fly. Rockets, almost invulnerable in the air, can carry charges of any power. They can be used in any weather, at any time of the year or day.

Our rockets possess unexcelled exactness in hitting a target. In tests, they reached the aiming point thirteen thousand kilometers from the starting point. Soviet scientists and engineers have made global rockets which could approach an object from any direction and carry powerful nuclear strikes with high accuracy. All these qualities of rockets made them the basic means of carrying nuclear charges to the targets.

The high combat qualities of nuclear rocket weapons, and also

176

their wide introduction into the army and navy, caused them to become the main means of destroying the enemy in battle operations and war as a whole. Here it is necessary to say that the task of all soldiers is the study and practice of possible actions of units and subunits in conditions using nuclear weapons.

Special significance in nuclear rocket war is acquired by the beginning period. The importance of this period is that the first mass nuclear attack in great measure predetermines all the following course of the war and carries losses to the armed forces and to the country as a whole such that might put it in exceptionally difficult circumstances. The results of using nuclear weapons might be so effective that the aims of the war will be achieved in this period. The imperialists are counting on a surprise attack in their aggressive plans for unleashing a war against the U.S.S.R. and other countries of the socialist camp. However, the Soviet Armed Forces are able to frustrate the aggressor's attack and carry to him shattering blows.

Characteristic of the beginning period of the war is the waging of the most active and decisive actions in warding off the attack of the enemy and in carrying to him blows with the maximum use of stocks of nuclear weapons. These actions make up the basic composition of the beginning period of the war. The main task will be decided by the Strategic Rocket Troops' carrying massive nuclear attacks on the armed forces and the economic centers of the enemy. Simultaneously, unrolling of active military operations of all the other services will begin in land, sea, ocean, and air theaters. The armed struggle will be bitter and decisive. In connection with this, enormous significance is given to the high combat readiness of all the services of the Armed Forces and service branches in order that no sort of accident can take us by surprise.

3. In discussing the *third* question, it is important to observe that the revolutionary changes which took place in military affairs caused radical changes in the method of military organization. Changes were accompanied by the rearming of the army and navy and their organizational reconstruction and by corresponding changes in the roles of the services of the Armed Forces in contem-

porary war. The main thing accomplished by the technical re-equipping and the reorganizing of the Armed Forces was the creation of the *Strategic Rocket Forces*. This is a new service of the Armed Forces, the decisive means of the Supreme High Command in fulfilling the more important tasks of armed battle.

The Strategic Rocket Forces are armed with intercontinental ballistic rockets and rockets of medium range having powerful nuclear charges. They are designated to decide such problems as the destroying of the main groups of the armed forces of the aggressor and, primarily, their strategic means of nuclear attack, destroying industrial and administrative centers and other important objects in the enemy's deep interior. The combat possibilities of the Rocket Troops are now such that they are in condition to simultaneously and in a short time decide all these problems. The Strategic Rocket Troops are troops of *constant combat readiness*. The use of an advantageous number of rockets is possible only on the basis of high military and technical training of the teams as a whole as well as of each soldier separately. From this follows the necessity for the heightened technical knowledge of all personnel.

Technical progress has also produced serious changes in the *Ground Forces*. Although earlier their basic firepower was artillery, now the chief means of firepower has become the rocket units, able to carry to the enemy decisive defeat with nuclear attacks on enormous areas and at great depths. Such possibilities of nuclear rocket weapons determine their role in the Ground Forces. This is not a support means, such as was and remains cannon-type field artillery. The team of the launch position of tactical or operational-tactical rockets is able to independently decide combat problems. Here it must be emphasized that this circumstance produces special demands on each member of the crew.

The role of the *tank forces* in battle has grown. As a result of technical progress, they possess good protective means from the penetration of radiation and antitank means, high maneuverability, and great firepower. Tanks are more able to withstand the effects of nuclear weapons, to utilize quickly the results of their use,

178

and, acting in conditions of radioactive contamination, to penetrate to great depths and to seize important regions and objects.

The development of means of air attack raised the role and the significance of the *National PVO* [air defense]. Here also serious changes took place. The basic means of air defense now are the surface-to-air missile complexes, which are able to annihilate air targets with the first rocket, while in the last war an average of five hundred shells were used to shoot down one airplane.

The successful waging of battle with air enemies would be impossible without *radio-radar devices* which allow the detection of flying apparatuses at great distances, the fixing of their co-ordinates and the guiding of surface-to-air missile troops and PVO fighter aviation, armed with air-to-air missiles, at them in good time.

Great changes have occurred in the *Air Forces*. Aviation has crossed the sound barrier and has significantly raised its ceiling. The speed of modern airplanes has reached more than twenty-five hundred kilometers an hour and the height of their flight is about thirty thousand meters. The arming of *bomber aviation* with nuclear-tipped rockets allows them to annihilate targets from great distances. This precludes the necessity of the entry of airplanes into the zone of the active means of air defense of the enemy who is protecting strike objectives. Bombers continue to be the main means of independent spotting and hitting of targets, especially small-sized and moving ones.

The position and significance of *air transport aviation* is growing. Its equipping with our own, more modern planes has increased the potential for making landings and for transporting rockets and various material and technical devices.

There have been essential changes in the role and significance of the *Navy*. Now the basis of its force is the *submarine* with atomic engines, armed with nuclear rocket weapons and long-range, self-guided torpedoes. Submarines can make long voyages under water, destroy ships of the enemy at sea or at bases, and carry out surprise nuclear rocket attacks on important objectives. *Naval rocket-carrying aviation* is developing and occupies a main place in the fleet's force along with submarines.

179

The introduction of nuclear rocket weapons and radio-electronics raises the effectiveness of using modern rocket-carrying surface ships, ships for antiship defense, and other fleet forces.

4. When examining the feature of military actions of subunits in conditions using nuclear rocket weapons it is necessary to focus the attention of the listener on the following considerations:

(a) the character of modern war;
(b) the basic aspects of combat operations;
(c) protection from weapons of mass destruction; and
(d) the increased role of each soldier in modern combat.

We will briefly discuss these considerations:

(a) New means of armed combat are showing a definite influence on the nature of combat. No matter where it takes place— on the ground, on the water, under water, or in the air—modern battle is characterized by decisiveness, dynamics, high maneuverability, and rapid and acute changes of circumstances. Combat actions will cover great areas. For example, the actions of the Ground Forces will take place on a wide front and at great depth. In modern battle special significance is given to the timely destruction of the nuclear weapons of the enemy and the means of their use and, also, to other weapons of mass destruction; to the struggle for winning and maintaining firepower supremacy over the enemy; to initiating actions of all elements; to the skillful use of one's own weapons, military equipment, terrain, weather, and nighttime conditions, and, also, to the ability to quickly overcome various areas of contamination and destruction.

(b) In combat with the use of nuclear weapons the defeat of the adversary is achieved only by decisive attacks, carried on at high tempos. In the course of attack, encounter battle will often arise, the significance of which has now been increased.

In the course of battle, subunits often meet with the necessity of temporarily going on the defensive for the purpose of economizing on strength and resources in one area and creating superiority in the other, lowering the combat possibilities of the enemy's troops, or holding some sort of important object or region. In all cases, in going on the defensive it is necessary to seek to use the forces available, the weapons and the terrain in such a way to provide superiority for one's own troops and to create unfavorable conditions for the troops of the enemy.

In speaking of waging war with the use of nuclear weapons, it is necessary to stress the high dynamics of battle when often one will have to adapt oneself to the quick premeditated change from attack to defense and back. In connection with the high tempo and maneuverable character of military operations, the role of marches to various distances has increased in significant measure. The swiftness of marches in its turn ensures the speed of maneuvers. In these circumstances the subunits must be ready to overcome natural and artificial barriers on the march.

The threat of the use of nuclear weapons by the enemy obliges the troops to act by dispersing, quickly approaching the enemy and skillfully using the protective means of the locality, and strictly observing the rules of camouflage. Operations will be carried out at night also. Night complicates the use of nuclear weapons, aviation, and other military equipment, and simultaneously permits the achievement of surprise, and it follows, fulfillment of the tasks with the fewest losses.

(c) The nature of modern war makes special demands of all personnel in the matter of the acquisition of strong habits of protection from weapons of mass destruction. In examining the content of this question, it is necessary to emphasize with all decisiveness that for preserving fighting efficiency, along with profound technical knowledge, strong practice habits are demanded from the soldiers, skillful actions on the field of battle, and the confident fulfillment of tasks in the individual means of protection from destruction by radioactive materials.

The attention of the student must be turned to the necessity of always keeping the individual means of protection and the table of means of special treatment in good repair, so as to be able quickly, without fuss, to take the necessary measures at the signal notification of radioactive, chemical, and bacteriological contamination of the locality, and to liquidate the traces of the use by the enemy of weapons of mass destruction.

The conversation about this must be carried on in such a way that it will be conducive to producing in the soldiers, sailors, sergeants, and starshinas psychological preparedness to act in the complicated conditions of modern war. To these ends, concrete instructive examples with tactical practice may be used, showing in them the merits and demerits of actions of separate soldiers and whole units in carrying out radiation, chemical, and bacteriological reconnaissance in different aspects of battle; in the special partial treatment of regular arms and equipment; in the use of individual means of protection; in fulfilling the mission and performing the combat service to contaminated areas.

(d) The nature of modern warfare acutely raises the significance of independent actions of subunits and the role of each soldier taken separately. The swift-moving, highly maneuverable, combat operations demand from the soldier inflexible will power, initiative, rapidity of orientation, correct evaluation of circumstances, and the ability to make an independent decision if it is demanded, without wavering, and to resolutely put it into action.

The equipping of our army and navy with new weapons and complicated military equipment, which in the final count is directed by man, in turn immeasurably raises the role of each soldier. Here, stress that it is not rockets, airplanes, and tanks, no matter how perfect they are, that will decide the outcome of battle, but man, masterfully possessing this technology, strong of spirit, with limitless devotion to the country, ready in spite of danger to fulfill the tasks set before him.

In conclusion, it is appropriate to note that our point of view on the raised role of soldiers in modern war is acutely different from views existing in the armies of the Western countries. The imperialists would like to have mechanical robots on the starting positions, behind the wheels of fighting machines, on submarines, doing everything that they are ordered to do. This explains why the masses of capitalist countries are more and more beginning to

182

understand the ruinous war which the imperialists are trying to unleash. A similar state of mind is also reflected among the soldiers of bourgeois armies.

5. On examining the *fifth* question, it is important that each student distinctly realize that constant combat readiness is the basic demand which is made by the Communist party and the Soviet government to the Armed Forces as a whole and to each soldier separately. It is necessary in order to preclude a surprise attack by the enemy on our country, to carry to him a swift, crushing retaliatory blow and achieve victory.

High military preparedness is guaranteed by the deep ideological convictions of the Soviet soldiers, their moral staunchness, constant vigilance, conscientious military discipline, excellent combat training, irreproachable conditions of arms and equipment, and the skill to master them to perfection. The study of this question, as with all themes, must be conducted in close connection with the life of the units, ships, and elements. It is desirable that the lecturer, group guide, soldiers, or sailors widely use examples from training and service in speeches, leaning on the experience of excellent combat trainees and victors in socialist competitions.

High combat readiness is inseparable from conscientious military discipline. Discipline was always the fundamental base of military preparedness of the army. Now its meaning is raised even higher. The significance of discipline must be pointed out in concrete examples from the life of the units and from elements. In connection with this, leaders must select such examples earlier and plan how best to present them to the listeners.

New means of armed combat have immeasurably raised the demands for moral and fighting qualities in soldiers. Each soldier, sergeant, and starshina must develop in himself these high qualities. Without them, it is impossible to act successfully in conditions of the use of nuclear rocket weapons.

Constant combat readiness is unthinkable without the knowledge by each soldier of his weapon and military equipment and the skill to use them in battle. The interests of victory over the enemy demand the thorough mastery of different technical means of battle, keeping them in excellent condition, and finding the best manner of their combat application. Concerning this, it is important that each soldier not only know to perfection his own weapon and military equipment and skillful use of them but also that he master the adjacent specialty in the event he may be asked to substitute for a comrade put out of action. In the course of studies, the soldiers, sergeants, sailors, and starshinas who have mastered one or two class specialties and have become genuine masters of their business, and thus are able to raise the combat readiness of their units, should be named.

LITERATURE
[for Soviet Students]

V. I. Lenin, "The Downfall of the Second International," *Works*, Vol. 21, 194–95: *Complete Works*, Vol. 26, 224.

Lenin, "About a Separate Peace," *Works*, Vol. 23, p. 117; *Complete Works*, Vol. 30, pp. 187–88.

Material of the XXII Congress of the CPSU, 298–304, 361–65, 403–405.

R. Ya. Malinovsky, *Vigilantly Stand Guard Over the Peace* (Moscow, Military Publishing House, 1962).

Problems of the Revolution in Military Affairs (collection of articles) (Moscow, Military Publishing House, 1965).

---

14. THE TASKS ARE IMPORTANT, CRUCIAL
BY MARSHAL OF THE SOVIET UNION V. I. CHUIKOV

Editors' Notes

THE CHIEF OF CIVIL DEFENSE in the Soviet Union, Marshal Chuikov, has the duty of providing a civilian shelter program to compliment the Soviet antiballistic missile systems. He clearly and concisely points out the task that is to be accomplished.

The outcome of nuclear rocket war will now be decided not only on the battlefield, it will in significant measure be predetermined by strikes on the rear areas and on important political and economic centers. Victory in such a war will depend to a large degree on the ability of the state to survive. Therefore, civil defense, the basic significance of which is to assist the government to survive in war, assumes in truth a state and national character.

Chuikov's article is directed primarily at schools; school officials are called on to give proper support to the civil defense program. Deficiencies of the past, which in the main seem to be an indifference to the need for civil defense, are pointed out. Chuikov emphasizes that a knowledge of civil defense might mean the difference between life and death.

Military Knowledge, the magazine in which the article appeared, is the official monthly journal of civil defense. There is nothing comparable with this publication in the United States. Readers are told, for example, how to make a simple device for measuring the amount of time they can be exposed to a given number of roentgens. Cutouts for making the device are provided, with full instructions for assembly. The expensive, elaborate family shelters—advertised in the United States some years ago—are unknown. A practical, inexpensive approach for protection measures, using materials readily available, is stressed.

It is hardly appreciated in the United States that the Soviet Union already possesses the world's finest shelters against atomic attack. These are the deep, elaborate subways in five of the largest cities—Moscow, Leningrad, Kiev, Tbilisi, and Baku. Many sections of the subways run well over one hundred feet below street level and are provided with heavy blast doors that can be used as desired to seal off sections of the subways. A large number of the total inhabitants of Moscow and Leningrad could be provided shelter in their subways alone.

Marshal of the Soviet Union V. I. Chuikov would appear well qualified to head the Soviet civil defense program. He is a former Soviet military adviser to Chiang Kai-shek and a founder of the Whampoa Military Academy. His legendary Sixty-second Army, which generally is credited with stopping the Germans at Stalingrad, was awarded the honorary title of the Eighth Guards Army.

In 1960 he became commander in chief of the ground forces, a post which was abolished in 1964 when the ground forces were reorganized.

Chuikov has been embroiled in a strange controversy with an even more famous Marshal of the Soviet Union, Georgi K. Zhukov. In the literary magazine, *Oktyabr*, in the spring of 1964, Chuikov published two articles attacking Marshal Zhukov's conduct of the last days of World War II. He followed this with another article in *Recent and Contemporary History*, an Academy of Sciences' journal, in March, 1965. To the complete surprise of most Western observers, an official publication of the Ministry of Defense, *Military Historical Journal*, printed Zhukov's reply. Subsequently, Zhukov has regained a great deal of his former stature, and his memoirs of World War II have been announced for publication.

Marshal Chuikov's book, *The Beginning of a Journey*, was one of the first popular accounts of World War II. It was published in 1958, an indication of the difficulty met in toeing the party line in the U.S.S.R.

THE SOVIET PEOPLE enter into the new year 1966 armed with the wise decisions of our own Communist party. Decrees approved at the March and the September plenums of the Central Committee of the Communist party of the Soviet Union (CPSU) and, also, laws adopted by the sixth and seventh sessions of the Supreme Soviet U.S.S.R. determined the path of the basic improvement of the managing of the peoples' economy, the perfection of planning and strengthening of the economic stimulus of industrial production. The transition to the principle of field management of industry and to new forms of guidance of agriculture opened wide possibilities for the further raising of the economic and the defense power of the Motherland.

The measures outlined by the party are inspiring the Soviet people to new accomplishments in building Communist society in our country. Now, everywhere, upsurges of labor are forming and socialist competitions are unrolling for the appropriate greeting to the XXIII Congress of the CPSU.

Important events are taking place in the international arena. The rotten colonial system is breaking up under the blows of national-liberation revolutions. Trying at any price to hold on to their slippery position, the imperialists, headed by the U.S.A., are openly resorting to force, to armed intervention into the affairs of other countries and other peoples.

The bestial bombing of peaceful cities and villages in the Democratic Republic of Vietnam, open intervention in South Vietnam, aggression against the Dominican Republic, and many other piratical actions of American militarists and her allies constantly hold the world on the brink of war.

The West German *revanchists* are persistently straining for the nuclear weapon, and the ruling circles of the U.S.A. are not only going toward them but are even themselves pushing for this step, which is exceptionally dangerous for the cause of peace.

All this cannot help but evoke legitimate fears in the Soviet people and all supporters of peace. The Soviet Union and all socialist countries must vigilantly watch the development of events. Now, with special force, rings out the order of Il'ich [Lenin], "Comrades, be alert, cherish the defense ability of our country and the Red Army as the apple of your eye."

While consistently following the Leninist policy of peaceful co-existence, the Communist party and Soviet government are doing everything necessary for the further strengthening of the defense power of the country, for education of the people and their valiant Armed Forces in the spirit of devotion to the Socialist Motherland and to the great ideal of communism. The technical equipping of the army and navy is being raised in every way possible; skills are being perfected, and the Soviet warrior is being ideologically tempered. They are ready, at any moment, to fulfill with honor their sacred duty to protect the Fatherland.

The party and government are also giving great attention to civil defense which has now become one of the most important aspects of strategic security of the vital activities of the state. The Central Committee of the CPSU and the Council of Ministers of the U.S.S.R. demand from all workers of civil defense and from all the population the achievement of high combat readiness.

The people played a decisive role in the last wars also. But in modern conditions this role has grown even more. The outcome of nuclear rocket war will now be decided not only on the battlefield, it will in significant measure be predetermined by strikes on the rear areas and on important political and economic centers. Victory in such a war will depend to a large degree on the ability of the state to survive. Therefore, civil defense, the basic significance of which is to assist the government to survive in war, assumes, in truth, a state and national character.

Therefore, it is necessary, first, that each Soviet person know the uses and the methods of protection from nuclear, chemical, and bacteriological weapons and how to use them; and, second, that the personnel of civil defense staffs from top to bottom be well trained.

In the last year we have done a great deal toward solving this crucial problem. However, it would be an unpardonable mistake to labor under a delusion about our achievements. Especially since we, as is shown by an analysis of the state of affairs in various areas, have not yet achieved high quality and genuine massiveness in training the population or in attracting them to the staffs of civil defense which have been formed. This especially applies to the rural areas and the residential areas of cities.

A sickness is spreading; there are oversimplifications and many conventionalities in carrying out studies. Often practical studying of devices, ways and means of protection, and methods of carrying out rescue work are replaced by conversations and lectures. People finish the program and do not know how to act under the threat of nuclear attack, how to construct the most simple shelters, and do not know how to act according to the signals of civil defense. In working out the study plan and the tactical background, they have allowed all sorts of "simplifications."

Moreover, there have been isolated instances of additions and plain "eyewash" in accounts about the fulfillment of teaching plans of the population which, of course, cannot be tolerated.

The preparation of the population for protection from weapons of mass destruction is the most important state task. It is now demanded of each citizen that he be able to protect himself and to save others or to render them necessary aid in the event of a nuclear rocket attack by the enemy. But that is not enough. We need trained, experienced cadres who are able to organize skillfully the protection of the people and also the rescue and restoration work.

Quality of preparation of cadres at all levels has become the most important part of the range of our problems. Therefore, only realistic evaluation of what has been done, and concentrated effort on liquidating serious insufficiencies in the organization of the training, will allow us to solve successfully the problems of the new year of study. For both command and regular personnel, the date of beginning and end has been formed differently than before —from November 1, 1965, through September 1, 1966. This period is better for intensive preparation of people occupied in the sphere of production, that is, the basic studying contingent.

The "nineteen-hour program" must be finished everywhere by the established day. In those places where the program is completed, knowledge and habits must be strengthened; systematic training and tactical-drill studies must be carried out, and studies of the basic theme repeated.

The question of teaching school children about civil defense is especially acute. Now, only the older grades carry on preparation. However, all ages must be protected, including students of the younger classes. Consequently, they, also, must learn to put on gas masks, know the signals of the alarm and how to act according to the signals.

The program of preparation for students of middle schools on civil defense in the 1965–66 study year produces great demands of directors, and of teachers, who are carrying out the study part. Results of the first half-year show that not all is being done in order to assure the successful learning of civil defense by the students. The subject is not included in the scheduled hours in all of the republics. Often lessons are carried out by teachers who have not had special preparation. Oral class lessons mainly predominate. Schools are poorly equipped with study materials, charts, and other special property. Expeditions to exhibits of civil defense are rarely prepared.

It is necessary to end decisively the underestimation of the need to prepare school children in this subject. Staffs of civil defense and DOSAAF [a Soviet paramilitary organization], and of Red Cross and Red Crescent committees must assist the schools in the selection and the training of instructors, in obtaining charts and other special property, and in creating exhibits of civil defense. It is necessary to leave the local study base, in its broad sense, to the arrangement of the school instructors: the games, exhibits, model protective works, and so forth. Also, all mass defense work and military patriotic education in school must take into account the interests of civil defense. It is advisable, for example in simulating military games, to train the participants to fulfill methods of protection from nuclear, chemical, and bacteriological weapons by rendering self-help and mutual aid and doing other things to effect civil defense habits.

For sharply improving the quality of preparation of the population for protection, it is necessary, first of all, to arrange the closest co-operation between the staffs of civil defense and DOSAAF and Red Cross and Red Crescent committees. The practice of past years indicates: where staffs of civil defense and the committees of the societies work together—co-operating in decisions on all existing problems—there the plans of preparation of workers and employees, and the population not occupied with production, have been fulfilled on time. People receive the basic knowledge in studies, learn well the methods of protection from weapons of mass destruction, and have basic habits in rendering aid to the suffering. On the other hand, dissociation, isolation, and shifting of responsibilities to others evoke stoppages in the studies, endlessly prolong the set date of finishing the preparation, lower the results of study and contribute to other insufficiencies. In the final result, the matter of protection suffers serious damage.

A great deal needs to be done to basically improve propaganda work, to free it from the eye of formalism, to overcome superficial and unreal approaches to the matter. It is hard to expect success if each citizen is not imbued with the understanding of the strict necessity of possessing ways and methods of protection from weapons of mass destruction, a feeling of personal responsibility for fulfilling the demands of civil defense and for establishing its measures.

If the imperialists decide to begin a new world war, our Armed Forces will mercilessly smash the aggressors. But there can be no guarantee that some sort or part of the rockets or the airplanes carrying deadly cargoes will not break through to our industrial and administrative centers. The *rear*, in the meaning that existed in previous wars, will not exist, since today there are no nontarget cities and regions. All the countries in the world will be exposed to fire—lengthways and crossways.

In this extremely complicated condition, only those who accurately fulfill orders and recommendations of civil defense and those who know how to act at one command or another can protect themselves.

Each Soviet citizen must know that the party and the government is constantly concerned about his life. The basic principles and methods of protecting people have been reviewed and studied, and the organs of civil defense have been ordered to fulfill them strictly. This must be put at the base of patriotic education of our people in order to strengthen in them confidence in victory.

The Central Committee demands that the great potential of press, radio, television, cinema, and means of graphic agitation be much more widely used than previously. Agitation, expediently added to propagation of knowledge of civil defense so that it encourages the reader, hearer, or viewer to join study groups, adds to the material of the program. In developing this work, the improvement of its content must be given assistance by the active support and help of local party, professional union, Komsomol (young Communists) organizations, and cultural establishments.

The chiefs of civil defense and their staffs, DOSAAF, Red Cross,

191

and Red Crescent committees, organizing combat training of formations for instruction of the population, must remember that the nineteen-hour program, as all other programs, is not the limit of but only a step to thorough learning of the effective use of ways and methods of protection and to mastering the organization by the forces of civil defense.

In the new year it is necessary that, along with fulfilling the current study plan, all-round preparation be directed at making a new, more modern, program. It is proposed that programs be shorter, fuller, directed mainly at independent study and practical mastering of the material. This means the programs will demand updated special literature and will require a good study material base. It is necessary to be concerned with this today. Measures must be devised, also, for raising the qualifications of teachers, committee instructors, and for adding specialists to their ranks.

To see the perspective of the development of civil defense, to assist creatively in its strengthening and perfecting in every way, to struggle so that all the Soviet people will know the ways and the methods of protection from nuclear, chemical, and bacteriological weapons, and to be able to effectively use these ways and methods —this is our duty.

Our lives and the interests of the further raising of the defense power of the Soviet Fatherland demand the fulfillment, responsibly and persistently, of this duty.

---

15. MILITARY ART IN THE POSTWAR PERIOD— FROM *THE HISTORY OF MILITARY ART*
EDITED BY COLONEL A. A. STROKOV
Doctor of Historical Sciences, Professor

Editors' Notes

THE HISTORY OF MILITARY ART is one of the seventeen books that will make up the *Officer's Library* series. Chapter seventeen, included here, was written by Colonel Strokov himself, and the chapter subheads give an excellent outline of the contents:

CONDITIONS AND STAGES OF DEVELOPMENT OF THE ARMED FORCES OF THE U.S.S.R. AND SOVIET MILITARY ART IN THE POST-WAR PERIOD
> *The Nature of the Contemporary Era. The Growth of the Might of the U.S.S.R., Its Material-Technical Base and Defense Potential*
> *The Stages of Development of the Armed Forces of the U.S.S.R. and Soviet Military Art*

THE NATURE OF THE REVOLUTION IN MILITARY AFFAIRS
THE CONCEPT OF SOVIET MILITARY DOCTRINE
THE ARMED FORCES OF THE U.S.S.R.
> *Strategic Rocket Troops and National PVO Troops*
> *The Ground Forces*
> *Air Forces (Military)*
> *The Naval Fleet (Military)—(the Navy)*

THE NATURE OF WAGING NUCLEAR ROCKET WAR
> *The Decisiveness of Political and Military Goals. The Scope and Beginning Period of War*
> *The Growth of the Role of Strategy. The Change of Strategic and Operational-tactical Methods and Forms of Fighting*

CONCLUSIONS

In the first section, the Western reader will have an opportunity to see what the Soviet officers are told about their own "material-technical base and defense potential." The account of the revolution in military affairs, which comes next, provides an excellent summary.

The section entitled "The Concept of Soviet Military Doctrine" is written in an unusually cumbersome and ponderous style. The last section, however, "The Nature of Waging Nuclear Rocket War," is clearly and forcibly stated. It is a sobering experience to read about Soviet perceptions of the United States and the doctrine taught Soviet officers for the conduct of a future war.

Strokov restates the usual dogma: "World war will inevitably assume the nature of a nuclear rocket war with the main means of destruction in the war being the nuclear rocket weapon, and rockets of various types being the basic means of delivering it to the target."

The primary danger to the Soviet Union, according to this author, is a massive and surprise attack by the imperialists using nuclear rocket weapons. "Soviet military doctrine considers the frustration of a surprise attack by the enemy and the carrying to him of a crushing blow as the main immediate task of the armed forces." What do the Soviets really mean when they speak of *frustrating* an enemy's nuclear missile attack? Can such an attack be *frustrated* by an antiballistic missile system, or is this the Soviet way of stating a pre-emptive attack? The reader might note the ambiguous use of the term by a number of Soviet authors and then make his individual analysis as to what the Soviets actually intend.

The History of Military Art contains 656 pages. The book went to press in December, 1965, and was on sale by the Spring of 1966. Thirty-five thousand copies were printed in the first edition and the price at the local military bookstore for a copy was one ruble, seventy-five kopeks, or about $1.90 at the current official rate of Soviet exchange between the ruble and the dollar.

We have deliberately translated the term "Voyenno-Vozdushniye Sili" as "Air Forces (military)" rather than "Military Air Forces," the reason being to prevent confusion with the Soviet "Civil Aviation Fleet," also under government control. The same concept holds true for the Navy, there being civilian sea and river fleets and a "military sea fleet." Ordinarily, we use the general terms, "Air Force" and "Navy."

Colonel Strokov is a doctor of historical sciences, a professor, and head of the Department of Military Art at the Lenin Military Political Academy.

Chapter Seventeen. The Structure of the Armed Forces of the U.S.S.R. and the Development of Soviet Military Art in the Postwar Period

CONDITIONS AND STAGES OF DEVELOPMENT OF THE ARMED FORCES OF THE U.S.S.R. AND SOVIET MILITARY ART IN THE POSTWAR PERIOD

The Nature of the Contemporary Era. The Growth of the Might of the U.S.S.R., Its Material-technical Base and Defense Potential

AFTER THE SECOND World War, basic changes took place in the alignment of forces in the international arena. The victory of the socialist revolution in a series of countries, the formation of a world system of socialism, and its transformation into a decisive factor in world development is the main world-wide event of significance after the Great October Revolution of 1917.

Second in importance in events of world development is the downfall of the system of colonial slavery and the victory of the national-liberation movement in many countries which had been enslaved by imperialism. The path along which the countries freed from the yoke of imperialism will go—the path of capitalist or non-capitalist development—is one of the basic problems facing their peoples. (*Material of the XXII Congress CPSU*, p. 355.)

Several of the young countries of Asia and Africa, differing in the level of development, in the relationship of class forces, and in the conditions of formation of different classes, have started on the noncapitalist path.

The world imperialist system is torn with acute and deep contradictions. World imperialism has entered into a period of decline and ruin.

In the Program of the CPSU, adopted at the XXII Congress of the party, an all-round description of our era is given. The contemporary era, the basic content of which, says the Program, is the change from capitalism to socialism, is an era of struggle of two opposed social systems, an era of socialistic and national-liberation revolutions, an era of the downfall of capitalism and the liquidation of the colonial system, an era of the change to the path of socialism of all new nations, and the triumph of socialism and communism on a universal scale. In the center of the modern era stands the in-

195

ternational working class and its chief offspring, the world system of socialism (*Material of the XXII Congress CPSU*, p. 322).

The formation and affirmation of socialism on an international scale is the basic content of the modern historical process. The mighty world system of socialism is constantly gaining strength and by its forward movement crowds the world system of capitalism and forces it back. After the revolution in Cuba in 1959 the world system of socialism included fourteen countries, a third of the world's population (more than a billion people). At the beginning of 1964, the population of the socialist world in comparison to the population of the world constituted 35.6 per cent (in 1919—7.8 per cent), and the population of the chief imperialist powers and their colonies, 16.2 per cent (in 1919—48.1 per cent); the population of former colonial and semicolonial countries, which have achieved independence, has reached 42.6 per cent. In 1964, 26 per cent (1919—16 per cent) of all the territory of the world belongs in the share of all the countries of the socialist camp.

In the world economy, the socialist countries occupy an ever larger place. The proportion of the world industrial production belonging to the socialist system in 1963 was 38 per cent (1917—less than 3 per cent, 1937—about 10 per cent, in 1950—approximately 20 per cent, in 1955—about 27 per cent). The average annual growth of industrial production in socialist countries from 1958 to 1963 reached 10.7 per cent, while in the developed capitalist countries, during this time the tempo of growth equaled 4.7 per cent and in the U.S.A. 3.6 per cent.

The Soviet people have performed great services for mankind. As a result of their self-sacrificing labor and the theoretical and practical activity of the Communist party of the Soviet Union, mankind has received a truly functioning socialist society and an experience-proved science on the building of communism. Many nations are already going this way. Sooner or later all countries will go this way. (*Op. cit.*, p. 332.)

Our people, fulfilling the legacy of the great Lenin, achieve new historical successes each year. They are going on the sure Leninist

196

course set forth by the XX, XXI, and XXII Congresses of the CPSU and the Program of the party.

The main thing in the development of the U.S.S.R. is that socialism has gained complete and final victory. The people of the Land of the Soviets are successfully building a Communist society. The government of the dictatorship of the proletariat has grown into a government of all of the people.

Economy, science, and technology have achieved enormous successes. The Soviet Union now produces almost 20 per cent of the world's industrial production, that is, more than England, France, and the FRG put together (*Pravda*, May 9, 1965). It is confidently overtaking the U.S.A., the most powerful capitalist country. In 1963 the volume of industrial production of the U.S.S.R. was about 65 per cent of the volume of American gross production (in 1950 it was less than 30 per cent). Our country has surpassed the United States in the mining of iron ore and coal, the production of coke, cement, prefabricated reinforced concrete, main-line diesel and electric locomotives, and in several other branches of industry.

In 1964, Soviet industry gave the country 85 million tons of steel, 62.4 million tons of cast iron, 224 million tons of oil, and 554 million tons of coal.

The Soviet Union surpasses by far the leading capitalist countries in the tempos of industrial production growth, and it has firmly taken the world's lead in the most important branches of science and technology. First place in conquering space belongs to the Soviet people. The new launching of the multiseated cosmic ship "Voskhod–2" is evidence of the might of the U.S.S.R. and its defense power.

The Soviet Armed Forces, military theory, and the art of waging modern war are developing under conditions of rapid growth of the Soviet socialist economy, science, and technology, and under the most powerful technical basis for war and modern means of defending the homeland—the atomic and thermonuclear weapon, rockets of all radiuses of action, radioelectronics, and other equipment. The Soviet Army is the most advanced in the world. It was announced at the XXII Congress of the CPSU that its rearming with nuclear rocket equipment was fully completed.

The Soviet Armed Forces are developing fighting co-operation with the armed forces of other socialist countries. The new rule of the fraternal union of socialist countries is constantly working in the socialist camp—all-round political, economic, and also military collaboration. Fighting co-operation of the armies of the socialist countries expresses itself in the joint working-out of problems of combat training and the strengthening of the defense potential of the socialist camp.

With the formation of the world socialist system and the development of the co-operation of the socialist countries, new problems connected with guaranteeing the security of all the countries of the socialist camp have been placed before the Central Committee of our party and the government. In the Program of the CPSU in a special section, "Strengthening the Armed Forces and the Defense Potential of the Soviet Union," it is said that the CPSU considers the defense of the Socialist Fatherland, the strengthening of the defenses of the U.S.S.R., and the might of the Soviet Armed Forces as the sacred duty of the party and of all the Soviet people, and as the most important function of the socialist government. The Soviet Union considers as its international duty, and that of the other socialist countries, the providing of reliable protection and security for all the socialist camp. (*Material of the XXII Congress of the CPSU*, p. 404.)

The Warsaw Pact of friendship, co-operation, and mutual aid, signed in 1955, has great significance for the upholding of the security of the socialist community and the peace in Europe. In contrast to the aggressive North Atlantic Pact, the Warsaw Pact has a purely defensive nature. The leading role in the struggle with the imperialist aggressors belongs to the U.S.S.R., the mightiest socialist power. The nuclear rocket shield surely guards the countries of the socialist camp from incursion of imperialist aggressors. The U.S.S.R. is the decisive front and a decisive force in the struggle with imperialist aggression.

*The Stages of Development of the Armed Forces of the U.S.S.R.
and Soviet Military Art.*

Guided by Leninist teachings, objective laws of social development, and the laws of armed conflict, the Communist party constantly strengthens the defense potential of the country.

Three stages can be distinguished in the development of the
Soviet Armed Forces and military art after World War II: the first
encompasses the eight postwar years, 1945–53; the second, from
the end of 1953 to 1959; and the third stage began in 1960.

In the first postwar stage, 1945–53, our Armed Forces, military
theory, ways and methods for conducting war, strategy, operational art, and tactics developed on the basis of the rich experience
gained from the Great Patriotic War and the Second World War,
and the use of improved (conventional) weapons and military
equipment, the increased firepower, and maneuverability and
striking force of the troops.

The Ground Forces, which have as arms of service the infantry
(riflemen) artillery and tank and special troops (the cavalry as an
independent arm of service was disbanded soon after the war),
received new forms of shooting weapons, tanks with improved
armor protection, firepower, speed, and maneuverability, and new
models of cannon artillery (heavy artillery, mortars, and recoilless
guns), and rocket artillery. Jet aircraft, light jet bombers and
fighters with sonic and supersonic speeds, and helicopters, were
introduced into the Air Forces. By the beginning of the 1950's jet
and turboprop long-range bombers entered the armaments of aviation. The Navy was also armed with new sorts of weapons. National
PVO Troops and paratroopers, which were made independent services of the Armed Forces, were equipped with more modern arms
and equipment, and the accuracy, rapidity of fire, and maneuverability of the fire of antiaircraft artillery was improved. National
PVO Troops were armed with jet fighter airplanes.

Military-theoretical and military-technical thinkers—while continuing to work on strengthening the firing power of the Armed
Forces, their mechanization and motorization, and on increasing

mobility, maneuverability, and striking power on the basis of conventional weapons and combat equipment—revealed the combat qualities of the nuclear weapon, which has the possibility of combining the destruction of shock waves, light radiation, penetrating radiation, and radioactive fallout, and proceeded in these years to work out its use.

In 1947, the government of the Soviet Union declared that the secret of the atomic bomb no longer existed. In August, 1949, the first atomic bomb was exploded in the Soviet Union. In 1953, a year earlier than the test by the U.S.A., the U.S.S.R. tested the first hydrogen bomb. In the first years after the war, work on creating rockets of various classes and designations intended to serve as carriers of nuclear charges progressed successfully.

When the nuclear weapon in the form of nuclear bombs first appeared, aviation was its carrier. By the end of the first postwar period, the U.S.S.R. had modern long-range bombers at is disposal as carriers of the atomic bombs. By this time computer equipment began to be introduced, and radio-technical means were being perfected.

Combat training of the troops and improvement in their organization were based on the experience of the Great Patriotic War. Rules and regulations reflected the experience of the last war and took into account the possibility of further perfection of the armaments system.

The theoretical generalizations and rules and regulations worked out in the first years after the war have real meaning for today also, especially for waging war with conventional weapons.

In the second stage, which began at the end of 1953, the Soviet Armed Forces changed over to the study of waging war by using nuclear weapons.

The second stage is connected with the perfection, accumulation, and introduction into the Armed Forces of the nuclear weapon, and the rockets of various designations. Atomic energy, electronics, automation, and other various forms of technical means of fighting rapidly appeared. The Soviet Armed Forces were equipped with intercontinental ballistic rockets and other modern military equipment.

A revolution in military affairs took place in those years—basic qualitative changes in the means of armed struggle and in the methods of their use (in military art) and in the structure of the Armed Forces.

At first the aviation bombs were the means of using the nuclear weapon. Since 1956 the Soviet Union has had intercontinental rockets. Different kinds of ballistic rockets were first made a few years earlier; they were in existence in the middle of the first postwar stage of development.

Military radioelectronics, also a new military-technical factor without which it would be impossible to use the complex and swift-acting equipment, including rockets, made headway. The wide introduction of radioelectronics led to new progress in military affairs. Radioelectronics assured the skillful use of technical means of combat and direction of troops; and its role in timely warning of an aggressor's attack, carrying out of reconnaissance, intercepting targets, and destroying objectives accurately, etc., is extremely important.

With the massive introduction into the troops of rockets of various systems and classes, new qualitative changes, not seen since the introduction of the nuclear weapon, took place in the structure of the armed forces and in military art.

The nuclear rocket weapon (nuclear charges and rocket carriers) became the basic decisive weapon. Aviation surrendered to rockets its role as the principal carrier of the nuclear weapon. But aviation continued and continues to develop, and airplanes have turned into rocket carriers.

The combining of the rocket and the nuclear weapon into a single whole, the nuclear rocket weapon, is a new phenomenon in military affairs.

In the third stage of the postwar period, from the beginning of 1960, the qualitative transformations in the army and in military affairs continued. A new service of the Armed Forces was created and developed, the Strategic Rocket Forces, and the nuclear rocket weapon and other continually improved means of armed struggle were widely introduced in the necessary amounts into all the services of the Armed Forces.

Today the military might of a country is determined by the nuclear rocket weapon, the combat qualities of its nuclear charges and strategic rockets, the level of development of its nuclear and rocket industry, the power of its strategic rocket troops, and by the nuclear rocket weapons of all other services of the armed forces.

The XX Congress of the CPSU, which took place in February, 1956, marked out a program for the further development of our country, the paths of continual technical progress, the planned introduction of the latest achievements of science and technology into production, opened new possibilities for the structure of the military, and the development of all military affairs on the basis of the new weapon and the new combat equipment.

In the years between the XX and the XXII Congresses of the CPSU, an intensive rebuilding of all military affairs took place in keeping with the new weapon and the new equipment. For our Armed Forces, this period of time, according to the Minister of Defense, Marshal of the Soviet Union R. Ya. Malinovsky at the XXII Congress, was filled with significant events connected with the rearming with new, modern equipment, the wide introduction into the troops of the nuclear rocket weapon, and the major improvement of all the older services of the Armed Forces. But the main thing was the creation of a new service of the Armed Forces, the Strategic Rocket Forces.

The time between the XX and XXII Congresses of the CPSU is considered as a turning point when "a real revolution in military affairs" took place.

Typical of the postwar period has been rapid military-technical progress, rapid development of nuclear and rocket weapons (strategic rockets: intercontinental and medium range, operational-tactical, naval rockets for underwater and surface ships, rockets of the class "air-to-ground," "air-to-ship," "air-to-air," "surface-to-air," and "guided antitank rockets"), development of radioelectronic equipment: electronic computers, calculating-computing apparatuses, radar and navigational apparatuses, means for reconnaissance, communication, and so forth; jet aviation, creation of atomic engines for submarines, development of means of antiaircraft and antirocket defense, the antirocket for intercepting and destroying enemy rockets in flight, and the appearance of ever newer forms of weapons and equipment.

Enormous achievements by the Soviet Union in the field of industry, science, and technology have permitted the creation of cosmic ships and have paved the way for exploration of space.

After the launching of several cosmic ships, Yuri Gagarin made the first space flight in the world on the cosmic ship "Vostok" on April 12, 1961.

Priority in rocket construction and in conquering space belongs to the U.S.S.R. Each new victory on this path has been more imposing, more outstanding, and has testified to the inexhaustible creative thought of Soviet scientists and technologists. During the period from 1961 to 1963, Soviet cosmonauts made six orbital flights in single-place satellite ships of the "Vostok" series. On October 12 and 13, 1964, the world's first multiplace cosmic ship, the "Voskhod," made a flight. On March 18 and 19, 1965, the Soviet cosmic ship "Voskhod–2" was orbiting about the Earth. During the flight, Soviet Cosmonaut Leonov left the ship and successfully carried out a series of planned experiments outside the ship in space and returned to the ship. Thus, for the first time in the world, the exit of a man from a sputnik-ship and free flight in cosmic space by him was performed. A new page was commenced in the conquering of space and the possibility of carrying out work outside a ship's cabin—to gather ships in orbit, to build cosmic stations, and to transfer to other space ships—was proven.

Global rockets, created by Soviet scientists and engineers, can fly around the Earth in any direction and carry out strikes with high accuracy on diverse objectives in any region of our planet. (See R. Malinovsky, "Program of the CPSU and Questions of Strengthening the Armed Forces of the USSR," *Communist*, No. 7, 1962, p. 20.)

As far as strategic ballistic rockets are concerned, their high combat quality and their reliability have been successfully proved by launches which have taken place. In January, 1960, space giants, powerful ballistic multistage rockets, were launched successfully into the aquatory of the Pacific Ocean, 12,500 kilometers from the starting place. On January 30, 1965, the successful launch of a new variant of the rocket carrier of cosmic objects was made into the aquatory of the Pacific Ocean 13,000 kilometers distant. The model of the last stage of the rocket carrier reached the water surface in the given region of impact with high accuracy and without any sort of deviation from the target. (In 1965 additional launches into the region of the aquatory of the Pacific Ocean were made of new variations of rocket carriers of space objects.)

The Soviet Union has nuclear weapons of unprecedented destructive force. In the beginning of the 1960's, nuclear charges were created equivalent to fifty and one hundred million tons of TNT. It is well known that the explosive force of a powerful nuclear charge surpasses the explosive force of all the ammunition used in the whole world during the years of the Second World War. One nuclear charge with the equivalent force of one hundred million tons of TNT is five thousand times more powerful than the atomic bombs dropped by the Americans on Hiroshima and Nagasaki.

In the postwar period the perfecting of arms and military equipment of conventional sorts continued. Conventional weapons can find wide application in nuclear rocket war and even wider application in nonnuclear war.

With the appearance of the nuclear weapons and rockets, Soviet military-theoretical thought worked out methods of their combat use. The problem was to comprehend the new laws lying at the base of the reconstruction of the armed forces and the development of military art. It was necessary to allow no gap between combat potentials of the armed forces armed with the nuclear rocket weapon and the methods and forms of using them in armed battle. Between the methods and forms of armed battle (military art) and the combat potential of the armed forces must be complete conformity. Broad and comprehensive theoretical elaboration was made of the problems of military affairs raised, and encompassed the revolution that had taken place. The characteristic fea-

204

tures of the beginning period of a nuclear rocket war were advanced to the forefront.

The XXII Congress of the CPSU (1961) has a special place in the military structure, in the development of Soviet military theory. It advanced many new questions of contemporary military affairs and adopted a great new program. In the Program is a special section, "Strengthening the Armed Forces and the Defense Potential of the Soviet Union." In it, it speaks of the need to maintain the defensive power of the Soviet government and the combat readiness of its Armed Forces on a level guaranteeing the decisive and complete defeat of any enemy which would dare to infringe upon the Soviet Motherland. And care is taken so that the Soviet Armed Forces will be powerful, will have the most modern means of protecting the country—atomic and thermonuclear weapons, with rockets of all radii of action—that all kinds of military equipment and weapons be kept at the necessary level. The CPSU is doing everything so that the Soviet Armed Forces will be a precise and well-co-ordinated organism, will have high organization and discipline, will carry out missions placed before them by the party, the government, and the people in an exemplary fashion, and will be ready at any moment to give the imperialist aggressors a shattering repulse.

Military affairs in our country are proceeding along the path marked out by the XXII Congress of the CPSU and the Program of our party.

The very basis of military construction, it says in the Program, is the leadership of the Armed Forces by the Communist party, the strengthening of the role and significance of the party's organizations in the army and navy. The growing role and significance of the party as a leading and directing force of our society and of the Soviet Armed Forces are in accordance with objective laws.

THE NATURE OF THE REVOLUTION IN MILITARY AFFAIRS

A real revolution in military affairs took place in the postwar years through the efforts of the party and the government.

Military art and all military affairs, as is known, are dependent on the method of production of a society, on the material basis of life in a society, on the social type of army (for example, capitalistic), and on the characteristics of weapons, military equipment, and other factors.

The development of military art is a complex process which leads to qualitative changes and to the replacement of the old with the new. The development of military art, as does all "actual life and actual history, includes in itself . . . both slow evolution and rapid jumps, interruptions of gradualness." (V. I. Lenin, *Works* (5th ed.), Vol. 20, p. 66.)

Basic changes (revolutions) in military affairs are connected with the replacement of one socio-economic formation by another and with new characteristics of weapons and military equipment, that is, they take place on the basis of social revolutions and of changes in the technical base of waging war.

The contemporary revolution in military affairs is connected with the appearance of nuclear weapons and rockets and the equipping of the Armed Forces with them. By the time of the XXII Congress of the CPSU, the fundamental qualitative reconstruction of military affairs was basically completed. Now the real turning-point stage, "the stage of reconstruction is basically completed," as the Minister of Defense of the U.S.S.R., Marshal of the Soviet Union R. Ya. Malinovsky said at the Congress. (*XXII Congress of the CPSU. Stenographic Notes*, Vol. II, M., 1962, p. 115.) The transformations evoked by the revolution continue even today.

Bringing about a revolution in military affairs became possible thanks to the successes of socialist production and Soviet science and industry (the creation of especially exact instrument-making, special metallurgy, nuclear, electronic, and rocket industries, jet aircraft, modern shipbuilding, and production of the means of automation).

The level of production growing at an unprecedented rate and the development of science and technology were the basis for the revolution in military affairs; the nuclear rocket weapon was created and its mass production organized. An unprecedented qualitative jump took place in the development of weapons, from conventional weapons (guns, airplanes, tanks, and others) to nuclear rocket. The creation of new means of destruction (nuclear weapons) and new means of delivering them to the target (rockets), which became the main decisive military-technical means of armed conflict, determined the origin, nature, and direction of the modern revolution in military affairs, that is, it was its essence. All aspects and indicators of the revolution in military affairs are connected with the changes in the military-technical base.

The changes of the material-technical conditions of armed battle evoked changes in the methods and forms of waging it (military art), in the organization and in the structure of the armed forces as a whole.

The revolution encompassed all areas of military affairs (this is the content of the revolution): the military-technical base of war; it led to the rearming of the troops with new weapons and military equipment; the methods and forms of waging war and military operations, military art; the structure of the armed forces which evoked changes in the organizational structure, in the correlation of the services of the armed forces and branches of the services (the appearance of a qualitatively new service of the armed forces); operational and combat training, the whole system of training and educating the troops. It evoked a revolution in military theory, in the views on the nature of waging contemporary war. Military-theoretical thought revealed new phenomena born of the revolution, explained their nature, their interrelationships, and practical meaning.

The revolution in military affairs advanced new demands for moral-combat qualities of the personnel, for political work in the troops.

The very complicated equipment with which the Armed Forces is now armed, and the new methods of waging military operations make immeasurably greater demands of the personnel. No matter how complex or perfected military equipment may become, victory in contemporary war will be achieved by soldiers who are ideologically hardened, courageous, and boundlessly devoted to their Motherland, and who have military and technical mastery, steadfastness, discipline, and physical endurance. The higher the soldiers' moral-combat qualities, their staunchness and fearlessness, the more fully the powerful military equipment will be used.

The role of man grows, along with the development of science and industry, and new prospects open before him. Man's participation is valuable and effective in modern, transformed production and military affairs. His destiny is not *Automation and the Obsolescence of Man* (the title of a book by the bourgeois author Luongo) and not hopeless labor in an era of cybernetic robots, as proclaimed in the works of many bourgeois researchers, for example in the work "The Monster of Doctor Frankenstein, a Thinking Robot Developed by the Navy" which belongs to the well-known American cyberneticist F. Rosenblatt, who fell under the influence of similar sociological formulations.

The Central Committee of the CPSU and the Soviet government in carrying out the revolution in military affairs were led by the ideas of providing a sure defense of the U.S.S.R. and the countries of all the socialist camp, of preserving peace on earth; this, too, forms the social-political base of the revolution. Turning the Soviet Armed Forces into a powerful factor for preserving the peace, into a reliable bulwark for the safety of the U.S.S.R. and the countries of the socialist camp and of all nations, this is the most important result of the revolution in military affairs.

The revolution in military affairs, which has taken place in the U.S.S.R., was carried out more rapidly, more purposefully and effectively than in the U.S.A. The socialist system, as the most advanced socio-economic system, and the policies and leadership of the Communist party and of leading Soviet scientists assured the achievement of military superiority over imperialism.

One recalls the forecast of V. I. Lenin who said: "New inventions in the realm of science and technology will make the defense of our country so powerful that any attack on her will become impossible." (N. K. Krupskaya, *Conversations with Il'ich—Recollections of V. I. Lenin*, Vol. 2, Moscow, 1957, p. 682.)

THE CONCEPT OF SOVIET MILITARY DOCTRINE

The revolutionary changes in military affairs found their reflection in the military doctrine of the Soviet socialist government.

Soviet military doctrine is a system of views adopted by the Soviet government on the nature of war, the methods and forms of waging it, on preparing the country and the Armed Forces for war against imperialist aggression. It contains guiding political, military-political, and military-technical provisions:

—on the social-political nature of a possible war;
—on the nature of waging war, its methods and forms, strategy, operational art, and tactics;
—on the structure and training of the Armed Forces for war, on preparing the people and the country as a whole for defeating the aggressors.

"The doctrine includes a comprehensive evaluation of the nature of a future war, that is, its socio-political nature, the probable methods of carrying out the armed struggle, and the demands which come from this for preparing the Armed Forces, the people, and the country as a whole for a decisive repulse to the aggressor." (R. Ya. Malinovsky, *Vigilantly Stand Guard Over the Peace*, Moscow, 1962, p. 17.)

The doctrine is a general government concept, and it is worked out by government, political (and military) leadership.

The doctrine determines the direction of the building of the armed forces, the services and service branches, the system of equipping them technically and developing military art, the methods and forms of waging war (strategy), and military operations (operational art and tactics). The rules and regulations of our Armed Forces reflect the provisions of Soviet military doctrine.

Military doctrine is the same for all the armed forces. It covers all kinds of armed forces and the waging of war on land and sea theaters and in the air.

Soviet military doctrine in contrast to bourgeois doctrine is dialectical-materialistic, and it is based on the theory of Marxism-Leninism, on the policies of the Communist party and on the achievements of leading Soviet military science; it expresses the laws of armed struggle and it answers the demands of contemporary war in the highest degree and corresponds to the wealth of possibilities of the socialist structure.

The policies of the Communist party and the Soviet government permeate the entire content of Soviet military doctrine. Military doctrine expresses the socio-political nature of war, the military-political goals and the missions of our government in the war, and it determines this on the basis of Marxist-Leninist teachings on war and the army.

M. V. Frunze remarked that the military affairs of a given government taken together are not a self-contained quantity but are wholly determined by the general conditions of life of this government; the nature of the military doctrine is determined by the general political line of that social class which heads it. (See M. V. Frunze, *Collected Works*, Vol. II, p. 13.) The basic condition of the vitality of the military doctrine is included "in its strict accordance to the general goals of the government and those material and spiritual resources which are at its disposal." (*Op. cit.*)

Military doctrine is based on military-scientific researches and it is inseparably linked with military science. Military doctrine must not be considered as a part of military science. Military science lies at the base of military doctrine; however, not solely. Military doctrine expresses the main achievements of military science and it is built on the objective laws of waging war (the laws of armed struggle are also the subject of military science—laws, indicating how, in what way, and with what methods the armed forces are trained and victory achieved in contemporary war.) Military doctrine and military science are correlated and interdependent.

The same thing can be said about military doctrine and strategy which, together with operational art and tactics, compose the subject of military art (the theory of military art is a part of military science). Military doctrine and strategy—these concepts are not identical. The most important role in military art belongs to military strategy. It concerns the ways and forms of armed struggle, the training and use of the armed forces in war. Military doctrine in these questions is based on the achievements of military strategy (the theory and practice of strategy). The positions of military strategy which are adopted become over-all government positions, that is, they go into military doctrine. In relation to strategy, it comes forth as a whole system of views on questions of the military protection of our government and of all the socialist camp from imperialist aggression, as containing general governing positions. Strategy originates from these. The subject of strategy remains unchanged but, expressing the laws of the methods and forms of armed struggle and the working out of actual questions involved in making war plans, in the proportional development of the services of the armed forces and the service arms and in organizing their co-ordination, and in selecting methods and forms of waging war and in the art of their use, and in regard to other questions connected with training and methods and forms of armed struggle, it is guided by military doctrine and puts it into practice.

Military doctrine and military science have a common material, political, class, and philosophical basis. In this is their unity; their unity is also in the subject itself, in that the positions adopted by Soviet military science become officially adopted by the government. Military doctrine, wrote M. V. Frunze, is built in relationship "with the basic positions of military science and the demands of military art." (M. V. Frunze, *Collected Works*, Vol. II, p. 13.) But this is only one of its bases, a direct military one.

The political basis of military doctrine is defined by the Communist party, the decisions of the party congresses, the plenums of the Central Committee on defending the Socialist Fatherland and all of the socialist camp, specific arrangement of forces and their correlation in the world arena, and the conditions of the international situation. It is founded on Marxist-Leninist teachings on war and the army which consider war as a historical socio-political phenomenon.

The economic and technological (military-technological) basis of the doctrine is determined by the level of development of production, economy, and technology, both general and specifically military (that is, by economic, technological, and military-technical sciences).

Soviet military doctrine takes into account changes in the political relationships between governments and between world social systems, the achievements of economics and technology, new means of fighting, the experience of the Patriotic and Second World War and the postwar practice in building the Armed Forces. Military doctrine is not an established system of views which is set once and for all; it is constantly developed. Changes in the international situation, in the specific arrangement of forces, in science and technology and in the means of armed struggle evoke changes in military doctrine.

Military doctrine cannot be considered as just practice and science as its theory. Military doctrine expresses objective laws. It is the realization of the objective and the subjective; the subjective factor, as history shows, does not always fully, sometimes even incorrectly, take into account objective factors and the existing political and economic possibilities of the country, its own possibilities and the possibilities of the enemy, the means, the forces and the range of armed struggle, the role of the services of the armed forces and other things. The effectiveness of a military doctrine is in the deepest reflection and the fullest use (in preparation and then in waging war) of the objective laws of war. The development of military doctrine, and also military science, proceeds along the lines of the fullest reflection of objective laws of preparation and waging war (in the conditions of a definite historical period which takes shape with its level of development of industrial production, science technology, and means of armed struggle). However, while science has the goal of discovering the objective laws, and showing their action, and giving explanations of phenomena, military doctrine is a system of views worked out on the basis of sciences, and in it emphasis is given to the skillful use of the discoveries and explanations by science of objective laws. But this subjective influence is stronger the more fully and deeply it corresponds to reality, when it proceeds in accordance with need, that is, rests on objective laws. The more deeply we know the peculiarities of objective processes, the more freely we will orient ourselves in the complicated conditions of armed struggle and the more effective will be the results of our actions.

Soviet military doctrine serves the interests of our socialist government and the governments of socialist countries.

An outstanding role in creating the bases of Soviet military doctrine belongs to the founder of the Soviet government and its Armed Forces, Vladimir Il'ich Lenin. The genius of the Lenin military heritage guides the Communist party in working out and perfecting Soviet military doctrine.

THE ARMED FORCES OF THE U.S.S.R.

The Strategic Rocket Troops and National PVO Troops.

The revolution in military affairs led to basic qualitative changes in the structure of the armed forces and in its organization; the correlation of the services of the armed forces and the service arms was changed, and an absolutely new service of the armed forces, the strategic rocket troops, appeared. All other services of the armed forces, the national PVO troops (air defense), ground troops, air forces (military), and the naval fleet (military), have undergone deep qualitative changes; they have been equipped with nuclear rocket and other contemporary weapons.

The Strategic Rocket Troops are the main service of the Soviet Armed Forces. They compose the basic defensive power of the U.S.S.R. and are the decisive force for achieving the main goals of war. The rocket troops are called *strategic* because they will decide the most important strategic missions; the targets of their strikes are directly connected with the goals of the war. They can carry out strikes at a distance of many thousands of kilometers over the entire territory of the enemy, destroy the military industrial potential of an aggressor, disorganize his government and military control, liquidate his means of nuclear attack, and also carry out strikes and destroy major troop groupings and operational centers.

213

In co-ordination with all the other services of the armed forces, they create by strategic strikes favorable conditions for attack.

The Strategic Rocket Troops have as armaments the most powerful nuclear weapons and rocket equipment in the world. The strategic rockets have almost unlimited range of action and can deliver nuclear charges of any power to any point on the globe.

Soviet military rocketeers control their weapons with skill. "Exercises which have been conducted," writes the commander in chief of the Strategic Rocket Forces, Marshal of the Soviet Union N. I. Krylov, "indicate growing combat mastery, high teamwork, and combat readiness of formations, units, and subunits." (See *Izvestia*, February 22, 1964.) They are in a position to rain down nuclear rocket strikes of crushing force on the aggressor at any moment.

The Troops of National PVO have been rearmed and reorganized. Now they are the troops of antiaircraft (designated to destroy enemy airplanes and winged rockets) and antirocket defense. The protection of the country's territory from nuclear strikes and from any means of aerospace attack of the aggressor and, thereby, the sure preservation of the country's vital activity and also the protection of the actions of the other services of the Armed Forces depend on their successful activities. The troops of PVO will solve their task in mutual co-operation with all other services of the Armed Forces and with the Troops of PVO of the ground forces. The Strategic Rocket Forces and National PVO Troops (which enter earliest into war) can predetermine all the subsequent course of the war.

The basis of the Troops of National PVO is the surface-to-air rocket troops, working closely with new interceptor aircraft. Surface-to-air rocket troops, which replaced troops with barrel-type antiaircraft artillery, according to the commander in chief of the Troops of National PVO, Marshal of Aviation V. A. Sudets,[1] are armed with rocket complexes of various designations, including long-ranged unmanned interceptors, and they are able to destroy all contemporary means of aerospace attack at maximum distances,

---

[1] General of the Army P. F. Batitsky replaced Marshal Sudets as commander in chief of National PVO in July, 1966.

at high and low altitudes, and at supersonic speeds of flight. (See V. Sudets. *The Reliable Shield of the Peaceful Skies. The Nuclear Age and War*, Moscow, 1964, p. 73.)

While earlier, using barrel-type antiaircraft artillery, the number of shells spent on an enemy airplane averaged four to six hundred, now, in spite of the development of high altitude flying and high speed airplanes, the rocket troops can destroy them, as a rule, with the first rocket. The complicated and extremely important problem of destroying enemy rockets in flight has been solved in the Soviet Union.

The development of the surface-to-air rocket troops is combined with the development of aviation and primarily with the supersonic rocket-carrying fighter interceptor, which has high maneuverability and the power to destroy winged rockets and airplane-carriers of nuclear weapons, in any meteorological conditions, at any altitude, and at any speed of flight.

The role of the radiotechnical troops of national PVO is great. Their task is to detect air targets and constantly follow their flights, effectively guiding surface-to-air rockets and interceptor aviation to these means of air attack. With the help of radioelectronic equipment they assure the interception and destruction of any means of enemy air attack by the surface-to-air rocket troops and rocket-carrying aviation.

The development of means of attack, the ballistic missile, new systems of aerospace weapons, and the development of aerospace defense proceed with incredible speed. Each of these weapon systems of attack and defense tries to improve so that its development will be superior. They are seeking development of antiaircraft and antirocket defense which will outstrip the means of attack of the enemy. And it must be mentioned that in combat with bomber aviation, especially long-range, such a superiority has been achieved. At the same time, long-range bombers, converted into rocket-carriers, will be able to destroy objects without entering into the zone of action of antiair defense means. Scientists and engineers are tirelessly working directly on equipment for anticosmic defense (PKO).

The Ground Forces.

The firepower, mobility, and striking force of the ground forces have grown considerably. They are fully motorized and armed with rockets with nuclear charges of diverse powers, superior tanks, the latest systems of barrel and rocket artillery, antitank guided rockets (PTURS) with great armor-piercing ability, and modern automatic small arms.

On the ground forces has been laid the task of destroying the enemy's manpower, his troop groupings which survive after the delivery of nuclear strikes. They must carry out headlong attacks at unprecedented high tempos to a great operational depth, seize and hold the enemy's territory, his important strategic regions, destroy his air and sea landings, and at the same time not permit the invasion of our territory by the enemy's army. The role of the ground forces is not confined solely to occupying enemy territory after nuclear strikes delivered by the other services of the armed forces. They must be able to solve the most complex tasks given them in the course of a war.

The basic force of the ground troops, their main means of destruction, is a new arm of service, the operational-tactical rocket troops. The task of the rocket formations and units of the ground troops is to destroy important enemy objectives, which are met on the path of attack and troop groupings, and by nuclear rocket strikes to create conditions for the swift, uninterrupted movement of tank and motorized infantry troops.

Tank troops are able to use effectively the nuclear strikes and by both fire and armored might break the enemy's resistance and move rapidly forward. Crews protected with powerful armored shielding in the tanks are in a position to withstand the destructive factors of nuclear explosions and, consequently, in the greatest measure, preserve combat readiness and high mobility and carry out strikes at a great depth with great masses. In their combat qualities, Soviet tanks surpass American and West German armored machines.

The combat potentials of the motorized infantry have grown, although the numbers of personnel in a motorized infantry division

216

have become fewer than the numbers in a division at the end of the Patriotic War. In a motorized infantry division, just as in a tank division, the number of tanks has increased, and the weight of one salvo, not counting rocket weapons, has increased by several times.

The artillery has been constantly perfected, and it is one of the strongest arms of so-called conventional weapons. Artillery is no longer the main means of firepower (the god of war) but its role remains significant, and it is called upon to assure the operations of tanks and motorized infantry, to destroy with its firepower, especially in close combat, group targets openly situated. Recoilless artillery, rocket artillery, and tank-destroying artillery have been greatly improved.

In connection with the adoption of nuclear rocket weapons by the ground troops, the role of troop PVO, which is called upon to destroy enemy air targets, his airplanes and his rockets, has grown. As a means of PVO of the ground troops, there are surface-to-air guided rockets and artillery mountings, and modern aircraft.

Airborne troops have acquired new qualities. They can independently accomplish missions of seizing and holding or destroying important objectives in the deep rear of the enemy. At the XXII Congress of the CPSU, R. Ya. Malinovsky gave this example for characterizing the possible range of action of paratroops in contemporary circumstances: during the course of an exercise, our military transport aviation alone dropped more than one hundred thousand parachutists, not including the transport of men and cargo.

Military-technical thought continues to work productively on increasing the maneuverability, mobility, striking and firing power of the ground troops, and on decreasing the weight and the caliber of operational-tactical means in the nuclear rocket arsenal. New types of weapons are being created and improved, and reconnaissance means, communications, automation, and control of troops are being perfected.

Air Forces (Military).

The Air Forces are armed with new jet airplanes (in place of

217

piston-engined), and gun and machine gun ordnance weapons have been replaced by rockets. Rocket-carrying aviation composes the basic combat power of the air forces. It can carry out nuclear rocket strikes on the enemy from a great distance, several hundred kilometers before reaching the target, without entering the zone of his antiair defense. Supersonic rocket-carrying airplanes have replaced bomber planes. The basic weapon of the rocket-carrier, fighter, and fighter bomber is the aviation rocket of the class "air-to-ground" and "air-to-air." The speed and ceiling (up to thirty kilometers and more) of supersonic airplanes has greatly increased. The commander in chief of the Air Forces, Chief Marshal of Aviation K. A. Vershinin, writes that the moving of aviation from dense layers of atmosphere to cosmic space and the going from sonic and supersonic speeds to cosmic speeds and altitudes of flight is assured. (See K. Vershinin. *Aviation and War. The Nuclear Age and War*, Moscow, 1964, p. 55.)

The mission of aviation in a possible war is the same as earlier (but now it is not the sole facility and not the means of longest range): the destruction and demolishing of important objectives in the enemy's rear, hitting naval targets (long-range aviation), destroying air targets, manpower, and equipment (and dropping airborne troops) in co-ordinated action with the ground troops (frontal, bomber, fighter-bomber, fighter, and transport) and with the navy.

The Naval Fleet (Military)—(the Navy).

The Navy also has been essentially transformed. Atomic engines, rockets, and nuclear weapons have qualitatively changed the fleet. Although at an earlier time the Navy consisted of battleships, cruisers, destroyers, and other ships, mainly surface, the basis of its power now is the submarine fleet, atomic underwater rocket-carrying ships armed with ballistic and self-navigating rockets and torpedoes. The combat possibilities of atomic rocket-carrying submarines are incomparable. In comparison with other forces of the fleet, they have such advantages as secrecy, concentrated firepower, unlimited radius of action, ability to remain for long periods in an underwater situation, high independence of action, low vulnerability, the ability to take part in lengthy operations at any time of the year in any weather, great speed of movement under water and under arctic ice, and the capacity to destroy enemy objectives with launches of rockets from under water. Along with underwater ships, rocket-carrying aviation belongs to the navy's power structure. It can carry out nuclear rocket strikes on ships and submarines of the enemy in the distant regions of the ocean. The surface fleet, also, has acquired new qualities (rocket ships and torpedo boats and antisubmarine forces) and the navy's shore defense consisting of rocket units. The revolution in military affairs led to the creation of —writes the commander in chief of the Navy, Admiral of the Fleet S. G. Gorshkov—a qualitatively new nuclear-rocket, submarine, and aviation navy, able to carry out any strategic mission in the distant regions in the ocean.

Our fleet has become an ocean fleet and has acquired ocean-going qualities closing the era of undivided rule of the oceans by the American and English navies.

The operations of the atomic submarines are harmoniously combined with the actions of rocket-carrying and antisubmarine aviation, which can search at sea and carry out destructive blows on surface ships and submarines.

"The Soviet Navy," Admiral of the Fleet S. G. Gorshkov said in 1962, "is more modern than the navy of any capitalist country."

The Soviet Navy can perform any strategic task in distant ocean regions; it can battle with the enemy's fleet on the sea and in bases, destroy his strike aircraft carriers and rocket-carrying submarines, and also disrupt and wreck his ocean and sea transportation. An important mission is the securing of simultaneous action with ground troops on the shore and the assuring of the landing of marines. The Soviet Union is a great sea power.

The services of the armed forces and the service arms continue to increase their combat power and perfect their combat mastery. The harmonious development of all the services of the armed forces and the service arms and their skillful co-operation in the course of waging war is a law on which victory depends.

The creation of the strategic rocket troops and the qualitative changes which have taken place in all the other services of the armed forces based on arming them with nuclear rocket weapons and other new equipment have evoked qualitative changes in the methods and forms of waging war and military operations.

THE NATURE OF WAGING NUCLEAR ROCKET WAR

The Decisiveness of Political and Military Goals. The Scope and Beginning Period of War.

The Communist party and its Central Committee, concentrating their activity on solving the problem of the reconstruction of all military affairs, worked out Soviet military doctrine. What are the basic positions which make up the content of Soviet military doctrine on the question of the nature of waging war?

A future war, if the imperialists unleash it against the socialist countries, will become a world war; the main forces of the world will be drawn into it, and it will be a war of two coalitions with opposing socio-political systems. It will be the decisive clash of two opposed socio-political systems. The basic contradiction of the modern world will be decided in it, the contradiction between socialism and imperialism. War is a continuation of politics. It is "politics through and through," V. I. Lenin wrote. The nature of the political goal, Lenin noted in the margin of Clausewitz' book *On War*, has a decisive influence on waging war. War between countries of the capitalist and socialist systems will have a violent and an acutely defined class nature of a fight to the death; it predetermines the extreme decisiveness of goals and plans, methods, and forms of waging it.

A new world war will take on unprecedented spatial range and intercontinental character. Strategic nuclear rocket weapons will permit the shifting of the center of gravity of the armed conflict out of the zone of direct troop engagement and out of the limits of the position of the front to the rear areas and the achieving of decisive military results at any distance and on vast territory. In the last war, Europe, Asia, and parts of Africa were theaters of military operations. Many countries will be pulled into a nuclear rocket war and it will encompass all continents. Although in the past, wars left the countries of Europe and Asia in ruins, now the fire of war will burn on the American continent. If the imperialists of the U.S.A. unleash war, it will be disastrous for them.

World war will inevitably assume the nature of a nuclear rocket war with the main means of destruction in the war being the nuclear rocket weapon and the basic manner of delivering it to the target being the rockets of various types.

The use of weapons of mass destruction will give war an unprecedented destructive character.

A future world war, in spite of the crushing power of the nuclear rocket weapon, will demand multimillion man armies and the participation in it of the people of the belligerent countries. The use of nuclear rocket weapons, the enormous spatial range of the war, and the inclusion in it of all the territory of the countries of the enemies will demand unparalleled exertion of all the strength and resources of the people and the army. A belligerent country will be turned into a military camp.

Victory will be achieved by the combined forces of all the services of the armed forces and the service arms, with the decisive role of the strategic rocket troops. Military operations will be characterized by dynamics and high maneuverability, crushing firepower, and lightning movement. There will be neither continuous stabilized fronts nor the former boundaries between front and rear.

Soviet military doctrine takes into account that world thermonuclear war might be swift-moving. Now no one can deny—Marshal of the Soviet Union R. Ya. Malinovsky writes—the possibility of swift-moving war, primarily because the first surprise nuclear rocket strikes could carry unprecedented destruction, annihilate an extremely large number of troops in places of their usual quartering, and destroy a great part of the inhabitants of the major cities. At the same time, it is absolutely clear that, depending on the conditions of the way the war starts, the armed struggle— not for life but to death—will not be limited only to strikes of the nuclear weapon but can be drawn out and can demand long and utmost effort of all the forces of the army and the country as a whole. (See R. Ya. Malinovsky. *Vigilantly Stand Guard Over the Peace*, p. 26.) War may assume a more or less lengthy nature. Therefore we must be ready for such a war and we must have prepared manpower reserves and material resources. In contemporary conditions, "We must prepare our Armed Forces, the country, and all of the people to struggle with the aggressor primarily and mainly in conditions of nuclear war." (*Ibid.*, p. 27.) We must seek to destroy the aggressor in a short period of time.

The most acute problem of contemporary war is the problem of its beginning period in which the attacking side seeks primarily to carry out a surprise strike and to seize the strategic initiative.

The experience of wars of the past century shows that the aggressor pounced on his enemy with surprise and treacherous blows. Seizing the strategic initiative, he tried to use it to the maximum and to achieve major successes. The victories of Hitler's Germany in the beginning period of the Patriotic War were achieved as a result of a successful surprise attack and led to losses by our people and country, of many lives and extensive territory. The wiping out of after-effects of the beginning period of the war and the depriving the enemy of strategic initiative demanded enormous exertion of the people and the army and took a long time.

The beginning of a new war will be qualitatively different. The content will be changed and the significance of the beginning period of the war will grow immeasurably. The main burden of the war will shift to the beginning period. The unlimited application of the nuclear rocket weapon and its maximum use in the very first crushing strike will encompass all the territory of the countries which are subjected to the nuclear rocket strike and will destroy and demolish their most important political, economic, and military objectives. From the very beginning of the war, strategic groupings of all the services of the armed forces will be brought in and it will assume an all-encompassing nature. Consequently, all the territory of the country, and not just the border regions and the immediate rear, will be subject to a surprise attack. There will not be, as there was earlier, a period of a threat of war; war will begin with the strategic groupings which are in being and not with armed forces mobilized beforehand, and it might spring up suddenly. The carrying out of a surprise attack permits the seizing of the strategic initiative. The beginning period of a war can have a decisive influence on the outcome of the war.

World thermonuclear war, if it breaks out, will be divided into the beginning and subsequent period. Particular significance is attached to the beginning period of the war, the duration of which the military leaders of imperialist states fix at approximately three days. The military leaders of imperialist states hope to predetermine the outcome of the war in their favor by means of nuclear strikes (the basic mass of nuclear charges which have been stock-piled) in this beginning period.

The massive and surprise use by the imperialists of the nuclear rocket weapon is the main danger. Soviet military doctrine considers the frustration of a surprise attack of the enemy and carrying to him a crushing blow as the main immediate task of the Armed Forces. The constant high readiness of our Armed Forces is the prerequisite for this. The concept of "combat readiness" has been considerably expanded, and its significance has grown immeasurably. The most important indicator of military preparedness of the Soviet Armed Forces is the high level of their training. "The main common mission for all of our Armed Forces," the Minister of Defense Marshal of the Soviet Union R. Ya. Malinovsky said at the XXII Congress CPSU, "in the course of combat and operational training, is set by us as the studying and working out of ways for the sure repulse of a surprise nuclear attack of an aggressor and also of ways to frustrate his aggressive plans by way of a well-timed carrying out of a crushing blow on him." (See *XXII Congress CPSU. Stenographic Report,* Vol. II., p. 118.) To frustrate the surprise attack of the enemy, [repulse must be] well timed. "[We must] frustrate such an attack, from no matter where it was planned, and completely defeat the enemy." (R. Ya. Malinovsky. *Vigilantly Stand Guard Over the Peace,* p. 27.)

The American imperialists are preparing a nuclear rocket war against the U.S.S.R. and other socialist countries. The declaration of former President Kennedy that the U.S.A. under certain circum-

223

stances will display initiative in a nuclear conflict with the Soviet Union is well known. [We must] in good time frustrate the plans of the aggressor and not allow the display of initiative in nuclear conflict by warning him "of our force and readiness to defeat him at the very first attempt to commit an act of aggression." (*Ibid.*, p. 25.)

The striving to apply military-technical might and the basic efforts of the armed forces in a crushing nuclear rocket strike on the aggressor determines the need to create all the conditions for its preparation in peacetime. Before the beginning of the war, all the necessary forces and means must be prepared, assuring the waging of war both in the beginning period and in the subsequent period. In the conditions of nuclear war, the significance of the economy of the country and the military-technical superiority over the enemy, achieved prior to entering into war, has grown. It is highly important to have at one's disposal the military-technical means which assure the use of technical surprise, that is, new means of armed struggle which the enemy does not have.

Soviet military doctrine considers that world war can break out growing out of a local conflict—a local war which is being waged in a limited territorial region (one or two countries) and with limited forces and means. It [Soviet doctrine] is built on the waging of war in conditions of using nuclear rocket and conventional weapons.

Soviet military doctrine correctly evaluates the ties and mutual dependence of material and moral factors, the ties and mutual dependence of man and equipment. It gives first place in waging war to man who has created the equipment and guides it. The destructive force of modern military equipment is unequalled. Unprecedented changes have taken place in the relationship of "man and machine." Man, with his social and moral-political qualities, having mastered the new powerful equipment, was, and remains as before, the decisive factor in war; to him belongs the decisive role in waging war.

The role of the moral-political qualities of the soldier in achieving victory is growing immeasurably.

224

The Growth of the Role of Strategy. The Change of Strategic and Operational-tactical Methods and Forms of Fighting.

The contemporary revolution in military art began directly in the sphere of strategy and then encompassed other branches of military art. In the past, revolutions in military art and in the methods of waging war, caused by changes in military equipment, appeared at first in battle and in tactics and then in strategy. The nuclear rocket weapon appeared as a means of strategy. Changes in operational art and tactics occurred with the arming of commands and divisions with it. While earlier strategy had weapons whose range of action did not exceed the framework of operations and battles, today nuclear weapons of colossal power, and intercontinental and global rockets, permit strategy to influence the armed struggle directly and immediately by raining down decisive nuclear rocket strikes on strategic objectives located in any region of the enemy's territory, in other words, to achieve strategic results as if independent of the operations and battles being waged (operational art and tactics). Consequently, with the appearance of a new weapon of strategic importance, the possibilities of strategy have grown. Formerly it could achieve goals placed before it only by means of carrying out operations with ground forces, aviation, and fleets. Now, this is only one side of armed conflict. Decisive results will be achieved by crushing nuclear strikes, that is, directly in the sphere of strategy. Before the nuclear rocket period of war, the armed forces of the enemy were strategic objectives of war, but now, simultaneously with them, industrial centers, communications centers, the basic means of waging war (nuclear weapons and rockets), and also systems of governmental and military administration of the belligerent sides will be the most important strategic objectives of war.

Although in past wars attack and defense were the basic kinds of military actions, carried out by ground forces with aviation support and, on occasion, naval support, in contemporary war the greatest importance will accrue to a new sort of military action—

the action of the strategic rocket troops (strategic strikes and strategic offense) and the troops of national PVO in frustrating the enemy's nuclear strikes (strategic defense). In ground theaters highly maneuverable offensive and defensive operations of ground forces will unfold simultaneously, in which the basic role will be played by rocket formations and units and armored tank and motorized troops.

The concept of "offense" and "defense" has changed. They encompass now not only the actions of the ground forces. The main factor in strategic offense in a future war is the nuclear strike, carried out by rocket troops, the rocket forces of the navy (the rocket-carrying submarine fleet), and rocket-carrying aviation. Another form of strategic offense will be strategic operations in theaters of military actions, carried out by the ground forces, aviation, and the fleet (in shore areas).

The main element of strategic defense is the protection of the country from nuclear strikes by the operations of the troops of PVO and other forces and weapons allocated for this purpose.

The nature of strategic deployment has changed. Although formerly deployment of troops was understood to include the various measures of protection, complete mobilization, and the combat deployment of troops along the borders of a country, now it takes the shape of a system of arranging strategic groupings in all of the territory of the country.

In ground theaters of military operations instead of position fighting full-scale maneuvering operations will unroll. The way for offensive movement will be paved by the nuclear weapon. A new proposition of armed struggle will acquire the greatest significance: the combination of nuclear rocket strikes with lightning offensive maneuvers.

The nature and ways of fighting on the sea have changed. The main actions of the navy will unroll not on inland seas but on the ocean expanses. Instead of the earlier single-combat of squadrons of large surface ships, strikes with nuclear means will be carried out by submarines and aviation.

The harmonious combination of actions of all the services of the armed forces and service arms and the combination (simultaneous) of nuclear strikes with all of the other means of armed struggle are the necessary condition for achieving victory in war.

Changes have taken place in operational art and tactics, in the methods and forms of carrying out operations and battles. In all the services of the armed forces, the main means of defeating the enemy both on the front and in the rear has become the nuclear rocket weapon, which allows the achieving of major results in a short period of time—the destruction of his important objectives and troop groupings; in this the most important mission of all of the services of the armed forces will be depriving the enemy of his means of nuclear attack.

The conduct of operations and battle is the sum total of actions of all combat means—the nuclear rocket weapon and conventional weapons which have been improved on the basis of modern science and technology. The conduct of operations and battle is possible also without the application of the nuclear weapon; in such a war (local) the role of ground forces and other "not new" services of the armed forces and service arms will grow sharply and the nature of armed combat will be more like the Great Patriotic War.

The wide use of new armaments and military equipment sharply increased the combat power of all the services of the armed forces and service arms, their striking force and mobility, and it gave operations a destructive and intense nature and caused the appearance of diverse forms of operational maneuver and in a decisive way it influenced the length of operations.

High mobility, maneuverability, and swiftness in the conduct of operations and battle are the necessary conditions for fulfilling missions of seizing and holding the initiative and for preserving combat effectiveness. The decisiveness of operations will be expressed in their crushing nature and in the swift defeat of the enemy. Operations will be characterized by large spatial range and will be decided in a short time but in great depth.

The interconnection and interdependency of units and formations have grown. The skillful combination of the use of the nuclear weapon and the actions of troops, the ability to exploit its results quickly and effectively, has become predominant in organizing operational and tactical co-operation. The artful combination of rocket strikes and movement is the reliable guarantee of victory. In nuclear rocket war, discrepancies between the possibilities of the nuclear weapon and the possibilities of the movement of troops, their dynamic and swift actions, are fraught with fatal consequences. The services of the armed forces and service arms will carry out forms of maneuvers inherent in their combat nature and corresponding to the demands of the assigned mission and the actual situation.

The role of reconnaissance and all other aspects of support operations has grown immeasurably.

The offensive operations of the ground forces will have great scope along the front and in depth and will be carried out along lines of advance without stopping, in the absence of continuous stable fronts, at a high tempo. Front lines will be temporary. Great gaps will exist between commands and divisions.

Defending groups will be subjected to strong simultaneous action throughout the depths of operational deployment. Major centers of fighting at different operational depths will occur. Troops on the offensive will be forced to attack and counterattack, operational and tactical air-landings will be widely used; and it will be necessary on separate lines of advance to break through the fortified defense of the enemy. Ground force divisions and formations will be able quickly to overcome wide zones of destruction, radioactive and chemical contamination. The forcing of water obstacles will be done without stopping.

Determining the main and auxiliary strikes and the choice of objectives for carrying out nuclear and conventional firepower strikes will acquire important significance. The principle of the use of superior forces and equipment in decisive areas has not lost its meaning. However, the carrying out of a nuclear rocket strike can bring to naught superiority of forces in any of the selected areas. The danger of exposing concentrations of troops to nuclear rocket strikes has led to dispersed and open formations of troops and has evoked new demands flowing from the actual conditions of nuclear rocket war: to shift from dispersion of troops along the line of attack (for conducting battles and engagements) to their concentration, and from that to shift again to dispersion. To answer this demand, troop action must be swift and accompanied by rapid thrusts of tank formations.

The methods and forms of conducting operations will be distinguished by great variety. Attacking troops, while carrying out deep blows, will aim at cutting through the enemy and destroying him by units and also at surrounding his forces.

Defense may be carried out in fortified regions to hold them and can be carried out to preserve personnel and fighting equipment on consecutive lines. Nuclear strikes, strikes of tanks and aviation and artillery fire, compose the basis of defense. It must have high antiatomic and antitank stability. Counterpreparation has acquired new qualities. The role of counterstrikes has grown, in the interest of which the nuclear weapon will be used. After successfully carrying out a defensive operation, the troops might launch a counterattack.

Modern combined arms battle will acquire new qualities and will be strained and fierce, swift and maneuverable to the extreme. Units and subunits almost all the time will be found in a situation of movement and in conditions of frequent and acute changes of surroundings.

The main distinguishing feature of modern tactics is the nuclear rocket and nuclear aviation strike. In this, in fact, is its new content. Nuclear rocket strikes are the means of independently deciding important combat missions and their role does not amount to the conventional support of troop combat actions.

Warfare and operations have become extremely complicated. One must not forget that the nuclear weapon with its destructive possibilities in waging war will be used by both sides and that this will allow either side in an extremely short period of time to achieve decisive results.

Contemporary combined arms battle includes primarily tactical nuclear strikes, fire strikes by conventional artillery, and highly maneuverable actions and swift attacks of formations, units, and subunits of tanks and motorized infantry. Attacking troops will have to conduct encounter battle and use various forms of maneuver: frontal strikes, outflanking, wide envelopment, and withdrawal; they must quickly use nuclear strikes, destroying on their way both enemy troops that survived their attack and those freshly arrived; they must attack chiefly along directions in the presence of gaps in combat formations, in conditions of mutual penetration, in free spaces, in gaps formed by nuclear strikes that create the danger of open flanks from the rear. Fighting in such conditions takes on an area nature. Areas of defense in tactical depths will be destroyed by nuclear strikes or by fire from other types of weapons. The time for attacks of formations on foot has passed. The methods of "eating away" the defense have also gone into the past; it will be overcome by tanks and motorized infantry troops on the march after the carrying out on it of nuclear strikes.

In the course of attack, it will be necessary to resort to defense, to counterattack, to wage a struggle in encirclement, and to leave the battle. The role of counterattack in contemporary defensive battle has grown greatly; its main purpose is the defeat of enemy units and formations which have penetrated the defense. Counterattack is the decisive action in defense. It commands great strike force; it can be carried out at a high tempo and in significant depth; it can be preceded by strikes of atomic weapons.

In war that is not nuclear rocket, combined arms battle will be carried out as before, with conventional means. The methods and forms of conventional battle, however, under the influence of new, perfected conventional weapons and combat equipment have also undergone changes in the limits of earlier qualities.

The control of troops has become more complicated, as have also the methods of leading troops by commanders and staffs, the equipment, and the means of communications, detection, guidance, the preparation of calculations, and so forth.

The new demands which have appeared for the guidance of troops—in leading them and in organizing their actions—have been caused by the changed military-technical basis of war, the new nuclear rocket weapon and complicated military equipment, the changed role of the services of the armed forces and the service arms in achieving victory over the enemy, and the changed methods, forms, and scope of waging war and military operations.

Purposeful and planned direction of troops is the most important link in the use of the objective laws of armed struggle. The decision which is adopted must objectively reflect the conditions which have been built up and must foresee the further course of the battle. Commanders and chiefs of all levels must master to perfection the art of organizing and conducting battles and operations, the combining of conventional means of struggle with nuclear rocket strikes, and the maintaining of the constant co-ordination of troops in the course of combat operations. They must quickly orient themselves to conditions, make rapid decisions, assign missions, and unwaveringly achieve their fulfillment. They must master the methods of directing troops and know the equipment for directing them.

The directing of troops must be strictly centralized, flexible, operative, steady, and firm from top to bottom. The successful direction of troops in our time is unthinkable without the wide use of technical means. The resolution of the contradictions between the constantly increasing dynamics of military actions and the existing systems of control depends on the high qualities of the command structure.

Conclusions

A new era in the development of military affairs began in the postwar period. In the first postwar years (the first stage, 1945–53) Soviet military theory thought, organization, and training of troops was based primarily on the experience of the Great Patriotic and Second World War, on the use of conventional but more perfected weapons. During this time, the nuclear weapon was created and the first kinds of rockets appeared. Study of the combat characteristics of atomic and thermonuclear weapons was begun and the theory of their use was worked out.

In the following years (second stage—the end of 1953 to 1959) nuclear and rocket weapons, radioelectronics, and other new equipment were introduced into the Armed Forces. Troops were trained to wage war in conditions of nuclear rocket weapons. Military-theoretical thought was working over the use of nuclear and nuclear rocket weapons and working out methods and forms of using the Armed Forces in the new conditions of waging war.

From 1960, in connection with the introduction into all of the services of the Armed Forces of the new means of battle, there began a new, third stage in its building, in the development of military art. At the beginning of 1960, a new service of the Armed Forces was created, the Strategic Rocket Forces. All the services of the Armed Forces and service arms, on the basis of the experience being acquired and the use on exercises and in maneuvers of the new means of combat, continued to work out methods and forms of waging nuclear rocket war.

The rapid development of production and of science and technology is the basis of the revolution in military affairs, and it evoked a qualitative jump, from conventional weapons to nuclear rocket ones, in the development of armaments. The new means of destruction—the nuclear weapon—and the new means of delivering it to the target—the rocket—became decisive in waging war and determined the origin and character of the modern revolution in military affairs.

The revolution encompassed: the military-technical base of war and the rearming of the troops with the new weapons and military equipment; military art, the methods and forms of waging war and military operations; the structure of the armed forces; the role, the place, and the mission (relationship) of the services of the armed forces and service arms; the organizational structure; operational and combat training, and all the other areas of military affairs. The revolution changed the art of conducting armed struggle (military art) and the organization and the structure of the armed forces as a whole.

The power of the armed forces has grown immeasurably, and its structure, as well as the relationship between the various services of the armed forces and service arms has changed. The main place was taken by a completely new service of the armed forces, the Strategic Rocket Troops.

232

The revolution in military affairs called to life new laws of armed conflict. The goals and objectives of war changed. The strategic goal of war is connected primarily with strategic nuclear rocket strikes, with destroying the economic and political centers, the rear of the belligerent countries as a whole. The nature of the beginning period of war is different. The role of surprise and the struggle for strategic initiative and also the demands for constant combat readiness of the Armed Forces has grown fantastically, bringing military alertness to the highest limits. The scope of war and military actions has changed. War encompasses enormous territorial space and the cosmos and acquires an intercontinental, destructive, annihilating nature. The question of the length of war will be decided in a different way.

Changes have taken place in the interrelation between the outgrowths of military art, strategy, operational art, and tactics. The role of strategy has grown greatly and its content has been filled out with a new and most effective quality. With the creation of the Strategic Rocket Forces it is as if it had acquired its own material force and received the possibility of directly, immediately influencing the course of armed struggle, where earlier it reached its goals indirectly through the conduct of operations, engagements, and battles carried out by ground troops and air and naval forces.

Modern war will be decided by the combined actions of all the services of the armed forces and service arms. The strategic forces must be directed toward the skillful organization of their co-operation, toward the achievement of high maneuverability of troops, crushing firepower, and lightning-like swift strikes, the combination of nuclear strikes with other means of armed struggle, and their timely use.

The distinguishing feature of of modern military doctrine is the use of conventional weapons along with the nuclear rocket weapon. Contemporary world war, if the imperialists unleash it, will be waged with all sorts of weapons. Local wars are being waged by the imperialists with conventional weapons.

In waging war, the decisive role will belong to man—his having mastered the new weapon, the new military equipment, and the art of waging war, and because of his moral combat qualities. Waging war with the new nuclear rocket weapon will raise the role of the system of the training and the education of the soldier.

The revolution in military affairs has been brought about under the leadership of the Central Committee of the Communist party in accordance with the ideology and policy of the party. The socialistic productive relationships and the policies of the Communist party assure the fuller, more effective, influence of production, science, and technology on the military field.

The U.S.S.R. is the most powerful military power. "The Soviet Army," the Chairman of the Council of Ministers Comrade A. N. Kosygin at the reception in the Great Kremlin palace on March 23, 1965, said, "has the most modern weapons, which are second to none in their power."

---

16. ACCORDING TO THE LAWS OF DIALECTICS
By COLONEL S. I. KRUPNOV
Candidate of Philosophical Sciences

Editors' Notes

THIS ARTICLE, with its inconspicuous title, perhaps provides the most perceptive insight into Soviet military thinking of any writing in this selection. It may suggest to the American reader why the Soviet Armed Forces do not always react as we expect. The introduction of Soviet antiballistic missile systems and increased numbers of intercontinental ballistic missiles reflect their dialectical analysis of strategy.

Dialectical materialism asserts that development always proceeds through the stages of thesis, antithesis, and synthesis. It follows, therefore, that "the appearance of new means of struggle always brings into being corresponding *countermeans*, which in the end also lead to changes of the methods of military operations. The 'struggle' of tanks and antitank means, submarines and antisubmarine means, airplanes and antiairplane defense, radio-means and

234

means of jamming, rockets and antirocket—this is the axis around which revolves the development in military affairs. . . . " In some respects the nature of both attack and defense has changed and "*the tendency to* rapprochement *is observed* on these basic aspects of combat actions. A strategic nuclear rocket strike *combines* in itself simultaneously the function of attack and defense."

Krupnov continues by listing contradictions, such as those between the concentration and dispersion of troops. At all times, whether on the march, in attack, or in defense, the troops "must act in dispersed groupings in order not to be a convenient target for strikes with nuclear weapons. At the same time they must remain strong, able to carry strikes to the enemy at any moment." Another contradiction exists between centralization and decentralization. Nuclear weapons require strict centralization of control, but at the same time military actions are so spread out that the commanders of units must be given an unusually wide latitude of independence.

According to Krupnov, "The revolution in military affairs evoked by the appearance of the new weapon has not been received by everyone in the same way." Nevertheless, "The key to the correct understanding of the problem is given by dialectical-materialism." Nuclear rocket weapons have changed the very nature of war, including strategy, operational art, and tactics. "Naturally, the nuclear rocket weapon has also brought to life such absolutely new methods of combat actions as *antirocket* operations. . . . Finally, a possible nuclear rocket war harbors the danger of armed conflict in *space*."

This article by Colonel Krupnov was published in *Red Star*, January 7, 1966. He is the author of *Dialectics and Military Science* (Moscow, Military Publishing House, 1963).

On the Development of Methods and Forms of Armed Conflict

THE QUESTION of the methods and forms of armed conflict has always occupied a most important place among the problems of military science. This is in order because the question is about the very vital search for and determination of the most effective path of achieving victory in war.

What lies at the basis of this process, and what are the dialectics of the development of methods and forms of armed conflict?

I

New methods and forms of armed conflict do not arise automatically by themselves. They are worked out by *people*. Engels wrote that tactics were worked out on the fields of battle. Naturally, a special role here belongs to the military leaders. The level of their knowledge, culture, talent—all of these have a great influence on the development of military affairs.

Does this mean that the creation of new methods and forms of armed conflict is only the result of the subjective activities of people? No, it does not. "It is not the 'free creation of the mind' of brilliant military leaders that has acted here in a revolutionary manner," remarked Engels, "but the invention of better weapons and changes in the living soldier material."

In other words, each new system of waging armed conflict in the final count is the product of *objective* conditions. These conditions are primarily *economic*. In this, economics, the level of development of production, in particular in science and technology, determines the methods and forms of conflict, not directly, but indirectly, *through armaments, military equipment, and the personnel*. In its turn, weapons and military equipment affect considerably the methods and forms of conflict, not at once, but only when the weapons have been collected in a sufficiently large quantity.

It is well known that in 1949 the atom bomb was tested in the Soviet Union. But at that time the production of nuclear ammunition was still not sufficient and, therefore, the basic power of the army and navy, as before, was composed of conventional forms of weapons. Troops were trained by already established methods of fighting. After 1953, nuclear weapons began to be introduced comparatively widely and the Soviet Armed Forces began to master new methods of waging military operations.

Radical transformations in organization, combat, and political

236

training began only when nuclear weapons and modern methods for their delivery were introduced into the troops in sufficient quantity. The necessity and the possibility emerged for creating a new service of the Armed Forces—the Strategic Rocket Troops. With a stock-taking of the properties and the colossal possibilities of the new weapon, fundamental transformations were carried out in the troops of PVO (air defense), in the Air Forces, and in the Navy. The nuclear rocket weapon also became the basis of the combat power of the Ground Forces.

Such transformations are closely connected with those changes which have taken place in the personnel of the Soviet Armed Forces. Their general educational, technical, and special training and political-moral condition have reached such levels today that it is possible to use most effectively the nuclear rocket weapon and other combat equipment for raising the combat readiness and combat potential of the troops and, in wartime, for defeating the enemy.

War is waged by people in the name of definite *political goals.* Their nature has a decisive effect on the range, the intensiveness, and the degree of effort of military actions; that is, it also determines the methods and forms of armed struggle. This connection between the nature of the political goals of war and the methods of armed conflict is necessary; it is repeated in all wars and therefore has the force of an objective law.

The influence of politics has an effect to the greatest degree, primarily, in selecting the moment to begin the war, in selecting the main objects of strikes, and in determining the sequence and the strength of these strikes. Politics, secondly, determines whether the war is waged to an unconditional surrender or whether its mission should bear a more limited nature. Thirdly, in keeping with the political goals, the tempo and tension of combat actions, the forces and means which are necessary for mobilization and so forth, are determined.

But these alone do not exhaust those objective conditions which influence the methods and forms of armed conflict. Their development and the nature of the actions of the troops on the field of

237

battle, in addition, depend *on the relationship of forces of the belligerent sides and on the possibilities of the enemy and of his military art.*

Finally, the methods and forms of armed conflict also depend *on geographical surroundings.* The extent of the theater of military operations, climate, the local terrain, the water barriers, the vegetable kingdom—all this has an essential influence on the nature of fighting, combat, and operations.

Thus, new methods and forms of armed conflict are made by the creative efforts of people, but their appearance and development are conditioned by a whole series of objective circumstances.

II

All the phenomena of nature, society, and thought have inherent internal contradictions. Precisely these contradictions are the source of all development. Therefore, the most important condition for the proper understanding of all of the processes of the world, V. I. Lenin taught, is "the understanding of them as a unity of contradictions."

The phenomenon of armed conflict is not an exception to this general rule. On the contrary, war is contradictory throughout. It arises from socio-economic and political antagonisms between classes, governments, and nations, and represents a degree of the highest aggravation of the contradictions, the sharpest form of their settlement. Therefore, only a *correct understanding of the nature of the social conflict which has evoked the war and realization of its political aims make it possible to determine with the greatest exactness the military-strategic nature of the armed conflict.*

The basic contradiction of the modern era is the contradiction between the two social systems—socialism and imperialism. And, naturally, if the imperialists unleash thermonuclear war, it will inevitably become a world war, a coalition war, and it will have an exceptionally violent and decisive nature. It will inevitably be marked by the final victory of the forces of socialism over the forces of imperialism. But wars can also be caused by other contradictions: between capitalistic monopolies and workers, between the metropolis and the colonies, between imperialist powers themselves. In this case, armed conflict might have a different nature.

Thus, the knowledge of social conflicts and of the political goals of the war makes it possible to foresee its nature. But such knowledge alone is not enough to determine with sufficient certainty all the diversity of those methods and uses which will be used by soldiers on the battlefield. For this, it is necessary to understand the *contradiction between weapons, military equipment, and methods and forms of armed conflict* which always exist in military affairs. This contradiction is explained by the fact that the material base, forces, and means of waging war change more quickly than methods and forms of conflict. Between them arises a disparity. Sooner or later it is detected, and people must eliminate it. It was thus, for example, after the appearance of firearms and after the invention and introduction of tanks and airplanes.

The contradiction between the means and forms of armed conflict in our time has acquired special acuteness. At first it seemed to some people that nuclear rocket weapons would not bring in any qualitative changes to the organization and direction of troops and in the methods of their actions. But tests of the new weapons and research of their possibilities convincingly showed that they were unconventional and different in principle than weapons of the past. The search was begun for new organizational forms and principles of waging armed conflict.

The problem is not limited to the search for the most effective way of using modern weapons. The appearance of new means of struggle always brings into being corresponding *countermeans*, which in the end also lead to changes of the methods of military operations. The "struggle" of tanks and antitank means, submarines and antisubmarine means, airplanes and antiairplane defense, radio-means and means of radio jamming, rockets and antirockets— this is the axis around which revolves the development of military affairs, including the development of methods and forms of armed conflict.

Or this contradiction. Since war began to be waged, armies have always had to attack or defend themselves. *Attack and defense* are two contrasting kinds of military action. But it is the kind of contrast which organically ties and depends on each other and the correct understanding of the development of each of them is possible only by examining attack and defense in close connection with each other.

In present-day war with the use of the latest means of attack, just as it was earlier, only attack can lead to the defeat of the enemy and victory over him. But even in such a war, one cannot manage without defense. It is another matter that *now the nature of both attack and defense has essentially changed and the tendency to* rapprochement *is observed* of these basic aspects of combat actions. A strategic nuclear rocket strike, for example, *combines* in itself, simultaneously, the function of attack and defense.

Since ancient times one of the principles of military art has been the concentration of force on the main direction of military actions. This principle preserves its significance in present-day war also. But now, both on the march, in attack, and in defense, troops must act in dispersed groupings in order not to be convenient targets for strikes with nuclear weapons. At the same time they must remain constantly strong, able to carry strikes to the enemy at any moment.

Thus, still another most acute contradiction arises—the *contradiction between concentration and dispersion.* Every kind of improvement in troop mobility is the chief form of solving this contradiction.

Present-day combat actions are distinguished by high maneuverability, waged on a wide front and at exceptionally high tempos. Such a nature of armed conflict significantly complicates the control of troops. Now the commander must make a decision and convey it to his subordinates in the shortest period of time. At the same time the quantity and the difficulty of questions to be decided by the military leader have increased. This contradiction is overcome by the method of seeking *new ways of control* based on the widest use of electronic computer machines and small mechanizations. These devices, of course, cannot replace the commander. Today, he, as never before, must have deep and all-round knowledge, extremely developed intuition, the ability for logical thinking, mathematical methods of knowledge, and high moral qualities.

A decisive influence on the development of the principles of systems of control of troops is rendered by the constant existence of *contradictions between their centralization and decentralization.* The use of the nuclear rocket weapon and the swiftest use of the results of its strike is unthinkable without strict centralization of control. At the same time military actions will be spread over a large area without set fronts and with great gaps between combat formations. This demands concessions of independence to commanders of subunits, units, and groups, which are significantly greater than in past wars.

Thus, contradictions and the overcoming of them are the vital source of the development of methods and forms of armed combat and of all military affairs. To notice, in time, emerging contradictions and to determine the proper course of their solution means to find the key to solving problems which are standing before military science and before the theoreticians and practitioners of military affairs.

III

The revolution in military affairs evoked by the appearance of the new weapon has not been received by everyone in the same way. Some have affirmed that the nuclear weapon is allegedly absolute and that it completely negates massive land armies and air and naval fleets. Others have supposed that the changes in military affairs must be gradual for, they say, the nuclear rocket weapon is no different in principle from the old, and will not bring in great changes in the methods and forms of armed conflict but will only add a few features to it.

These different points of view reflect the age-old question: How does the process of development of methods and forms of armed conflict proceed—gradually and smoothly, or by leaps in a revolutionary manner?

The key to the correct understanding of the problem is given by dialectical-materialism. It teaches that *the development of military affairs, as all development, is subject to the actions of the law of the transformation of quantitative changes to qualitative ones.* New weapons lead to qualitative changes of methods and forms of armed conflict, not at once, but only at the time when its quantity reaches a significant size.

As gradual as the development of military affairs seemed in the past, it still moved ahead by jumps. But these jumps were far from being equal in their range and significance. Some of them were relatively prolonged and led to qualitative changes of a specific nature; others were accomplished more quickly and encompassed *the whole realm of military affairs.* Just such a fundamental military-technical transformation is taking place now in the armed forces of the major countries of the world. The present powerful jump in the development of weapons and military equipment brought in with it fundamental qualitative changes in the nature of combat actions.

Nuclear rocket strikes are now the main and basic method of armed conflict. They represent an absolutely new phenomenon and they cannot be compared to conventional firing actions. The nuclear rocket weapon with its unlimited possibilities allows the achieving of decisive results in war in the very shortest period of time. In contemporary conditions, for achieving, let us say, operational goals, it is not obligatory to create groupings of personnel in the former dimensions, and a long period of time is not needed for the "gnawing through" of the defense of the enemy, and so forth.

The appearance of the nuclear rocket weapon changed the very *correlation* of strategy, operational art, and tactics. Strategy, for the first time, took on such a quality as the ability of direct action on the enemy. Operational art and tactics are now called on to decide problems connected with finishing up those main results which must be achieved by nuclear rocket strikes.

Thus, nuclear rocket strikes are leaving a considerable imprint *on all aspects* of military art. An attack now begins with carrying out these powerful strikes on on the whole depth of the enemy's defense. Ground troops, especially tank and airborne troops, quick-

242

ly exploit the results of these strikes. Attack is usually waged with dispersed formations, at a rapid tempo, by methods of deep, swift blows, combined with operations along the flank and rear of the enemy with the aim of breaking him up and destroying him in parts. The bases of military actions of the defenders today are composed of the highest activity, maneuvers with forces and means along the front and in depth, counterattack and counterstrikes. Both for the defenders and the attackers there should be such absolutely new sorts of combat protection as *antiatomic and antibacterial defense.*

Naturally, the nuclear rocket weapon has also brought to life such absolutely new methods of combat actions as *antirocket* operations. The actions of the troops of PVO have started to be organized in a different way. Fundamental changes have taken place also in the methods of combat in aviation and the navy. Finally, a possible nuclear rocket war harbors the danger of armed conflict *in space.*

In a newspaper article it is impossible to disclose everything new that has appeared in the methods and forms of armed conflict as a result of the revolution in military affairs. But what has been said is enough to draw the conclusion: present-day military-technical revolution cannot be regarded as a single phenomenon. It represents a many-sided process in which one may see the appearance of new methods and the "withering away" of old methods and forms, or their being filled with new content. It is important to remember and take into account that old methods of conflict cannot be discarded, for armies have conventional weapons alongside the nuclear rocket ones.

In connection with this, another currently topical question arises: What should be our relationship with the *experience* of the past and to military history?

Soviet military science is both against fetishism of historical experience and against the underestimation of history. Based on the laws of dialectics, it teaches that the new arises only from the old and in no other way, that the present-day revolution in military affairs was brought about by all of the past development of science and technology. The study of military history, the experience of the past, allows "the discovery" of the general laws of development of

243

methods and forms of armed conflict; it expands the horizon and helps one better orient oneself in the contemporary directions of science.

But it would be unreasonable to search in history for a ready answer on all questions brought forward by our times. "It is necessary to recognize this indisputable truth," taught V. I. Lenin, "the Marxist must take into account real life, the exact facts of *reality*, and not continue to cling to the theories of yesterday."

To the question of what to take from past experience, and what to decisively reject, military practice must give the answer. In this, by "practice" is meant not only armed struggle but also maneuvers and various exercises and war games and tests on the firing range and the shaping of military processes and many other things. It is necessary not to cling to the past but with the greatest attention to turn to contemporary troop and naval practices, analyze them constantly, generalize, taking material from research, and then again to try out the results of this research in practice.

Military affairs are in a stage of rapid revolutionary development. The perfection of the nuclear rocket weapon and complicated military equipment continues to have a decisive influence on the methods and forms of armed conflict as well as on the organization and the combat and political training of troops. To understand the dialectics of this development it is necessary to explain the essence; to find the path of successful solution of those problems which stand before officers, generals, and admirals.

---

17. THE TIME FACTOR IN MODERN WAR
By Colonel I. A. Grudinin
Professor, Doctor of Philosophical Sciences

Editors' Notes

Colonel Grudinin is a lucid writer whether or not one agrees with his conclusions. Much of his military theory is difficult to dispute. In his opinion, military decisions, which formerly took months or years to determine, may be decided in minutes, hours, or a few days in modern nuclear rocket war. Forces must be combat ready at all times to "frustrate the aggressor's attempts to carry out a strike and to achieve the decisive goals of war in its initial period." There is also the possibility of a long, protracted war. The Soviet Armed Forces must be ready for either. In the event of a long war, the state must be capable of expanding the production of military equipment while the war continues, and this military equipment will include "conventional sorts of weapons."

The most important factor, however, is being prepared for a nuclear rocket war. *"The growing significance of the beginning period of a possible thermonuclear war makes exceptionally high demands for achieving the level of combat readiness . . . .* Winning and keeping military technological supremacy over the probable enemy, in times of peace, has decisive significance."

Grudinin shows that technological progress has made difficult the training of personnel in the new equipment. In the United States some fifteen years ago a ten-day course was required for training a certain specialist; modern equipment is so complicated that fifty-four weeks are now required for the same type of training. New equipment is introduced so rapidly that there is a danger of a lag in the technical preparation of personnel.

In the past, according to the author, it sometimes was stated that "to learn to fight is possible only during a war." This can no longer be the case. "In a short, swift-moving war, when the beginning period acquires decisive meaning, it would be too late to learn to fight. Those who do not learn to fight the enemy in peacetime are destined to be defeated in war." In combat troop training special attention must be given to studying the strong and the weak sides of the probable enemy. One must know his armaments, organizational structure, military art, training, and other factors. "Deep and constant study of the probable enemy serves as one of the main conditions of combat readiness of the armed forces . . . ." The time of peace must be used for the preparation of war.

245

In the actual course of armed conflict, time is equally significant. "Swiftness of action and surprise paralyze the will of the enemy, stun him, and lead to confusion." To "delay in war is like death." For swift strikes to be successful, rapid follow-up action must be taken. If swift action is taken, the enemy's nuclear counterstrike will be late "and do less damage to attacking units."

"The efficient use of time [is] the most important combat quality of a commander." Timely, correct decisions save lives and serve to guarantee victory with minimum losses. Untimely decisions lead to defeat. The introduction of computers, mathematical methods, and cybernetics increases the role of the commander and makes even more necessary the perfecting of the art to evaluate quickly and accurately the information provided by machines.

This article was published in *Communist of the Armed Forces* in February, 1966. Among Colonel Grudinin's other works are *Questions of Dialectics in Military Affairs*, published in 1960, "On Dialectical Negatives in Military Affairs," *Communist of the Armed Forces*, February, 1965, and "The Subjective Factor and Chance in War," *Military Historical Journal*, June, 1965. Another of his articles appears at chapter 24.

WHEN WE SPEAK of the revolution in military affairs, we mean primarily the qualitative jump in the ways and means of armed conflict. This jump has forced our cadres to approach anew the solving of problems of military theory and practice, to work out actively the ability to use for their own interests all actual conditions in which war is conducted, including such an important factor of actions as time.

Time, like space, is a basic form of every being. Being outside of time, F. Engels stressed, is the same sort of nonsense as being outside of space.

Time expresses duration and sequence of existence of objects, processes, and events, and also the rise of new ones and their development along an ascending line. Its basic property is irreversibility. Time flows only forward. It cannot be stopped. The past, present, and future cannot change places. The possible at one time can become the impossible in another. There is a true folk saying: "Lost gold may be found; lost time cannot be restored."

The role of the time factor is exceptionally great in modern war. New kinds of weapons and fighting equipment have made possible the solution of strategic, operational, and tactical problems in a significantly shorter time than in the last war. The rocket weapon, carrying nuclear charges, permits the carrying out of powerful strikes on targets situated at any point in the world and the putting out of action of whole industrial regions and major groupings of troops in the space of minutes. The growing mobility of armies and navies makes it possible to travel great distances in compressed time periods.

The correct use of time in modern war has become one of the most acute problems. Research and elucidation on the subject encompass an extremely wide circle of questions connected with the development and strengthening in peacetime of the economic, moral-political, and military might of the state, with methods of beginning and waging war, and with other questions.

THE TIME FACTOR AND THE COMBAT READINESS OF TROOPS

In a new world war, if the imperialists unleash it, the beginning period will have the most important significance for victory. Those problems of armed conflict, which earlier were solved in months and years, can be decided in minutes, hours, or a few days in modern nuclear rocket war. The first mass nuclear strikes can in large measure predetermine all of the subsequent course of the war and lead to such losses in the rear areas and in the troops that the people and the country could be placed in an exceptionally serious situation. In connection with this, basic changes in the content of the definition of combat readiness of the Armed Forces of the U.S.S.R. have taken place. Now the Armed Forces are combat ready so that at any time of the year, at any minute of the day or night, they can repulse a surprise enemy attack, frustrate the aggressor's attempts to carry out a strike, and achieve the decisive goals of war in its initial period.

War, if the aggressors unleash it, will be a war of two world systems, encompassing dozens of countries. Along with the possibility of a short swift-moving war, the possibility of a long, drawn-out war exists. From this comes the necessity to simultaneously prepare our Armed Forces for winning victory in a short time or in a long battle.

In the event of a drawn-out war, the early preparation both of human reserves and of material resources are needed, plus the ability of the state to expand the production of the means of waging armed conflict quickly in time of war, including conventional sorts of weapons. In these conditions, exceptionally great importance is given to the possibility of augmenting the fighting potential of the army by way of adding reserves to it in good time.

Imperialist governments are carrying out active military preparations. Therefore, socialist countries must be prepared in every way to repulse an aggressor. *The growing significance of the beginning period of a possible thermonuclear war makes exceptionally high demands for achieving the level of combat readiness of the Armed Forces by the given time.* The army and navy must be armed in sufficient quantity with the latest means of fighting and modern equipment for the frustration of a surprise attack of an aggressor and for carrying to him a retaliatory strike. At the present level of development of science and production the superiority of one country in quality and quantity of new weapons might place the opposing side in an incomparably more serious situation than in the past.

As is known, the Soviet Armed Forces began to receive new equipment and weapons long before the Great Patriotic War [World War II]. However, this process was not finished by 1941, which was one of the reasons for our failure in the beginning period of the war. Certain time was needed to liquidate the superiority of the enemy in quantity of new equipment.

In conditions of nuclear rocket war, it will be very difficult or altogether impossible to solve problems of mass production of new equipment and their mastery by the troops in a short time. More *time* is needed now for the production of the latest armaments, and more reserves and qualified working hands are needed. In the foreign press it states that in the 1940's, forty thousand engineering hours were needed to make the German ME–109 fighter. In the 1960's, four million hours were spent on the construction of the American F–104 plane, that is, one hundred times more hours. Because of this, today, winning and keeping military technological supremacy over the probable enemy, while still in time of peace, have decisive significance.

The rapid development of our economy and science is very important for the safety of our Motherland. Creating the material-technical base of communism, speeding up the tempo of industrial production, and raising the production of agriculture directly affects the strengthening of the economy, and the moral-political and military potential of our country.

With the presence of modern ways of delivering the nuclear weapon to the target, the economic structure, side by side with the armed forces, becomes the main objective of strikes. From this comes the necessity for the timely preparation of the territory of the whole country to repel an aggressor.

From the growing role of the time factor comes the necessity for the swift mastery of new equipment, the perfection of the military preparedness of our Armed Forces. High military preparedness grows out of exact calculations, numbers, time periods, hours, and minutes which cannot be violated without running the risk of being taken by surprise. Deviation from the scientifically calculated norms of military preparation can only be for the purpose of further shortening the periods. Nonfulfillment of these norms is fraught with the most serious consequences.

One of the most important trends of the efficient use of peacetime for raising combat readiness of units and subunits is the excellent mastery of weapons in the shortest possible time period. Without this, there cannot be combat readiness; without this, the best organization of the armed forces cannot be worked out to find the most effective method of the combat use of military equipment, and the enemy cannot be defeated.

Now the question of timely mastery of the armaments entrusted to the forces has its specific features. The first of these consists of the fact that at the present time they are receiving exceptionally complicated combat equipment. Thus, a modern ballistic rocket has almost thirty thousand parts. It is completely understandable that this, in large measure, also dictates the term of preparation of corresponding specialists. A similar picture can be seen in mastering other kinds of modern weapons and equipment. In the American newspaper, *Air Force Times*, it was reported, for example, that fifteen years ago a ten-day course of training was needed for the preparation of a specialist in the technical servicing of bombsights, but now fifty-four weeks are needed to prepare a similar specialist for servicing of the B–58 airplane.

The second specific in mastering modern means of warfare consists of the fact that the new equipment is rapidly replaced with still newer equipment. *In these conditions a contradiction arises between the rapid replacement of new equipment with the latest, and the achievement of a level of technical preparedness of personnel.* Without the timely solution of this contradiction, the enemy cannot be defeated in battle and victory in war cannot be won. The possibility of serious lags in the level of technical preparedness of personnel, combat skill, and military art comes up every time a qualitatively new form of weapon or of military equipment comes into service. In order not to permit the lowering of combat readiness, the personnel must master the new armaments and methods of their use in a short time-period. As never before, it is necessary to perfect constantly the training method. Contradictions between the training time of the soldiers and the constantly increasing volume of knowledge which they must master can be resolved only by introducing new technical means and methods of training them.

From ages of practice in the development of military affairs, the formula arose and spread that "the enemy is the best teacher." It follows from this that to learn to fight is possible only during a war.

Of course, there is always something to learn from a strong enemy. But this study cannot be postponed to a period of war. The probable enemy can and must be well known in peacetime. For the armed forces and for military art, the period of peacetime is always highly crucial. The soldier, according to a saying by A. V. Suvorov, is in peacetime what he is in war.

Now, peacetime has decisive significance for the development of military art and the combat training standard of troops. Earlier, insufficiencies in the combat training standard of troops and in the development of military art, which were permitted in peacetime, could be worked out under the blows of the enemy during the course of the war, but now this cannot be done. In other words, what is possible in one set of conditions is impossible in another. In a short swift-moving war, when the beginning period acquires decisive meaning, it would be too late to learn to fight. Those who do not learn to fight the enemy in peacetime are destined to be defeated in war. That is why, indeed, the carrying out in combat training of the principle "learn that which is necessary in contemporary battle" is now a question of life or death. Troops well trained in peacetime can fight the enemy and then perfect their training standard by the experience of conducting combat actions.

Successful combat troop training presupposes the fullest calculation of the strong and the weak sides of the probable enemy. In studying the enemy, it is important to uncover in time the leading tendencies in the development of his armaments, organizational structure, military art, methods of conducting local wars by the imperialists, and methods of training and educating troops. Deep, constant study of the probable enemy serves as one of the main conditions of combat readiness of the armed forces and the preparedness of the country as a whole to repel an aggressor.

THE TIME FACTOR IN THE COURSE OF ARMED CONFLICT

For achieving victory over the enemy, the correct use of time in the course of military actions has exceptionally important significance. The whole of the history of wars shows that time won in transferring troops and in maneuver and attack leads in conjunction with other conditions to the achievement of victory. Swiftness of action and surprise paralyze the will of the enemy, stun him, and lead to confusion.

V. I. Lenin explained that "it is necessary to be able to take the moment into consideration and to be bold in decisions," that "attack on the enemy must be most energetic." Speed of action is impossible without indomitable energy and bold daring. Favorable conditions might be lost. Therefore the choice of the moment of the blow on the enemy is a very important condition for the achievement of victory.

The exceptional significance of the right use of time in armed conflict is expressed in the popular expression "delay in war is like death." The loss of time gives the enemy the chance to concentrate forces, to place them advantageously, to make surprise attacks, to impose his will, to force the acceptance of battle in conditions advantageous to him.

Swiftness of military actions presupposes exact calculation and high mastery. Swiftness of action must not be confused with hastiness and rashness. In the days of the battle against the mutiny of Krasnov-Kerensky, V. I. Lenin stressed: "Not losing a single hour, a single minute, it is necessary to organize ourselves, organize the staff; this must be done today. After organizing, we will be able to secure victory for ourselves in a few days, and perhaps, even sooner." (*Works*, Vol. 26, p. 236.)

During the Great Patriotic War, the swift actions of units and formations of the Soviet Army served as one of the most important conditions of the full defeat of the troops of Fascist Germany and militarist Japan.

Although speed of combat actions and swiftness of attack always played a big role in achieving victory, now they have acquired paramount importance. The destructive force of the nuclear bomb is well known to everyone. Even this weapon, because of insufficiently swift actions, might not produce the right effect. This takes place when time in preparation and realization of the nuclear blow is more than that which the enemy troops spend on dispersion, or when reconnaissance detects corresponding targets and reports them late. In the foreign press, on the basis of experiments, scientists noted that atomic strikes sometimes were delivered to empty or sparsely settled places. The reason for this was that, as a rule, if

252

too much time, up to four hours or more, passes between detecting a target and carrying out an atomic strike on it, the contemplated objective usually changes its location and the nuclear blows are delivered to the place abandoned by the troops.

There is little sense in a nuclear strike when its results are not used before the enemy manages to pull up reserves and repair defenses. In order not to permit him to restore the broken defenses, the attacking formations and units must use the results of their nuclear strikes as soon as possible. Swift advance of troops also leads to delay of the enemy's nuclear counterstrike which results in less damage to attacking units. It follows that speed of action is one of the main conditions for defeating the enemy and for preserving one's own forces.

Speed, speed, and more speed multiplied by decisive and skillful actions—this formula of military art becomes full of new meaning. Now the struggle to gain even a minute will have the most acute character on both sides. It will find expression in attack, defense, meeting engagements, and in frustration of the enemy's counterstrikes. A nuclear blow does not eliminate the necessity of defeating the enemy, especially his reserves, directly in battle. In connection with this, foreign military ideologists widely discuss the question of raising the mobility of troops on the battlefield. In part, they point out that infantry must be able to wage war without getting out of their machines, that all artillery must be self-propelled and possess high mobility and swiftness for concentration and dispersion. It is considered expedient that engineer subunits have the same sort of transport means as the combat arms which they serve. All these and many other measures, in the opinion of foreign military specialists, will permit the tempo of attack to be increased.

Attack operations even in the last war, especially toward the end, were carried out at high tempos. In the campaign in the Far East, Soviet troops covered 50 to 80 kilometers a day and sometimes 100 kilometers or more. In a future war, if one starts, the tempo of attack, in the opinion of several foreign researchers, will grow to 160 kilometers a day.

Even today there is much proof that the law of swift combat actions, in nuclear rocket war, will be given unseen scope. The use of this law is unthinkable without the timely solution of the contradictions between the possibilities of the nuclear rocket weapon acting on the whole depth of the enemy and the possibilities of tanks and motorized infantry swiftly using the results of this action. The further rise in the mobility of combined formations is necessary and also the development in every way of airborne troops.

For achieving success in many aspects of battle, minutes, seconds—even tenths of seconds have become very significant. This refers to bombing with supersonic planes, to air battle of modern fighters, to the actions of surface-to-air missilemen who are called on to destroy the target with the first rocket. The extremely limited time will determine the outcome of tank attacks in co-operation with other service arms which possess great speed of movement without roads.

From artillery is demanded the ability to fire accurately, on the move, without topographical bases, and to begin hitting the target after the first shot. It is important in this to use correctly modern computer means and automatic equipment for directing the fire. The habits of the officer-artillerist of quickly making all possible calculations in the mind and also the habits of clear-cut actions by gun commanders, gun layers, loaders, operators, communications men, and scouts retain their significance.

The dynamics and high tempo of battle evoke the necessity of shortening drastically the time spent on changing the firing position of artillery. This demands from the operators of machines and artillery tractors exact habits to act swiftly in any local condition, time of year, or day. It is important to be concerned in time about the professional preparation and good moral-psychological hardening of this category of servicemen.

Modern equipment and weapons call forth the wide use of nighttime for conducting battle. In this, it must be taken into account that night simultaneously facilitates and hampers the actions of troops. It facilitates by creating great possibilities for secretly carrying out regroupings, occupying forward positions, and carrying out surprise strikes. It hampers by complicating orientation, carrying out of aimed fire, direction of troops, and the prediction of the basic strength of the enemy.

Night actions demand strict camouflage and exceptional co-ordination and accuracy in fulfilling the given missions. In night conditions, it is harder to organize co-operation—especially to co-ordinate the order of use of the atomic weapon with the maneuver of units and subunits. Darkness complicates the organization of combat maintenance. That is why it is important to carry out systematic night exercises, to struggle with indulgences and simplifications in their course, to achieve co-ordination in the actions of subunits and units and the skills of the men to act at night as in the daytime.

THE EFFICIENT USE OF TIME—THE MOST IMPORTANT COMBAT QUALITY OF A COMMANDER

According to the development of means of armed conflict, the influence of the military leaders on the course and the outcome of battle, operations, and on the war as a whole becomes stronger. Their activities serve as one of the chief causes determining the transformation of the possibility of victory into a reality. Timely, correct decisions of the commander effectively given to the troops and accurately brought into action guarantee victory with minimum losses. The untimely decision, as the experience of war testifies, leads to defeat even when superiority over the enemy in forces and means exists.

It can be frankly stated that victory over the enemy at the present time is secured by the high combat readiness of the troops and by swiftness of action by the commander in changing circumstances. These two conditions make it possible to frustrate the intentions of the enemy, to forestall him in the use of nuclear rocket means and in combination with active troop operations, to defeat him in the very shortest time.

Now the contradictions between swiftly changing conditions and the ability of the commander to make correct decisions in a short time become first and foremost. The introduction of complex automatic processes of directing troops, using technical means, permitting the collection, working out, and giving of information in the most efficient form (for example, on an electronic map with colored representations) will make possible the making of decisions in the minimum time. Turning the given possibilities into action calls for the greatest art from the commander, an excellent knowledge of the properties of modern weapons, the correct use of methods of direction, including apparatuses of automatic communications, computers, and the complex conducting of all sorts of reconnaissance.

The introduction of automation into the direction of troops and the use of mathematical methods and cybernetics does not lessen but raises the role of the commander in guiding the troops. And with the presence of the latest equipment, the deciding role in making decisions which meet actual conditions and in putting them into action belongs to people. In other words, the dependence of victory on highly qualified military cadres who are thoroughly prepared in sufficient numbers while it is yet peacetime has grown sharply.

The contradictions between the possibilities of machines which give an enormous quantity of information and the ability of man to master it in a limited time can be solved by way of the further raising of the quality of equipment for automatic direction of troops and by way of perfecting the art of the commander to evaluate quickly and accurately information given by machine.

The timely neutralization of the enemy by nuclear weapons, the quick landing of air troops just after the nuclear blows and also the swift movement of tank units and formations, the wide maneuvers of troops, and the readiness of comparatively small fighting groups to carry out independent actions at great depths depend in large measure on the skill of the military leader.

Slowness in the use of forces and weapons available to the commander, as experience shows, most often leads to failure. On the Voronezh front in the spring of 1942, our troops, possessing superiority in tanks over the enemy, had the chance to upset the plans of Hitler's command. However, because of slowness in organizing active combat operations and in taking sufficient initiative, boldness, and firmness in directing the troops this chance was lost.

The experience of exercises indicates the exceptional importance of training our officers and generals in the skill of creatively analyzing facts and uncovering the essence of appearances. The simple mastering of material is based primarily on keen contemplation, and this does not need deep logical (abstract) thought. In practice, the actions of the commander at each step conflict with the necessity to know independently the nature of conditions in the shortest time.

Each battle and operation has its own special features flowing from actual conditions. In the conditions of war, it often happens that the orders of the senior commander are not worked out in detail and all the responsibility must be taken on by the commander himself without delay. In this sense, the successful combat action of the Forty-first Rifle Division in the first days of the Great Patriotic War might serve as a highly instructive example. On the order of General Major N. G. Mikushev, the division was fully concentrated and brought to combat readiness two days before the attack of the "Hitlerites." The initiative of the commander allowed them to meet the German Fascists' attack with organization and to defend successfully for five days the border area they held from the superior forces of the enemy on the Rava-Russian line. The division left the border only after an order from a higher commander in connection with the general unfavorable condition on the front.

In combat conditions and in the absence of an order of a senior chief, the commander must not wait but act. Meanwhile the experience of tactical studies shows that we still meet commanders who, even after receiving orders, act irresolutely. In one exercise, the subunit commanded by Officer Medvedyev was given the task to defeat the retreating "enemy" with bold and decisive actions and force a crossing of a water barrier on the march. Conditions were favorable for successfully fulfilling the mission; in front of the subunit which had the necessary means of force was a small group of the "enemy." His reserves had not yet managed to reach the river and take up defense positions on the opposite side. The subunit had

257

the chance to move up swiftly to the river and cross it on the march. However, this chance was allowed to slip by. In order to report the circumstances and to receive an order from the higher commander, Officer Medvedyev stopped the vanguard three miles from the river for nearly an hour. In this time the "enemy" brought up reserves, occupied the opposite shore, and the mission had to be fulfilled in more difficult circumstances.

It is not the one who does not achieve the goal of annihilating the enemy who deserves reproach, but the one who, fearing responsibility, does nothing and does not use the favorable moment for success in battle. The commander's initiative must be developed and encouraged in every way possible. Fear of independent actions without higher orders is one of the chief reasons for indecisiveness in the most acute moments of situations. Unnecessary guardianship of a subordinate and particularly blaming him for his independent decisions and actions in the framework of a given problem is the result of not understanding the necessity of initiative in fulfilling orders.

The correct use of time in the course of military operations is one of the most important conditions of winning victory over the enemy. In the century of the rapid growth of military equipment, many complicated questions of directing troops and waging combat operations must be decided in the course of a few minutes or even seconds. To achieve decisiveness is possible only under the skilled organization of combat training, political studies, tactical exercises, and training. All Soviet soldiers are called on to use each minute of study with maximum effectiveness for mastering military affairs and for raising the combat readiness of the Armed Forces in every way possible.

AS LEADER AFTER LEADER in the U.S.S.R. is denounced for "personality cults" and "hare-brained" scheming, the current leadership becomes faced with the problem of explaining how such terrible men could have established and pursued "the wise course" followed in the past by the Soviet Union. The answer is in an understanding of the faceless party and its Central Committee. The Soviet government merely executes party decisions.

The Communist party holds a congress frequently to select new members for the Central Committee, which numbered 360 members in 1966 compared to 330 in 1961. The Central Committee in theory selects the presidium, renamed Politburo, which contains 11 men. The secretariat, also with 11 members, has four of its group, Brezhnev, Kirilenko, Suslov, and Shelepin,[1] who have dual membership in the Politburo. These bodies do the daily work of the party. Periodic plenums of the Central Committee affirm their activities. No one is sure how much power the Central Committee wields, but the pretense is maintained that it represents the 12,000,-000 Communist party members of the U.S.S.R. After nearly fifty years of Communist rule the Central Committee has amassed considerable influence. Therefore the military representation on the Central Committee becomes of some importance. The Soviet Armed Forces' officer corps has a 93 per cent party or Komsomol (Young Communist League) membership. The armed forces as a whole are over 80 per cent Communist party or Komsomol members.

The top ten men of the defense ministry are full members of the Central Committee, as are another nine marshals of the Soviet Union. Another five marshals are candidate members. (There were

---

[1] At the June, 1967, Plenum of the Central Committee CPSU, Shelepin seems to have been dropped from the secretariat.

19 living "marshals of the Soviet Union" on January 1, 1967.) Ten other military members of the Central Committee are commanders of critical military districts or fleets. The chief of civil defense, the minister of communications, the minister of civil aviation, and the chief of DOSAAF (the paramilitary youth organization) are also represented on the Central Committee.

General of the Army Yepishev had a seat on the Central Committee also, as did two other of his political officers. This was an increase in political officer representation, which had been rather severely restricted under Khrushchev. The increase may be a reflection of Leonid Brezhnev's brief tenure (1953–54) as a deputy chief of the Main Political Administration. Like Khrushchev, Brezhnev holds the rank of a general lieutenant (two stars) and was active in World War II as a political adviser.

Thus, through its officer representation, the Soviet Armed Forces took an active part in the XXIII Party Congress held in Moscow from March 29 to April 8, 1966. Marshal Sokolovsky's article, published in the *Communist of the Armed Forces* in April, apparently was timed to coincide with the Congress. This writing, together with the speeches delivered to the Congress by Marshal Malinovsky and General Yepishev, shows a continuation of the nuclear path that had been so openly disclosed to the West by Marshal Sokolovsky's *Military Strategy* of 1962.

---

18. ON CONTEMPORARY MILITARY STRATEGY
BY MARSHAL OF THE SOVIET UNION V. D. SOKOLOVSKY
AND GENERAL MAJOR M. I. CHEREDNICHENKO

Editors' Notes

IN AUGUST 1962, some two months before Soviet missiles were detected in Cuba, *Military Strategy* appeared in Moscow bookstores. In this now-famous book Soviet military theoreticians announced their doctrinal concepts of the all-out nature of future war involving nuclear powers, the global scope of modern war, and the advantages of surprise and of making the first strike. In retrospect, Soviet doctrine as outlined in this book helps to explain their Cuban missile adventure. The authors of the above article, which appeared in *Communist of the Armed Forces* in April, 1966, also contributed to *Military Strategy* while Marshal Sokolovsky himself was editor.

At the time *Military Strategy* was written, the roles and missions of the various components of the Soviet Armed Forces had not been clearly defined. A new command, the Strategic Rocket Forces, had been created in 1960. Missiles were given the primary role in the Soviet force structure. However, there was still the controversy between the "traditionalists" and the "modernists," the former placing emphasis on conventional warfare and the latter advocating nuclear forces. *Military Strategy* was a collection of articles from sixteen different contributors and not all had the same conception of war in a nuclear age.

"On Contemporary Military Strategy" appeared almost four years later and was timed to coincide with the XXIII Party Congress. Marshal Sokolovsky was again selected to restate Soviet military doctrine and strategy. The coauthor of this selection is General Major M. I. Cherednichenko, who also was one of those who criticized, in an article in *Red Star*, the English language version of this book published by RAND[1] and edited by Dinerstein, Gouré, and Wolfe.

The authors reiterate the Communist view that "A new world war would be a decisive armed conflict of two world systems—capitalist and socialist—excluding any sort of compromise." From the side of the "imperialists" such a war would be "unjust"; from the side of the socialist countries it would be a "just war, insofar as it would be directed at the liquidation of imperialism—the sole cause of war. . . ." Any such war "inevitably will acquire global scope; it will be fluid; victory in such a war . . . will be shaped by the high combat readiness of the armed forces, first and foremost by the strategic nuclear forces."

---

[1] RAND has been labeled by the Russians as a "factory of military thought" controlled by the Pentagon.

In 1962 the authors of *Military Strategy* accused the United States of planning a nuclear attack upon the Soviet Union. This current article points up "the danger of surprise nuclear attack" and states that Soviet Armed Forces must be able to "frustrate the aggressive designs of the enemy and to bring defeat to him in a short time." (One wonders if the Soviets hope to "frustrate" the enemy through an antiballistic missile system or by means of a pre-emptive attack.)

"The most acute problem of strategy in contemporary circumstances" the article stresses, *"is the working out of means of waging nuclear rocket war."* Target selection, as given in this Soviet military philosophy, is opposite that of the United States political-military leadership. The Soviet doctrine calls for "the simultaneous action on populated centers and the armed forces of the enemy with nuclear weapons," as stated by these authoritative writers. United States doctrine stresses highly accurate weapons' delivery intended to limit damage to nonmilitary targets.

There is no ambiguity in the basic theme of this article. The authors have stated with emphasis. *"The beginning period of nuclear rocket war, in our opinion, consists of the segment of time from the moment of the breaking out of war to the fulfillment of the basic military, political, and strategic tasks.* Making a retaliatory nuclear strike is its main content, one which might be directed at frustrating a nuclear strike, disorganizing government and military administration, and destroying the economy and armed forces of the aggressor. As a result of the retaliatory nuclear strike on the aggressor, such defeat might be inflicted, after which he could not continue aggressive actions." The delivery systems for these nuclear weapons are rockets, submarines, and aircraft.

Since the publication of *Military Strategy* in 1962, followed by the revised edition in 1963, Marshal Sokolovsky has maintained a position as one of the chief spokesmen of the Ministry of Defense. In February, 1966, he accompanied Premier Kosygin to Tashkent for the settlement of the Indian-Pakistan dispute, and in April, 1966, he was re-elected to the position of candidate member of the Central Committee.

Sokolovsky and Cherednichenko have also coauthored the following articles:

"New Stage of Military Art," *Red Star*, August 28, 1964.
"Some Problems of Soviet Military Development in the Postwar Period," *Military History Journal*, March, 1965.

Red Star reports that the next book by these coauthors will be *Military Art in Nuclear Rocket War* to be published in 1967.

IN CONNECTION with the outfitting of the armies of the largest countries in the world with nuclear rocket means of fighting, the role of military strategy has grown immeasurably and its substance has been radically changed. And it is no wonder that the problems of contemporary strategy became the center of attention of the political and military leadership of the imperialist governments. Politicians and scientists, military theoreticians, and leaders of these countries are occupied with the questions:

Of what do the changes in military strategy consist as compared with the period of classic military art?
What is the role of strategy in contemporary conditions?
What is the interrelationship of strategy with politics, economics, and doctrine?

It is quite understandable that Soviet military thought must also be occupied a great deal with the urgent problems of contemporary strategy. In conditions when the imperialists are speeding up nuclear rocket armaments and are preparing an attack on the Soviet Union, the development of military strategy, the identification of its contents, and the resolution of its problems acquire paramount significance for preparing our country for the sure frustration of a surprise attack and the defeat of the aggressor.

The military ideologists of imperialism create strategic concepts one after another that have directed, on the basis of the aggressive course of imperialism, the preparation of war against socialist and other peace-loving countries. Replacing the bankrupt

263

so-called doctrine of "containment," which had been proclaimed by the ideologists of imperialism soon after the end of World War II, the doctrine of "deterrence" was advanced, which in turn was replaced by the concept of "massive nuclear retaliation" and "flexible response." Now the imperialist militarists are counting on the strategy of "escalation," or the gradual, step-by-step strengthening of military actions, and the accumulation of armed forces and the involvement of many governments in participating in the military conflict. Events in Vietnam convincingly unmask the mankind-hating nature of the policy of the U.S.A., the strategy of "escalation," and all the multiplicity of actions of the theoreticians and the practitioners from the Pentagon in preparing for a new world war.

In the aggressive plans of the imperialist militarists, a large place is allotted to the analysis of modern military strategy.

A famous specialist in the realm of strategy, the French General Beaufre, in the book, *Introduction to Strategy*, asserts that the former concept of strategy as the art of using armed forces to achieve political aims is outmoded; that now a new strategy is being advanced as a means of instilling fear; that is, the strategy of threatening the employment of nuclear weapons. By this is meant that instilling fear might be effective in the face of a real threat of nuclear attack.

The opinions of a Harvard professor of economics, T. Schelling, have much in common with the opinions of Beaufre. In his book, *The Strategy of Conflict*, he presents strategy as a means of developing a method of action, of imposing it persistently on the enemy under the threat of a nuclear strike, and of achieving the goals of American imperialism. In essence, it is an attempt to find theoretical basis for the arms race, to justify the strategy of "flexible response" and "escalation of war" of American imperialism, and to justify the nuclear solicitation of the West German *revanchists*. The strategy of instilling fear, in the final analysis, is the strategy of deterrence.

The English military theoretician, Liddell Hart, treats the content of modern strategy in a somewhat different sense. By military strategy he means the art of deployment and employment of armed

264

forces for achieving objectives set by politics. The same point of view is held by the American military writer H. Baldwin. In the article, "The Global Strategy of the U.S.A.," he writes: "Strategy, like war, is an art and not a science." "National strategy," Baldwin stresses, "supposes the application and not the simple formulation of a definite form of action." In other words, military strategy is imperialist aggression in action.

In the opinion of the chief of staff of the armed forces of France, Army General Ailleret, it is improper to apply to the concept of "strategy" a sense of either science or art, or any other discipline having a quite definite content. "Strategy," he writes, "is the area of the practical activities of the higher military leadership." In this definition, one side of strategy is taken—"the activities of the heads of the government carrying out the leadership of war," and the chief of staff's developing "for the heads of government, military aspects of the common strategy." The activity of millions of people united in the armed forces is left in the shadow.

General Ailleret skeptically views attempts to develop a theory of strategy. In his opinion, such a theory would present elementary truths having no practical meaning. However, many bourgeois military leaders do not deny the important role of strategy and are making great efforts in the theoretical working out of its problems.

Of course, one could bring in other examples of the interpretation of the content of modern military strategy in the West. But the question here is not about the quantity of statements of bourgeois military ideologists, but that all the different interpretations of strategy by them in the final analysis lead to one thing—to the attempt to introduce into the concept a rationale which would justify preparation for aggressive wars. While disclosing the ideological factors of bourgeois military theoreticians and political figures, it is important to see the real content of the aggressive military strategy of imperialism, to thoroughly analyze this content, and to make the right conclusions.

Military strategy is a complicated social phenomenon. It includes the theory and practice of the preparation and the waging of war, the area of activity of the higher military leadership of the govern-

265

ment in the co-ordinated use of the armed forces of a country for achieving the goals of any war.

Being a component part of military art, contemporary military strategy concerns all of the armed forces and first of all the strategic nuclear forces. Its object is the co-ordinated action of all the forces and equipment for achieving the goals of war and of the creative activities of people united in the army and navy. Strategy which ignores the creative activities of millions of people is doomed to failure.

Military strategy embraces the military actions on a strategic scale. Operational art and tactics determine more concrete forms and methods of armed struggle, and direct the forces of subunits and units in the achievement of strategic goals of war. Thus, between strategy and operational art and tactics there is a close relationship and interdependence; however, strategy plays the principal, determining role.

At the same time military strategy is the realm of practical activities of the higher political and military leadership. It represents the art of the higher organs of direction in the organization of the necessary forces and means, their preparation for war, and in the co-ordinated employment of armed forces, primarily strategic nuclear forces, for the solution of military-political and strategic problems of any war. Strategic leadership must organize millions of people united in the armed forces, must purposefully direct their active military efforts toward the accomplishment of military tasks.

Military strategy is unthinkable without scientifically based theory. Summarizing historical experience, evaluating the international and internal political conditions, the economic potential of the country, the characteristics of the equipment used in fighting, the capabilities and the nature of the enemy's actions, the theory of strategy works out the ways of preparing and waging war, in agreement with the use of the armed forces as a whole and also of each separate arm of service.

Theoretical research permits the exposure of the class nature of military strategy, its ties with, and its interdependence on the politics and economics of the government and with all aspects of society. As is known, in contemporary conditions, the strategy of imperialistic government is aggressive, mankind-hating, primarily directed at preparing and unleashing nuclear war against the socialist countries. Simultaneously, there is the military strategy of socialist countries, pursuing in the highest degree just and progressive goals—it must ensure the security of the socialist camp, curb the aggressive aspirations of imperialism, and be directed at frustrating and warding off imperialist aggression. Even young governments and nations, who have recently won their independence and are struggling against imperialism for freedom and national independence, have their own military strategy.

V. I. Lenin stated that war was the continuation by violent means of those policies which guided the belligerent powers and the ruling classes long before the war. From this follows the subordination of strategy in relation to politics, the full dependence of strategy on politics.

Military strategy is inseparably linked with the social and political structure of any government. The political leadership of a country determines the military, political, and strategic goals, selects the ways and forms of waging war, ensures the conformity of the political aims of the war to the military and economic potential of the country, creates conditions for achieving the established goals, mobilizing for this human and material resources. Military strategy finds and puts into practice the ways of achieving established political goals through armed struggle. In turn, politics is often forced to reckon with the demands of military strategy. The converse influence of strategy on politics occurs.

The use of armed forces in war is in direct dependence on economics. The economic conditions determine methods and ways of waging armed battle, that is, military art; strategy is also in this category. The appearance of nuclear weapons and strategic rockets —these main decisive instruments of war—is the result of the achievements of economics, science, and technology. This led to changes in the structure of the armed forces and evoked a deep revolution in military affairs, especially in strategy.

In addition, one must take into account that economics also

267

cannot now be developed without a stocktaking of strategic considerations. This is reflected in the production of combat equipment, in the distribution of production forces, in raising the stability of economics in conditions of nuclear war, in developing technology, creating reserves, reconstructing the economy for the war effort, and so forth.

Let us take up the relationship between military doctrine and military strategy. Military doctrine, as is known, determines the main direction of the military structure, the preparation of the country and armed forces to repulse aggression for the decisive defeat of the enemy in the event of war. It is a scientific system of views on war, raised to a degree of mandatory direction in any given government. It determines the general principles, the propositions for ensuring a reliable defense for the government's security and the ensuing requirements for building and preparing the armed forces, and for personnel training. Military strategy issues from these principles and propositions, is governed by them, works out and researches concrete questions guaranteeing the realization of the doctrinal premises. In its turn, military doctrine uses the achievements in the development of military strategy, converts some of the most important of its premises, proved by practice, into doctrine.

Guided by the propositions of Marxist-Leninist teachings about war and armies and also by military doctrine, our strategy always takes into account the nature and character of various types of war. A new world war would be a decisive armed conflict of two world systems—capitalistic and socialistic—excluding any sort of compromise. From the side of the imperialists, this would be a reactionary, unjust war, a continuation of the aggressive policies of imperialistic government, directed at annihilating socialist countries. And the result of such a war would unavoidably be the death of imperialism. From the side of socialist countries subject to imperialist aggression, it would be a just war insofar as it would be directed at the liquidation of imperialism—the sole cause of war—and at securing the gains of socialism. However, such a war inevitably would lead to unimaginable destruction, enormous sacrifices, and suffering of the people of the world. Therefore, the people not only of socialist countries but of all the countries of the world are vitally interested in preventing the unleashing by imperialism of a world nuclear war.

For a long time the imperialist governments have directed the preparation for a new world war along all lines—political, ideological, economic, and especially military. With each year this preparation becomes more and more sinister and dangerous. The imperialists are trying to do everything beforehand, in peacetime, in order to achieve their goals in war in a short time.

The socialist countries must take corresponding measures in preparing their own armed forces, economy, and people to frustrate the criminal plots of the imperialists. The constant readiness of socialist governments to deliver a crushing blow in retaliation for the aggression of the imperialists is the sure restraining factor in the path of the predatory aims of imperialism. Military strategy of socialist countries is also called on to decide these complicated problems.

The range of problems of military strategy includes the determination of the bases of the building of the armed forces, its structure, the equipping of it with combat equipment and armaments and with material, the principles of using the armed forces as a whole and each service of the armed forces separately. This problem, both in theory and in practice, is determined by the results of demands for guaranteeing the security of the country in any situation, taking into account the levels of economic development, scientific and technological achievements, and also the aggressive measures of the probable enemy.

Strategy must determine in time the trend in the development of the armed forces and of the means of armed conflict; it must work out the necessary recommendations for application. It can cope with this only in the event that it is armed with the scientific method of dialectical materialism and if it studies all the phenomena and processes of military affairs deeply and from all sides and if it boldly glances into the future. In the contrary case, its recommendations might turn out to be in error, so that it will unavoidably cause damage to the defense potential of the country.

Perhaps *the most crucial task of strategy is strategic planning.* This question always stands in the center of attention of the military leadership of any country.

The experience of history teaches that the successful conduct of combat actions, especially in the beginning period, in significant measure depends on the art of strategic planning, on the skill of the political and military leadership in realistically evaluating the enemy's and one's own potential and, in the event of war, in using these capabilities for victory over the enemy.

It is known that great significance is given in imperialist countries to the question of strategic planning. In the U.S.A. this work goes on under the leadership of the National Security Council and the President himself. The immediate leadership of strategic planning belongs to the Joint Chiefs of Staff who carry out the planning for employment of strategic nuclear forces in world nuclear war, conventional forces in nuclear and in local wars, and also the coordination of plans of military blocs in various theaters. Thus the working out of plans is made more exact each year and is tested in numerous exercises and maneuvers and is recomputed on electronic computers, about which the responsible military leaders of the U.S.A. openly speak quite often.

In the aggressive bloc of NATO, the strategic planning is carried out under the leadership of the NATO Council. Under the Supreme Headquarters of NATO a special group of planners was created consisting of a large number of generals and officers of all countries that are partners of the bloc. A more and more sinister role in strategic planning is being played by the *revanchists* of the FRG. Already supervision for all planning, including planning in the area of nuclear weapons, for a rather long time has been carried out by a West German general—a deputy chief of staff of the supreme headquarters for plans and operations of NATO. Being discussed in NATO is a United States proposal for creation, from the war departments of the basic bloc member countries, of a spe-

270

cial committee on planning, which is calculated for the admittance of the representatives of FRG to planning the employment not only of the operational-tactical but also of the strategic nuclear weapons now in the hands of the U.S.A.

The strategic planning of NATO bears an openly aggressive character. It is built on the dictates of American militarists and on the disregard of the interests of many members of the bloc, which leads to disagreement inside this aggressive organization. Nevertheless, the system of strategic planning of the imperialist camp functions and presents a serious threat to the cause of peace.

The planning of a repulse of imperialist aggression in contemporary conditions has become an immeasurably more complicated problem than in the past. This is because a new world war, if it is unleashed by the imperialists, will use weapons of unseen destructive force; such a war inevitably will acquire global scope; it will be short and swift-moving; victory in such a war, in significant measure, will be determined by the high combat readiness of the armed forces, first and foremost of the strategic nuclear forces, with the art of their effective employment. The planning of military actions now has turned into a highly complicated scientific problem.

The determination of the composition of the armed forces for peacetime and especially for time of war; the making of a reserve of arms, military equipment, and, primarily, nuclear rocket weapons as the main means of war, as well as material reserves, deploying strategic groups and organizing the all-round security of the armed forces in time of war—this is the crucial task of military strategy. In the past, the big governments usually kept a comparatively small number of armed forces in peacetime, planning for the securing of a minimum protection of the border and for securing their mobilization deployment in the event of war. The general staff worked out plans of mobilization deployment, for moving troops into the theater of military operations, and for making strategic groupings, and also plans for mobilization deployment of all the economic resources and plans of transporting material and troops to theaters of war. In contemporary conditions all these questions must be solved in a different way.

271

The aggressive imperialist governments have rejected the previous principles of mobilization deployment of their armed forces immediately before the war and also at the beginning of it. For the implementation of aggressive plans, the imperialists are making efforts, in order to have the necessary groupings of armed forces in corresponding regions while it is still peacetime, for deciding the chief missions of war in a short period of time. The U.S.A. and the military bloc of NATO have already prepared, in essence, the grouping of strategic nuclear forces—intercontinental rockets, atomic rocket submarines, and strategic aviation; groupings of operational-tactical nuclear forces and land forces in Europe and in other regions; fleet groupings in the Atlantic, the Mediterranean Sea, the Pacific Ocean, and groupings of forces and means of air defense in North America and in Europe. At the same time, the imperialist governments are preparing large reserves for the deployment of mass armed forces in the course of the war.

The danger of surprise nuclear attack of an aggressor is forcing the Soviet Union to have in constant combat readiness such Armed Forces as would be able in time to deliver a shattering retaliatory nuclear strike, to frustrate the aggressive designs of the enemy, and to bring defeat to him in a short period of time. These Armed Forces are made up of Strategic Rocket Troops, atomic rocket submarines, long-range aviation, the National PVO [air defense] Troops and also the necessary composition of Ground Forces, Air Forces, and Naval Forces.

The most acute problem of strategy in contemporary circumstances is the working out of methods of waging nuclear rocket war. This problem has been found in the center of attention of military theorists and practitioners of many governments for a long time. There are sharp polemics on this which have fundamental significance because the deepest changes have taken place in this field.

First of all the question arose as to what is the main object of armed conflict. In the past, combat actions led to the mutual annihilation of the armed forces of the belligerents in the theaters of military action. In contemporary conditions, the position has radically changed. For rockets with nuclear charges, the front line saturated with troops is not an obstacle and distance plays no practical role. The economy of the country, the system of government administration, the armed forces, including strategic nuclear forces —all these are easily accessible to modern means of battle and could be destroyed in a very short time. The simultaneous action with nuclear weapons on vital centers and on the armed forces of the enemy is the basic method of waging nuclear rocket war. The main and most reliable force now is the Strategic Rocket Troops.

With this question is connected the question of aspects and forms of strategic actions. The basic aspects of strategic actions in the past were the strategic assault and the strategic defense, in which the ground forces came forth as the main force. In nuclear rocket war, an aspect of strategic actions new in principle—the strikes of strategic nuclear forces on military, economic, and political objectives of the enemy, that is, the operations of the strategic rocket forces, atomic rocket submarines, and long-range aviation—moves out into the forefront. One of the main aspects of strategic action is that of national PVO in protecting the country and armed forces from the nuclear blows of the enemy. It is completely probable that in nuclear rocket war the previous forms of strategic action, such as strategic attack in ground theaters, defense in isolated sectors, and also the active operations of the forces of the fleet on ocean and sea theaters, will find a use, although the modes of their use have been basically changed insofar as here the main problems will be solved by nuclear strikes.

Each aspect of strategic actions and armed conflict as a whole will be conducted in concrete form, limited by missions, space, time, forces, and means. Military strategy must work out forms of combat actions having valid application. As already noted in the press, the working out and the mastering of such forms as nuclear strikes of strategic forces, the operations of the troops of national PVO and PRO [antirocket defense], strategic assault operations in land theaters, naval operations in ocean theaters, and also airborne operations, have most important significance in nuclear rocket war.

It is known that nuclear rocket weapons and other new combat equipment open great possibilities for surprise attack. It has become possible to deliver enormous destruction and devastation to the territory of the enemy in an exceptionally short time, literally to be counted in days and hours. The imperialists are taking this into account and therefore are counting on a surprise nuclear strike. From the numerous statements in the overseas press, it is known that the military leadership of the imperialist bloc is planning to employ the primary stockpile of nuclear charges in the first few days after the beginning of nuclear war and by this to predetermine its outcome in their favor. Military theoreticians of the West figure that this will make up the beginning period of world nuclear war. In this period it is proposed to carry out so-called nuclear attack or aerospace operations involving both strategic and operational-tactical nuclear forces. Strategic nuclear forces are for strikes on targets deep in the territory of the socialist countries for the purpose of creating "atomic chaos" or, in the definition of McNamara, "the assured destruction" of socialist countries as "an organized society." Nuclear forces in theaters are designed to be used for winning nuclear superiority and to guarantee the first strategic attack operation.

Along with the increased possibilities for surprise attack, the possibilities are growing for the timely detection not only for the beginning of an attack but also of the beginning of the direct preparations by the enemy of an attack, that is, there are possibilities of preventing a surprise attack.

The beginning period of nuclear rocket war, in our opinion, consists of the segment of time from the moment of the breaking out of war to the fulfillment of the basic military, political, and strategic tasks. Making a retaliatory nuclear strike is its main content, one which might be directed at frustrating a nuclear attack, disorganizing government and military administration, and destroying the economy and armed forces of the aggressor. As a result of the retaliatory nuclear strike on the aggressor such defeat might be inflicted after which he could not continue aggressive actions. Simultaneously with the retaliatory strike or soon after it, active military actions of all forces will be launched with the aim of warding off nuclear blows of the enemy with the forces and means of

274

PVO and of completing the crushing defeat of his armed forces with land forces, aviation, and naval forces.

Military strategy must contribute to the solution of complicated and crucial tasks of the beginning period of nuclear rocket war. The ensuring of high combat readiness of the nuclear forces, the forces and equipment of PVO and PRO, all systems of intelligence service, detection, and warning now takes on special significance. Victory in contemporary war may be achieved by active, decisive actions and full use of the combat capabilities of all forces and means of struggle and by efficient co-operation between them.

The use, by strategy, of our moral and political supremacy over the enemy and the calculation of his weak points in this relation will have great significance for the successful waging of war. In modern war the people with high morale will win—those who are convinced of the rightness of that cause for which they are fighting. In these conditions, exceptional significance is acquired by the all-round ideological work of strengthening the moral and fighting spirit of the troops and the creation in our soldiers of great aggressive spirit and the readiness to fulfill their obligation in any circumstance of battle.

Within the realm of questions of war strategy falls the securing of firm and continuous direction of the armed forces. Successful management of the army and the navy is now possible under the conditions of equipping all systems of management with modern computer equipment, high-speed communications equipment, and equipment for automating the basic work of management. It is important to provide for the constant high combat readiness of all systems of control.

The role of strategy in achieving victory in war has not always been the same. As is known, previously strategic success somehow came about from operational and tactical successes, from results of actions on an operational and tactical scale. For wars employing conventional weapons, this proposal, to a certain degree, remains in force even for modern conditions. As concerns nuclear rocket war, then the role of strategy fundamentally changes. Under the

275

immediate control of strategic leadership are such powerful weapons of battle which may decide the basic missions of war.

The outcome of armed combat in nuclear rocket war will take shape mainly through use of strategic nuclear rocket weapons. In connection with this, strategy in a greater degree than ever before has become the main decisive part of military art. The working out of the questions of military strategy in the contemporary stage acquires paramount significance for the preparation of the armed forces and for all the country to repulse aggression.

It is known that in the U.S.A., and in other countries that are partners in NATO, special attention is being given to working out questions of military strategy. For this, scientists of different specialties have been attracted on a wide scale to carry out research on the problems of strategy, using the achievements of science and technology and computer machines, under the instructions of the ruling circles of the imperialist governments. A special corporation has been set up under the Pentagon called RAND—an original factory of military thought where engineers, mathematicians, physicists, philosophers, economists, astronomers, and so forth, work. The mission of the corporation—the scientific working out of plans for thermonuclear war. The Hudson Institute, headed by the famous military theoretician and ideologist of imperialism, H. Kahn, and many other scientific institutions have been drawn in for the solving of many military problems.

In England, a special institute for strategic research has been established, headed by a scientist, A. Buchan. Side by side with these are unofficial institutes such as the British Institute for Strategic Studies, headed by the former prime minister of Great Britain, Lord Attlee. Under the NATO Supreme Command, there is a technical center in which models of military actions are worked out and consideration is given to all factors.

The higher organs of military leadership of imperialist governments—the military departments, committee of the chiefs of staff, general staffs, staffs of armed services, and so forth—are constantly occupied with the questions of military strategy. They constantly refine and renovate the strategic plans of war, the plans of the construction of the armed forces, the development of means of fighting, and the questions of strategic deployment; they develop doctrinal and strategical concepts; they conduct studies and maneuvers, and create and play model war. All this huge army of scientific, military, and political figures of the imperialistic countries work by the sweat of their brows on the tasks of their own monopolistic masters at planning openly aggressive strategy.

The strategy of the socialist countries opposes the aggressive strategy of imperialism and is able to assure the frustration of any intention of the imperialists. From this comes the great demand to work out the contemporary problems of strategy, both on the theoretical and on the practical plane.

Military strategy and its theory are component parts of military science. The working out of the theory of military strategy, in essence, represents specific social research.

As in other social sciences, the theory of military strategy is called on to expose pressing problems and tasks and to indicate the valid path of their solution, to serve as a scientific basis of party policy in questions of protecting the country. It is fully understood that the deficiencies of social sciences, being printed in our periodical press, are inherent in military strategy as well. Without a scientific approach, no sort of problem of modern strategy can possibly be decided. For this, it is required that practice be actively generalized, the chief tendencies in the development of military affairs be determined, and the conclusions for practical work be extracted. The great advantage to be gained from the broad application of mathematical methods of solving theoretical and practical problems in strategy is now already apparent to everyone.

Contemporary Soviet military strategy is built on a scientific Marxist-Leninist basis and has close ties with practice; it takes into account the development of foreign military strategy, and bases itself on the level of development achieved by other sciences. Expanding the front of strategic research makes necessary a bolder involvement in this work of scientists of different specialties, generals, admirals, and officers having corresponding preparation. The collective comparison of different points of view in order to rule out erroneous opinions has important significance in the discussion of the problems of strategy.

Experience itself has brought forth the problems. Their successful solution will play an important role in further strengthening our defense capabilities and in raising the readiness of our Armed Forces to repulse a possible imperialist aggressor.

---

19. ADDRESS TO THE XXIII CONGRESS CPSU
By Marshal of the Soviet Union
Rodion Ya. Malinovsky (1898–1967)
Minister of Defense, U.S.S.R. (1957–67)

Editors' Notes

THE FIRST CHAPTER of our book was an article by Marshal Malinovsky, written in 1964. The following is a speech by the same marshal, who in his capacity as minister of defense reported to the XXIII Congress of the Communist party of the Soviet Union during the session in April, 1966.

The initial part of his speech contains standard polemics against the United States. Because this is only indirectly concerned with the "Revolution in Military Affairs," we considered deleting it. However, since *détente* is a word frequently used by many United States officials when referring to relations of the United States with the Soviet Union, we included the entire address.

Marshal Malinovsky provides a summing up of the changes within the Soviet Armed Forces over the past several years. Attention is first directed to the strategic nuclear forces and to the strategic rocket forces in particular, for which "has been built a large quantity of new, and even more important, . . . *mobile launchers*."[1] Notice is then given to "new atomic rocket-carrying submarines" and "long-range rocket-carrying aviation." Finally, somewhat more cursory reference is made to all other arms of the Soviet military forces. The mysterious "blue belt" is mentioned also.

1 Emphasis has been added.

Because Marshal Malinovsky was reporting to the Congress of the Communist party, he gave specific attention to ideological matters. "About 93 per cent of the officers, generals, and admirals in the Armed Forces are Communists and Komsomols." Throughout the armed forces as a whole, when all ranks are considered, 80 per cent are either Communists or Komsomols. "The command staff, political organs, and party organizations are the conductors of party ideas, skillfully and purposefully educating the personnel in . . . hatred for imperialist aggressors."

If Marshal Malinovsky's writing in this chapter is compared with his views in chapter 1 the reader can see a continued commitment to the concept of the decisive role which nuclear rockets will play in any future war.

COMRADES: The soldiers of the Soviet Armed Forces, Communists of the army and navy, like all of our people, have come to the XXIII Congress CPSU closely united around the party, the Leninist Central Committee and the Soviet government, in readiness to fulfill any order of the Motherland.

The troops of the army and navy have received the draft directive for the new five-year plan with great enthusiasm and approval.

In these days all the minds and thoughts of our soldiers are concentrated on the work of the XXIII Congress as an event of genuine historical significance. The Congress plays a great role in the further strengthening of the economic and defensive might of the Soviet government.

Permit me to give to you, delegates of the Congress, the warm fighting greeting from our glorious Armed Forces.

Comrades! We have all listened with deep attention to the report of First Secretary of the Central Committee CPSU, Comrade Leonid Il'ich Brezhnev. The activity of the Central Committee shows with extreme clarity that the fighting headquarters of our party holds high the banner of the revolutionary ideas of Marxism-Leninism and firmly leads the country along the Leninist way.

Again and again is revealed to us the timeliness and the vitalness of the decision of the October (1964) and subsequent plenums of the Central Committee, which exerted an exceptionally beneficial influence on the activity of the party and the people. They have raised still higher the authority of the party, the energy of the Soviet people—our working class, collective farmers, intelligentsia, and the soldiers of the Soviet Army and Navy.

The results and the perspectives of the building of communism in the U.S.S.R. gladden all of us and our foreign friends.

Of course, our successes go against the grain of the ruling circles of capitalist states. The imperialists can in no way be reconciled with the triumphant procession of the Soviet Union to communism, with the building of socialism in the countries of the people's democracies, with the widening range of the liberation struggles of the peoples. They have not abandoned the delirious idea of destroying socialist countries by force.

Especially raging are the American imperialists who have taken on themselves the role of "saviors" of the capitalist system. The ruling circles of the U.S.A. are stubbornly whipping up the arms race, persistently perfecting their military machine, equipping it with predominantly offensive fighting means—intercontinental ballistic missiles and atomic submarines with "Polaris" missiles. In this arms race, other Western powers also take an active part.

The leaders of Washington with all their might are trying to strengthen the aggressive military-political blocs and primarily NATO. But the facts tell of serious contradictions becoming more and more acute in the North Atlantic aggressive bloc. Many partners of the bloc do not want to be reconciled with the dictates of American militarism; they do not want to be drawn into world nuclear war. A sufficient indicator of the unceremonious dictates of the U.S.A. is the stubborn striving, in spite of the catastrophe over Spain, to continue flights of their strategic bombers with nuclear bombs over Western countries. These daily flights by no means demonstrate the force and might of the American imperialists, but rather they indicate their weakness.

In carrying out a colonial policy, the U.S.A. insolently interferes in the internal affairs of the peoples of other countries, organizes reactionary revolutions, especially in young national states, and sets up regimes in them to please themselves. They attack independent states at their own discretion and do unheard-of barbarities there, evoking by this the hatred and condemnation of the whole world.

The unleashing by the American imperialists of a war in Vietnam, the ground of which has been turned into a sort of testing area by the overseas robbers for trying out all kinds of poisonous gases, modern weapons, and military equipment, is a serious threat to the peace. Recalling to people's minds the dark days of fascism, the bosses of the Pentagon subject the cities and villages of the Democratic Republic of Vietnam to barbarian bombardment and are carrying out the tactics of "scorched earth" in South Vietnam.

We are deeply convinced that the latter-day "conquerors" will not succeed in breaking the will of the Vietnamese patriots and in forcing them to their knees. The Vietnamese people are not alone. The people of the socialist countries, millions and millions of people in the whole world, are on their side. The U.S.S.R. has rendered and will render unselfish and decisive aid to the heroic Vietnamese in their just and courageous struggle for their freedom and independence.

Speaking of events in Southeast Asia, one should not forget about Europe. Here the coals of the last war continue to glow; they can light the fires of a new war, which would be nuclear and still more destructive and catastrophic in its results.

The U.S.A. is trying to legalize the access of FRG to the nuclear arsenal. In turn, West Germany is taking every measure to become one of the leading members of the "nuclear club" of NATO and is pretending to leadership in it. In the last ten years Bonn's military expenditures have been two hundred billion marks, which is twice what the Hitlerites spent on preparing for the Second World War.

The ruling circles of FRG are openly demanding the approval of the Western allies for their policy of revenge and for the recognition of their hegemony in NATO side by side with the U.S.A. including "full equal rights" in the planning and the use of nuclear weapons. All these pretensions have been raised to the rank of

Bonn's state policy. This becomes especially clear in the program statement of Erhard in the *Bundestag*, November 10, 1965, in which demands were put forth to review the results of the Second World War and to remove the responsibility for it from German imperialism and its West German heirs. Demands were made for a review of the postwar boundaries in Europe and for the removal of any restrictions on the FRG in the area of nuclear armaments.

The Central Committee CPSU and the Soviet government firmly and consistently pursue a Leninist peace-loving course, persistently struggle for the creation of favorable conditions for the building of a Communist society in the U.S.S.R. and for the development of the world system of socialism, for preventing new world war. In this the party cannot fail to take into account the growing aggressiveness of the imperialist powers headed by the U.S.A. Concerned about the security of our people and the peoples of other socialist countries, the party is taking all the measures for strengthening the defense potential of the Soviet Union.

The Soviet Union cannot be apathetic to the military preparations of the imperialists. Under these circumstances we consider it our main task to raise with unremitting persistence the military power of the army and the navy and their readiness to defeat any enemy if war is imposed on us.

For the Soviet Armed Forces, the period since the XXII Congress of the party was attended by the solution of many highly complicated and extremely important problems of military organization. The measures carried out in this direction permitted an increase of the reserves of nuclear ammunition of various designations and also sharply strengthened the equipping of the services of the Armed Forces with means of its delivery.

Considerable attention during these years was given by the Central Committee of the Communist party and the Soviet government to the development of our Strategic Rocket Troops and atomic rocket submarines. The basic efforts of the chief branches of our military industry were subordinated to the rapid build-up of these forces which compose the chief means of restraining the aggressor and of decisively defeating him in war. All of the newest achieve-

282

ments of Soviet science and industry were used in the interests of the perfection of these [branches of the armed services].

By the heroic labor of our workers, engineers, constructors, and scientists, a series of essentially new aspects of rocket armaments has been created. In a short time, a whole complex of various strategic means of battle has been put into operation. In the Strategic Rocket Forces there has been built a large quantity of new, and even more important, mobile launchers, for which we give the constructors, engineers, and workers of the defense industry our deep thanks.

Along with the Strategic Rocket Forces, we have created during these years an underwater rocket-carrying fleet which is able to fulfill strategic missions of destroying enemy objectives both on sea and on land. It includes new atomic rocket-carrying submarines armed with ballistic rockets having underwater launch capability and great range. Our long-range rocket-carrying aviation has also increased its nuclear power.

Simultaneously with the development of strategic nuclear weapons, tactical-operational nuclear means were also developed, especially for the Ground Forces and the Navy. The arming of the Armed Forces with conventional means of fighting has also been intensified proportionally. Tanks and motorized infantry divisions have received more modern armored tanks, artillery, and special equipment in armaments. Soviet tanks, in a number of important aspects, are superior to the latest sorts of tanks of the U.S.A. and the other countries belonging to NATO. The per cent of armored protection of the troop personnel from the action of the lethal factors of nuclear weapons has been increased much more. The mobility and maneuverability of the Ground Forces have been increased. The signal corps, the engineers, and others have received further development.

New, highly effective surface-to-air rocket systems and aviation complexes of interceptor aircraft have been worked out and adopted into armaments. Our PVO weapons guarantee the reliable destruction of any airplane and many rockets of the enemy's. Long-range aviation has qualitatively changed. A significant part of the stock of military airplanes, frontal, naval rocket-carrying, and especially military transport aviation has been renovated.

Our airborne assault troops have been significantly strengthened. During recent years they have shown good results in the combat training of personnel. In 1965 and the first months of 1966, paratroopers have made half a million jumps and have dropped by parachute many heavy pieces of equipment and cargo. Soviet paratroopers can appear in the rear of the enemy with everything necessary, even medium tanks, for a successful waging of battle; and they are able to resolve great strategic tasks in modern war.

New rocket ships, forces, and means of antisubmarine defense especially made for battle with rocket submarines of the aggressor have been added to the equipment of the navy.

The technical equipping of all the branches of the Armed Forces was accompanied with the constant perfection of their combat readiness and by the raising of the level of their combat and political training. Personnel of the army and navy are successfully mastering new military equipment and have the ability to use it in battle and operations.

In recent years we conducted a great quantity of rocket launchings, combat firings, large operations, and troop practices. The overwhelming majority of them were completed successfully in spite of complicated conditions in fulfilling the combat tasks. It is sufficient to note, for example, that almost all rocket launchings made in the past year were rated "good" or "excellent."

In recent years the quantity of long voyages by our atomic submarines has increased five times, which dramatically demonstrates the ability of our glorious sailors to successfully fulfill any combat task in the ocean expanse from the arctic to the antarctic. A few days ago, a round-the-world voyage of a group of atomic submarines in a submerged state was successfully completed.

All this makes it possible to say with assurance that the Soviet Armed Forces can fulfill any combat task which might be placed before them by the party and by the government for the defense of our Motherland.

I would especially like to stress that in the last few years military

284

collaboration has been widened and strengthened with the fraternal armies of the countries who are members of the Warsaw Pact—created for the protection and defense of the peaceful labor and development of its people and permeated by the unity of interests of the socialist countries. Collaboration finds its reflection in the jointly-carried-out exercises and maneuvers, in the systematic exchange of experience in the operational and combat training of troops, and, also, in achievements in the area of military-technical and theoretical research. All this contributes to better mutual understanding and unity of views on questions of training and conducting contemporary operations.

The basic qualitative changes which have taken place in the Soviet Armed Forces have now forced the leaders of the Pentagon to evaluate our military might more soberly and to approach differently the estimate of the established relationships of military forces in the world.

The Secretary of Defense of the U.S.A., Robert McNamara, in his report last year to the Armed Services Committee of the House of Representatives had to admit that an attack of Soviet strategic rockets on just two hundred cities in the U.S.A. might in a few hours result in the annihilation of 149,000,000 people and two-thirds of the industrial potential of the country.

True, McNamara still tries, as before, to substantiate the alleged unlimited military power of American imperialism. As before, his militant and bragging statements—in which he, in a sensational way, boasts the creation by the Americans of a means for annihilating millions of people and makes cannibalistic assessment of victims and destruction—have not ceased.

We do not have to advertise our Armed Forces. They are made not for attack but for defending the borders of our country and for assuring the safety of our people and countries friendly to us.

We quietly and confidently stand on guard over the peaceful labor of our own people more staunchly now that the creation of a blue belt of defense of our government has been created. In any event, if the imperialists try to unleash war against the Soviet Union and other socialist countries, there can be no doubt then that our

285

blow will prove to be devastating for the organizers of the war. In connection with the complicated nature of the contemporary international situation and of the uninterrupted war provocations of the imperialist powers, we, in the interest of guaranteeing the peace and safety of the peoples, will continue in the future to perfect our Armed Forces, to strengthen their power and combat readiness.

Comrades! The power of our Armed Forces is included not only in first-class weapons which we have on our hands. It is also composed of the strength of spirit of the troop personnel, their selfless devotion to their people, and their loyalty to the ideas of the Communist party.

The Soviet Armed Forces possess highly qualified, well-educated officer cadres who are absolutely devoted to the party and the government and are qualified to lead troops in peace as well as in war.

Our officers, generals, and admirals are the backbone of the army and the navy. They are the real golden fund of the Armed Forces. Much has been done and is being done in the way of training politically and theoretically mature military cadres who are highly qualified and devoted to the Motherland. Now, in the army and navy every fourth officer has a high military or special education. Among the troops the proportion of engineer-technical staff grows steadily higher.

The presidium of the Central Committee CPSU gives us constant help and support in work with the cadres. On its orders, many young officers, generals, and admirals with good prospects, having good political and military-technical training, recently took over leading command posts in the troops, the central apparatus, and the military schools. As a result of this, a significant strengthening of all basic sections of the leading cadres of the army and navy was achieved. The commander engineer is now becoming the central figure in our Armed Forces, especially in the Strategic Rocket Troops, the Navy, and the Air Forces. Their ideological-political training level has improved. About 93 per cent of the officers, generals, and admirals in the Armed Forces are Communists and Komsomols.

The command staff, political organs, and party organizations are the conductors of party ideas, skillfully and purposefully educating the personnel in the spirit of socialist patriotism, proletarian internationalism, boundless devotion to their people, and hatred for imperialist aggressors.

With feelings of special satisfaction, I report to you of the remarkable qualities of our soldiers, sailors, sergeants, and petty officers. Characteristic of them is high political consciousness, boundless devotion to our own Leninist party and people, heroism, and readiness for self-sacrifice for the sake of the protection of their Motherland. Each day of their service involves tenacious training and the will to excel in military and political training. And, as always, Communists set the tone in this. Now 60 per cent of the members and candidates for membership in the party who are serving in subunits are rated "excellent" and as class "specialists." Communists and Komsomols—these are the enormous strength of our army and navy. They compose more than 80 per cent of the personnel of the Armed Forces and are the basis on which is founded the high political and moral condition of the troops.

It must also be noted with satisfaction that well-educated, technically knowledgeable, and physically trained draft-age youth are joining the Armed Forces. In 1965 out of a general contingent called into service in the army and navy 80 per cent of these young people were Komsomols. Among the draftees, 65 per cent had sports ratings and 98 per cent wore the GTO badge, "Ready for Labor and Defense." Now in the Soviet Army we have more than 90 per cent of the soldiers and sergeants with higher, middle, or incomplete middle education. Filling out the ranks of the army and the navy with such youth guarantees in a short period the mastery of modern, complicated military equipment, which in no small degree helps raise the combat readiness of the Armed Forces.

At the same time it must be mentioned that among the draftees youths are still met who are poorly prepared for military service. It is necessary to activize the education of our youth in the revolutionary, fighting, and working traditions of our party and our people. We salute the decision whereby the VII Plenum of the Central Committee VLKSM (Komsomols) placed before the Komsomols the task of the wider extension of education in these traditions.

The basic power of our Armed Forces is the unbreakable unity of the army and the people. Therefore, we consider as one of the main conditions for raising the combat potential of our Armed Forces the all-round expansion and strengthening of the ties of the army and navy, party organizations, political organs, and military councils with local party, council, and trade union organizations.

The Soviet people surround their Armed Forces with deep respect and concern; they correctly see in them the reliable shield of the Motherland. In this unity with the workers of the country lies the inexhaustible spring of the strength of our army, the superiority over armies of imperialist states.

The interests of strengthening the defense potential of the country demand the constant attention to the military patriotic education of the Soviet people, especially the youth, the wider dissemination of military knowledge among the population of the country, and the attraction of them to an active part in the perfection of all systems of civil defense. Here is a big field of action for the army and the navy as well as for local party and Komsomol organizations and also for all Soviet and trade union organizations.

The further strengthening of the brotherly ties and unity of the Soviet Armed Forces with the armies of countries who are members of the Warsaw Pact and of all the socialist community must be the object of our unremitting concern.

Comrades! The soldiers of the army and navy, like all the Soviet people, link their successes and plans for the future with the activities of the Communist party and its Leninist Central Committee. In the leadership of the party is the decisive source of the strength and might of our Armed Forces.

The constant concern of our Leninist Communist Party for strengthening the defense power of the country and for our glorious Armed Forces is clearly reflected in the report of the Central Committee to the XXIII Congress CPSU.

"The Communist party and the Soviet government and all our

people," pointed out Comrade Leonid Il'ich Brezhnev in the report, "highly value the honorable and difficult work of the soldiers, sailors, sergeants, petty officers, officers, generals, and admirals; they dearly love their Armed Forces, are proud of their fighting glory. The party in the future will strengthen the all-round defense capability of the Soviet Union, increase the power of the Armed Forces of the U.S.S.R., and support that level of combat readiness of the troops which will reliably guarantee the peaceful labor of the Soviet people."

These words of the party inspire the Soviet soldiers and fill their hearts with pride and thanks for the great concern of the Central Committee for the defenders of the Motherland. At the same time, it rings out like a battle cry obliging all of the personnel of the Soviet Army to give all their energy to the cause of raising their fighting mastery and obliging them to preserve unremitting vigilance so that, as it says in the report of the Central Committee, the aggressors, if they try to break the peace, will never catch us by surprise and retribution will overtake them inevitably and without delay!

Permit me, comrade delegates, in the name of the personnel of the army and the navy, to assure the XXIII Congress of our own Communist party and all of our friends that the Armed Forces of the Soviet Union, infinitely devoted to the cause of the party and to relying on the support of all of the Soviet people, will henceforth, with honor and dignity, fulfill their sacred military duty in defending our dearly-loved Soviet Motherland!

---

20. ADDRESS TO THE XXIII CONGRESS OF THE CPSU
By GENERAL OF THE ARMY A. A. YEPISHEV
Chief of the Main Political Administration of the Soviet Army and Navy

---

Editors' Notes

THE MAJORITY of the selections in this book have been taken from

Communist of the Armed Forces, the official organ of the Main Political Administration of the Soviet Army and Navy. The chief of this organization is General of the Army A. A. Yepishev, one of the most powerful men in the Soviet Union.

General Yepishev's career to date has been remarkable. He served as a political officer during World War II in units commanded by General K. S. Moskalenko. From 1951 to 1953, as a deputy to the notorious Beria, he served with the famed Soviet secret police, the MGB. In the days after the death of Stalin, Beria was arrested when he tried to take over power. Yepishev's former military colleague, General Moskalenko, took part in the trial. From 1955 to 1962 Yepishev served two tours as an ambassador, first to Rumania and then to Yugoslavia. After this, he was appointed to his present position as chief of the Main Political Administration, becoming the ideological guard over the Soviet Armed Forces. In November 1964, in a surprisingly short time after the ouster of Khrushchev, General Yepishev received a promotion in the Communist party structure.

General Moskalenko was designated a marshal of the Soviet Union in 1955 and in 1960 became the commander in chief of the strategic rocket forces. For reasons not quite clear, Moskalenko moved to the post of inspector general in April, 1962, at which time General Yepishev took over the Main Political Administration. In some ways, Moskalenko's fortunes seem to have been close to those of General Yepishev.

This address is quoted frequently and is required reading for Soviet officers. For those in the outside world who hope for increased freedom in the Soviet Union, General Yepishev's words may be read with dismay:

> The least slackening of attention to ideological work and any lowering of demands for arming cadres with revolutionary theory and for the ideological content of works of literature can cause annoying misfires. Obviously this laxness is also the reason why sometimes "works" emerge which bear the marks of indifference to politics and of ideological improbity and some which are even, frankly, anti-Soviet. We cannot ignore such cases, although they

290

may be isolated, because this could damage the interests of the Communist education of people.

The advocates of lack of principles and ideals and of *petit bourgeois* licentiousness are also displaying their worth in the fact that some under the flag of freedom of creativity, others under the pretext of combating the consequences of the personality cult, and still others under the disguise of "champions" of historical truth and authenticity are, in essence, flirting in front of the mirror of history and are trying to run down the heroic history and struggle of our party, our people, and their army, and the glorious combat and revolutionary traditions of the older generations, to slander Soviet reality, and to detract from the grandeur of our victory over fascism in the past war.

Yepishev goes on to call for more education and for intensification of "the scientific-theoretical processing of the problem of war and peace as connected with past wars and particularly with the nature of a possible thermonuclear war."

COMRADES, every day the work of the Congress merges into a thrilling demonstration of the unbreakable unity of the party and the people and evokes a great tide of political and creative activity of the broad masses of people in all corners of our immense Mothcrland. The Soviet people regard the XXIII Congress CPSU as a new landmark on the road of the country's move toward a great goal—communism. Its work and the decisions adopted will have great significance not only for our party but also for all world Communist and workers' movements.

Like all the Soviet people, the servicemen of the Armed Forces of the U.S.S.R. have received with profound satisfaction the accountability report of the CPSU Central Committee in which was given a profound analysis of the beneficial activity of the party and its Central Committee in all spheres of party, state, and economic construction and which outlined grand perspectives for our forward movement.

In the period which has elapsed since the XXII Congress CPSU,

291

the Soviet people have made great new strides in the building of communism, in the strengthening of the economic might of our Motherland, and in raising the well-being of the Soviet people.

The Central Committee's work on accomplishment of the tasks in the sphere of strengthening the country's defense capability and of perfecting the Armed Forces also has been many-sided. Taking into account the essence of the processes which have been caused by the radical changes in military affairs, in the nature of a possible war, the party has scientifically formulated the principles of Soviet military organization at the current stage and has determined the means and methods of conduct of an armed struggle. In this it proceeded from the great Lenin's instruction that " . . . we must accompany our steps for peace with the straining of all our military readiness to its utmost . . . ."

Relying on gains in the economy, science, and technology, the party has implemented a series of important measures for future strengthening of the combat power of the army and the navy and for equipping them with the most modern weapons and combat technical equipment. As a result the power of the Soviet Armed Forces has risen to a new, higher level.

The training of command, political, and technical engineering cadres and the inculcation in personnel of class self-consciousness on the basis of the ideas of Marxism-Leninism and their education in the spirit of selfless service to the Motherland and to the cause of communism also was an object of the party's untiring attention.

Covering a glorious and heroic path, our Armed Forces have grown and become stronger, as has the whole country, in the years of Soviet power. Powerful atomic and thermonuclear weapons, rockets for various combat designations, supersonic airplanes, atomic submarines, radioelectronics, and many other things—this is what determines the Armed Forces' present image. The army and the navy have made a gigantic leap also in improving the spiritual and cultural cast of mind of the soldiers and the commanders and of party-political and technical-engineering workers.

The servicemen of the army and the navy well understand that the source of their strength and invincibility lies in the leadership

292

by the party and in the unbreakable unity with the people, and that this is a guarantee that they will continue to be a reliable guard of the peace and security of our Motherland and the entire socialist brotherhood. Therefore, evaluating the great achievements of the party and tangibly feeling the fruits of its far-seeing policy, including the area of the country's defense, the Communists of the army and the navy and all Soviet soldiers fully approve and support the political line and practical activity of the Central Committee of the CPSU and the party's plans for the future.

The decisions of the October (1964) CPSU Central Committee plenum and subsequent plenums as well as the peaceful steps of the party and the government on the international scene, including the organization of the Tashkent meeting, the friendly contacts with the leaders of fraternal parties which were established in the interests of the further strengthening of the unity of the countries of the socialist brotherhood, and the cohesion of the international Communist movement, as well as other important political events, have evoked ardent approval from army and navy personnel. All servicemen of the U.S.S.R. Armed Forces wholeheartedly support the domestic and foreign policy of the party and the government.

The growth of the political and creative activity of the Communists and the raised role of scientific management of the country have beneficially affected the development of our Armed Forces and the styles and methods of the work of military cadres. In the past few years the Party Central Committee has adopted a series of principle measures concerning specific sectors of military organization, the training and education of military cadres, and the intensification of political work in the troops. Military councils, commanders, political organs, and party organizations are organizing their activities in the spirit of new, higher party demands.

The high training and the moral-political hardening of the Soviet soldiers are being tested in daily strenuous military service. Combat duty at rocket launching positions, flights on supersonic airplanes, voyages of thousands of miles on underwater and surface ships, exercises of many days in hard frost and burning heat and service in the most remote corners of our country puts the officers and soldiers in peacetime in conditions close to combat. And they are worthily fulfilling their complex and responsible duties.

This is good reason to report to the Congress that the army and navy personnel are ready at any moment to go decisively to the defense of the security of their native land and to honorably discharge their military obligations.

Soviet soldiers, educated in the spirit of internationalism, rejoice with all their hearts at the successes of the working people of brother socialist countries, strengthen the combat friendship with soldiers of their armies, and shoulder to shoulder with them vigilantly stand guard over the peace and security of the peoples.

The yearnings and hopes of all peoples who are struggling for freedom and national independence against the forces of international imperialist reaction are close and understandable to our soldiers. Together with all Soviet people they wrathfully condemn the aggression of American imperialism in Vietnam and express feelings of brotherly solidarity with the heroic Vietnamese people. In answer to the piratical acts of the American militarists, thousands of our people, the personnel of whole units, are reporting their readiness to go to Vietnam as volunteers to fight for the freedom of the long-suffering Vietnamese people.

Comrades! The growing combat readiness of our Armed Forces and the firm political and moral state, good organization, and discipline of the personnel are the result of intense work of military councils, commanders, political organs, and party organizations and of an intensified party influence on all aspects of troop life and activity.

Extensive work is being conducted in the army and the navy on the ideological and organizational strengthening of the party organizations as the supports of the commanders. Their contacts with the non-party masses have broadened. There are party organizations at almost all starting batteries of the rocket troops. The party organizations of the national PVO troops, ground forces, air forces, and the navy have become stronger, especially in the latter's submarine forces and on rocket-carrying ships. A majority of the personnel of the Armed Forces are Communists and Komsomols.

294

Soldier Communists with feelings of great responsibility fulfill their obligations and serve as examples in mastering combat skills.

One of the many discharging his military duties in an excellent way is a delegate to this Congress, Major Georgii Ivanovich Voronovich. He is a pilot first class and the commander of an outstanding aviation squadron. In the regiment where he serves, four-fifths of the personnel are Communists and Komsomols. They are outstanding in combat and political studies. Such a phenomenon is typical of our Armed Forces.

With us, combat training is closely linked with the ideological-political education of the soldiers. A harmonious system of Marxist-Leninist studies for officers, generals, and admirals and a system of lessons for soldiers and sailors, sergeants, and starshinas has been set up for this purpose. Hundreds of Marxist-Leninist universities, party schools and circles, officers' clubs, and soldiers' and sailors' clubs are operating in the army and the navy; the stocks of books in libraries, the number of film projectors, television sets, and radio sets are growing; and military newspapers and magazines are being published in large numbers. This enables our cadres to systematically enrich their knowledge in the field of Marxist-Leninist theory and in the political and practical activities of our party and to study deeply the problems of military science and organization.

During the years of service in the army, the servicemen acquire all-round knowledge and physical hardening. Their strenuous military work is not only useful but socially necessary. It can be said with good reason that our army and navy, together with their main purpose, the armed guarding of the country, is a school for training and educating youth.

Increasing contacts with working peoples' collectives and with local party, council, and Komsomol organizations are being used in educational work with the soldiers. We are certain that these contacts will be developed in the future also.

Each year tens of thousands of young Communists who have received their initial party training in the army and navy party organizations leave the ranks of the Armed Forces for the national economy. The army each year gives the country well-trained machine operators, diesel experts, electricians, builders, and other specialists. In the past few years alone, hundreds of thousands of servicemen transferred to the reserves went to shock construction projects in various areas of the country under Komsomol assignments or under organized recruitment. This is a natural process since the people and the army are one.

In speaking of the positive aspects of our activities, we clearly realize that quite a few shortcomings and unsolved problems exist in the work of military councils, of commanders, of political organs, and of party organizations. We see these omissions of ours and are undertaking the necessary measures to correct them and not to permit them in the future.

Comrades! Our life and work proceeds under conditions of aggravated international conditions created by the aggressive activities of the imperialist powers, primarily the U.S.A. Because of them, a dangerous situation is emerging in various parts of the world and in several places the imperialists are waging war. Blinded by hatred for people who are building socialism, imperialist reaction, together with threats of a military attack on our country and the other socialist countries, is also trying to attack us on the ideological front. It is counting on ideological diversion, on moral and psychological corruption of the Soviet people. Without hiding their spite, our enemies say frankly that "an aggressive strategy in the political, economic, and psychological fields is necessary" in order to "blow up Russia from the inside."

The intensification of the aggressiveness of the imperialists and the activization by them of various kinds of ideological diversion demands from us unweakened vigilance; we must strengthen the security of our country from the point of view both of perfecting the Armed Forces and of educating the people, especially the younger generation, in the spirit of readiness to resist the ideological onslaught of the apologists of imperialism.

Comrade Brezhnev's report gave a high value to the ideological-educational work of the party and of all detachments of the cultural front including the creative intelligentsia. We see the results of this work in the growth of the social consciousness of our society and in the education of the new man. A splendid replacement for the older generation is growing up in our country and undoubtedly the glorious Soviet youth will worthily stand any test in the struggle for our just cause should this be necessary.

Nevertheless, the increasing tasks of building for communism and of its protection demand a further improvement of the people's ideological-political education. Hence it is absolutely legitimate that many delegates have given great attention to this question.

The front of the ideological struggle and the cause of our people's ideological tempering form a most important sector of party activity. The struggle between the two ideologies is not a theoretical argument but a real struggle which concerns all of us. And every Communist must be an active fighter against the ideological attacks of imperialism.

Sometimes our ideological foes succeed in exerting an evil influence on the minds and actions of some inadequately conscious members of our society, particularly in those places and times where and when education is conducted unsatisfactorily and complacency and lack of principles are permitted. As a result of this, cases of political immaturity, of amoral conduct of individuals, of faulty understanding of their civic duties, and of loss of a feeling of responsibility to the collective, to society, and to the government are sometimes found.

It is impossible to live in a society and not to have obligations to it. Our road to communism does not lie in weakening but, on the contrary, in strengthening individual responsibility to society, in strengthening its organization and discipline, in raising the authority of our state and social organs in solving problems concerned with the building of communism.

In this ideological struggle, just as in any other struggle, all kinds of weapons must be in a state of constant readiness to operate efficiently and faultlessly. And it must be said that our ideological weapon, containing the great charge of the immortal ideas of Marxism-Leninism, unfailingly hits the target and mercilessly exposes the reactionary ideology of imperialism and anticommunism. It reliably serves the cause of building a Communist society.

The least slackening of attention to ideological work and any lowering of demands for arming cadres with revolutionary theory and for the ideological content of works of literature can cause annoying misfires. Obviously this laxness is also the reason why sometimes "works" emerge which bear the marks of indifference to politics and of ideological improbity and some which are even, frankly, anti-Soviet. We cannot ignore such cases, although they may be isolated, because this could damage the interests of the Communist education of people.

The advocates of lack of principles and ideals and of *petit bourgeois* licentiousness are also displaying their worth in that some under the flag of freedom of creativity, others under the pretext of combating the consequences of the personality cult, and still others under the disguise of "champions" of historical truth and authenticity are, in essence, flirting in front of the mirror of history and are trying to run down the heroic history and struggle of our party, our people, and their army, and the glorious combat and revolutionary traditions of the older generations, to slander Soviet reality, and to detract from the grandeur of our victory over fascism in the past war.

Whether the authors of such "works" realize it or not their "writings" are playing into the hands of our ideological enemies who are trying to disarm our people spiritually and to sow poisonous seeds of doubt about our heroic past and the greatness and nobleness of the present.

The party has never concealed the fact that our road toward the victory of socialism was not strewn with roses. There have been rifts and difficult passages on this road. And the party has properly assessed it at the proper time. We have never been against criticism of our shortcomings, but we were and are of the opinion that criticism must be party-minded and objective; it must be beneficial to the common cause and must not be detrimental to it. And when individual damaging creations emerge which distort our reality this, of course, can only evoke justified indignation from the Soviet people both at the authors and at those people who willingly or unwillingly, because of their lack of principles, afford every possible opportunity for the publication of such works. This indignation is also joined by the voice of the army public, since the servicemen of the Soviet Army and Navy are an essential and inseparable part of the people.

Did our revolutionary people struggle on the barricades of Krasnaya Presna; did they, under Lenin's leadership upon a signal from the *Aurora*, storm the old world; did they heroically fight at Perekop and Kakhovka, overcome difficulties and privations, erect the edifice of socialism; did millions of Soviet people sacrifice their lives in the deadly encounter with fascism so that individual authors, who have hung on to the splendid detachment of our creative intelligentsia, could use freedom of speech for jeering at the most sacred concepts of Soviet man—the Motherland, the party, and Leninism? Our people have obtained genuine freedom and democracy at too great a price to permit ideological turncoats to slander the historical gains of socialism and our beloved Soviet power. Therefore we shall wage a resolute struggle for the purity of Marxism-Leninism ideology and for the further strengthening of our social and state system. And the attempts to charge us with "violation of democracy" are futile.

At the XX Congress, the party embarked on a correct course in these matters and it will also continue to follow unswervingly the Leninist line in the future. And no one will succeed in using in the struggle against us the shortcomings and errors connected with the personality cult and which were revealed by the party and resolutely condemned.

We firmly believe that our creative intelligentsia will still create many works that are worthy of the heroic exploits of the Soviet people and their Armed Forces. These works will serve the noble cause of the education of youth, strong in spirit and ready to perform noble deeds on behalf of the Motherland.

A prominent place in the formation of high civic qualities in the working people, particularly of the rising generation, and a correct understanding of their importance to society is occupied by military-patriotic education which the party considers an inseparable part of the ideological-political training of our people. The Komsomol as well as the All-union Society "Knowledge" and our other social organizations are conducting considerable work in this respect. The fruitful work of DOSAAF in the field of youth education and training of army cadres must be particularly mentioned. It can be expected that this work will be even more intensified.

The interests of the protection of the socialist Fatherland and of the peoples' patriotic education oblige us to intensify the scientific-theoretical processing of the problems of war and peace connected with past wars and, particularly, with the nature of a possible thermonuclear war. This is the more important because sometimes incorrect, confused opinions still exist in this area, and extremes are permitted in the interpretation of the possible consequences of the use of new means of armed struggle. Under the flag of an "innovator's" approach to the development of theory, sometimes attempts are made to cast doubts on the fundamental views of the classical writers of Marxism-Leninism on the laws of the development of military affairs.

Working out the problem of war and peace from a position of Marxism-Leninism will promote a really creative development of military theory and practice. This will enable us to better educate the Soviet people and all military cadres in the spirit of optimism, in a firm belief in their own strength, and in the inevitable defeat of any aggressor.

Comrades! Army and navy Communists absolutely support the proposals of the introduction of changes and supplements in the CPSU statutes as expounded in the report of the Central Committee of the CPSU and consider that their acceptance by the Congress will promote the further strengthening of the party and the improvement of its organizational and political activities.

The servicemen of the army and the navy are deeply touched by the warm and cordial words addressed to our Armed Forces in the report of Leonid Il'ich Brezhnev. His words inspire them to new successes in combat and political training and to raising the troops' combat readiness.

Permit me, on behalf of the army and navy Communists and of

the entire personnel of the Armed Forces, to assure the delegates of the Congress that the Soviet servicemen are always with the party. They will in the future reliably stand guard over the historic gains of the Soviet people, building communism.

V · A Blueprint for the Future

IN APRIL, 1966, during the meeting of the XXIII Party Congress, Vietnam was a predominate theme. Underlying this obvious development was the split with Red China. Thus, the main subjects found in the Soviet military press in the months following the Congress discuss these problems in a more or less indirect fashion. The primary concern was the ideological struggle between the two major Communist powers. The articles here deal with the basic differences that exist in their philosophy, refuting charges of "revisionism," softness toward the West, economic reforms, and—of primary interest to us—with the revolution in military affairs. In calling the United States and its nuclear weapons a "Paper Tiger," the Chinese indirectly pasted this label on the Soviets.

The blueprint for the future in our selections includes an article on foreign policy. Next, the blueprint ties the revolution in military affairs to the dialectical philosophy espoused by communism. Another article lauds the economic plans of the XXIII Party Congress, stressing the military aspect of every part of the plan. Then the really fundamental question of whether nuclear war can be fought and won is discussed, and Mao Tse-tung's ideas on people's wars are indirectly attacked. This is cleverly done under the guise of criticizing a lecture given by a fellow officer.

The following two articles deal directly with ways and means of achieving military victory in future war. Victorious means will be produced by obtaining military-technical superiority, a goal which the Soviets are now pursuing with single-minded intentness and which they feel is guaranteed by their superior system. Another article deals with the manner in which wars will be fought; in other words, how the revolution in military affairs has affected tactics. The final article is on Soviet military doctrine.

As of 1967 Communist China was in the midst of a chaotic "cul-

302

tural revolution." Although the Soviet blueprint for its revolution in military affairs has some very clear and precise details, the reader will note that Soviet military writing becomes definitely hazy when Vietnam and Red China are discussed.

In the Soviet assessment there are two nuclear super-powers and three other nations, Britain, France, and Communist China, who possess limited nuclear capability. Only two countries have the proven rocket technology, as evidenced by space programs, and only two have the advanced electronic systems to make the nuclear-tipped missiles truly effective. This, in part, accounts for the continued belittling of massive manpower, such as Red China possesses and which the Soviet Union lacks in comparison. The Soviet leaders measure military superiority by the quantity and the quality of nuclear weapons and the means of their delivery. Their only competitor for superiority is the United States.

---

21. THE LENINIST COURSE OF FOREIGN POLICY OF THE U.S.S.R.
By V. V. ZAGLADIN
Candidate of Historical Sciences

Editors' Notes

THE AUTHORITATIVE *Communist of the Armed Forces* for May, 1966, recommended this article for the "Marxist-Leninist preparation of officers, generals, and admirals for studying the theme, 'The International Posture of the U.S.S.R.: Foreign Policy Activities of the Communist Party of the Soviet Union (CPSU).' "

The study presents political doctrine as interpreted by the XXIII Party Congress. Its purpose is to give the trends in the foreign policy of the Soviet government which change "depending on circumstances in the world arena, on the correlation of forces, and on the growth of the possibilities of world socialism and its allies."

At the present time "There are three basic types of governments existing in the world arena: the countries of socialism, the countries struggling for their national liberation, and capitalist countries. The countries of socialism are united in a common social structure, a single goal—the goal of building socialism and communism." Since 1961 the political, military, and economic cooperation of these socialist and Communist governments has been strengthened.

Zagladin considers it unfortunate that relations between the Soviet Union and China, as well as between the Soviet Union and Albania, have developed unsatisfactorily. However, according to Comrade L. I. Brezhnev at the Party Congress, "We are convinced that in the final analysis, our party and our people will overcome all difficulties and will go in a single rank to struggle for the common revolutionary cause."

For those countries "where the flame of national-liberation struggle still blazes, where bloody skirmishes with colonizers go on, the course of our country is defined by the Congress in the following words of the summing-up speech: 'to continue to render every kind of support to people struggling for their liberation, to secure the urgent share of independence for all colonial countries and peoples.' "

Special note is made of the "close friendly relations" with the UAR [United Arab Republic], Mali, Guinea, and Burma. "Good fruitful relationships" can be had with revolutionary-democratic parties of many different types, and they do not have to be Marxist-Leninist.

Zagladin states that over the last two years the American imperialists have taken aggressive actions against the countries of the socialist community and against national-liberation movements. This characteristic feature of the international gendarmes, the main source of world reaction, "was quite clearly described by V. I. Lenin in his 'Letter to the American Workers.' " In Vietnam, Zagladin asserts, the American militarists are using bombs, rockets, poisonous substances and napalm. Second to the United States as a threat to world peace is the Federal Republic of Germany.

The article specifically points out that "the principles of peaceful coexistence, affecting the area of intergovernmental relations, is inapplicable between oppressors and the oppressed, between colonizers and the victims of colonial oppression."

Judging from the content of this article, Vietnam has a special relationship with the Soviet Union, and "No one will ever dare put out the flame of socialism which the Democratic Republic of Vietnam raised on high."

The reader will notice that the Soviet writers frequently write about the support given to national-liberation movements, but are never specific on how such wars should be fought or the exact degree of Soviet commitment.

This article is recommended for use in the course of Marxist-Leninist preparation of officers, generals, and admirals for studying the theme "International Posture of the U.S.S.R.: Foreign Policy Activities of the Communist Party of the Soviet Union (CPSU)."

IN THE DECISIONS of the XXIII Congress of the CPSU, the foreign policy course of our party and government was clearly defined and thoroughly substantiated. The conclusions of the Congress on the questions of international policy attracted the earnest attention of the whole world. Truly now, on the threshold of the fiftieth anniversary of Soviet power, our country plays such an important role in the world arena that not one serious politician, even if he is the most thorough opponent of communism, can fail to take into account its intentions, its plans, and its decisions.

The decisions made by the XXIII Congress are now known in the farthest corners of the earth, and were preceded by great serious work. Based on the principal position of the guidelines of the Communist movement, embodied in the declaration of 1957 and the statement of 1960, on the aims of the XX—XXII Congresses CPSU, taking into account all the complicated international conditions, the contradictory tendencies of its development, the XXIII Congress of the party brought out a program of meas-

305

ures, directed at the solution of the most important questions of world policy, on strengthening universal peace and the security of nations.

The Internationalism of the Foreign Policy of the CPSU and Soviet Government

In the first years of Soviet power, in determining the main tasks of the foreign policy of our country, V. I. Lenin wrote "from the time of the victory of a socialist government in one of the countries, it is necessary to resolve questions . . . solely from the point of view of the best conditions for developing and strengthening the socialist revolution which has already begun." (*The Complete Collection of Works* Vol. 35, p. 247.)

Following Lenin's advice, today, when the Soviet people are building communism and the other peoples of the socialist community are successfully building a socialist society, our party sees the main task of the foreign policy of the U.S.S.R. in assuring the best conditions for developing the socialist and Communist structure, for accomplishing this in the shortest historical time-period. The resolution of this problem answers first of all to the highest interests of the Soviet people, to the national interests of our government, and to all the countries and peoples of the socialist community. At the same time, and this is the distinguishing feature of Soviet foreign policy, it is fully in keeping with the interests of all the revolutionary forces, the interests of all the fighters for peace, democracy, national freedom, and socialism.

Our party and our people have never forgotten and will never forget their international obligations. While developing their own foreign policy, the CPSU invariably is "proceeding from the basic interests of the Soviet people, of the international revolutionary obligations before brother socialist countries and workers of all countries." (Resolution of the XXIII Congress in the report of the Central Committee of the CPSU.) And in this relation, our party strictly follows the advice of the great Lenin.

It is well known that in their time "Leftist" Communists tried to artificially separate the national tasks of Soviet foreign policy from the great international tasks of the countries of victorious socialism and set one against the other. They suggested false and harmful theories as if the international mission of socialist foreign policy were the "instigation" of revolution in other countries. V. I. Lenin gave a shattering rebuff to such "theories."

The most important, decisive revolutionary obligation of countries of victorious socialism, Lenin said, is the building of the economy. Not the "export of revolution" but successes in the business of building a new society, thoroughly surpassing capitalism, and by this undermining its social basis—this is the main channel of revolutionary influence of socialism on world development, the main weapon of the power of socialism in the liberating struggle of all people. Therefore the strengthening of socialist countries and the protection of their achievements, guaranteeing the best conditions for their development, fully answers the interests of all peoples and of the world revolutionary movement.

The deep rightness of these Leninist attitudes is fully supported by almost half a century of experience in the Soviet Union and by twenty years of experience of developing the world socialist system. New evidence for this was given by the speeches of the representatives of brother Communist parties and also national-democratic and leftist socialist parties from the tribune of the XXIII Congress of the CPSU.

"The impending five-year plan of development of the economy of the Soviet Union is a new source of inspiration for the peoples of brother socialist countries, of the workers' class, for working and oppressed peoples of all the world in their struggle against aggressive imperialists led by the U.S.A., in the struggle for peace, national independence, democracy and socialism" according to the letter of greeting of the Central Committee of the Workers' Party of Vietnam, which was read out at the XXIII Congress by its First Secretary, Comrade Le Duan.

"The great universal contribution of the Soviet Union is the cause of liberating mankind," the General Secretary of the Central Committee of the Communist Party of Chile, Comrade Louis Corvalan, declared from the tribune of the Congress, "but its most significant contribution is the building of communism." And a member of the national Politburo of the party of the Sudanese Union of the Republic of Mali, Comrade Madeira Keita, said, "The successes of the Soviet people in the building of a socialist government exerts a great influence on the development of the world revolutionary movement."

In providing the most favorable international conditions for the building of communism in our country and the building of socialism in the countries of all the socialist community, Soviet foreign policy thus makes its own contribution to the common revolutionary cause of all nations.

The Main Trends of the Foreign Policy of the Soviet Government

The main national, and at the same time international, task of the foreign policy of the CPSU and the Soviet government is to determine its concrete aims at each given stage of development. These aims, naturally, are not immutable. They change depending on circumstances in the world arena, in the correlation of forces, and in the growth of the possibilities of world socialism among its allies.

In our day, as it was defined by the XXIII Congress of the CPSU on the basis of the analysis of the established conditions, the U.S.S.R., together with other socialist countries trying to secure favorable international conditions for building socialism and communism, places before the foreign policy the following concrete goals: strengthen the unity and solidarity of socialist countries, their friendship and brotherhood; support national-liberation movements and bring about all-round co-operation with young developing governments; consistently advocate the principle of peaceful coexistence with governments of different social structures; give decisive repulse to the aggressive forces of imperialism, and save mankind from a new world war.

As is obvious, the XXIII Congress outlined the concrete tasks of the Soviet foreign policy in relation to each of the three basic types of governments existing in the world arena: the countries of socialism; the countries struggling for their national independence; and capitalist countries. The differentiating character of the governments of these three groups determines the features of Soviet foreign policy in relation to each of them.

The countries of socialism are united in a common social structure, a single goal—the goal of building socialism and communism. By their relations with these countries the Soviet Union builds on a basis of socialist internationalism, mutual support, all-round brotherly co-operation on the principle of equal rights and noninterference, the independence of parties and of governments.

Just such an approach assured the essential strengthening and widening of relationships with almost all brother socialist countries which were achieved during the period between the XXII and the XXIII Congresses of the CPSU. During these years, as noted in the summing-up speech of the Central Committee of the CPSU, the political, economic, and military co-operation of these governments was strengthened. Further steps were taken on the path to perfecting the mechanism and activities of the Soviet Economic Mutual Aid (SEV) and the organization of the Warsaw Pact.

Unfortunately, relations between our country and China, and also between our country and Albania, have developed unsatisfactorily. But this happened through no fault of our country. "Our Party and the Soviet people" Comrade L. I. Brezhnev declared at the Congress, "sincerely want friendship with the people of China and its Communist party. We are ready to do everything possible to improve relationships with the people of Albania, and with the Albanian Workers' party as well. . . . We are convinced that in the final analysis, our party and our people will overcome all difficulties and will go in a single rank to struggle for the common great revolutionary cause."

In present conditions, when imperialism is intensifying its aggressive activities, special meaning is gained by the agreement of the foreign policy activities of the countries of the socialist camp, and the co-ordination of their defense policies. The CPSU considers that the unity of the countries of socialism and the establishment by them of common actions in the face of the threat from the side of the class enemy are, in our day, the highest obligation of the Communists of the socialist community.

Issuing from this, the XXIII Congress puts forward also in the future, *as one of the main directions of foreign policy actions of the party and Soviet government, the developing and strengthening of the ideological and political ties with Communist parties of all countries of socialism on the principles of Marxism-Leninism, the development and strengthening of political, economic, and other ties of the U.S.S.R. with socialist governments and every kind of assistance to the unity of the socialist community, strengthening its power and influence.*

From the times of "Great October," our party has considered and will consider brotherly union with countries and nations struggling for their national and social liberation as one of the cornerstones of our international policy. During the period between the XXII and the XXIII Congresses, the Central Committee of the CPSU consistently and unflinchingly followed a course of every kind of support of the struggle of peoples against colonial oppression, of all-round co-operation with young national governments on a basis of equality of rights, strict respect for sovereignty and noninterference in their internal affairs. Our country has followed and will follow in this the great Lenin principle of self-determination of nations, which is intended to protect the rights of all nations to independently determine their own fate.

Now, after the disintegration of the colonial system of imperialism in the area of the national-liberation movement, three basic types of countries have been formed. One type are those which, having received independence, start on the path of noncapitalist development and in time may lead more strongly to socialism; the second, those which are enticed to the path of capitalist development or still have not finally decided their orientation; the third, those countries which are still not freed from colonial oppression.

In relation to the countries of the third group, where the flame of national-liberation struggle still blazes and where bloody skirmishes with colonizers go on, the course of our country is defined

310

by the Congress in the following words of the summing-up speech: "to continue to render every kind of support to people struggling for their liberation, to secure the urgent share of independence for all colonial countries and peoples."

The Congress with satisfaction noted that in the years after the XXII Congress our relations with the overwhelming majority of independent countries of Asia and of Africa have been successfully developed. Mutually beneficial trade and also economic and cultural co-operation have been significantly widened. Many Soviet specialists work in those countries to give the people their experience and knowledge. Thousands of young people from the countries of Asia and of Africa are studying in high and middle-level schools in the U.S.S.R.

Our party and our government are rendering all possible support to countries which are becoming free. The CPSU actively opposes the interference by the imperialists in the internal affairs of young national governments or attempts by the neocolonialists to set off independent governments one against the other causing them to exhaust their strength in internecine struggle.

The position of the Soviet Union and the majority of independent countries of Asia and of Africa on basic international problems is this—in the struggle for peace, against colonialism and neocolonialism, for national freedom and independence—the positions of the countries either coincide or are close. And this forms a good basis for the further fruitful collaboration in this area.

In its resolution, the Congress noted as an important problem for the future: "the developing of the all-round co-operation with countries achieving national independence."

Especially close friendly relations were made by our countries with those governments of Asia and of Africa which, like the UAR, Mali, Guinea, and Burma, are making serious social reforms and are steering a course toward socialism. Characteristic features of recent time consist of this, that the Central Committee of the CPSU has established friendly relationships along party lines with a series of revolutionary democratic parties which are in power in these countries. Good, fruitful relationships have been developed by the

311

CPSU with several revolutionary-democratic parties of other governments. It is well known that these parties are not Marxist-Leninist. However, they advocate progressive ideas and promote policies in the interests of peace and social progress.

In line with the decisions of the Congress, the Central Committee of the CPSU henceforth will widen ties with Communist and revolutionary-democratic parties of young national governments. All-round development of these ties will promote the strengthening of the fighting union of world socialism and the national-liberation movement in the struggle against imperialism. "One of the most important results of the XXIII Congress of the CPSU," wrote the Guinea newspaper *Horoya*, "is that it still further cemented the great coalition of peoples who are building socialism, and peoples who are waging national-liberation struggles. As a result, a new powerful obstacle has been placed on the path of imperialism, colonialism, and neocolonialism."

In regard to relations with countries of the capitalist world, then it must be mentioned that the XXIII Congress, summing up the development of these relationships for the past four years, defined the perspective for the future as *coming from the Lenin principle of peaceful coexistence of states with different social systems.*

Peaceful Coexistence and Problems of Averting World War in Contemporary Circumstances

On the eve of the XXIII Congress of the CPSU, the bourgeois press and different sorts of imperialist propagandists excelled, as much as they could, in prophesying concerning the perspectives of the Soviet foreign policy. Significantly, many of these false prophets almost hinted at the possibility of repudiation by the CPSU of the Leninist principle of peaceful coexistence of states having different social systems. Now all these gloomy prophesiers are caught in the web of their own provocations.

The XXIII Congress of the CPSU, continuing the tradition of Lenin and the course of the XX–XXII Congresses, took up a firm line on confirming the principles of the peaceful coexistence of governments belonging to opposing political systems. The Con-

312

gress noted that the policy of peace flowed from the very nature of our government, all of whose actions were determined by the interests of the workers. Durable peace and stable peaceful coexistence of two systems—this is one of the most decisive foreign policy conditions of the successful building of communism, the forward movement of the great revolutionary cause of the working class.

It is well known what enormous forces were placed in its time in the Lenin-guided Soviet foreign policy in order to win peaceful respite and peaceful conditions for building the socialist society. And this peaceful respite was won in acute and irreconcilable struggle with imperialism. The "Left" dogmatists and sectarians attacked the Leninist policy of peace many times in that period. Then they brought out alternatives: either struggle for peace or struggle against imperialism. Not taking into account conditions or the desires of the masses, they called for thoughtless bellicosity, hiding their adventurism under the slogan "revolutionary war." Lenin, and together with him all the party, rejected the false alternatives of the Leftists.

Lenin showed that in conditions of the coexistence of two opposing social systems the struggle against imperialism was tied by the most inseparable forms with the struggle for peaceful conditions of building a new society and for universal peace, that this as a matter of fact was not two struggles, but one and the same great struggle, having great revolutionary significance. The struggle for peaceful coexistence is one of the forms of class struggle having as its aim the unyielding accumulation of forces of the socialist structure, the strengthening of the unity of all the revolutionary ranks and the decisive unmasking and international isolation of reactionary imperialist forces.

Attempts to smear and to discredit this struggle are unworthy of a revolutionary. "Can a Communist with any understanding of the conditions of life and of the psychology of the worker and the exploited masses," V. I. Lenin wrote, "slip into that point of view of the typical intelligentsia, *petit bourgeois,* or *déclassé* with the attitude of a fine gentleman or lord, which the 'psychological world' describes as 'inactive,' and by waving a box of swords be considered as 'active'?" (Complete *Collection of Works* Vol. 36, p. 288.)

Nevertheless, the concrete form of struggle for peaceful coexistence and of the anti-imperialist struggle is different at different times. These forms are determined on the basis of scientific analysis of the given concrete situation, an exact account of objective conditions and of their changes. During the past four years, periods of a certain easing of tensions have more than once been replaced with periods of acute aggravation. In a series of instances, bloodletting conflicts dangerous to the interests of universal peace have succeeded in being unloosed by imperialist aggressors.

As a whole, however, international relations continue to develop in the same general direction as in the earlier period. The gradual change of the relative forces for the side of peace, national liberation, and social liberation has continued. Between 1961 and 1965, the people succeeded in holding back the most aggressive forces of imperialism and in averting the beginning of a world thermonuclear war. The decisive role in this belonged to the foreign policy of the Soviet Union and other governments of the socialist community.

The strengthening of the power of socialist countries, while progressively widening the international front of the battle for socialism and increasing the pressure of the national-liberation movement, evokes more and more persistant attempts from the side of imperialism to find new ways and means to build a dam on the path of the great stream of the renovation of the world. These attempts are becoming more and more active, for life is frustrating, one after another, all the recipes brought forward by ideologists and politicians of imperialism in struggling with social progress.

While developing new plans for the struggle against the forces of democracy and of national and social liberation, imperialism lays special hopes on the appearance of discord in the anti-imperialist front, on the temporary weakening of the unity of the socialist camp, and of the Communist movement.

Such are the basic circumstances causing the activation in the last two to two and one-half years of the aggressive actions of imperialism against the countries of the socialist community and

314

the national-liberation movement. The most activity is shown by American imperialism, the most important international exploiter. It displays, again and again, those most characteristic features of the international gendarmes, the main source of world reaction which was quite clearly described by V. I. Lenin in his "Letter to the American Workers." There is no part of the world where the activation of American aggression could not be observed now. Special resentment of the nations is evoked by the insolent actions of the American militarists in Vietnam. By widening the intervention in South Vietnam, the ruling circles of the U.S.A. started on the path to open aggression against a brother socialist country, the DRV [Democratic Republic of Vietnam]. Bombs and rockets, poisonous substances, and napalm—all have been used by the brutal colonizers.

The ruling circles of the Federal Republic of Germany have advanced as the main ally of American imperialism in Europe. They are straining for nuclear weapons; they are trying to expose to review the results of the Second World War. The aggressive union of Washington and Bonn is a serious threat to the peace of Europe and of all the world.

The foreign policy of our party since the time of Lenin until our day consists of this, that it always told people the truth, unmasked the maneuvers of the enemies of peace, the initiators of war. The XXIII Congress of the CPSU tore off the mask of the enemies of peace. In the whole world the voice of the party of Lenin resounded its call for the mobilization of societies in the struggle against the dark designs of imperialism.

The Congress showed that mankind is now living in the most crucial period of our history. The imperialists needed twenty years after the end of the First World War to start the Second World War. Now more than two decades have passed after its conclusion. To-day, judging by everything, the imperialists calculate that they can use a new young generation that still does not know the horrors of war as "cannon fodder." Their actions have already led to a worsening of the world situation, to a growth of international tension. The Congress urged the joining of all forces in order to prevent the further development of this process and to block the path of war.

Taking into consideration the correlation of the forces in the world, our party considered and will consider that the averting of a new world war is a real problem. But for its solution no small amount of work is necessary. The possibility of averting war is dependent on the power of the world system of socialism, national-liberation movements, and the international working class. However, for converting this possibility into actuality, it is necessary that the powerful forces of the fighters against imperialism act jointly. A united front of all the forces of peace and social progress must oppose the aggressors. Or else, as the experience of recent years shows, the cause of repulsing aggression and of preventing universal nuclear rocket war will be placed under serious threat.

In contemporary circumstances it is especially important to ask questions specifically about the ways of struggle against world war. What action does our party consider necessary for its prevention? What is the real path of the struggle against the growth of the military threat? The Congress gave an exact answer to these questions.

We well understand that the present "new course" of imperialism in international politics is revealed in the progressive weakening of its position in the world arena. It would be a mistake, however, not to consider that in our day the aggressive policies of imperialism rest on its growing military-economic potential, on the achievements by them of renowned successes in the military science field. Taking into consideration this circumstance, the Congress came to the following conclusion: "In conditions when the aggressive forces of imperialism are intensifying international tensions and creating the breeding ground of war, the CPSU will in the future raise the vigilance of the Soviet people and strengthen the defense capability of our Motherland so that the Armed Forces of the U.S.S.R. will always be ready to protect reliably the achievements of socialism and to give a shattering repulse to any imperialist aggressor." Let no one be mistaken, the Soviet Union and its powerful Armed Forces are always ready for a decisive fight with imperialism. And if the imperialists choose the military way of deciding the general controversy between socialism and capitalism, then we will lay on the scales of history all our economic and military power.

The Congress decisively stated: The carrying out of the Lenin line on peaceful coexistence and on strengthening the security of peoples assumes today, first and foremost, a firm and decisive repulse of the aggressive attempts of those forces which are trying to strain international relations and to create a new breeding ground of military danger. The solidarity of all peace-loving forces in the struggle to defend Vietnam and revolutionary Cuba, to defend the rights and interests of peoples subject to imperialist aggression—there is that border on which the tense struggle is now going on for peace and for peaceful coexistence of governments with different social systems.

The Program of the CPSU, in conformity with contemporary circumstances, settles a definition of the idea of peaceful coexistence. *"Peaceful coexistence"* it says, "supposes: giving up war as a way of settling issues between governments; resolving issues by negotiations, equal rights, mutual understanding, and trust between governments, with due regard for the interests of each other; noninterference in internal affairs, the acknowledgment of each people's right to independently decide all questions in their own country; strict regard for the sovereignty and territorial integrity of all countries; the development of economic and cultural cooperation on the basis of full equality and mutual interest. Peaceful coexistence serves as the basis of peaceful competition between socialism and capitalism on an international scale, and it is the specific form of class struggle between them."

Coming from this definition, the Congress brought out a concrete program of measures, the adoption of which could considerably normalize the international situation and lead to a turn in the development of events favorable for the people, for the side of the cause of peace. This program provides for, in part, serious steps in pursuit of nuclear disarmament, preventing the further spread of the nuclear weapon and forbidding its testing in all spheres. It also

317

provides for measures on strengthening the European security and for strengthening the effectiveness of the UN as an important instrument of universal peace.

Bourgeois ideologists often use the argument that the policy of peaceful coexistence is incompatible with supporting the liberation struggles of peoples. As a matter of fact, such a sort of argument is none other than returning to new ground that false alternative against which V. I. Lenin struggled in his time. Then it was shouted "either peace or struggle with imperialism." Today it is shouted differently; either support the liberation struggles of people or carry on a policy of peaceful coexistence. However, today, as yesterday, in actual practice such alternatives do not exist.

To whom is it not clear that, for example, the liquidation of American aggression and the withdrawal from Indochina of all American troops and the restoration of peace in Vietnam is an important condition for averting world war, and at the same time for the subsequent successful development of the national liberation struggle of the peoples of this region? The interests of the struggle for softening international tensions and for strengthening peaceful coexistence fully coincide with the interests of the struggle for national and social liberation of peoples. This circumstance was settled in their collective documents of 1957 and 1960 by the fraternal Communist parties.

It is absolutely clear that the principles of peaceful coexistence, affecting the area of intergovernmental relations, is inapplicable in relations between oppressors and the oppressed, between colonizers and the victims of colonial oppression.

The Soviet government has supported and will support the liberation struggles of oppressed peoples against imperialism. It is known to the whole world that our country unconditionally opposes the aggression against the heroic Vietnamese people. In a special declaration on the occasion of the aggression of the U.S.A. in Vietnam the XXIII Congress decisively denounced the shameful actions of American imperialism. The declaration says: "In the carrying out of 'escalation' of the shameful war against the Vietnamese people, the aggressors will meet ever-growing support of the Vietnamese people from the Soviet Union and other socialist friends and brothers. The Vietnamese people will become masters of all their land. And no one will ever succeed in putting out the torch of socialism which the Democratic Republic of Vietnam has raised on high."

Almost half a century ago, mobilizing all the forces of the young Soviet republic to repulse the interventionists, V. I. Lenin paid what was at that time exceptional attention to the necessity for achieving normal political and diplomatic relations with capitalist countries, and first of all, with the United States of America. He often stressed that the development of such relations was an important condition for basically strengthening international peace.

Following Lenin's advice, the XXIII Congress of the CPSU oriented the socialist foreign policy on the further all-round improvement of relations with the capitalist world. At the same time it decisively opposed conceptions having wide circulation in the West concerning the belief that the sphere of normal relations can supposedly be limited to relations of the great powers. The world is indivisible. Complications of circumstances in one region of the world without fail are reflected in the state of international conditions as a whole. And normal interrelations, constructed on the principle of peaceful coexistence, must be spread to all governments, independent of their size and geographical location. One cannot provoke war against one of the socialist countries and plan on bettering relations with other socialist countries.

Foreign policy lines, approved by the XXIII Congress of the Lenin party, compose the necessary basis for the struggle for decisive normalization of international circumstances. The peoples of the world are convinced that carrying this out will strengthen still more the international position of the Soviet government and its authority; it will promote the further change of the relationship of forces in the world arena in favor of the forces of peace, democracy, national-liberation, and socialism.

319

22. THE DIALECTICS OF DEVELOPMENT AND CHANGE IN FORMS AND METHODS OF ARMED CONFLICT
BY GENERAL MAJOR V. VOZNENKO
Candidate of Military Sciences

Editors' Notes

WE DISLIKE cutting out parts of an article, since we might have omitted the very point that the author was trying to establish. Three-fourths of Voznenko's article, however, would be of interest only to a student of dialectics. The latter portion, presented here, could easily have been written by a different author.

Translation of this work was made difficult by the author's choice of words. *"Vooruzhennaya bor'ba,"* which is used more than seventy times, literally means *armed struggle*, or *fight*, or even *conflict*. The word for war is *"voina,"* which the Soviets define as "an armed struggle between states," so there seems to be little difference between "war" and "armed struggle." However, General Major Voznenko makes it clear in the text that he does not exactly mean "war" when he uses the words. Another term, used fifty-seven times, is *"sposobi vooruzhennoi bor'bi,"* or "methods of armed conflict." This seems to be used to relate to nuclear weapons. The Soviet *Dictionary of Basic Military Terms*, 1965 edition, defines the following:

METHODS OF CONDUCTING ARMED CONFLICT—various applications of military operations of the armed forces directed at fulfilling strategic missions and achieving strategic goals. In present-day conditions, methods of conducting armed conflict means: the simultaneous influence of the means of armed conflict on the interior of the country and the basic groupings of the armed forces of the enemy by means of conducting simultaneous or consecutive deep operations on land, on sea, and in aerospace and in delivering massed, group, or single nuclear strikes on strategic objectives of the enemy, and so forth.

Voznenko has summed up the problem clearly and concisely.

"The appearance of the nuclear rocket weapon and the arming of the leading governments of the world with it evoked a modern revolution in military affairs. It signifies a profound qualitative jump not only in armaments and military equipment but also in the methods and forms of conducting armed combat."

The author considers "the question [that] arises about what sorts of methods of armed combat will be used if a new world war begins without the use of the nuclear weapon." Should this happen, the portions of the forces armed with nuclear weapons must be maintained at a high state of readiness because the nuclear means might be introduced at any time. The commanders cannot copy the methods used in past wars.

This article appeared in *Communist of the Armed Forces*, in June, 1966. Therefore, having been written after the adjournment of the XXIII Congress of the CPSU, it reflects any change in direction of the armed forces that might have been given as a result of that Congress.

THE DEVELOPMENT of methods of armed combat and of military art goes on continuously just as changes in quality and quantity of weapons and other factors continually accumulate. However, noticeable changes in tactics, operational art, and strategy, or definite jumps in their development take place only when these changes reach a certain level after which one can see improvement or disappearance of certain methods of action and the beginning of others. In this the law of dialectics finds its own manifestation, the law of transition from quantity to quality.

The recognition of the continuity of development of methods of armed combat does not mean that this process takes place uniformly. In military art, changes decisively transforming the methods of armed combat have taken place in the past and are taking place at the present. Thus, Soviet military art at the beginning of the thirties was marked by rapid development of tactics and operational art, which was connected with the important changes of armaments, and the organization of troops as well as the working

321

out of the theory and practice of battle in sufficient depth of the defense zone and operational rear, combat actions of mechanized and tank formations, the air forces, airborne troops, and so forth.

The appearance of the nuclear rocket weapon and the arming of the leading governments of the world with it evoked a modern revolution in military affairs. It signifies a profound qualitative jump not only in armaments and military equipment but also in the methods and forms of conducting armed combat.

The process of the further perfection of the nuclear weapon and its carriers—rockets of various designations, aviation, submarine fleets—and also of radioelectronics and other kinds of weapons and military equipment is taking place today. All this and other factors are evoking the swift process of development and change of the methods of armed combat, the growth of their activity, complexity, and diversity. While in the past new weapons changed the methods of armed combat at a comparatively slow rate, the nuclear weapon in a short period of time has become the basic and decisive weapon which is able to fulfill the main mission of a battle, an operation, and armed combat as a whole. It has brought to life absolutely new methods of operation of all the services of the armed forces and has fundamentally changed all of their structures and military art itself.

The essence of these changes in methods of armed combat is that in present-day conditions ideas about the main objectives of armed force are changing. Such objectives now are not only strategic nuclear weapons and groupings of armed forces but are also objectives composing the basic military-economic power of the enemy, the organs of his government, and organs of higher military command as well as those of his moral potential and will to fight.

It is known that in the past for the achievement of strategic goals the method used was that of successive solution of a large number of intermediate problems. It is sufficient to recall those numerous strategic tasks which were fulfilled by the Soviet Army during the attack from the Volga to the Dnieper, and from the Vistula to Berlin. Now there is the possibility of deciding the main tasks and of reaching the goals of war or strategic operations by means of the simultaneous striking of all of the enemy's main objectives, thus the most decisive and active offensive operations of all kinds and of all scales move to the forefront. Strategic actions will be primarily determined by strategic nuclear strikes, operations in the theaters of military actions, and also operations on a large scale of long-range aviation, the navy and the combat operations of the troops of PVO [air defense].

The methods of armed combat in nuclear war at all levels— strategic, operational, and tactical, will not be similar to the methods of armed combat in wars even of the not distant past. They will be distinguished by great territorial sweep, a growth of forces and means participating in battle, operations, and in war as a whole, by maneuverability and swift-moving action, in quick and sharp changes in the relationship of forces and of means, and also by radical changes of conditions, complicating the whole process of directing troops and forces, their mutual actions and close support.

Sometimes the question arises about what sort of methods of armed combat will be used if a new world war begins without the use of the nuclear weapon? Even in this case, it is unthinkable that we will repeat those tactical and operational ways which were characteristic for the campaigns of 1944 and 1945. The structure and armaments of the services of the armed forces and also the branches of services and forces, both qualitatively and quantitatively, have changed, so that new tactical and operational ways and methods of combat are needed.

At the same time it is necessary to keep in mind that the nuclear weapon of tactical, operational, and strategic designation will be in constant high combat readiness and might be used at any time. This, too, will not permit commanders to copy methods of action used in the last war, but will inspire them to search persistently for new methods in keeping with the qualitatively different character of armed combat.

In studying the objective laws of development and change of methods of armed combat, our cadres can with a high degree of probability foresee the perspective of the further development in weapons and in military equipment and the improvement of the organizational structure of the armed forces. Knowledge and a stocktaking of the tendencies and the directions in the development of military affairs will permit Soviet officers, generals, and admirals to fulfill successfully the raising of the combat readiness of our Armed Forces and the decisions of the XXIII Congress of the CPSU on strengthening the defense potential of our Motherland.

23. THE XXIII CONGRESS OF THE CPSU ON THE MILITARY THREAT AND THE PROBLEMS OF STRENGTHENING THE DEFENSE POTENTIAL OF THE COUNTRY
BY GENERAL OF THE ARMY V. D. IVANOV, GENERAL MAJOR A. OVSYANNIKOV, AND COLONEL M. I. GALKIN

Editors' Notes

FROM THE TITLE alone, it is apparent that this article, appearing in *Communist of the Armed Forces*, June, 1966, represents an official viewpoint. Its purpose is to inform the Soviet Armed Forces of the decisions and views of the XXIII Party Congress.

General Ivanov, the senior author, is well qualified professionally from both his ideological and his military background. He is the commandant of the General Staff Academy, a member of the Communist party since 1919, a veteran of the Spanish Civil War and a former first deputy chief of the General Staff.

This article seems to be directed at Communist China as well as to its Soviet audience and the United States. The theme is the relationship between economic and military power. "The growth of the military threat primarily appears in the increasing militarization of the capitalist economy and the arms race." The point is made several times that economic achievements are the basis of progress by military forces.

Specific figures are given on economic growth rates of various capitalistic nations, on the percentage of the national budget of

324

the United States going for direct and indirect military expenditures, and on the numbers of U.S. intercontinental ballistic missiles and atomic submarines. As is usual in Soviet publications of this type, no Soviet statistics are given from which meaningful comparisons can be made.

"In contemporary war the role of economics is changing its essence. The timely creation of reserves of nuclear weapons is acquiring exceptional significance, by the use of which the military-political goals of war might now be achieved in the beginning period." The authors then go on to show how "the basic directions in the development of our socialist economy have a great influence on the strengthening of the defense potential of the country." As they state, "It is scarcely worth pointing out that steel and other metals are used not only for machine-tools, tractors, combines, and other machines of peaceful labor but also for rockets, submarines, airplanes, tanks, and so forth."

Electric power, machine building, the chemical industry, oil, gas, coal, modern transport, and agriculture—all contribute to the defense potential of the country. The reader might note that one aspect of the "Five-year Plan" emphasizes the importance of agriculture "to create the necessary food reserves" for military needs. These concepts are worth serious reflection by persons who think that the economy of the Soviet Union is being rapidly oriented toward consumer needs.

Following an analysis of the economic basis of military power, the article examines some of the principles of the organization of the Soviet Armed Forces as well as the armed forces basic direction. The usual emphasis is given to the Strategic Rocket Forces, with specific mention being made about new mobile missile launchers. Again, in order, the atomic submarine and aircraft are discussed. Throughout, the importance of nuclear weapons in all of the Soviet services is stressed. This is in accordance "with the demands of the revolution in military affairs."

Colonel Galkin, one of the coauthors of the article, is a candidate of philosophical sciences and one of the authors of the textbook *The Bases of Military Pedagogy and Psychology*, 1964, which was written by the Department of Military Pedagogy and Psychology of the Lenin Military-Political Academy. He also wrote an article entitled "Know and Take Into Account the Psychological Features of Subordinates in Their Training and Education."

ALL LIFE and activity of the Soviet people is filled with the enthusiasm of the active struggle for the realization of the plans of the XXIII Congress of the CPSU. The party Congress examined the main problems of the building of communism on the basis of the scientific analysis of our successes in the struggle for communism and of international conditions, which determined the internal and external policies of the Soviet government. Great attention was given to questions of the further strengthening of the defense potential of the country and of the reliable safeguarding of the security of the socialist system. "In conditions when the aggressive forces of imperialism are aggravating international tensions and are creating a breeding ground for war, the CPSU will henceforth raise the vigilance of the Soviet people and strengthen the defensive power of our country so that the Armed Forces of the U.S.S.R. will always be ready to protect reliably the achievements of socialism and to give a shattering repulse to any imperialist aggressor."

The Aggressiveness of Imperialism—the Reason for the Intensification of Military Danger

The Soviet Union firmly and consistently follows a peace-loving foreign policy which flows from the very nature of our structure, persistently fights for preventing new world war, for decreasing international tension, for creating conditions under which each nation can freely develop. While occupied with peaceful construction, our party and our people cannot be distracted from what is taking place in the world arena. The XXIII Congress pointed out the presence of two contrary tendencies acting in modern international conditions. "The relative forces in the world arena," states a resolution of the Congress, "are continuing to change in favor of

326

socialism, workers', and national-liberation movements. Together with this, the current period is characterized by the intensification of imperialist aggression and the activation of reaction. The deepening of the general crisis of capitalism and the aggravation of contradictions are strengthening the adventurism of imperialism, its danger for nations, for the cause of peace and social progress."

The party takes into account both of these tendencies in deciding questions of internal and external policy of the Soviet state.

The firm confidence in the triumph of socialism and communism and the resolve to overcome all difficulties on the path to the bright goal inspire the conclusion of the party that in the modern epoch the world social system and forces struggling against imperialism and for the socialist rebuilding of society determine the main direction of historical development. The socialist community of nations is showing its more powerful influence on the course of history primarily by successes in the development of productive forces. The industrial production of the socialist countries during the period from 1961 to 1965 increased 43 per cent. In 1965 the U.S.S.R. produced almost one-fifth of all the world's industrial production, whereas on the eve of the Second World War the whole of the U.S.S.R.'s industrial production composed less than one-tenth. The political, economic, and military co-operation of the socialist countries has gained strength.

The increase of the economic power determines the steady growth of the international authority of the socialist system, its influence on the fate of mankind. Under the influence of the victory of socialism, a further aggravation of the class war in capitalist countries is taking place. Rallying around the working class are more and more social layers—masses of farmers, workers in mental work, and also persons protesting monopoly. In the world the process of the further development of the national-liberation movement is going on. Nations, having won state independence, are struggling to liquidate the heavy consequences of the rule of the colonizers.

The growth of the forces of socialism cannot but be admitted by the imperialists themselves. The words, written not long ago, of one reactionary French magazine are noteworthy: "In fifteen years democracy (read 'capitalism') has lost half of the free world. If events develop the same way, in another fifteen years the free world will cease to exist."

The XXIII Congress of the CPSU analyzed in depth the social processes which are taking place in the capitalist world, and noted the further sharpening of contradictions of imperialism. The capitalist economy continues to be unsteady. It cannot escape irregularities and cyclical development. Capitalism has gone through two periods of economic crisis in the postwar years: 1948–49 and 1957–58.

The law of irregularity of economic and political development of the country continues to act in the capitalist world. After the Second World War the U.S.A. had absolute predominance in the volume of production in the capitalist world (53.9 per cent of the industrial production). Subsequently, their proportion of production was reduced. During the period from 1953 to 1964 the level of industrial production in the U.S.A. grew only 44 per cent while in the FRG it grew 125 per cent; in France, 116 per cent and in Italy, 141 per cent. FRG by 1962 had already overtaken England in volume of industrial production. FRG now has an industrial production two times greater than that of France. Japan has left Italy and France behind. All this gives rise to economic rivalry among capitalist states and increases the instability of their economies.

In the present-day bourgeois world, the basic contradictions of capitalist society are being intensified with full force as are also the contradictions between labor and capital. Scientific technical progress and the growth of labor productivity associated with it is being used by monopoly for its own enrichment. In 1965, for example, the monopolies of the U.S.A. received forty-five billion dollars of pure profit; that is four times more than the annual average in the period of World War II.

The intensification of the contradictions of capitalism is clear testimony that capitalism is outliving its age and is becoming more and more reactionary. The words of Lenin about imperialism being ready for any savagery, brutality, and crime in order to defend the dying capitalist enslavement sound especially real today. (See *Works* Vol. 19, p. 77.)

Imperialism always saw its salvation in predatory wars. Thus, under the guise of German imperialism, it plunged mankind into two world wars in the life span of one generation.

In evaluating modern imperialism, the XXIII Congress of the CPSU reached a very important conclusion about the growth of the military threat. In the last few years the imperialists have brazenly interfered in the affairs of other countries and nations and have not hesitated to use armed intervention. The military threat which is being evoked by the aggressive actions of the imperialists, and primarily the U.S.A., has grown.

The growth of the military threat primarily appears in the increasing militarization of the capitalist economy and in the arms race. F. Engels wrote that "militarism rules over Europe and devours it." This tendency is a hundred times greater today. Militarization has now turned into a constant factor in the development of the capitalist economy. The direct and indirect military expenditures of the U.S.A. in 1939, for example, were 3.5 per cent of the national budget; in 1949, 11.4 per cent; and in 1962, 17 per cent. During the last fifteen years the expenditures of the U.S.A. have surpassed by forty times military costs of the fifteen prewar years.

The lion's share of military expenses of the U.S.A. is going for production of strategic means of attack particularly for the development of nuclear rocket weapons. In 1960 the proportion of rockets in the armed forces of the U.S.A. compared to strategic bombers was 5 per cent higher and in 1965 it was already higher than strategic bombers. In 1961 the U.S.A. had thirty-five rocket installations and one rocket-carrying atomic submarine. At the present time it has more than seven hundred intercontinental rockets and thirty-two rocket atomic submarines. Not long ago Secretary of Defense McNamara of the U.S.A. stated that the strategic rocket forces scheduled for production between 1967–71 will assure the "guaranteed" destruction of the Soviet Union and other countries of socialism.

Militarism more and more subordinates science to its influence in capitalist countries. More than 50 per cent of all science personnel in the capitalist world are being used in military areas. Sixty per cent of the artificial satellites of Earth launched from the U.S.A. have direct military purpose.

The creation by imperialist states of multimillion man armies in peacetime is without precedent in history. In April, 1966, the number of men in the armed forces of the U.S.A. passed 3,000,000 (of these about 1,000,000 are located outside the boundaries of the country). In 1962, there were already 8,200,000 men in the regular armies of capitalist countries belonging to military blocs.

A direct outgrowth of the existence and the growth of the military threat is the creation of aggressive military blocs and groups. This new phenomenon is characteristic for the postwar period. Earlier military blocs of states usually existed in war years. In peacetime only diplomatic and political prerequisites of military coalitions were made. This coalition strategy now exists in full measure in peacetime.

The main aggressive bloc, NATO, is a military-political supranational organization which is kept in a state of constant military readiness. The U.S.A. in every way is trying to use NATO to turn western Europe into an armed camp, a military base for an attack on the socialist countries.

The imperialist bloc, SEATO,[1] in the plans of the ruling circles of the U.S.A., must secure the southeastern flank of its aggressive plans and must also serve as a weapon of struggle with the national-liberation movement. At the present time the U.S.A. is holding in southeast Asia a greater quantity of her own troops than the number held there during the period of the war with Japan. A third military bloc, CENTO,[2] according to the American magazine *Col-liers*,[3] was created to have a military base "close to the interior regions of the Soviet Union."

Such are the actual facts. They testify to the practical prepara-

[1] SEATO, Council of Southeast Asia Treaty Organization.

[2] CENTO, Central Treaty Organization.

[3] *Collier's*, the national weekly, was published from April 28, 1888, to January 4, 1957.

tion of a new world war by the imperialists. The most sinister role in this is being played by the ruling circles of the U.S.A. who long ago adopted a course for gaining world supremacy.

The aggressive aims of American imperialism have taken on a special sweep in recent years. With the coming to power of President Johnson, there was a noticeable review of American policy. A cult of brute force was revived, a policy of movement along a path of aggression and adventure, dangerous for peace. Events of recent years clearly show what an unscrupulous sham the pre-election program of Johnson's was, hiding the true aims of the rulers of the U.S.A. When Goldwater proposed the bombing of North Vietnam in his pre-election campaign Johnson called his demand criminal adventurism. But it is no one other than this same Johnson, who, on becoming president, gave the order to bomb the Democratic Republic of Vietnam.

The earth of Vietnam has been turned into a sort of range for testing all kinds of poison gases, modern weapons, and military equipment by the overseas robbers. The dark days of fascism are brought to the minds of people as the bosses of the Pentagon subject the cities and villages of the Democratic Republic of Vietnam to barbarian bombardments and follow tactics of "scorched earth" in South Vietnam.

War in Vietnam, like other predatory actions of American militarists, represents a serious threat to mankind. It carries in itself the constant threat of turning into world war. Aggression, if it is not stopped, always has a tendency to spread. That is why the peoples of the whole world are demanding an end to the American imperialist crimes in Vietnam and at other points in the world.

Since the beginning of 1966, American imperialism has stimulated feverish activity directed at rebuilding and strengthening the aggressive blocs and at expanding the union with the FRG. At the present time West German imperialism is coming forth as the main partner of the U.S.A. in Europe in the business of aggravating international tension. West Germany is becoming more and more the seat of the military threat. The FRG is now the only country in Europe advocating a review of the postwar boundaries. Nurturing

331

the idea of revenge for defeat in World War II, West German leaders openly come out with pretenses for receiving the nuclear weapon, for the beginning, if only under the guise of creation of joint nuclear forces. It must also be kept in mind that the FRG at the present time has the economic and technical potentials for independent production of a nuclear weapon.

Imperialism is still strong and it has become craftier. In its attempts to prevent social progress, the imperialists may enter into any adventures. One must not fail to take into account the danger of the unleashing of a world war by them.

Our party attentively follows what is taking place in the world and in capitalist countries. It is constantly concerned with strengthening the defense of the U.S.S.R.—a necessary condition for the building of communism in our country and for protecting the gains of socialism and preserving peace in the whole world.

The Growth of the Defense Might of the Country, One of the Main Tasks of the Five-year Plan

The defense potential of the Soviet government is determined by many factors of socio-political, economic, and strictly military nature. In present-day conditions the solution of all national economy problems in unity with the problems of national defense is acquiring special significance. The successful economic development of our country creates the prerequisite for the constant improvement of the fighting might of the Soviet Armed Forces.

The determining dependence of the course and the outcome of war on economic conditions, as pointed out in the classics of Marxism-Leninism, is fully confirmed by the experience of war. It is absolutely obvious that this is true in nuclear rocket war too, if the imperialists succeed in unleashing it. Only those governments or union of governments whose economics will be in condition to resolve the problems of mobilizing all the branches of the national economy and of science and to unite the people in moral-political terms can count on victory.

In contemporary war the role of economics is changing in its essence. The timely creation of reserves of nuclear weapons is acquiring exceptional significance, by the use of which the military-political goals of war might now be achieved in the beginning period. The significance of reserves of other material means, collected in peacetime, has grown tremendously. In present circumstances the economy itself is becoming the object of armed attack because of the availability of strategic rockets carrying thermonuclear charges to the opposing sides. However, it is not excluded that war might assume a prolonged nature also. Then no less significant than the timely creation of reserves will be the vitality of the most important branches of the economy and the ability to restore those branches during the war.

The CPSU takes into account the new conditions of preparing the country for the repulse of imperialist aggression and on this basis determines the task of developing the national economy and the direction of perfecting the Armed Forces. "The Five-year Plan," according to the directive of the XXIII Congress CPSU, "must guarantee the further growth of the defense might of the Soviet Union, which will allow the still more reliable protection of the Soviet people and all of the socialist community from the danger of imperialist aggression and will strengthen the position of the peace-loving and liberating forces in the whole world."

The rapidly developing socialist economy has a decisive role in strengthening the military power of the Soviet Union and the other socialist countries. "It is especially true in our times," Comrade A. N. Kosygin remarked in his report at the XXIII Congress of the CPSU, "when weapons are becoming ever more complicated and costly and a high level of science and technology is needed for their production."

The economic potential of the U.S.S.R. is determined by the harmonious development of all growths of the national economy. All the basic directions in the development of our socialist economy have a great influence on the strengthening of the defense potential of the country.

In the new Five-year Plan, great aims are set out for developing metallurgy, electrical energy, chemistry, and machine building. These are the most important branches which are determining the sure step of the Soviet people to communism. These branches of industry also create the firm base for perfecting the defense of the Soviet government. It is scarcely worth pointing out that steel and other metals are used not only for machine-tools, tractors, combines, and other machines of peaceful labor but also for rockets, submarines, airplanes, tanks, and so forth.

The party considers, as an important task of the new Five-year Plan, the providing of a high tempo of development of metallurgy, giving special attention to improving the quality of metals which are especially important in modern military equipment.

The years of the new Five-year Plan will be marked by further development of electrical power. The main direction in the development of energy is the building of large thermal electropower stations and economical hydroelectric stations, the creation of unified energy systems, the improving of the effectiveness of the use of electrical power stations and also of their survivability in case of war.

The heart of industry is, as is well known, mechanical engineering. It is at the service of all branches of the national economy without exception, including, of course, the defense industry.

A branch of industry which is revolutionizing production is the chemical industry. The plan of big chemistry in the new Five-year Plan calls for doubling the output of chemical products. The development of chemistry, especially the chemistry of polymers, is leading to the creation of new materials having great significance for defense.

Oil, gas, and coal are the basis of the fuel of the country, at the same time they are the most important source for providing the Armed Forces with fuel, lubricating oil substances, and so forth.

It is hard to overestimate the significance for defense of all aspects of modern transport. It is planned to increase the freight turnover of the railways between 1966 and 1970 by 23 per cent; water transport, 1.8 times; and automotive, 1.7 times. Approximately seven thousand kilometers of new railway will be added to the existing network of means of communication, twelve thousand kilometers of pipeline, and about sixty-three thousand kilometers

334

of auto highways. Undoubtedly these planned measures will promote the satisfaction of the growing demands in contemporary war for the rapid transport of troops, equipment, and weapons on rail and highways, by air and sea lines.

The growth of all branches of the national economy in many ways determines the development of the material well-being of the workers, and, also, the raising of the defense potential of the country and the development of our agriculture. The fulfillment of the main task which is placed before the country in the new Five-year Plan will increase significantly the production of agricultural and animal products, secure a high and stable tempo of development, permit the satisfaction of the growing demands of the population for food products and of industry for agricultural raw material, and, also, create the necessary food reserves.

The Communist party is giving great attention to science and to the use of the achievements of scientific-technical progress.

In the directive for the new Five-year Plan the basic direction of speeding up the development of scientific-technical progress is indicated; it has enormous significance for the national economy and also for raising the might of the Armed Forces. Research in the areas of theoretical and applied mathematics will raise to a new level the use of mathematical methods in various areas of science and technology. In military affairs this will have a certain influence on the perfecting of methods and equipment for guiding troops and for the solution of other problems.

The research of cosmic space will be widely used for perfecting long-range radio communications, television, meteorological service, and for other practical goals. We must keep in mind that the strategists of imperialism are directing basic efforts in the exploration and use of the cosmos for the resolution of military tasks.

The further strengthening of the socio-political unity of socialist society, the growth of political consciousness, and the education and culture of the Soviet people have enormous significance for raising the defense potential of the country. The directive for the new Five-year Plan adopted by the XXIII Congress of the CPSU provides for the solution of such important socio-political problems as raising the well-being of all the peoples of the Soviet Union and the further erasing of the differences between town and country, between workers in mental pursuits and in physical labor, and the developing of the economy and of the culture.

The realization of the program of economic and cultural building planned by the Congress will raise still further the economic and defense might, the international authority, and the influence of the Soviet Union.

Constant Combat Readiness of the Armed Forces—the Most Important Condition for the Security of the Country

The XXIII Congress of the CPSU, after examining the course and results of the building of communism in the U.S.S.R., summed up the strengthening of the combat power of our Armed Forces and raised the problem of the further perfection of them. These results show that our party is religiously observing the legacy of Lenin—to cherish the defense of the country as the apple of one's eye. It consistently and persistently translates the demands of its program into reality and determines the basic direction and principles of the organization of the armed protection of the socialist Fatherland.

Comrade L. I. Brezhnev stated in the report of the Central Committee of the CPSU to the XXIII Congress of the party that "the party will henceforth in every way possible strengthen the defense potential of the Soviet Union, increase the power of the Armed Forces of the U.S.S.R., and maintain that level of military preparedness of troops which will reliably guarantee the peaceful labor of the Soviet people."

For the Soviet Armed Forces the period which has passed since the time of the XXII Congress has entailed the resolution of many highly complicated and exceptionally important problems of military organization. Along what basic direction did the Soviet Armed Forces develop?

In present-day conditions, the basic means of restraining the aggressor and of defeating him decisively in nuclear war is the nuclear rocket weapon. The measures taken by the Central Committee of the party and the Soviet government made it possible to

336

increase significantly the reserves of nuclear ammunition of various designations and also sharply reinforced the equipment of all of the services of the Armed Forces with the means of using these stores.

A great deal of attention was given to the development of the Strategic Rocket Forces. New means of fighting were introduced into this main service of the Armed Forces of the Soviet Union and mobile launchers were created. This is a new and a very important circumstance; it has great significance for the successful fulfillment of the missions by the Rocket Troops.

An underwater rocket-carrying fleet was created in the Navy— a fleet capable of destroying not only sea targets of the enemy but also objects on land located far from shore. Soviet rocket-carrying atomic submarines are able to carry out launches of ballistic rockets to a great distance from an underwater location. In recent years the number of long voyages taken by our submarines has increased five times. The statement of Minister of Defense of the U.S.S.R., Marshal of the Soviet Union R. Ya. Malinovsky about the successful completion of the around-the-world voyage of a group of atomic submarines while submerged resounded like a combat report of Soviet sailors to their party. During the time required for the voyage almost 40,000 kilometers were traveled without coming to the surface. This, once again, convincingly confirms the excellent combat possibilities of Soviet atomic ships created by the labor of scientists, engineers, and workers and also confirms the exceptionally high moral-political qualities of the submariners.

A significant part of the fleet of combat airplanes for frontal and especially for military transport aviation in the Air Forces has been renewed.

Operational-tactical nuclear means have been developed for the Ground Forces and, along with this, in corresponding proportion, conventional combat equipment of the troops has been improved. New, more modern, armored, artillery and special equipment have been introduced into tank and motorized infantry formations. For troop personnel armored protective cover from the action of the destructive factors of nuclear weapons has been increased by a large percentage. The mobility and the maneuverability of forma-

337

tions and units of the Ground Forces have been increased. The organizational structure of the troops is being improved in conformity to the demands of battle and of operations in nuclear war.

Our airborne troops have been significantly strengthened. Soviet paratroopers have everything necessary, even medium tanks, for successfully waging war. They can solve strategic problems in contemporary war.

The troops of National PVO [air defense] are at a level on which they can guarantee the reliable destruction of any airplane and many rockets of the enemy. This service of the Armed Forces is equipped with the latest highly effective surface-to-air rocket system and aviation complex for the interception and destruction of enemy means of attack.

Thus, thanks to the tireless concern of the party and of all of the Soviet people, our Motherland has Armed Forces equipped with first-class, present-day combat equipment and weapons.

The powerful equipment and awesome weapons have been given to Soviet soldiers, the true sons of our people. The Lenin party calls upon the soldiers to improve constantly their political and combat training, to perfect order and organization, to raise vigilance and combat readiness of units and ships.

Thanks to the constant attention of the Central Committee of the CPSU, a remarkable cadre of commanders, political workers, and engineers having good political, military, and military-technical training has grown. At the present time each fourth officer in the army and navy has a higher military or special education than formerly. Commanders, political organs, and party organizations, all army Communists and Komsomols, composing 93 per cent of the officers, generals, and admirals, are educating the personnel in the spirit of socialist patriotism, proletarian internationalism, in the spirit of constant readiness to go to the defense of the interests of socialism.

Among the many problems placed before us in connection with the resolutions of the XXIII Congress of the party, the further improvement in the practice of troop management, style, methods of work of the commanders, political organs, and party organizations has special significance and there is increased concern that the management of the troops will have a scientific basis, free from the smallest trace of superficiality. In present-day conditions, scientific management is an indispensable and important condition of the combat capability of the troops and the achievement of victory in armed battle.

New tasks stand today before Soviet military thought. Guided by scientific technological progress and by the achievements of modern science in leading areas, military thought is called upon to solve more effectively the problems of military theory and practice. The perfection of available weapons and the creation of new means of armed struggle and the working out of new forms and ways of waging war acquire special significance.

For the development of modern military art, much of value comes from the deep study of the experience of past wars. The scientific elaboration of the history of the Great Patriotic War also helps to unmask the bourgeois falsifiers of history, the *revanchists* and the militarists. In the battle against bourgeois ideology, every sort of ideological weapon must work accurately and smoothly.

The decisive source of the might of the Soviet Army and Navy is the leadership of the party. In contemporary conditions the leading role of the party in strengthening the defense capability of the U.S.S.R. and the combat power of the Armed Forces has grown significantly. This is stipulated by a series of factors, including the complication and enlargement of the problem of the timely economic and military preparation of the whole country to repulse the imperialist aggression; the necessity for improving the structure and the organization of the Armed Forces, the training and education of their personnel, in accordance with the demands of the revolution in military affairs and with the nature of a possible nuclear rocket war; the growing significance of the moral factor in this war; the widening of the international tasks of the Armed Forces; and the necessity of strengthening the military co-operation of the U.S.S.R. with the other socialist countries.

An important condition for the successful solution of problems which the party is placing before the Armed Forces is the further rise of party-political work among the troops and the strengthening of the influence of the party on all sides of the life and activities of the army and navy. Man must always be on top in party-political work, since party work is work with people.

Soviet soldiers are filled with pride for the high value which the XXIII Congress of the CPSU placed on their military labor. In answer to the concern of the party for strengthening the defense potential of the country, they are expressing unwavering resolve to achieve new successes in combat training, in political tempering, and in raising the readiness for performance of their sacred duty to the Motherland.

---

24. ON THE QUESTION OF THE ESSENCE OF WAR
By Colonel I. A. Grudinin
Professor, Doctor of Philosophical Sciences

Editors' Notes

ONE SIDE OF A CONTROVERSY that for some reason the political and military hierarchy decided to put into print is presented in this article. The spokesman is Colonel Grudinin and his writing "The Time Factor in Modern War" is chapter 17 of this book. In the following article Grudinin is presumably attacking a lecture given by Lieutenant Colonel Ye. Ribkin entitled "Nuclear Rocket War and Politics," which was "distributed by the Frunze Central Club of the Soviet Army as material to help propagandists." A copy of Ribkin's lecture is not available, but judging from Colonel Grudinin's comments the lecture would seem to follow Lieutenant Colonel Ribkin's article "On the Nature of World Nuclear Rocket War," included as chapter 9.

On the surface, at least, the controversy centers around very obscure points of Marxism-Leninism. The most specific issue is Grudinin's scathing condemnation of General Major N. A. Talensky for an article called "Thoughts on Past Wars," written in *Inter-*

national Affairs,[1] April, 1965, in which Talensky stated: "In our time there is no more dangerous illusion than the notion that thermonuclear war might still serve as an instrument of politics, that political goals can be achieved by using nuclear weapons."

Grudinin claims that "Such an assertion is not only in error, but it is harmful because it can shake one's assurance in our victory over the aggressor and the consciousness of the necessity to be ready at any moment for armed struggle with the use of the nuclear rocket weapon."

Ribkin, in his article "On the Nature of World Nuclear Rocket War," attacks the identical paragraph found in Talensky's writings. Grudinin praises Ribkin for this attack, stating, " . . . the lecturer's criticism of those who deny all possibility of victory in a world nuclear rocket conflict is highly appropriate." The reader may wonder if the real purpose of Grudinin's article is to criticize Ribkin, as it appears on the surface, or to condemn the outmoded views of Talensky. The issues on which Ribkin and Grudinin agree are probably more important than those on which they differ.

This writing typifies the firmness with which Communists must hold to the party line. "Without question, world nuclear rocket war, in the event it breaks out, will lead . . . to great destructive consequences, and the very existence of some countries will be risked. However, no matter what the consequences of a given war, this in no way changes the position that war would be a continuation of the policies of the government and the classes taking part in it by forceful means. And in this is the essence of any war."

It is interesting to note the reference that V. I. Lenin wrote: "War is a continuation of policy by other (that is, violent) means." Readers of Clausewitz will understand the source.

Grudinin's article appeared in *Red Star* on July 12, 1966.

THE QUESTION of the essence of modern wars is a real theoretical and political question. The question is about what is chief and

---

[1] Note Ribkin's reference to the same article by Talensky in "On the Nature of World Nuclear Rocket War," chap. 9.

decisive in war, what becomes apparent in all its processes. But that which is the main thing does not lie on the surface. It is hidden behind varied phenomena and in addition is thoroughly camouflaged and distorted by the imperialist advocates of new world nuclear rocket war in order to justify their criminal, man-hating designs. This determines both the urgency of the given question and that increased attention which is being given to it in recent times in our press and by verbal propaganda.

In particular, the lecture of Lieutenant Colonel Ribkin "Nuclear Rocket War and Politics," distributed by the Frunze Central Club of the Soviet Army as material to help propagandists, is devoted to this question. The lecture was distinguished by the independent approach of its author to the working out of the complicated and important problem selected by him. In this article we would like to dwell in a little more detail both on the merits and on certain demerits of the lecture which, in our view, has an essential character.

Even in the introductory part of the lecture, it is clear that Comrade Ribkin has made it his aim to answer the questions concerning "what has remained unchanged and what is new in the formula 'war is the continuation of politics,' " and "Has the nature of war changed, and if it has, how?" In criticizing the erroneous assertions that, supposedly, war has now ceased to be a continuation of politics, the author dwells in detail on how this formula should be understood.

He recalls that war arises on the basis of deep contradictions of antagonistic society, based in their economies; that in contemporary conditions the cause of world wars is the aggressive policy of imperialism, primarily of the Americans; and that politics determines the historical meaning, the nature of war, its essence. The author stresses the teachings of Marxism-Leninism on just and unjust wars, which give a correct orientation to the understanding of the historical role of each given war and work out the right relationship to any actual war.

Here is given a characteristic of the contemporary epoch, and it speaks of the changes in the correlation of class forces in the international arena in favor of socialism. But from these correct premises, in our view, a deeply erroneous conclusion is made. In the possibility that the socialist countries and the peace-loving forces of the planet can restrain the imperialist aggressors, in the fact that certain socio-historical conditions limit the actions "of the basic law of the correlation of war and politics (that is, the possibility of continuing politics by means of war)," the lecturer sees something new which, allegedly, changes the very essence of war.

In other words, the possibilities of preventing a new world war and the possibilities and conditions of its arising are identified with war *itself;* an attempt is made to combine the uncombinable, war and peace, the condition of society in peacetime and its condition in wartime. But such an assertion is theoretically indefensible and politically harmful. To adhere to it would mean voluntarily or involuntarily to agree with those bourgeois ideologists who spread in every way possible the story that there allegedly is no difference between war and peace, and thus they attempt to camouflage, to hide from the masses, the policy of imperialism aimed at preparing for a new world war and at distorting the class essence of this war in the event it should break out.

Yes, we have always stressed and will stress that the possibility of preventing world war exists in the contemporary epoch, just as there exists the possibility and the danger of its breaking out. In the Resolutions of the XXIII Congress of the CPSU it is written: "The deepening of the general crisis of capitalism and the sharpening of its contradictions increases the adventurism of imperialism, its danger for peoples, for the causes of peace and social progress."

But the possibility of the preventing and the possibility of the breaking out of a new world war do not change and cannot change the essence of war.

The lecturer is absolutely right in saying that if imperialism forces a world nuclear rocket war on us, then from the side of the imperialist powers it would be a continuation of the aggressive, antinational, reactionary policy directed at liquidating socialism and at establishing world imperialist rule, but from the side of the socialist governments, it would be a continuation of the policy of

343

the heroic defense of the gains of socialism and communism, freedom and independence of peoples.

The author of the lecture convincingly demonstrates the danger and deep erroneousness of opinions that war in defense of the socialist Fatherland and the socialist camp, which we would be forced to wage in the event of a nuclear attack by the imperialists, would allegedly "lose" its just nature as the result of the use by us of nuclear rocket weapons. Such an opinion actually has nothing in common with the idea of the reliable defense of the gains of socialism and communism, with the problem of defeating the aggressor. The use by us of the nuclear rocket weapon would be a forced act and would be by the most just means, which would permit the bringing down on the aggressor the superior power of the same sort of weapons with which he will attempt to annihilate our country and other socialist countries.

But from these opinions it follows that the use of the nuclear rocket weapon cannot change the essence of war as a continuation of the politics of certain classes and governments by violent means. And if the lecturer recognizes the correctness of these opinions, and they are, indisputably, correct, then he must recognize also the erroneousness of his assertion that "noticeable changes took place in the essence of war with the massive introduction into the troops of the nuclear rocket weapon." Otherwise the lecturer would be contradicting himself and simply confusing the question.

Later Comrade Ribkin dwells on the question of the correlation of politics and military strategy in a possible nuclear rocket war; of the dependence of strategy on politics; of the guiding role of politics in relation to planning and conducting military actions. But here also he identifies two different questions and again brings confusion into the understanding of the main point of war.

It is indisputable that the appearance of the nuclear rocket weapon raised to a new high the role of politics and political leadership. Realizing a high responsibility for the fate of the Motherland, the cause of socialism and communism, and firmly following a line to prevent new world war, the Communist party attentively follows the intrigues of imperialism, exposes its per-

344

fidious plans, points out to the masses how and in whose name the imperialists are carrying out a mad arms race. It is taking all necessary measures so that the defense potential of the country and the combat power of the Armed Forces of the U.S.S.R. will always be on that level which will guarantee the decisive, swift, and complete defeat of any aggressor.

It is also indisputable that world war with the use of the nuclear rocket weapon would not only raise the role of the leadership of combat actions but would also greatly complicate putting strategic plans into action. In this war, it will not be easy to work out and take one decision or another concerning the conduct of armed conflict. This is why we are paying great attention now to mastering the laws of armed struggle, to raising and perfecting the level of scientific leadership of the combat actions of the army and navy.

But has all this brought "noticeable changes" into the essence of war as such? No, it has not. The question of strategic leadership, no matter how complicated and difficult the appearance and use of the new weapon has made it, is a question of *manifestation* of the main point of war, of what ways the belligerent governments will direct the combat actions of the armed forces, and what forms and means they will choose for achieving their political goals in war. But this does not change the position that war was, is, and will be a continuation of the policies of classes and governments by forcible means, and its class essence remains as before.

In the last section of his lecture, Comrade Ribkin examines the question of results of world war, in the event it breaks out, and the possibility of victory in it. In themselves, the opinions of the lecturer on this score do not evoke any doubts. No one will contradict the fact that war with the use of nuclear rocket means will demand enormous sacrifices and cause serious destruction to the productive forces. Therefore, the most nearly correct and direct conclusion drawn from the assessment of the possible results of world nuclear rocket war is the conclusion that it is necessary to prevent such a war and that such a war must not serve as a method of solving international quarrels.

In speaking of all this, the author quite correctly stresses the

345

other side, that the imperialists have not renounced war as a method of achieving their political goals and, therefore, we must have great vigilance and a high level of constant combat readiness.

The lecturer's opinions on the possibility of victory in nuclear rocket war also deserve attention. He rightly asserts that the possibility or impossibility of victory cannot be reduced to just the properties of weapons, but that the question must be made broader, and the correlation of all enemy forces must be examined. It is also true that if imperialist reaction tries to unleash a new world nuclear rocket war then civilization will not be destroyed but the capitalist structure will be destroyed as a source of all wars. In spite of the sacrifices, the peace-loving socialist forces will win in continuation of the just, revolutionary policy in a war forced on them.

In this connection, the lecturer's criticism of those who deny all possibility of victory in a world nuclear rocket conflict is highly appropriate. This point of view is expressed not only by several foreign figures but also by individual Soviet authors of articles on war. Indeed, Comrade N. Talensky, for example, in his article "Thoughts on Past Wars," published in the fifth number of the magazine *International Affairs* (1965), wrote: "In our time there is no more dangerous illusion than the notion that thermonuclear war might still serve as an instrument of politics, that political goals can be achieved by using nuclear weapons."

Such an assertion is not only in error, but it is harmful because it can shake one's assurance in our victory over the aggressor, and the consciousness of the necessity to be ready at any moment for armed struggle with the use of the nuclear rocket weapon.

It is well known that our party, our government, and our people have decisively spoken and are speaking out against a world nuclear rocket war's serving, as it says in the Program of the CPSU, "as a method of solving international disputes." But imperialism is conducting an absolutely different policy. Actual fact shows that imperialist reactionists and, primarily, the imperialists of the U.S.A. are openly preparing for world nuclear rocket war. Consequently, the possibility is not excluded that the imperialists *might* try to achieve their political goals by using the nuclear weapon. Consequently, nuclear-rocket war *might* serve as an instrument of politics both for those governments which unleash it and for those governments which, because of it, are forced to take up arms in order to defend themselves and to crush the aggressor.

We repeat that in his lecture Comrade Ribkin correctly considers the given question. But his mistake is that here also he mixes two different problems, two qualitatively different phenomena: war and its essence and the conditions for the development of society after the war.

The results of different wars are most diverse, as history testifies. Certain classes and governments achieved their political goals in them, others suffered defeat. There were instances when, say, a stronger imperialist government subjugated an entire country by means of war, depriving its people of their independence and sovereignty. But this did not change the fact that each war is actually a continuation of the policy of certain classes and governments by means of force.

Without question, world nuclear rocket war, in the event it breaks out, will lead, as we have already said, to great destructive consequences, and the very existence of some countries will be risked. However, no matter what the consequences of a given war, this in no way changes the position that war would be a continuation of the policies of the government and the classes taking part in it by forceful means. And in this is the essence of any war.

From all of the above the following conclusions can be made.

First. The questions formulated in the lecture—"What remains unchanged and what is new in the formula 'war is a continuation of politics'?" and "Has the essence of war changed and, if it has changed, how?"—are artificial and forced. And the assertion of the lecturer that "noticeable changes have taken place in the essence of war with the massive introduction of nuclear rocket weapons into the troops" is in error.

Second. The methodology of the study and explanation of the main point of war, as is known, consists in proceeding in this from the classic position, from the understanding of the close interdependence of war and economics, which determines politics, from

347

the position of Marxism-Leninism on the unbreakable unity of the essence and its manifestation, and on the stability of the essence. Unfortunately, the author of the lecture neglected the methodological position of the unbreakable unity between the essence and its manifestation and, especially, of the stability of the essence.

If the "noticeable changes" were to take place in the essence of war in connection with the appearance of a new weapon, if this essence were to be unstable, then there would be not one but many definitions of war. The history of man has known an enormous number of the most diverse wars. Many of them were waged with the help of different weapons. Take, for example, the First and Second World Wars. The Second World War was distinguished from the First in particular by the fact that, along with many older means of armed struggle, new, more powerful weapons were used in large quantity. It was a "war of machines"; a war with the use of very destructive means. But, nevertheless, all this did not shake the essence of war; it was a continuation of the politics of governments and classes taking part in it by forceful means.

A new weapon, as a rule, causes revolutions in the methods and forms of armed conflict, in military art, and in the forms and methods of strategic leadership in war. However, even this does not change the essence of war; all wars have been the continuation of politics of the governments and the classes taking part in them by violent means.

Yes, the nuclear rocket weapon brought about a revolution in the methods and forms of armed conflict. Nuclear rocket war, if it breaks out, will be fundamentally different from all wars of the past. It will be a bitter, destructive and highly maneuverable war. It, in effect, will erase the difference between the front and the rear. But this cannot serve as a basis for the assertion of "noticeable changes" in the essence of war. To assert this means to retreat from Marxist-Leninist dialectical materialism which teaches us to see always the difference between essence and its manifestation, between form and content.

The essence of war is manifested in all elements making up its contents and form, namely, in armed, economic, ideological, and

348

diplomatic struggle. In this, the armed struggle represents the main manifestation of the essence of war, its specific reflection. It is namely, the *manifestation* and the *reflection*, and not the essence *itself* of war (and even more emphatically it is not the unity of war and politics as the author of the lecture asserts).

The content of war as a phenomenon of social life can change. War can take on various forms and can be waged with the use of various means of armed, economic, ideological, and diplomatic struggle, and different political goals can be pursued in it. V. I. Lenin always stressed that for determining a type of war and for revealing its just or unjust nature, "it is necessary in each instance, for each war, particularly to determine its political content" (*Works* Vol. 23, p. 187).

The author of the lecture is right when he says that the essence, in general, is mobile. However, one must not forget the position of Marxist-Leninist philosophy that the essence is stable, that under the influence of quantitative changes in the framework of a given qualitative definition the essence can change, but this change is immaterial from the point of view of the characteristic essence of the subject. We know, for example, what great changes have taken place in the system of capitalism in the monopolistic stage of its development. But capitalism did not cease being capitalism because of this. Its exploiting, aggressive, reactionary essence was preserved. And this essence of capitalism will disappear only when capitalism disappears and is destroyed.

The same thing may be said of the essence of war. It is highly stable. No new means of armed conflict can shake its inner basis. The essence of war as a continuation of politics by forceful means will disappear when wars and the reasons bringing them about disappear.

Third. The author of the lecture apparently feels the precariousness and inconsistency of his opinions and, therefore, at the end of his lecture he declares: "The changes in the essence of war oblige us to also take into account that war remains a continuation of politics." But it should be clear to everyone, including Comrade Ribkin, that if "war remains a continuation of politics" that means its essence remains stable. And the thing here is not just casually to take into account that "war remains a continuation of politics," but to be guided undeviatingly by this attitude always, and in everything, in every investigation of present-day war.

In his time V. I. Lenin wrote: "In applying to war the basic attitude of dialectics, it consists of this: '*war is a continuation of policy by other* [that is, violent] *means*'." And this was always the point of view of Marx and Engels, *each* war was considered as "a *continuation* of the politics of certain interested powers and of *different classes* inside it, at a given time." (*Works*, Vol. 21, p. 194–95.)

This formula is accurate and scientific in the highest degree. It was and remains the stable definition of the essence of war. And there is no sort of necessity to subject it to revision without running the risk of falling in with those who at times, under the guise of a creative approach to theory, try to cast doubt on one or another fundamental and stable attitude of Marxism-Leninism.

The creative development of the Marxist-Leninist theory, including the teachings of Marxism-Leninism on war and the army, is an important, complicated, and responsible matter, a task of enormous political and practical importance. And our obligation consists not in engaging in research to determine "what remains unchanged" and "what new things have appeared" in one position or another or in one fundamental formula or another of Marxism-Leninism when solving a given task. No. It appears that the basic obligation and the duty of scientific workers consist of discovering and correctly explaining—on the basis of the positions and principles of Marxism-Leninism, Marxist-Leninist methodology that has been tested in practice and confirmed by history, and on the basis of a comprehensive and genuinely scientific analysis of actual reality—the new phenomena in social life, in the world revolutionary process, in the development of military affairs, and in enriching the theory and practice by really new conclusions and positions. At the same time, we must piously defend the purity of Marxism-Leninism and be guided by it always and in everything, and stand on fundamental class and party positions always and in everything.

This demand of the party is an immutable law for the activities of workers on the ideological front.

All the history of our party serves as a model of creative application and creative development of the revolutionary teachings of Marxism-Leninism. The XXIII Congress of the CPSU was another convincing and clear testimony of this. In its Resolution, the Congress wrote: "The basis of all ideological work of the party is propaganda of the ideas of Marxism-Leninism. The creative development of the Marxist-Leninist theory on the basis of the experience of Communist construction and the development of the world revolutionary movement and the struggle with all manifestations of bourgeois ideology is of very great importance for all the activity of the party."

Military-theoretical workers of the army and navy persistently work on the fulfilling of this task, on the development of the teachings of Marxism-Leninism on war and the army. And the higher our demands in the ideological content of military-theoretical works, brochures, and lectures on questions of theory, the more concern we will display for the genuine scientific working out of new problems of military theory and practice, the more successfully this task will be resolved.

---

25. MILITARY-TECHNICAL SUPERIORITY: THE MOST IMPORTANT FACTOR OF THE RELIABLE DEFENSE OF THE COUNTRY

By Lieutenant Colonel V. M. Bondarenko
Candidate of Philosophical Sciences

Editors' Notes

At the time the *Communist of the Armed Forces* published this article, in September, 1966, the United States public was not yet generally aware of the scale of the Soviet Union's antiballistic missile system and of the accelerated increase in the numbers of Soviet

351

intercontinental ballistic missiles. Colonel Bondarenko's work would appear as a clear indication that an arms race is a reality insofar as the Soviet Union is concerned and that, furthermore, the Soviet leaders are confident of successfully winning the race.

Bondarenko points out that in the past, superiority in military equipment could change from one side to the other during the course of a war. However, since the revolution in military affairs, technological superiority in times of peace becomes increasingly important, if not decisive. New weapons make the beginning of a war crucial, and the possibility is remote of obtaining a change in the relative status of equipment after a war has started.

Emphasis throughout is given to nuclear weapons. "In spite of the fact that conventional weapons, as before, occupy an important place in the technical equipping of armies, the decisive means of fighting in contemporary war is the nuclear rocket weapon . . . ." The basic military-technical superiority of one side over another is determined by "the quantity and quality of nuclear ammunition and means of delivery."

Bondarenko does not believe that a plateau in weapon system development has, or will, be reached. "The achievement of military-technical superiority of one side over another is no guarantee of its preservation in the future. The stern dialectics of development are that the struggle for superiority must be waged *continually*." For the nation that might be in front at one particular time, "any weakening of attention in this field, excessive admiration for successes achieved, might lead to a loss of superiority."

Although a long industrial effort is normally required to achieve quantitative and qualitative superiority, it is recognized that new weapons, "secretly nurtured in scientific research bureaus and constructors' collectives can in a short time sharply change the relationship of forces." In fact, "The *surprise* appearance of one or another new type of weapon is advancing as an essential factor, especially in contemporary circumstances."

In Bondarenko's view, there is a danger that the military professional will limit military science to the mere perfecting of weapons already existing. Military specialists of the past would "never have invented firing weapons if they had been ceaselessly occupied with the perfection of the construction of just bows and arrows . . . ." It is important "to combine the development of old forms of equipment with a really revolutionary break with former views and ideas."

With the emphasis given to military-technical matters, "the central figure in the troops has become the commander-engineer." New methods of teaching have been adopted, such as programmed learning. It has been necessary to work out the optimum relationship between quantity of equipment and quantity of people controlling them. This is reflected in organizational structure of the various services.

In this respect, Bondarenko claims that the Soviet Union is ahead of NATO. There, for a division of nineteen thousand men almost thirty-five thousand are required in supporting roles. The Soviet Union "with the same means and the same manpower reserves could support several divisions."

Colonel Bondarenko is one of the authors of *Methodological Problems of Military Theory and Practice* (The Military Publishing House, Moscow, 1966), and he is on the faculty of the Lenin Military Political Academy.

THE COMMUNIST PARTY has displayed and will display constant concern for the military power of the Soviet government. Led by Lenin's advice on the defense of the socialist Fatherland, the party always considers the task of strengthening the defense of the country as one of the vital necessities. Thanks to just this, the Soviet Armed Forces with honor withstood the severe tests which were forced on them by the imperialists in the years of the civil and Great Patriotic Wars, convincingly demonstrating their military superiority over the armies of the aggressors.

The international situation and the development of events in the world demand the further raising of the defense potential of our Motherland. The deepening of the general crisis of capitalism, the aggravation of its contradictions, has led to a still greater intensification of the adventurism and aggressiveness of imperialism. The imperialists so far have not managed to push the world into the hell of thermonuclear war because there exists on our planet such a powerful force as the Soviet Union and its Armed Forces and the armies of other socialist countries.

Recently, several generals, and even responsible government figures in the U.S.A., very thoughtlessly and imprudently extolled the military might of the U.S.A. However, the real state of affairs is such that our superiority in the latest kinds of military equipment has become a reality. "Successes in the development of the economy, in science and technology," the General Secretary of the Central Committee of the CPSU, Comrade L. I. Brezhnev, said at the reception in the Kremlin in honor of the graduates of the military academies, "have allowed us to create a powerful, qualitatively new material-technical base for equipping the army and the navy with the latest armaments and to carry out a basic reorganization of the Armed Forces. The Soviet Army now has the most modern military equipment in sufficient quantities to preserve the superiority over the armies of the imperialist governments."

Military-technical superiority, along with moral-political superiority, is one of the most important factors in our time for the reliable defense of the country. The development of modern military affairs demonstrates the failure of the views of theorists who consider, it is said, even the most powerful weapons useless in the struggle against the masses of the people. That sort of opinion ignores that circumstance that the use of the nuclear rocket weapon, which is new in principle, can hamper and limit the actions of other factors and can have a decisive influence on the whole course and outcome of a war.

The recognition of this truth by no means lessens the role of moral-political factors, since the very production and use of the nuclear rocket weapon, as well as defense from it, to a great extent depends on the high moral spirit of the troops and of all the population of the country and on their readiness and ability to carry on a struggle in new conditions. But it is important to explain that along with moral-political factors, the significance of military factors themselves, in particular military-technical superiority over the enemy, has grown in contemporary circumstances as never before. Even during the Great Patriotic War an outstanding soldier with a grenade could face an enemy tank, but in the event of the use of the nuclear rocket weapon one cannot wage a victorious struggle with the enemy without having the most modern and powerful technical means.

The growth of the significance both of military-technical and military-political factors follows a law such that a lag of either one in contemporary war cannot be made up by the strenuous development of the other. Proceeding from this, our party not only constantly educates Soviet soldiers in moral staunchness, ideological conviction, and readiness for any difficulty and trial, but it also arms them with the most first-class equipment. Just such an army is the reliable guard of our Motherland and of all the socialist camp.

In the past the relationship of strength in military equipment could be changed in the course of the war itself. This was characteristic even for the Second World War. Now, in connection with the revolution in military affairs, the significance of military-technical superiority in peacetime has increased sharply. Under the influence of the new weapon and other new means of destruction, the importance of the beginning period is enhanced and the possibility of a change in the relative forces in the course of the war itself is seriously hampered.

In our time it is necessary to represent beyond all doubt the correlation at any moment of the military-technical equipment of our own army and the army of the probable enemy. Without a sober stocktaking of the military-technical possibilities of the opposing sides, it is impossible to carry out not only one's own military organization but also to carry out correctly a foreign policy and, also, to a great degree, an economic policy.

In researching the problems of military-technical superiority, two important aspects of its consideration can be distinguished. The first is connected with research of the dependence of the relationship of forces in the military-technical area on economics and on

355

the productive and scientific possibilities of the sides. The close tie of a country's military-technical superiority with its economic and scientific potential is absolutely obvious. The economic potential comprises the base of the military-technical superiority. Without a high level of economic development it is impossible to achieve superiority in military technology.

In the Resolutions of the XXIII Congress of the CPSU in the Summary Report of the Central Committee it was stated that the achievements of Soviet science and industry permitted the arming of our Armed Forces with the latest military equipment. "It is necessary to perfect further the production of military equipment," states the Resolutions, "so that the Soviet Army will be equipped with the most powerful and modern means of armament." (*Material of the XXIII Congress of the CPSU*, p. 188.)

The second aspect comes from the demands of practice. It is based on thorough research of the very meaning of military-technical superiority, its nature, its determining indicators, and their interdependencies. Such an aspect of examination of the problem is basic in the given instance.

Of what should military-technical superiority consist? How is it achieved? The complexity of the given questions comes primarily from the fact that the idea of military-technical superiority of one side over another is not absolute, its truth can be verified in the end only by a direct armed clash. But insofar as such "proof" in contemporary circumstances cannot be brought about and is also undesirable, then military theory and practice acutely need carefully worked out structures of those indicators which reflect the actual relationship of the military-technical possibilities of the sides and which permit the scientifically based conclusions of the superiority of one of the sides over the other.

In our view, it is advisable to distinguish three of the most important indicators which determine military-technical superiority: (1) the quality and quantity of weapons and military equipment; (2) the degree of training of the troops for using the given equipment; (3) the effectiveness of the organizational structure of the army which permits the fullest exposure of its combat potentials.

356

In brief, the essence of the problem can be formulated thus: *Military-technical superiority is such a correlation of quantity and quality of military equipment and weapons, of the degree of troop training in using them, and, also, of the effectiveness of the organizational structure of the army that the given side has the advantage over a real or potential enemy, and can defeat him.*

Let us look at the first indicator, the quantity and quality of weapons and military equipment. It is understood that the quantity and quality of the military equipment of each side is found in close dialectical unity. In spite of the fact that conventional weapons, as before, occupy an important place in the technical equipping of armies, the decisive means of fighting in contemporary war is the nuclear rocket weapon which is new in principle. Therefore, precisely the quantity and the quality of nuclear ammunition and means of their delivery compose the basic military-technical superiority of one side over another.

The qualitative perfection of nuclear ammunition, as is evident from the press, goes along two basic directions: widening the range of their power both on the side of increasing as well as on the side of decreasing—decreasing the sizes, simplification of the conditions of storage, and use. It is well known that the power of nuclear ammunition is already in the range from one hundred megatons down to several tons of TNT equivalent. For example, in the U.S.A. an atomic explosion with the TNT equivalent of only six tons has been tested. The recent significant decrease of the weight of ammunition is connected with the use of californium as a nuclear supply. However, judging from admissions in the foreign press, the practical problem of producing this rare element has so far been difficult to solve.

Considerable activity is also evidenced in the qualitative perfection of the means of delivery of the nuclear warhead. Here the leading role belongs to Soviet science and technology which have created and supplied the army with rockets of various designations in sufficient quantity. The first intercontinental and orbiting rockets were created in our country. In the last few years the attention of scientists and military specialists has been riveted on making rockets which could start from mobile launchers. The Soviet Union achieved considerable success in solving this problem by having created the world's first small-sized intercontinental rocket using solid fuel, the launch of which takes place from caterpillar-tred cross-country vehicles. The clearest indicator of improving Soviet technology and the rapid development of native means of automation is the unarguable priority of our country in opening up space.

Together with the origin and development of forms of military equipment which are new in principle also goes the further perfection of conventional forms of weapons. This perfection is being brought about by means of the automation of the guidance of weapons which leads to a significant raising of their effectiveness; by means of raising their reliability, exactness of aiming, and rate of fire; and also by means of widening the possibilities of the action of the fighting equipment in conditions of radioactive contamination, and so forth. Many sorts of conventional weapons with which the Soviet Army is equipped also surpass similar weapons of governments belonging to the aggressive bloc of NATO. This refers primarily to tank equipment.

The achievement of military-technical superiority of one side over another is no guarantee of its preservation in the future. The stern dialectics of development are that the struggle for superiority must be waged *continually*. Any weakening of attention in this field, excessive admiration for successes achieved, might lead to a loss of superiority. Therefore, in the Summary Report of the Central Committee of the CPSU at the XXIII Congress of the party it was stressed that "the party considers it necessary to assure the further development of defense industry, to assure the perfection of the nuclear rocket weapon and all other kinds of equipment." (*Material XXIII Congress CPSU*, p. 78.)

The achievement of quantitative and qualitative superiority over the enemy usually demands long industrial efforts. At the same time, the creation of a weapon that is new in principle and secretly nurtured in scientific research bureaus and constructors' collectives can in a short time sharply change the relationship of forces.

The *surprise* appearance of one or another new type of weapon is advancing as an essential factor, especially in contemporary circumstances. Surprise in this area not only demoralizes the enemy, it also for a long time deprives him of the possibility of using effective means of protection from the new weapon.

Military equipment, as any phenomenon of the objective world, passes in its development through periods not only of gradual change but also periods of sharp qualitative change, or jumps. A century ago, F. Engels stressed that the development of military affairs takes place under conditions of constant revolutionizing of its technical base. A new qualitative state in the development of military equipment begins when the law (or principle) underlying the construction or the power source used in it is superseded by another.

Basic, qualitative changes, to a large degree, are distinguished from each other by their range and, subsequently, also by that role which they play in the general process of the development of military equipment. Several of the jumps affect only one sort of armament; others encompass a large quantity of kinds of equipment; a third has the essence of a military-technical revolution. The most essential sign of such a revolution is the changeover to the mass use of a means of destruction which is new in principle, and which greatly exceeds the old in its power. The appearance of such destructive weapons of necessity evokes basic changes in the delivery equipment and guidance facilities.

Naturally, for making a weapon which is based on new laws of nature—laws which are either little studied in our time or perhaps, in general, still unknown—a sufficient historical perspective is needed. To foresee an actual scientific discovery is impossible because this would signify its realization, but to take into account the development of the more promising directions of science, their influence on the development of military technology and weapons is fully possible and necessary. For this, it is necessary to take as a

359

basis the real achievements of science and industry. Hence the close connection of military-technical superiority with the scientific potential of the country.

From the sum total of questions which characterize the tie of science and military equipment, it is necessary to stress the problem of the organic union of research work and the results of research in the theoretical and basic sciences with the daily perfection of equipment. One of the dangers here is excessive practicalism under which military science cadres would be limited just to perfecting already existing weapons and to adapting them with more versatility to generally accepted ways and methods of waging war. With such a narrow approach, the chances of the appearance of a kind of equipment that is new in principle would be very small. Looking back into the past, it can be confirmed with confidence that military specialists could never have invented firing weapons if they had been ceaselessly occupied with the perfection of the construction of just bows and arrows, never going beyond the principles of their action. The outstanding Soviet aviation constructor, S. A. Lavochkin, correctly asserted that although streamlining and perfecting existing machines is a necessary business, it is also important to break away more boldly from accepted schemes, to combine the development of old forms of equipment with a really revolutionary break with former views and ideas.

The solution of this problem is possible only in a state of good organization of scientific research work. The questions of the development of science have become more and more real for the achievement of military-technical superiority over a potential enemy.

The exceptionally high tempo of the development of science and technology, the enormous possibilities of production, and the complicated opposition of forces hostile to each other in the world arena create the tendency to constant and rapid change of weapons which one has with more modern and effective ones. From the other side, the process of working out, designing, testing, and mass-producing new weapons, and also the technical and tactical training of troops to work with them, demand a definite period of time. It is necessary to recognize clearly that the imperialists are trying in their own way

to solve this contradiction. For example, it was established by research specialists in the U.S.A. in 1955 that a complete change of
armaments in the troops took place in fourteen years on the average. According to figures of the American press, this period after-
wards was reduced to ten years.

The discrepancy of these two tendencies in practice appears in
the relationship of projected test forms of weapons and forms introduced into the armaments. The latter are selected from the most
favorable which correspond to the contemporary technical science
facts of tested forms, passing through all the tests and having a
relatively long prospect of military use. Test forms are made more
often for thorough verification of this or that technical science
idea and for preservation of the necessary succession between forms
and so forth. The relationship between testing and introducing
forms into armaments is determined not only by technical-science
and troop demands. Often a decisive influence on forcing the introduction into the armaments of some sort of weapon is indicated
by the foreign policy situation, the successes of potential enemies
in developing military technology, or other causes.

The strategy of military-technical construction in our time can
be a very important element which permits, with the correct evaluation of the prospective development of military equipment, not
blindly following all known forms but letting some intermediate,
transitional stages pass in order to concentrate the attention
and forces on more promising types of weapons. An example of
such a bold scientific strategy might be the military-technical policy
of the Central Committee of the CPSU and the Soviet government.
That policy allowed our country—which had concentrated efforts
on creating a means of delivery which was new in principle, the
rocket—to overtake the U.S.A., which in that period had concentrated its efforts on the development of intercontinental bombers as
the sole (in their opinion at the time) means of delivering nuclear
charges.

The contemporary nature of the development of military equipment gives rise to the necessity of the combination of new and
comparatively obsolete weapons which with skillful use also help

361

support the high combat power of the army. The problem of a skillful combination of new and comparatively old military equipment has not only a military-technical but also a moral-political aspect. The system of training and educating Soviet soldiers is called on to impart to them love and respect for all military equipment, and to have them achieve the proper understanding of and utilization of the combat potentials of any kind of weapon. Well thought out and skilled propagation of technical science knowledge, a full explanation to the personnel of the nature and essence of contemporary war and the place and significance in it of each type of weapon must serve this end.

Military-technical superiority does not come from the mere availability of definite forms of arms and equipment. It is obvious that without man even the most dread weapon will not decide the fate of a war. Arms and equipment act only as artificial organs of man, increasing many times his natural strength and capabilities. Man and military equipment are indivisible; there are organic ties between them; they act as one mechanism of armed conflict in which the decisive role belongs to man.

In the course of military-technical progress, gradual changes in the relationship of material (equipment) and personal (man) components of armed struggle take place. However, extension of potentialities of equipment and its automation and the apparent "independence" and "self-sufficiency" of action of many technical means constitute not a lessening of man's role and an exclusion of him from armed conflict, but primarily constitute a change in his duties and functions. New ways of waging armed struggle demand the formation of new habits in man, new abilities, and changes in the content and form of his actions in the course of fighting.

The more complicated the military equipment and the greater the quantity of functions it can fulfill, then the more demands are made of people, attendants, and directors. And now the degree of training troops to operate with this equipment has become more significant in the achievement of military-technical superiority.

In order to achieve an advantage in this very important area, it is necessary to solve a whole series of problems. Primarily we are talking about the qualitative changes in the personnel of the army. Only those who have a high general educational training are able to master the new military equipment to perfection. And it must be said that in the last few years in our army a genuine revolution has taken place in this relation. Reporting to the XXIII Congress of the CPSU on the qualitative changes in army personnel, the Minister of Defense, Marshal of the Soviet Union R. Ya. Malinovsky emphasized that now each fourth officer of the army and navy has a higher military or special education. The central figure in the troops has become the commander-engineer. Now more than 90 per cent of the soldiers, sailors, sergeants, and starshinas have higher, middle, or incompleted middle educations. All this represents a most important condition for rapid and thoroughgoing mastery by the personnel of the army and navy of complicated military equipment, and serves as a solid basis for the systematic raising of the military preparedness of the troops.

For all the importance of high general training of troops, the special knowledge received directly from the process of military studies has decisive significance for the skillful mastery of military equipment. It must be remarked about this that the ever-growing volume of knowledge and skills cannot be achieved just by increasing the quantity of hours devoted to the study of military equipment and methods of its use in battle. It is possible to resolve this problem only by means of optimizing the process of troop training. Programmed learning, in particular, has the greatest promise. The presentation of material, its volume, and tempo, according to the preparation of the student, gives the instruction maximum individualization. Thanks to modern technical equipment the inverse tie between student and teacher has changed from an incidental to a systematic one.

Optimizing the teaching process does not come just from the use of technical equipment. The creative initiative of servicemen also prompts other ways. The experience of a series of units and formations of National PVO [air defense] Troops in introducing individual methods of training might serve as an example of the

363

skillful approach to the perfection of the training process. It consists of dividing the students into small groups, taking into account their training and abilities. For each group an individual program of training is established which is a modification of the general program. In the process of mastering the new material, the students who go ahead are drawn in to work with the less prepared. The initiators who introduced individual teaching methods correctly consider that they have succeeded to a large degree in overcoming the main deficiencies of the old methods under which it was necessary, in essence, to equate to the average pupil or even to the backward ones.

The skillful mastery of military equipment and weapons also depends on the general technical science outlook of the soldier, sailor, sergeant, starshina, and officer, on the understanding by them of the physical processes on the basis of which has been constructed this or that sort of weapon. The detailed knowledge of physics, chemistry, mathematics, mechanical, and other sciences has become the essential and compulsory side of professional training of Soviet soldiers. Naturally, such depth and breadth of knowledge can be achieved if the framework of programmed combat training is widened by carrying out technical science instruction closely connected with the program of combat training on a fascinating and highly scientific level. Thereby the general military-technical culture of all servicemen will be raised, so that it is a real factor of the further growth of the combat readiness of the troops.

The high training of the troops for operating with the latest military equipment is determined to a decisive degree by the level of political consciousness of the soldiers, and their creative relations to combat studies. Patriotism, the understanding of public necessity and the importance of military labor to the government, inherent in Soviet soldiers, creates the most favorable conditions for the constant raising of the level of combat training of the troops. These objective conditions must be skillfully used in the interests of the further strengthening of the defense potential of our country.

One of the indicators of military-technical superiority is the establishment of the optimum relationship between quantity of equipment and quantity of people controlling it. This relationship is expressed in the organizational structure of the troops.

Characteristically, the creation of the latest military equipment and weapons, as well as the automatic arrangements for their direction, led to a whole series of contradictions in the solution of this problem. Several foreign specialists think that one of these contradictions is included in the disproportion between the quantity of fighting units and the significant broadening of the number of servicing subunits. Such a breach is explained both by a deficiency or a surplus of military equipment and people and by a lack of knowledge of combat possibilities, of ways of combat usage, and of conditions of technical servicing of several kinds of new equipment. The combat possibilities of nuclear rocket weapons, which have been studied only under the limited conditions of the testing range, in the opinion of many specialists are really not known to this day and this causes difficulties in determining the organizational form of army structure.

In capitalist countries these difficulties are further complicated by the simultaneous struggle between monopolies which, led by their own interests, sometimes try to give the troops as much auxiliary equipment as possible. One must not leave out of one's reckoning the traditional spheres of service, which in capitalist countries, especially in the U.S.A., bear a hypertrophic aspect. They also have an influence on the organization of the army's rear services. For example, for one division of NATO numbering about nineteen thousand men almost thirty-five thousand men must be in the rear. The well-known military theorist F. Miksche calculated, and not without reason, that the Soviet Union with the same means and the same manpower reserves could support several divisions.

The qualitative relationship between equipment and people is closely connected with the problem of the correct relationship between the services of the armed forces. Reality disproves all theories which are based on imaginary independence and absolutism of one service of the armed forces or another.

Soviet military doctrine objectively investigating the nature of modern war considers that final victory over the aggressor can be achieved only as a result of the combined and co-ordinated actions of all the services of the armed forces. This truth is also understood by the most far-seeing bourgeois military leaders.

One cannot approach the questions of military-technical superiority and the development and relationship of the indicators which form it as something settled once and for all. The role and significance of the various sides of military-technical superiority, the specific weight of separate services of the armed forces, the organizational structure of the army, and other factors change under the influence of actual historical conditions, new missions placed before the army, and the rapid perfection of arms.

And our party, while giving great attention to the development of the Soviet Army and Navy, constantly takes into account this circumstance. It proceeds from the fact that at the contemporary level of development of military affairs, the solution of the problem of maintaining military-technical superiority is possible only with the mobilization of all economic, technical-science, and moral-political forces of the country.

The Communist party and its Central Committee are doing everything necessary for the constant strengthening of the defense potential of our country, for securing superiority both in military-technical and also in other areas of military affairs.

---

26. CHANGES IN THE CONTENT AND NATURE OF MODERN COMBAT
By Colonel N. F. Miroshnichenko
Candidate of Military Sciences

Editors' Notes

In October, 1966, this article appeared in the *Military Herald*, a professional journal of the Soviet Army. It reflects a number of the concepts contained in the preceding article by Lieutenant Colonel Bondarenko. The author points out that: "The role and significance of *surprise* has grown still more. For example, the surprise use of the nuclear weapon permits the bringing of very great losses to the enemy; it depresses his troops morally, sharply lowering their combat ability; it quickly changes the relationship of forces and upsets command, thus creating conditions for completing his defeat."

Surprise cannot be achieved without secrecy. To obtain secrecy is difficult and requires countermeasures of the enemy's reconnaissance, constant improvement in the methods of camouflage and disinformation, and continuing study of the enemy in order to learn his tactics and his strong and weak sides.

In Miroshnichenko's view, the most important factor in contemporary warfare is *"the constant struggle against means of nuclear attack."* Before the nuclear weapon appeared on the battlefield, it was not always necessary to destroy guns and mortars as soon as they were located. "Now the situation has radically changed. A nuclear strike sharply affects the combat ability of troops. Therefore measures must be taken swiftly to destroy nuclear ammunition and guns (mountings) which could use them."

Even the principles of war, according to the author, have been changed as a result of nuclear weapons. The *principle of concentration of forces* has a new meaning, since nuclear firepower is a concentrated force, instead of a large number of military units. There is a new principle of *dispersion*, resulting from the fact that the nuclear weapon can simultaneously destroy troops over a large area. Both subunits and units must disperse along the front and in depth.

A previous article on tactics by Colonel Miroshnichenko, "The Fire System in Defense," appeared in the *Military Herald* in December, 1965. The colonel is a senior scientific assistant at Frunze Military Academy and is one of the authors of *Tactics*, another volume of the *Officer's Library* series published in 1966.

THE NUCLEAR WEAPON is the most powerful means of mass destruction in modern battle. It permits inflicting great losses on the enemy's manpower and military equipment in a short period of time, exerting a strong moral influence on his troops, destroying strong points, pockets of resistance, and also other objects; creating zones of contamination, destruction, and flooding. With the appearance of this means of fighting, earlier component elements of battle did not fully reflect its content. In particular, a new element of battle—the nuclear strike—arose, and the role of the old—fire, strike, and maneuver—changed.

The power of fire, for example, grew significantly. From a means of preparation and accompaniment of strikes, fire has become, in an ever larger degree, an integral part of war. Now, strike implies the combination of fire with the movement of tank and motorized infantry subunits with the aim of completing the defeat of the enemy. Its base is composed of gun, machine gun, and automatic fire of great density. Hence the force of the strike of the attackers is determined primarily by their firepower.

The nuclear weapon affects not only the content but also the nature of the combined arms battle. It becomes distinguished for growing decisiveness, dynamics and high maneuverability, rapid and acute changes of conditions, unevenness of development along the front and in depth, great spatial range, and complexity of radiation, chemical, and bacteriological conditions.

Decisiveness was characteristic for troops even before the appearance of the nuclear weapon. A future war, if the imperialists succeed in unleashing it, will be an armed clash of two opposed social systems. The possibility of any sort of compromise between them will be excluded since the struggle will acquire an extremely acute class character and this will give combat actions exceptional decisiveness. This will become apparent in the striving to win and hold fire superiority over the enemy, and also in energetic, bold and selfless actions of troops following nuclear strikes for the purpose of completing the defeat of the enemy in a short period of time and of achieving victory.

High *maneuverability* also is not a new feature of battle. Troops have always aspired for wide maneuver although conditions for this have been different. In the not distant past, in order to accomplish an envelopment or to make a turning movement for the purpose of striking along the flank or in the rear of the enemy the continuous front of his defense often was broken through. But now great gaps and breaks in the fighting order of the troops made by the nuclear weapon, their wide dispersion and the marked intervals between subunits will create the prerequisites for maneuver at the very beginning of combat actions and not just during the battle in depth. Moreover, the high mobility of subunits and the significantly growing possibilities for transferring them by air permits the quick use of the results of nuclear strikes and the penetration into the depths of the enemy's position. Consequently, movement, marches, highly dynamic and mobile methods of battle, and rapid change-over from combat formation to prebattle marching order will prevail in their operations.

The aims of maneuver have also widened. At its base now lie the quick use of the results of the nuclear strikes, the timely removal of the troops from under the nuclear strikes of the enemy, the replacement of subunits which have borne great losses and lost combat ability, the overcoming of zones of contamination and destruction, transferring efforts to a different direction and repulsing the blows of the superior forces of the enemy.

Maneuver with nuclear strikes is new; it might be accomplished in a short period of time at practically any distance without shifting rocket mountings.

Swift and acute changes of conditions are peculiar in full measure only to modern battle with the use of the nuclear rocket weapon. In the last war the tempo of break-through was comparatively low even in operations in its closing period. Consequently essential changes in troop location in an hour's time usually did not take place. Now the situation is completely different.

Because of the nuclear weapon, the relationship of forces and means in one direction or another (section) might be instantly changed and the opposition of the enemy rapidly broken or his change-over from one sort of fighting to another forced. Motorized subunits with their high mobility permit the accomplishment of movement at great distances in a short period of time, carrying

369

out strikes on the march, and carrying out combat operations at tempos several times above the tempos of attack in the last war. The absence of a solid front and the presence of intervals and gaps in the combat order also enables the sides to carry out surprise strikes on the flanks and in the rear. All this testifies to the fact that conditions in modern battle can sharply change in minutes and even in seconds.

This is concretely expressed in qualitative change in the composition of groupings and the relationship of forces, by the rapid bringing up of reserves, airborne landings, and as a result in sharp change of the character and methods of action, going from one type to another, redirecting efforts, changing the mission of the troops and their combat order. From this comes the growing role and significance of the time factor. Now even an insignificant delay in taking urgent measures in any section might become the cause for unjustified losses of people and of military equipment and for the frustration of the fulfillment of the combat mission.

Unevenness of the development of combat actions along the front and in depth appeared in battles in the period of the Great Patriotic War, primarily during an attack of tanks, mechanized formations, and units in an operational depth.

In nuclear rocket war combat operations from the very beginning will deploy on lines of advances: On some, subunits using the results of nuclear and fire strikes will swiftly push forward into the interior. On others, where the use of the nuclear weapon will be limited, stubborn fighting will go on; on still others, either the advancing will be slowed down or temporarily halted for the removal of traces of the nuclear attack of the enemy, or they will go over to defense, repulsing strikes of superior forces, or even withdrawing. This means there will be no solid front line.

The unevenness of the development of battle will raise the role of independent actions of subunits, advancing along lines, the initiative of the commanders at every level and also the significance of securing the flanks and the rear of one's own troops. At the same time bold and daring actions will be demanded of them—

370

swift break-throughs into the interior and wide use of outflanking and turning movements.

Great spatial range of battle is the result of the growing range of the weapons of destruction and also the increase of the combat potential of the troops. Although in the battles of the last war the enemy struck with fire to a depth of ten kilometers on the whole, not counting raids of aviation, now rockets can assure the enemy's destruction on the whole depth of his location. In addition, airborne landings will be widely used and thus combat actions, almost simultaneously, will embrace the full depth of the combat formation including the second echelon and the reserves.

The growing combat potentials of the troops and the necessity to disperse them has led to an enlargement of the width of the zone (area) of attack and defense and, also, of the depth of the combat mission and tempo of movement.

A new feature of modern war is *the complexity of radiation and chemical conditions*. It is well known that the aggressive circles of the imperialist states are preparing for the wide use of nuclear, chemical, and bacteriological weapons. This leads to the formation of a vast zone of contamination. Troops will be forced either to withdraw or to overcome the zones, to take protective measures or to wait for an abatement of the high level of radiation or to carry out combat operations in contaminated places.

Thus the content and nature of modern combat has been basically changed. It has become more complicated, deep, maneuverable, dynamic, and extraordinarily tense. All this affects the content of several principles of war and calls to life new ones.

Thus the well-known *principle of concentration of forces*, for the purpose of creating superiority over the enemy on the decisive direction at the right time, in present-day conditions is somewhat different. Now there is no necessity to concentrate large forces in comparatively small areas, because this is fraught with serious consequences. Superiority over the enemy can be created by nuclear strikes and concentrated conventional fire with subsequent swift movement in the direction (area) by motorized infantry and tank subunits located in a comparatively large area.

371

In modern warfare the role of such principles as *dispersion* has grown acutely. Earlier the limits of dispersion of the troops on the battlefield were determined primarily by the probable destruction of the fighters by rifle fire or within the radius of destruction of a single shell (mine, aviation bomb). Therefore it was calculated on the protection of the individual soldier and not of units and subunits. Close ties between subunits and units were preserved in battle.

At the present time, because the nuclear weapon can simultaneously destroy troops in a great area, to settle in a place or to move compactly regardless of the distance of the enemy is forbidden. In order to reduce as much as possible the losses from nuclear attack, subunits and units must disperse along the front and in depth. The limits of dispersion depend on the power of the nuclear ammunition, the extent of troop cover, and the ability to fulfill the combat mission (preservation of fire and tactical cooperation, the maintenance of steady guidance, and so forth).

However dispersion does not deny the necessity to concentrate subunits in the necessary place at the right time. But now this is done from the march, secretly, rapidly, and from different directions immediately before or during the strike itself. After the strike, the subunits again disperse in order not to be a convenient target for the enemy.

The ability to combine correctly the principles of concentration of forces and their dispersion in the most important direction is the sign of a commander's great skill.

The content of such a principle as *co-operation* has also changed. It consists, as is known, in agreement on missions, borders, and times of combat efforts, and in mutual help of the subunits of all services, special troops, and neighboring troops in the interests of the more successful fulfillment of the combat mission.

Insofar as the nuclear weapon is the most powerful means of destruction, then co-operation is now organized primarily for the most effective use of its results. But one must not deny mutual aid between subunits of all services, and special troops, between elements of the combat formation and of neighboring (units).

For supporting continuous co-operation, the initiative of the commanders has taken on special significance. In a break of co-operation, they must establish communication with neighboring (units) and with senior commanders, not waiting for special orders.

The role and significance of *surprise* has grown still more. For example, the surprise use of the nuclear weapon permits the bringing of very great losses to the enemy; it depresses his troops morally, sharply lowering their combat ability; it quickly changes the relationship of forces and upsets command, thus creating conditions for completing his defeat.

An indispensible condition for achieving surprise is secrecy. However, achieving it is not easy. For this, along with arrangements for countermeasures of the enemy's reconnaissance, it is necessary to perfect constantly the means and methods of camouflage and of disinformation, to raise the tactical training of officers, their knowledge of the enemy, his tactics, and his strong and weak sides.

The significance of *continuity of combat operations* is now difficult to overvalue. Even a short halting of attack means loss of advantage: the enemy might carry out nuclear strikes or bring up reserves and create a solid defense. The constant waging of battle at high tempos will not permit the enemy to determine exact objectives for the use of the nuclear weapon and will force him to change frequently the ways of its delivery.

In order to assure constant actions, there is a demand for great effort of moral and physical forces, deep combat formations, the presence of reserves of various designations, and the skill of commanders to prepare conditions for solving subsequent combat tasks in the course of fulfilling the previous [ones].

The most important content of this principle is *the constant struggle against means of nuclear attack* with all available equipment and methods.

Before the appearance of the nuclear weapon, guns and mortars, because of their comparatively limited firing possibilities, might not be destroyed right after their discovery. Now the situation has radically changed. A nuclear strike sharply affects the combat ability of troops. Therefore measures must be taken to swiftly destroy nuclear ammunition and guns (mountings) which could use them.

The content of such a principle as *comprehensive security of combat operations* has been expanded. Along with earlier known measures, the necessity has arisen to create protection against weapons of mass destruction. This protection has become a decisive factor, without which success in battle is impossible.

The decisive and tense character of modern war is producing higher demands for education, training, discipline, and the physical hardening of the troops. The chief force in battle always was and will remain man.

Commanders of all degrees must have high moral and fighting qualities. They must quickly evaluate conditions, make sound decisions and persistently strive to put them into action, preserve bravery and calmness, and show decisiveness and initiative.

---

27. ON SOVIET MILITARY DOCTRINE
By General Lieutenant I. G. Zavyalov

Editors' Notes

ON THE 30TH and 31ST of March, 1967—exactly one year after the meeting of the XXIII Party Congress—*Red Star* published an article, "On Soviet Military Doctrine," in two installments. The author, General Lieutenant Zavyalov, a prominent Soviet military theoretician, was a contributor to Marshal Sokolovsky's *Military Strategy* in 1962. In July, 1965, he wrote a series of articles which appeared in *Red Star* under the title "Speed, Time, and Space."

"On Soviet Military Doctrine" restates much of what already has been emphasized in previous selections of this book. General Zavyalov points out that Soviet military doctrine has two aspects, the political and the military-technical, and that "it goes without saying that the military-technical side of doctrine occupies a subordinate position in relation to the political side."

The author's initial views on nuclear weapons appear to be but a repeat of what other Soviet military writers have been saying over the past several years. "Now all military organization and methods of waging war are under the determining influence of the nuclear rocket weapon. . . . The nuclear weapon demanded not partial changes as had happened earlier, but a fundamental revolutionary break with all established views and positions in all areas of military affairs."

After this, Zavyalov modifies, only slightly, the usual Soviet position. For example: "However one should not, as has been done by several bourgeois military ideologists, make a fetish of the nuclear weapon." He goes on to state, "In this respect a possible world nuclear rocket war will not be excluded. . . . Soviet military doctrine takes into account all factors, all the possibilities of victory, and gives full preference to the most active and decisive methods of action."

In any war, "The decisive type of military operation always was and remains the *offensive*." After a discussion of the need for offensive actions, Zavyalov adds, "However, Soviet military doctrine does not leave the possibilities of defense out of the reckoning. In this it should be stressed that we recognize not passive but active defense, built on a new technical basis brought about by the appearance of modern means of waging war—defense directed primarily against the means of nuclear attack of the enemy. Such defense takes on extremely important national and stategic significance. . . . The application of such defense in no way contradicts the offensive character of military doctrine. This is especially true in respect to contemporary PVO and PRO defense (antiaircraft and antirocket defense) against the means of nuclear attack of the enemy."

Zavyalov again takes a slightly different view of the nature of a future war than generally has been expressed. He asks: "What kind of armed forces are necessary for waging present-day war?" He answers his question by asserting: "For waging modern war such armed forces are demanded as would be able to wage both world nuclear war and any other war."

375

These statements differ in minute details from the writings of the majority of the Soviet authors. The acknowledgment that a future world war might be other than nuclear, while pointing out the need of an antiballistic missile system, could be but another one of the contradictions to which the Soviets so frequently refer. Or would an antiballistic missile system combined with both nuclear and nonnuclear forces enable the Soviet leaders to better demonstrate that "war is the continuation of politics by other, that is, violent means"?

UNDER THE LEADERSHIP of the Communist party, we have worked out a modern, genuinely scientific military doctrine which issues from the new arrangement of class forces in the world arena and from those fundamental changes which have taken place in all areas of military affairs. Soviet military doctrine determines the means, ways, and methods of the reliable defense of the Soviet government and the gains of socialism and communism from imperialist aggressors. It includes a thorough evaluation of the socio-political essence and nature of a future war, the probable methods of its waging, questions of the organization of the Armed Forces and of training methods.

On a series of these questions, including the essence of war, articles have already been printed in *Red Star*.[1] While not repeating what has been said, but taking into account the importance, the urgency, the complexity of the problem, we would like to dwell in more detail on the interdependence and mutual conditionality of the two sides of military doctrine—the socio-political and the military-technical—which have important theoretical and practical significance for the fruitful activity of our military cadres.

1. The Main Thing—Scientific Validity

What goes into the concept of modern Soviet military doctrine? *Soviet military doctrine is the sum total of scientifically based views accepted in the country and by its Armed Forces on the na-*

1 See chap. 24.

376

ture of contemporary wars which might be unleashed by the imperialists against the Soviet Union, on the goals and missions of the Armed Forces in this war, the methods of its waging, and also on the demands, which flow from such views, for the preparation of the country and the Armed Forces for war.

Military doctrine is worked out by the political and military leadership of the state and has a clearly expressed class nature. Its basic demands and positions are embodied in state laws, in decrees of the party and of the government concerning military organization, and in military regulations, manuals, and directives of leading military organs.

At the base of Soviet military doctrine lie the claims of objective laws of social development, the laws of war and Marxist-Leninist principles of the military policy of the party and the government. The posture of military doctrine is determined by the socio-economic, political, historical, and other features of the country and depends on the arrangement of forces in the world arena. Clearly, in determining the nature of a future war, the methods of its waging and the direction of the organization and training of the Armed Forces, Soviet military doctrine is guided by the conclusions and positions of military science.

It is generally accepted that military doctrine has two sides—political and military-technical. The first includes positions disclosing the socio-political essence of war, the nature of its goals and missions, and demands issuing from these for the organization of the armed forces and for methods of preparing for and waging war. The second side includes questions of direct organization, of the training, equipping, and the use of the armed forces in war and determines the basic directions in the development of military art, the nature of military-technical measures necessary for strengthening the defense might of the country and for raising the combat readiness of the troops.

These two sides of military doctrine are inseparable from each other. They are closely tied and mutually conditioned. The military-political goals which the government pursues in each given war must in full measure be secured by its economic potential and by

377

the potential of its armed forces. In other words, military doctrine rests on a realistic basis if it truly reflects in its military-technical aspects the combat potential of the armed forces and if the views on the methods of preparing for and waging war correspond to the forces and means of the state.

It goes without saying that the military-technical side of doctrine occupies a subordinate position in relation to the political side. The organization and training of the armed forces is wholly subordinate to the military-political goals of the state.

The political position of doctrine issues from the social system of the government and from the policy carried out by it and is more stable than the military-technical position of doctrine. But if definite changes take place in the social structure of a state and in its economics, this means that there naturally and lawfully takes place one change or another, both in the political positions of the doctrine and in the military-technical side of the doctrine which is enacted through people, weapons, and military equipment.

But the interrelation between the two sides of doctrine is expressed not only in that its political posture influences the military-technical but also in that a reverse influence takes place. And this is completely natural because military-technical changes in a definite manner affect the nature of military-political goals and missions of the state and of its armed forces in a given war, and bring in new elements to the mechanism whereby politics influences military organization and the methods of preparing for and waging war. The political goals of a state in war are commensurate with its military potential and with the changes which are taking place in it.

When speaking of determining role, of the primacy of political views and of the political side, it should at the same time be stressed that Soviet military doctrine in the military-technical part also embodies highly important economic, ideological, and military-scientific features.

First, it strictly takes into account the latest scientific-technical and production achievements and the constantly growing economic potentials of the Soviet Union. A reflection is found in it that on the basis of successes in the development of the economy

378

and of science and technology we created the powerful nuclear rocket weapon and other modern military equipment, accomplished the complete rearming of the army and the navy, and carried out fundamental organizational transformations in all the services of the Armed Forces. The growing might of the socialist economy is creating all of the conditions to develop further and to perfect the Armed Forces, to increase their combat capabilities, and to keep the army and the navy in a state of constant, high combat readiness.

Second, our doctrine issues from the Marxist-Leninist position that man is the chief productive force and that the outcome of war in the final analysis is decided on the battlefield by people having strong spirits, possessing all the modern means and methods of waging armed struggle. In its military-technical section, Soviet military doctrine rests on qualitatively different, in comparison with capitalist countries, "human material." The personnel of the Soviet Armed Forces are people of the new socialistic social structure, highly conscientious people who well understand their civil and military obligations. Soviet soldiers possess exceptionally high moral and fighting qualities; they love their country ardently and, for the sake of protecting it, they will undertake any noble feat.

Third, the military-technical concepts of our doctrine are based on the more important positions and conclusions of Soviet military science. Having disclosed the nature of a possible war, its laws and regularities, military science thereby predetermines the main trends of military organization and influences, through doctrine, the development and the adoption into the Armed Forces of fundamental strategic concepts and views on the technical equipping and the preparing of the army and the navy for war.

Thus, Soviet military doctrine is created on the granite foundation of Marxism-Leninism, which permits it to reflect quickly and correctly and to respond to all changes in the economy, in the relationship of political forces, and in weapons. Soviet military doctrine is the embodiment of the scientifically based policy of the Communist party, the inexhaustible possibilities of the highly developed economy of the country, the inflexible will and greatness

379

of spirit of the Soviet people and of the achievements of advanced Soviet military science.

A pivotal question of military doctrine is determining the nature of future war. "When we place before ourselves the question of what form should be adopted in the organization of the Armed Forces of the Soviet Union," M. V. Frunze said, "we must first of all ask another question, the question of the nature of those military clashes which are possible in the future and in which our Red Army will have to take a part."

The correct understanding of the socio-political essence of war and its nature from a military-technical point of view, and, too, a knowledge of the armed forces and the military-economic possibilities of the probable enemy are the starting point of Soviet military doctrine in the realm of the organization of the Armed Forces. Indeed, just consider well what kind of enemy will have to be dealt with, and one can correctly determine what forces and means and what quantity we need for achieving victory, how to co-ordinate these demands with the economic, moral-political, scientific-technical, and other potentials of the state. The deeper and more fully these questions are exposed, the more purposefully the organization of the Armed Forces and their preparation for a possible war will progress, and the fewer mistakes there will be in resolving these questions, and the closer the research and conclusions of military science and military art will be to reality.

Military doctrine cannot be indifferent to the price of achieving victory. It prefers the most advantageous and effective methods of waging war, taking into account in this that the methods of waging war depend on the nature of the social structure and the policies of the state, on the level of development of its productive forces, the state of the economy, the moral spirit of the people, and on the nature of the political goals of war. The influence of all these factors on the methods of waging war occur through weapons, military equipment, and people. They directly influence the methods of waging combat actions and this means also the organization of the troops. "All organization and combat methods of the army and, at the same time, victories and defeats," remarked F. Engels, "indicate dependencies on the material, that is, economic conditions: from human material and from weapons and, consequently, from the quality and quantity of population and equipment." This Marxist position does not lose its great significance even in our day.

Now all military organization and methods of waging war are under the determining influence of the nuclear rocket weapon. By possessing colossal destructive and strike possibilities, it produced a fundamental revolution in all areas of military affairs and demanded absolutely new methods of waging fighting actions and new forms of troop organization; and it brought to life new principles of military art and radically changed the old. The nuclear weapon, demanded not partial change, as had happened earlier, but a fundamental revolutionary break with all established views and positions in all areas of military affairs—this was the chief result of its influence.

However one should not, as has been done by several bourgeois military ideologists, make a fetish of the nuclear weapon. Speaking of the influence of weapons and other military equipment on the methods of waging war, one must always keep in mind in whose hands these weapons are found. Historical experience reminds us that new methods and forms of armed struggle, weapons, and military equipment best serve to win victory over the enemy when they are used by a people and an army who are waging a just, liberating war and defending the cause of freedom and independence, the gains of socialism and communism, and who have high moral and political qualities.

In the years of the Civil War our Red Army, although it was more poorly armed and trained than the enemy, defeated the mercenaries of the interventionists and the White Guards. In the Great Patriotic War, the Soviet Armed Forces, having suffered great losses in the beginning period, managed in incredibly difficult circumstances to withstand the enormous Fascist German Army, to stop its attack and then to go over to the counterattack and fully crush the Hitlerite military machine. The Soviet people waged the most just war, defended the most sacred thing—their socialist Fatherland, the gains of the October revolution, and the cause of

381

socialism which gave birth to mass heroism and unheard of fortitude. In addition, victory was the result of the revolutionary work of the masses, creating their own special methods of fighting, which permitted the most effective use of the weapons which they possessed.

In this respect a possible world nuclear rocket war will not be excluded. And in it creative possibilities—raised in the just struggle of peoples who realize the goals and tasks of war, and are correspondingly prepared—will appear with unabated force. One cannot doubt that people opposing aggression will oppose the enemy with such methods of action as will lead to victory.

Before the aggressive aspirations and the growing military danger from the side of the imperialists, primarily the imperialists of the U.S.A., a defensive union on the basis of the Warsaw Pact had to be created for the purpose of securing the safety of our own people and the countries of socialism. Every day and every year the fighting co-operation of the fraternal armies of the countries, which are parties to this pact, grows. The exercises and maneuvers carried out together, the systematic exchange of experience in the operational and combat training of troops, achievements in the realm of military-technical and theoretical research—all this promotes the strengthening of the defense capability of the countries of socialism and raises the might of their armed forces.

Soviet military doctrine takes into account all factors, all the possibilities of victory, and gives full preference to the most active and decisive methods of action. Only with the skillful use of all forces and all modern means of waging war, and only with their close co-operation, can victory over a strong and perfidious enemy be achieved.

2. Types and Forms of Military Operations

The methods of waging war find their concrete manifestation in the types and forms of combat operations.

All diversity of military actions—offense and defense, attack and counterattack, withdrawal and pursuit, reconnaissance and protection, strike and counter-strike—are divided into two basic types: offensive and defensive.

The decisive type of military operation always was and still is the *offensive*. Only with powerful strikes and the skillful use of forces can full defeat be brought to the enemy and in the end the goals of war be achieved. Defense in the best of circumstances serves only to weaken the offensive possibilities of the enemy to secure the holding of fortuitous conditions for going over to a counteroffensive. It is impossible to achieve victory in war by defense alone.

Our country has never attacked anyone and does not plan to attack. But this does not at all mean that in the event of the unleashing of a war by the imperialists against the Soviet Union that our Armed Forces will wage only actions which are defensive in character. If the imperialists commit an act of aggression against us, we will answer with the most decisive, the most active offensive actions, with the use of all the might of our Armed Forces.

However, Soviet military doctrine does not leave the possibilities of defense out of the reckoning. In this it should be stressed that we recognize not passive but active defense, built on a new technical basis brought about by the appearance of modern means of waging war—defense directed primarily against the means of nuclear attack of the enemy. Such defense takes on extremely important national and strategic significance. But, speaking of the recognition of the objective regularities of defense as an aspect of military operations, one must not mix it up with or identify it with a defensive strategy.

Defensive doctrine and defensive strategy mean the complete or almost complete rejection by the armed forces of decisive offensive operations. Defense as a type of military action can be used by militarily strong states. It is used in separate areas and in different spheres of waging war for the solution of definite operational and strategic tasks, not by all of the armed forces, but only by a certain part of them.

The application of such defense in no way contradicts the of-

383

fensive character of military doctrine. This is especially true in respect to contemporary PVO and PRO (antiair and antirocket defense), defense against the means of nuclear attack of the enemy.

Speaking more briefly, our doctrine proceeds from the recognition of all types of military actions, giving preference to those which permit the most effective use of the combat possibilities of the Armed Forces for the full defeat of the aggressor. Such effectiveness can be achieved when the type of military operation assumes the corresponding organizational *form*.

In examining the question of the forms of combat actions it must be noted that in contemporary conditions any actions of a more or less major scale will unavoidably take the shape of *complex operations*. In its course war will demand the most accurate agreement of actions of the most diverse forces and means; it will demand agreement in time and space and in methods of fulfilling assigned tasks. Such operations demand all-round combat and material-technical support and uninterrupted operating systems of control.

The most characteristic type of operations in present-day war might be the independent and simultaneous operations of formations and major commands of one or several services of the armed forces, directed at achieving operational or strategic goals.

In all the diversity of modern operations, methods, types, and forms of military actions, several *general* demands appear for their organization and execution. These general demands appear as principles of military art.

Principles of military art are component parts of doctrine. And what is more, its military-technical side represents, one might say, a code of the most important positions and principles of military art adopted by the Armed Forces as practical guides for teaching and training troops, and for the organization and waging of combat operations.

Under principles are understood not separate, private positions of military art but central, basic generalizations flowing from objective laws of war and suitable for practical use in all basic types of activities of troops. They—these positions and principles—are established in corresponding regulations and manuals and are obligatory for all personnel of the Armed Forces. In addition, the regulations demand not blind, but creative application of these positions.

Here remains the basic position, expressed by F. Engels in his time, that "the principal thing is not the starting point of research but its concluding result; these principles are not adapted to nature or to man's history but are abstracted from them; nature and mankind do not conform with principles but the reverse—principles are true only insofar as they correspond to nature and to history."

The principles of military art issue from the practice of war and are confirmed by practice. They are objective and true insofar as they correspond to the objective laws and conditions of development in nature and society. And they are mobile: if the objective conditions change, the principles also change. This means that to guide the actions of troops with skill, one must know the objective laws of war and the principles of military art which flow from them, and must understand the nature of the actions of the first and the sphere of application of the second.

The basic principles and the most important demands of Soviet military art are:

—constant high combat readiness;
—decisive and active operations;
—correlation of the goals and missions in war to the forces, means, and planned methods of military actions which one possesses;
—the achievement of the goals of war by the combined efforts of all the services of the armed forces and branches of service with the decisive role of the nuclear weapon;
—close co-operation of forces and means which are taking part in battle and in operations;
—simultaneous action on all groupings of the enemy;
—surprise of actions;
—concentration of basic efforts on decisive areas at the decisive moment with subsequent dispersal of troops under the threat of a nuclear attack by the enemy;
—economy of forces at the expense of secondary theaters of military actions or operational directions;
—all-round fighting and material-technical support;

385

—the creation of reserves and their maintenance in a condition of constant readiness for the resolution of any unforeseen task;

—timely consolidation of achieved successes;

—the combination of central direction of troops with sensible initiative and independence of subordinates in fulfilling set tasks.

Of course, one must not think that these principles are suitable in all cases. They represent the sorts of rules which must be applied to strict conformity with conditions. They must not be considered abstractly or separately from each other. Taken separately they represent only links; little steps on the thorny path to victory. The use of the whole chain or the whole complex of principles and postures of military art is demanded, in conformity with concrete conditions, in order to reach the heights of victory.

It has already been pointed out above that the most important component part of doctrine is the view accepted by the state on military organization. In the wide meaning, included here are all questions connected with the organization of the Armed Forces: with recruiting them, technically equipping and training them; with indoctrination of personnel; with the working out of basic positions and demands of military art; and with the mobilization and combat readiness of the troops.

Soviet military organization is an integral and important part of the general governmental structure put into practice under the leadership and continuous control of the Central Committee of the Communist party of the Soviet Union. This structure is determined by many factors which can be divided into factors of internal and external form.

To the first group can be attributed the social structure of the state and the policy followed by it; the level of development of production, science, and technology; the economic potential of the state; the quantity, the moral-political quality, and the national features of the people; the geographic situation of the state; and the size and character of its territory.

The second group of factors is made up of international conditions: the character of the war which might be imposed on us; the

386

combat possibilities and the trends in the development of the armed forces of the probable enemy; the nature of his military doctrine and strategic concepts.

The influence of all of these factors on the organization of the Armed Forces of the U.S.S.R. must be viewed not in isolation from each other but in close interaction and in general connection with political lines and economic development of the state.

What kind of Armed Forces are necessary for waging present-day war? This question may be briefly answered thus: For waging modern war such Armed Forces are demanded as would be able to wage both world nuclear war and any other war. The army and the navy must be armed with all of the latest means of fighting and be well trained for actions both with the use and without the use of nuclear weapons.

What is necessary for the creation of such Armed Forces?

First, they must be recruited on the basis of the general military obligation of the citizens.

Second, the military system of the state must be built on a cadre basis of recruitment of the armed forces, guaranteeing the creation of a permanent, centralized, strictly disciplined army. Such a system permits the preparedness of highly qualified military cadres and builds up the necessary reserves of trained personnel for mobilization of new formations in the event of war.

Third, the Armed Forces must possess exceptionally high constant combat readiness and have the ability to mobilize quickly, deploy, and go into action.

Fourth, the organizational structure of the Armed Forces, that is, the internal arrangement and organizational form of commands and units must strictly correspond to the nature of the war and the technical equipping of the troops. In working out the organizational form, the goal of the most advantageous combination of combat equipment and men is pursued; that sort of combination which would guarantee the maximum effectiveness of the use of one or another sort of weapon and of fighting equipment.

In addition, the organization of formations and units is built with a calculation to assure the maximum combat and administrative-management independence, the ability to wage long operations in complicated conditions and circumstances, and to preserve high vitality. The organization must be extremely flexible, permitting the establishment of clear-cut co-operation between all elements of combat and operational formation and the rapid creation of the necessary troop groupings for carrying out maneuvers with forces and equipment. The organizational forms are selected taking into account the ease of operation and reliability of troop control.

Fifth, it is necessary that the organizational structure of the Armed Forces in peacetime have maximum conformity to the organizational form in wartime in order to assure the swift change-over from the first organization to the second.

And yet another factor. The interests of the security of the Motherland and the achievement of victory in war, in the event it arises, demand the preparation of reserves of trained personnel and the stock-piling of reserves of material-technical equipment in such quantity and such quality as to guarantee the full fighting ability of the Armed Forces.

This question closely borders on the problem of preparing the country to repel aggression. Soviet military doctrine proceeds from the fact that in nuclear war the whole country will be an enormous theater of military operations and that its outcome will depend not only on the Armed Forces but also on the preparation of *the whole country* for war.

Measures in this area are being carried out along at least three main directions: the preparation of the Armed Forces, the preparation of the economy, and the preparation of the population of the country. The solution of each of these problems depends on the economic possibilities of the country, on the level of ideological, including military-patriotic work, and on measures in civil defense.

Finally, Soviet military doctrine assigns a large place to the question of leadership in war. The doctrine stresses that in modern war the *unity* of political and military leadership is necessary, and a collective agency is necessary which would manage to unite *all* the efforts of the state and direct them toward the achievement of the established goals.

From all that has been said these conclusions can be made.

Soviet military doctrine is being developed in strict conformity with the Marxist-Leninist understanding of the essence, nature, and content of war, in strict conformity with party and state organization, and policies of the Communist party and the Soviet government—taking into account the international conditions which are taking shape. The realism of our military doctrine is that it proceeds from economic and moral-political resources of the country and from sober stocktaking of the combat possibilities of the Armed Forces, and that it is strictly guided by Marxist-Leninist teachings on war and the army and the positions and conclusions of Soviet military science.

Soviet military doctrine is being enriched with new theses. This is why officers, generals, and admirals who study military doctrine must attentively follow these developments.

To know doctrine means to understand what sort of war and what means and methods are necessary to prepare for and to wage war in order to achieve victory. To know military doctrine means to prepare—purposefully, with the consciousness of full responsibility before the government, the party, and the people—each subunit, each unit, each ship, and all of our Armed Forces for the defense of the Motherland, for the repulse and full, crushing defeat of the aggressor no matter from where he appears.

SUMMARY

FROM THESE SELECTIONS of Soviet military writings over the course of the past several years, one major conclusion appears inescapable. The Soviet Union is unswervingly committed to a nuclear strategy. Once a revolution is under way, whether it be to overthrow a government or to completely restructure a nation's military force, it is difficult to turn back. The revolution in military affairs is not a vague concept in the minds of a few military theoreticians; it is a planned transformation of the Soviet Armed Forces.

We now know that Soviet writers on doctrine and strategy have not gone in one direction, and Soviet allocations for research, development, and production in another. They have written of military-technical superiority defined as "the quantity and quality of nuclear weapons and their means of delivery." They have argued that antimissiles must be developed to counter missiles. They stress the requirement for civil defense. Toward the close of 1966 the American press announced a large increase in the number of Soviet ICBM's[1] and the deployment of a Soviet antiballistic missile system. The Soviet doctrinal and strategic concepts are being matched with weapons that could make possible the execution of their policies.

When the nuclear weapon was large in size and few in number, the Soviets gave first priority to its strategic use, with delivery by long-range aircraft and ballistic missiles. Now the nuclear weapon exists in various sizes and for many purposes, for deployment throughout their nuclear armed forces. The use of tactical nuclear weapons on the battlefield is being carefully studied. But first place still is given to strategic nuclear forces, consisting of thermonuclear weapons and their delivery systems—missiles, nuclear submarines,

---

[1] ICBM, Intercontinental ballistic missile.

and long-range aircraft. High priority also is given to the strategic defensive forces.

As these writings show, Soviet strategists approach the problems of war and peace in a nuclear age in a fundamentally different fashion than do the military theoreticians in the West, particularly in the United States. One reason for this, perhaps, is because almost all of their writers are officers on active duty. They are not necessarily officers of the combat arms, but they constantly are exposed to a military environment. Most of their counterparts in the United States work on the campuses of universities and in research institutions. The Soviet writers, especially in the rank of colonel and below appear to be highly educated, trained in the practical aspects of military art, and thoroughly conversant with the ideological wellsprings of Marxism-Leninism.

We must assume that Soviet military writers are constrained by the Communist party, acting through its military watchdog, the Main Political Administration. In like manner, party approval must be given to the publications of all writers. The similarity of many of the phrases repeated throughout these selections, especially those dealing with the beginning period of the war, the global nature of a future war, and the importance of the first strike, would, in the non-Communist world, border on plagiarism. These repeated phrases serve to highlight the key elements of doctrine.

Significant is the fact that the Soviet Politburo, which gives its blessings to the doctrinal writings of these military writers, is the same authoritative group which allocates resources between military and civilian sectors of the Soviet economy. The Politburo has consistently sought to provide the means to execute the military doctrine which bears its stamp of approval. One should not, therefore, be surprised to find that the dominant theme running through these military writings is the constant Soviet drive for superiority, waged by the party, in all of the manifest forms which military power might develop.

There is a belief among many people in the United States that the Soviet military leaders form a group distinct and apart from the

391

leaders of the Communist party. Some Westerners even believe that the two groups are hostile and that the Soviet Union is weakened by a continued conflict between the Soviet officer corps and the Communist party hierarchy. The Communist party came to power by force of arms and retains its position by force. The senior military leaders also are senior members of the Communist party. Military promotion is directly affected by political advancement. The top marshals and the commanders in chief are members of the Central Committee. There is a close intermarriage—both figuratively and literally—between the political and the military leadership and one supports the other.

The significance of the political-military relationships can be seen in some of the Soviet writings. For example, there were sixteen different contributors listed by the Soviets as having made inputs into the 1962 edition of *Military Strategy*. The only one, however, to whom a specific part was attributed was General Gastilovich, and his contribution presented a strong "modernist" view, emphasizing nuclear weapons. It is of importance that General Gastilovich's political commissar during World War II was General Major Leonid I. Brezhnev. In 1961, Brezhnev was given the title Hero of Socialist Labor, for "outstanding service in the development of rocket equipment and for assuring the successful flight of Soviet man in space on the spaceship 'Vostok.' "[2]

Undoubtedly there are factions among the Soviet marshals who dislike each other for both personal and professional reasons. Certainly there are such factions within the Politburo itself. Groups within the Politburo may argue about the allocations of resources, even those assigned to the military, in the same manner as the senior marshals and generals argue and disagree among themselves. However, there is nothing to indicate a division along the lines of the military versus the Communist party.

There are many Americans who will view these Soviet military writings as opinions expressed by private individuals in the Soviet Union who write with the same freedom and for the same purpose

2 *Bolshoi Soviet Encyclopedia Annual* (Moscow, Soviet Encyclopedia Publishing House 1966), 579.

as would a Henry Kissinger or a Herman Kahn in the United States. Many persons will feel that the views expressed in these selections would be contrary to the views held by more responsible members of the Soviet government. The authors whose works are listed here are writing both as members of the Communist party and as military theoreticians. What they have written is not only official military doctrine but also the military view approved by the leaders of the Communist party.

For reasons of military security, Soviet military writers rarely disclose anything of operational significance concerning their own forces. Soviet security practices take a pathological approach where new equipment is concerned, and Soviet writers explain the technical characteristics of missiles and antimissiles through the use of illustrations from the non-Communist press. Even a concept such as possible military operations in space is publicly presented to Soviet officers through the reprint of articles and books from the United States and elsewhere.

Despite such constraints and direction, Soviet writers exhibit a great deal of military professionalism. It is particularly important to note that Soviet writers are future-oriented. They do not subscribe to some American theories of a "technological plateau." Instead, they are able to visualize a cyclical application of basic scientific discoveries to technological application from which the superiority they seek may one day emerge.

"Wars of national liberation" are discussed by Soviet military writers, but they say very little as to how these wars actually are to be fought. Soviet writers are vague also concerning the amount and kind of military equipment that the Soviet Union might give to an insurgent group or in support of a "national-liberation war." There are, no doubt, several reasons for this. One would be that the Soviets want to maintain the fiction that all insurgency is a "spontaneous" movement. Another would be the possible conflict of interest with a second Communist group which might be operating in a developing nation, such as Communist Chinese groups which are found in many nations of Africa.

Soviet theoreticians are also very reticent about forces and weapons for limited wars. They have argued that any local war, especially if nuclear powers are involved, is likely to spread into world nuclear war. Should the Soviet Union openly send forces to fight in a local war, there would be the possibility of a direct confrontation with the United States. Based on their own theory, the danger of escalation into a nuclear war would be great, and in some cases, such escalation might "become inevitable."[3]

Soviet military equipment, particularly aircraft, has been engaged in both of the major "limited" wars in which the United States has fought since 1950. In neither have Soviet military personnel actually admitted to other than an advisory or training role. Is the Soviet Union likely to change this pattern in the future?

Soviet military forces have operated outside Soviet borders in the past. Many of the most promising officers in the Soviet Army were sent to Spain in 1936. They called themselves "volunteers" and fought in the international brigade. Aliases were used as a general rule.[4] Among the volunteers was the late Soviet Minister of Defense Marshal R. Ya. Malinovsky. "Volunteer" pilots went to China in 1938 to fight the Japanese.[5] In August, 1939, one month before Hitler and Stalin moved into Poland, full-scale Soviet military units were fighting in Outer Mongolia. The famous battle of Khalkin Gol, in which over half a million Soviet and Japanese soldiers were engaged,[6] took place at the exact time the Hitler-Stalin nonaggression pact was signed. After World War II, when East Germany and Hungary tried to break the Soviet yoke, the U.S.S.R. applied military power swiftly and ruthlessly.

The basic direction of Soviet military development appears to be a concentrated drive to achieve military-technical superiority. To use a large share of her total military resources to wage limited warfare, as the United States has done in Korea and in Vietnam, could

---

3 General Colonel Nikolai A. Lomov, "The Influence of Soviet Military Doctrine on the Development of Military Art," chap. 12.

4 Chief Marshal of Artillery N. N. Voronov, *In Military Service* (Moscow, Military Publishing House, 1963) 79. Voronov served in Spain as "Volunteer Voltaire."

5 Colonel N. G. Kozlov, *In the Sky of China*, Moscow, "Nauka" Publishers, 1966.

6 P. N. Pospelov (ed.), *History of the Great Patriotic War of the Soviet Union, 1941–1945*, I, 236–45. For a vivid personal report of Khalkin Gol, see also the account of Chief Marshal of Artillery N. N. Voronov, *In Military Service*.

detract from that objective. This is not to suggest that the Soviet Union would not commit her forces if she thought her vital interests were at stake or if major gains could be achieved with little cost and risk. But the Soviet leaders probably want the "revolution in military affairs" continued until military-technical superiority is assured. If, and when, this condition comes about, the United States will be forced to look at limited war in a new light.

An underlying American policy hope is that a genuine *détente* can be reached with the Soviet Union. But while we hope, we must at the same time be aware of the message which the leadership in the Communist party is presenting to the members of the Soviet Armed Forces to read and study. As one reads official Soviet military doctrine, the strategic orientation given the members of the Soviet Armed Forces ceases to be a mystery. If the threat implied by Soviet military doctrine and matching Soviet military capabilities is better understood in the West, this book will have served its purpose.

GLOSSARY

CANDIDATE OF SCIENCES—A learned degree conferred in the U.S.S.R. upon persons having higher education who have passed a candidate's examination and have defended a candidate's dissertation (U.S. equivalent—Master's degree). [Source: *Encyclopedia Dictionary* (Moscow, "Soviet Encyclopedia" Publishing House, 1964).]

DOCTOR OF SCIENCES—A learned degree conferred on persons having, as a rule, the learned degree of Candidate (in the U.S.S.R.) or Master of Sciences who have defended a doctor's dissertation (U.S. equivalent—Ph.D). [Source: *Encyclopedia Dictionary* (Moscow, "Soviet Encyclopedia" Publishing House, 1964).]

DISCLOSING OF THE PREPARATION OF THE ENEMY FOR USING WEAPONS OF MASS DESTRUCTION—The complex of measures directed at depriving the enemy of the possibility of the surprise use of weapons of mass destruction of our troops. Disclosing the preparation includes: the timely detection by all means of reconnaissance of the presence and grouping of means designated for nuclear, chemical, and bacteriological attack; the location of the stocks of ammunition of these means; the establishment of the time, place, and nature of the preparation of the enemy to use weapons of mass destruction. The timely disclosing of the preparation of the enemy for using weapons of mass destruction allows the carrying out of powerful nuclear rocket strikes or strikes with aviation forces and long-range artillery on the groupings of means and ammunition stores of nuclear, chemical, and bacteriological attack of the enemy [Source: Colonel P. I. Skuibedia (ed.),

Explanatory Dictionary of Military Terms (Moscow, Voyenizdat, 1966), 103.]

MILITARY ART—The theory and practice of conducting battle, operations, and armed struggle as a whole with the use of all means of the service branches and services of the armed forces and, also, ensuring combat actions in every respect. Military art as a scientific theory is the basic realm of military science and includes tactics, operational art, and strategy which is found in organic unity and interdependency. [Source: Faculty of the General Staff Academy of the Armed Forces of the U.S.S.R., *Dictionary of Basic Military Terms* (Moscow, Voyenizdat, 1965), 44.]

MILITARY DOCTRINE—The system of scientifically based views accepted by the government on the nature of modern war and the use in it of the armed forces, and also the demands for the preparation of the country and the armed forces for war which flows from these views.

Military doctrine has two sides: Political and military-technical. The basic postures of military doctrine are determined by the political and military leadership of the government in conformity with the socio-political system and the level of development of the economy, science, and technology, and with the military-technical equipment of the armed forces of the country, and also with a stocktaking of the conclusions of military science and the views of the probable enemy. [Source: *Dictionary of Basic Military Terms*, 41.]

MILITARY SCIENCE—The system of knowledge about the nature, essence, and content of armed struggle, about the forces, means, and ways of waging combat actions with armed forces, and about their all-round maintenance.

Military science investigates the objective laws and conforms with laws of armed struggle, works out questions of the theory of military art which compose the basic content of military science, and works out questions of the structure and training of the armed forces and their military-technical equipment, and of military-historical experience also.

Soviet military science comes from Marxist-Leninist teaching, and is governed by methods of dialectical materialism and historical materialism, taking into account and using with it all the achievements of the other sciences which promote the constant perfecting and progressing of military affairs. [Source: *Dictionary of Basic Military Terms*, 42.]

MILITARY STRATEGY—The higher area of military art which represents a system of scientific knowledge of the laws of war as an armed conflict in the interests of definite classes. On the basis of the studying of the postures of military doctrine, the experiences of past wars, military and political conditions, the economic and moral possibilities of the country, new means of battle, and the views of the probable enemy, military strategy investigates the conditions and nature of a future war, works out methods of its preparation and conduct, the bases of the strategic use of the services of the armed forces, and also the bases of the material and technical maintenance and the leadership of war and the armed forces. Military strategy in the conditions of modern war is becoming the strategy of deep nuclear rocket strikes in combination with the actions of all the services of the armed forces with the task of the simultaneous defeat and destruction of the economic potential and the armed forces of the enemy throughout the whole depth of his territory for the achievement of the goals of war in a short period of time. Occupying a subordinate position in respect to military doctrine, military strategy works out and investigates the concrete questions concerning the character of a future war, the preparation of the country for war, the organization of the armed forces, and the methods of waging war. Military strategy is in close correlation with operational art and tactics—in relation to which it is leading, since it determines the general goal of actions,

398

forces, means, and methods of solving problems. The mutual conditionality of all component parts of the theory of military art and the leading position of military strategy is explained by the fact that in war each separate success is subordinate to a common goal. Soviet military strategy is guided by the advanced scientific theory of Marxism-Leninism which allows the knowing and the correct use of objective laws which determine victory in modern war. Military strategy in imperialist countries is directed at preserving and consolidating the obsolescent capitalist system and at a struggle with the advanced and progressive system of human society—the socialistic. [Source—*Explanatory Dictionary of Military Terms*, 71.]

PVO (AIR DEFENSE)—Defense from an air enemy. It includes antiairplane (PVO), antirocket (PRO), and anticosmic defense (PKO). It is divided into National PVO, Troop PVO, and Fleet PVO. 1. National PVO—The sum total of national measures and combat operations of the troops of PVO which guarantees an active defense for the vitally important regions, administrative, political and industrial centers, businesses, transportation routes, strategic, and other objectives in the territory of the country from actions on them from the air. The task of National PVO is fulfilled primarily by National PVO Troops. 2. Troop PVO—Represents the complex of combat actions of various forces and means of PVO composing the armaments of formations (units, subunits) of the Ground Forces and fulfilling their mission in co-operation with National PVO Troops. Troop PVO is organized by all commanders to carry destruction to the means of air attack of the enemy, to repulse the strikes of his aviation and rockets on the troops and objectives in the rear and also to prohibit the conduct of air reconnaissance. 3. Fleet PVO is affected by National PVO Troops and ship means in co-operation with forces and means of PVO of the Ground Forces. [Source: *Explanatory Dictionary of Military Terms*, 347.]

Component parts of PVO are:

PKO (Antispace Defense)—A component part of air defense (PVO), designated for destroying the enemy's cosmic means of fighting which are being used for military purposes (in the capacity of a carrier of nuclear weapons, for carrying out reconnaissance, and so forth) in their flight orbits. Special space ships, satellite fighters, and other flying apparatuses, armed with rockets and radioelectronic apparatuses are the basic means of PKO. [Source: *Explanatory Dictionary of Basic Military Terms*, 348.]

PRO (Antirocket Defense)—A component part of PVO, designated for detecting, intercepting, and destroying enemy ballistic rockets (missiles) in the trajectory of their flights and creating jamming for them. PRO fulfills its mission with the help of antirocket and special jamming equipment. [Source: *Explanatory Dictionary of Military Terms*, 351.]

REVOLUTION IN MILITARY AFFAIRS, THE—The whole sum of fundamental, qualitative changes in the means of armed conflict, of methods of combat actions, in the organization of troops, their training and education, which has come into being in the last fifteen years in the more developed countries relative to science and industry and which is primarily connected with the creation of the nuclear rocket weapon. Going along new paths in the business of strengthening the defense potential of the country, and raising the preparedness of the Armed Forces to repulse an aggressor, the Soviet Union was the first to achieve the organic combination of a thermonuclear charge with a ballistic intercontinental and global rocket. The basic fire and striking power of our Armed Forces now is the nuclear weapon and the chief means of delivery to the target is the rocket. The revolution in military affairs enveloped all the basic branches. Simultaneously, the further perfection of troop organization and methods of armed conflict took place on all scales with the creation of automatized guidance systems, the most important of which were the electronic computer, radiolocator, and radiotelevision apparatuses. The methods of training and educating the troops have also been adapted to the solution of new problems. As a result of the contemporary revolution in military affairs, all services of the Armed Forces and branches of service of our country are equipped with first-class military equipment and powerful weapons. [Source: *Explanatory Dictionary of Military Terms*, 393.]

SERVICES OF THE ARMED FORCES—Component parts of the armed forces of a state designated for waging combat actions mainly in any kind of geographic surroundings: On land, on sea, and in the air. The services of the Armed Forces of the U.S.S.R. are:

> Strategic Rocket Troops
> National PVO (Air Defense)
> Ground Forces
> Air Forces
> Naval Forces.

Such a division of the Armed Forces is connected with the combat properties and designation of various sorts of weapons, the type of combat missions fulfilled by them, and the methods of their combat use. Each service of the Armed Forces includes in its structure different branches of service or fighting arms, and special troops, and each has as armaments special military equipment belonging only to it, which is uniform in basic principle but different in combat properties and potentials. Depending on the character of the mission being fulfilled, each service of the Armed Forces has a special organization peculiar to it, as well as recruitment, training, service for personnel, and also methods for the most effective combat use of weapons and military equipment belonging to them. [Source: *Explanatory Dictionary of Military Terms*, 75.]

SURPRISE—One of the basic conditions for achieving success in battle. Surprise in battle permits catching the enemy unawares, bringing him great losses in a short period of time, evoking panic, paralyzing his will, and depriving him of the possibility of showing organized resistance. Surprise is achieved by the use of various ways and methods of troop combat actions, by leading the enemy into error concerning one's own intentions, by preserving in secret the plan of battle, by speed and decisiveness of action, by hidden artificial maneuvers, by the unexpected use of the nuclear weapon and other new combat means, and by new methods of conducting battle. In order to escape surprise enemy attack, it is necessary to have high vigilance and combat readiness of the troops constantly, to organize their guard reliably, and to carry out constant reconnaissance of the enemy. [Source: *Explanatory Dictionary of Military Terms*, 75.]

APPENDIX

SOVIET MILITARY LEADERS AND RANKS

EXACT COMPARISONS of ranks between the armed forces of the United States and the Soviet Union cannot be made. For example, the Soviet minister of defense is roughly the equivalent of the United States secretary of defense and the chairman of the Joint Chiefs of Staff. The commander in chief of the Soviet Air Forces corresponds to the United States secretary of the air force and the air force chief of staff.

The civilian secretaries, undersecretaries, and supergrades, who play a major role in the armed forces of the United States, are unknown in the Soviet Union. In a sense, the "political officers" in the Soviet Armed Forces, responsible to the "Main Political Administration of the Soviet Army and Navy," fulfill some of the functions of the United States secretary of defense and his civilian appointees.

After the death of Marshal Malinovsky,[1] changes were made in the Ministry of Defense as follows: (April 12, 1967)

Minister of Defense—Marshal of the Soviet Union Andrei A. Grechko

First Deputy Minister of Defense—Marshal of the Soviet Union Ivan I. Yakubovsky (named commander of the Warsaw Pact forces in July, 1967)

First Deputy Minister of Defense and Chief of Staff—Marshal of the Soviet Union Matvei V. Zakharov

First Deputy Minister of Defense—General of the Army Sergei L. Sokolov

[1] Malinovsky died March 31, 1967.

Chief of the Main Political Administration of the Soviet Army and Navy—General of the Army Aleksei A. Yepishev

Deputy Minister of Defense, Commander in chief of the Strategic Rocket Troops—Marshal of the Soviet Union Nikolai I. Krylov

Deputy Minister of Defense, Commander in chief of National PVO (aerospace defense) troops—General of the Army Pavel F. Batitsky

Deputy Minister of Defense, Commander in chief of the Air Forces—Chief Marshal of Aviation Konstantin A. Vershinin

Deputy Minister of Defense, Commander in chief of the Navy—Admiral of the Fleet Sergei G. Gorshkov

Deputy Minister of Defense, Chief of the Rear—Marshal of the Soviet Union Ivan Kh. Bagramyan

Deputy Minister of Defense, Inspector General—Marshal of the Soviet Union Kirill S. Moskalenko

Deputy Minister of Defense for Combat Training—General of the Army Valentin A. Pen'kovsky

Deputy Minister of Defense—General of the Army Ivan G. Pavlovsky

(Comments: (1) General of the Army Yepishev, as chief of the Main Political Administration, takes precedence over the commanders in chief. (2) There has been no known commander in chief of the Soviet Ground Forces since the position was abolished in the Spring of 1964.)

There are a total of nineteen "Marshals of the Soviet Union" and one "Admiral of the Fleet of the Soviet Union." There are an additional twenty-six marshals, chief marshals, and admirals of the fleet, as, for example, Chief Marshal of Tanks P. A. Rotmistrov and Marshal of Aviation Ye. Ya. Savitsky.

It may be noted that we have used in our translations such terms as "general major" and "general lieutenant" instead of the United States designations of "major general" and so on. Our wording was deliberate, since the ranks are not the same. Comparisons are as follows:

UNITED STATES	SOVIET UNION[2]
General of the Army	Marshal of the Soviet Union
Admiral of the Fleet	Admiral of the Fleet of the Soviet Union
(no equivalent)	Chief Marshal of Aviation, Artillery, etc.
General	General of the Army
Admiral	Marshal of Aviation, Artillery, Tanks, etc., Admiral of the Fleet
Lieutenant General	General Colonel, General Colonel of Aviation
Vice Admiral	Admiral
Major General	General Lieutenant, General Lieutenant of Aviation
Rear Admiral (upper half)	Vice Admiral
Brigadier General	General Major, General Major of Aviation
Rear Admiral (lower half)	Rear Admiral
Colonel	Colonel (Polkovnik)
Captain (Navy)	Captain, 1st Rank (Navy)
Lieutenant Colonel	Lieutenant Colonel (Podpolkovnik)
Commander (Navy)	Captain, 2nd Rank (Navy)
Major	Major
Lieutenant Commander (Navy)	Captain, 3rd Rank (Navy)

[2] The highest Soviet rank is Generalissimus of the Soviet Union, a rank achieved only by Stalin. All information on Soviet ranks was taken from the *Explanatory Dictionary of Military Terms*, 97.

THE OFFICER'S LIBRARY

In 1965, Voyenizdat, the Soviet Military Publishing House, began a series of books called the "Officer's Library." The first volume published was *M. V. Frunze—Selected Works*. The well-bound, light blue books carry the notation *Biblioteka Ofitsera*—Officer's Library—on the cover in colorful red and gold.

Some revisions in the titles have been made from time to time. For example *Krasnaya Zvezda* [*Red Star*] announced that the *Program of the CPSU on the Defense of the Socialist Fatherland* would be a part of the series. However, it was published separately. *Military Doctrine*, announced for 1966, was unpublished and appears on the list for 1967. *Military Strategy*, although mentioned, names no author, so one cannot tell if this will be a third edition of the work edited originally by Marshal Sokolovsky. *Military Psychology*, the *Speeches of M. I. Kalinin*, and *Party-political Work in the Soviet Armed Forces* are all slow in appearing.

It is fairly obvious from the reviews in various publications that the books in the "Officer's Library" series are of an official nature, having the approval of both the Ministry of Defense and the Main Political Administration, which represents the Communist party in the armed forces. There have been criticisms, of course, and some were quite sharp. *Marxism-Leninism—On War and the Army* was cited at the awarding of the Frunze prizes in 1966. Earlier books were put out in modest editions, 29,000 copies or less. Later editions generally ran to 40,000 copies, and *Marxism-Leninism—On War and the Army*, 50,000.

It is quite significant that the first volume on Frunze is dated two weeks after the ouster of Khrushchev and thus reflects the currentness of the series. Nine books of the seventeen volume series announced for publication appeared prior to February 1, 1967. The following list is in order of publication, and both the phonetic spelling and the English translation are given.

M. V. Frunze—Izbrannie Proizvedeniya [*M. V. Frunze—Selected Works*].
(Moscow, Voyenizdat, 1965.)

Slovar' Osnovnikh Voyennikh Terminov [*Dictionary of Basic Military Terms*].

Military Order of Suvorov Academy of the General Staff of the Armed Forces of the U.S.S.R. Edited by General Lieutenant S. N. Krasil'nikov and General Lieutenant A. Ye. Yakovlev, under the leadership of General of the Army V. V. Kurasov. (Moscow, Voyenizdat, 1965.)

V. I. Lenin—O Voine, Armii i Voyennoi Nauke [*V. I. Lenin—On War, the Army, and Military Science*].

(Moscow, Voyenizdat, 1965.)

Marxism-Leninism—O Voine i Armii [*Marxism-Leninism—On War and the Army*], 4th ed., revised and enlarged.

Military-political Order of Lenin, Red Banner Academy named for Lenin, the Marxist-Leninist Philosophy Department. Edited by General Major N. Ya. Sushko and Colonel S. A. Tyushkevich. (Moscow, Voyenizdat, 1965.)

Organizatsiya i Vooruzheniye Armiy i Flotov Kapitalisticheskikh Gosudarstv [*Organization and Armaments of the Armies and Navies of Capitalist States*].

(Moscow, Voyenizdat, 1965.)

Osnovi Sovyetskovo Voyennovo Zakonodatel'stva [*The Bases of Soviet Military Law*].

Edited by General Lieutenant of Justice A. G. Gorniy. (Moscow, Voyenizdat, 1966.)

Istoriya Voyenovo Iskusstva [*History of Military Art*].

Edited by Doctor of Historical Sciences, Professor, Colonel A. A. Strokov. (Moscow, Voyenizdat, 1966.)

Taktika [*Tactics*].

Frunze Military Academy. Edited by Candidate of Military Sciences, General Major V. G. Reznichenko. (Moscow, Voyenizdat, 1966.)

Voyennaya Pedagogika [*Military Pedagogics*].

Edited by Candidate of Pedagogical Sciences, Lieutenant Colonel A. V. Barabanshchikov. (Moscow, Voyenizdat, 1966.)

Voyennaya Doktrina [*Military Doctrine*].

Voyennaya Psychologiya [*Military Psychology*].

Partiyno–politicheskaya Rabota v Sovyetskikh Vooruzhennikh Silakh [*Party–political Work in the Soviet Armed Forces*].

Spravochnik Ofitsera [*Officer's Guide*].

M. I. Kalinin "O Kommisticheskom Vospitanii i Voinskom Dolge" [*The Speeches of M. I. Kalinin "On Communist Education and Military Duty"*].

50 Let Vooruzhennikh Sil U.S.S.R. [*Fifty Years of the Armed Forces U.S.S.R.*].

Voyennaya Strategiya [*Military Strategy*].

Technicheskii Progress i Revolutsiya v Voyennom Dele [*Technical Progress and the Revolution in Military Affairs*].

INDEX

409

417

UNIVERSITY OF OKLAHOMA PRESS
NORMAN